Public Opinion and Democracy

Vox Populi–Vox Dei?

The Hampton Press Communication Series
Political Communication
David L. Paletz, Editor

Eastern European Journalism
   *Jerome Aumente, Peter Gross, Ray Hiebert, Owen Johnson,
   and Dean Mills*

The In/Outsiders: The Mass Media in Israel
   Dan Caspi and Yehiel Limor

Islam and the West in the Mass Media:
   Fragmented Images in a Globalizing World
      Kai Hafez (ed.)

Eden Online: Re-inventing Humanity in a Technological Universe
   Kerric Harvey

Civic Dialogue in the 1996 Presidential Campaign:
   Candidate, Media, and Public Voices
      Lynda Lee Kaid, Mitchell S. McKinney, and John C. Tedesco

Mediated Women: Representations in Popular Culture
   Marian Meyers (ed.)

Political Communication in Action: States, Institutions,
   Movements, Audiences
      David L. Paletz (ed.)

Glasnost and After: Media and Change in Central and Eastern Europe
   David L. Paletz, Karol Jakubowicz, and Pavao Novosel (eds.)

Gender, Politics and Communication
   Annabelle Sreberny and Liesbet van Zoonen (eds.)

Strategic Failures in the Modern Presidency
   Mary E. Stuckey

War in the Media Age
   A. Trevor Thrall

forthcoming

Governing from Center Stage: White House Communication Strategies
   During the Age of Politics
      Lori Cox Han

Business as Usual: Continuity and Change in Central and
   Eastern European Media
      David L. Paletz and Karol Jakubowicz (eds.)

Public Opinion and Democracy

Vox Populi–Vox Dei?

edited by

Slavko Splichal
University of Ljubljana

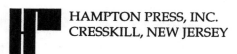

HAMPTON PRESS, INC.
CRESSKILL, NEW JERSEY

Printed in the United States of America

Library of Congress Cataloging-in-Publication Data

Public opinion and democracy : vox populi-vox dei? / edited by Slavko Splichal.
    p. cm. -- (The Hampton Press communication series. Political communication)
  Includes bibliographical references and indexes.
  ISBN 1-57273-340-3 -- ISBN 1-57273-341-1 (pbk.)
   1. Public opinion. 2. Democracy. I. Splichal, Slavko. II. Series.

HM 1236 .P83 2001
303.3'8--dc21

00-053560

cover design: © 1994 Margaret McCarthy c/o Mira

Hampton Press, Inc.
23 Broadway
Cresskill, NJ 07626

Contents

Introduction:
Public Opinion and Democracy Today

Slavko Splichal

The essays collected in this book examine the relationship between two concepts—public opinion and democracy—central to social and political theories at least since the Enlightenment. Controversies over the function of public opinion for democratic political process are as old as the idea of public opinion itself, and they represent an enduring issue in theorizing public opinion and democratic government. As the Latin saying goes, "*vox populi, vox dei*"; the voice of the people is supposed to be equal to the voice of God. Yet public opinion is also believed to be like an ignorant, vulgar person who reproves everyone and talks most of what he understands least, as Hegel quoted Italian Renaissance poet Lodovico Ariosto. On the eve of the twenty-first century, the "mutual action and reaction of the makers or leaders of opinion upon the mass, and of the mass upon them" is still "the most curious part" of the process of public opinion formation and expression, as it was a century ago in James Bryce's (1888/1995: 915) original wording. For over a century and a half, controversies on the nature and functions of public opinion have cen-

1

tered on the problems of the tyranny of the majority, lack of competency in citizens, parliamentary representation, domination by elites, exclusion of nondominant social classes, manipulation of the masses by persuasive communication and propaganda, and many others. What the most recent history of public opinion specifically "contributed" to these discussions, both in theory and practice, is primarily the (changing) role of the mass media and public opinion polling. Clearly, these developments are related to broader social, political, and economic changes that are commonly labeled "postmodernity," which somehow incorporates the alleged emergence of "information societies" as the historical negation of industrial capitalism and the poststructuralist critique of the heritage of the Enlightenment.

This volume is deliberately not designed to refine one single theme, to develop one single paradigm, or to prioritize any particular approach or method within the scope of the overall topic of public opinion. The solicited contributions to the book may challenge mainstream empirical "public opinion research" as administrative research, yet they equally build on theoretical and empirical perspectives. Both the initial discussions at the colloquium organized by the European Institute for Communication and Culture in 1997 in Piran, Slovenia, and the subsequent design of this volume were primarily concerned with forms of political institutionalization of public opinion and the relationship between the mass media, opinion polling, and broader issues of democracy and democratization. This is clearly reflected in the organization of the book. The first part presents new perspectives in theorizing public opinion, focused on the issues of social representation, domestication of public opinion, rationality, political learning, and civic competence. The second part includes discussions of three historical "deviations" from the prevailing traditional Western understanding and practice of public opinion—Islamic, socialist, and postmodern. The third and the fourth part specifically deal with the empirical world of opinion polls and mass media as two forms of political institutionalization of public opinion in contemporary societies.

The notion of public opinion is closely related to both participatory and representative democracy, but the two models of democracy are often seen as mutually exclusive. However, due to the widespread belief of the inapplicability of forms of direct democracy to present-day conditions, much of the contemporary debate has been framed by the notions of representative democracy, in which legitimacy is conferred on representative lawmakers through the electoral process and rational deliberation of laws by elected representatives accountable to a more or less politically involved citizenry.

Representative democracy (government) that can only be created from above has been from the very beginning not a means of a direct reproduction of majority opinions and decisions. It has rather been an attempt to secure government from any simple majority: as Burke insisted, the representative had to be accountable to his or her conscience rather than loyal to his/her constituents. Representative democracy excludes "the people" from direct influence on national power. At the same time, it ensures that citizens give their consent, loyalty, and obedience (even under the threat of their "isolation"), which legitimize the government. If direct democracy is the *ideal model* of democracy, then representative democracy seems to be a form of "quasi-democracy" because of its elitist roots. Nevertheless, once it is recognized and supported as a form of government, people can identify with, and feel themselves to be represented by exactly those who exclude them from a direct influence.

Recent developments have unsettled this "quasi-democratic" framework of public opinion processes at key points. Despite going through the usual campaign routines, the legitimacy of elected leaders is no longer taken for granted—there are high levels of public disenchantment with politicians in many democracies. Although it may be true that the idea of representation saved democracy as the guiding ideology of the modern state—due to the insurmountable difficulties in the implementation of direct democracy—it is also true that the implementation of the representative principle caused a great many citizens to become (structurally) excluded from participation in day-to-day decision-making. The question of structural exclusion is particularly important because it pertains to the core of the formation of the public sphere since the seventeenth century.

Correlative with the disenchantment with politics, institutions that previously organized meaning, identity, and authoritative information for many people, structured their political preferences, and simplified the process of democratic power-seeking (political parties, mainstream religion, the nuclear family, the workplace, neighborhood, and social-class groupings) have waned in salience and influence. Mass media have emerged as autonomous power centers, and media-based strategies for shaping public opinion and winning support have become more important. The rise of polling, which is often indicted for manufacturing instead of monitoring public opinion, perhaps debilitated democracy, but at the same time it provoked intense discussions and controversies regarding the social and political consequences of polling and its normative validity. Consequently, polling stimulated the questioning of the nature and functions of public opinion in society and democracy of the twentieth century.

On the eve of the new millennium, populism as a political doctrine and practice has become fashionable. Modern technology has significantly stimulated populism. Politicians are becoming more sensitive to feedback information through new computer-mediated communication channels. There is a growing interest in public opinion polling. George Gallup, one of the founders of polling, was among the first to believe that polls ought to compensate for the growing limitations of a parliamentary democracy. Opinion polls certainly cause people who are interested in political life to become more sensitive to shifts in the popular temper and awareness of significant issues. But at the same time they have, as Leo Bogart noted, "a pernicious effect on political candidates who follow the precepts of market research rather than their own considered and conscientiously arrived-at policy choices" (Bogart, 1995: 9).

Modern personalized communication technologies—telephone, telefax, and increasingly electronic mail—enable politicians to establish contacts with the electorate, to measure its pulse, or even to subordinate themselves dysfunctionally to it by passing dubious laws, not attempting to solve societal problems but merely reacting to "electronic pressures." In this perspective, we may talk not only of the coming period of "cyberdemocracy" or "virtual democracy" but rather of "hyperdemocracy." Thus a new democratic rhetoric may be emerging in legislatures and in public discourses (and even in public relations, which strive for the same public status) drawing primarily on public sentiment. We can typically observe such a trend in the broadcast media: the experiences, views, and priorities of ordinary people are being presented more often, and they are being stimulated to participate in discussions on social and political problems in various new modes introduced in/by the mass media, for example, call-in-programs, electronic town meetings, televised citizen juries, and, especially, talk shows.

Yet along with rising populism in politics, popular dislike of political representatives and mistrust of democratic procedures grow. These developments have also revived direct democracy models. In the book *Creating a New Civilization*, for example, Alvin and Heidi Toffler condemn to death the old-fashioned, "physical" Congress of the United States and call for a wholesale rethinking of the Constitution because the spectacular advances in information and communication technologies ought to open universal possibilities for direct citizen participation in political decision-making. Accordingly, the people must begin to "shift from depending on representatives to representing ourselves."

These ideas are most reminiscent of Dewey's Aristotelian dream of community empowerment and the development of Great Community, in contrast to Lippmann's unscrupulous Platonian questioning of the "omnicompetence" of citizens in the 1920s. Yet, theorists such as John

Stuart Mill, Alexis de Tocqueville, James Bryce, and Walter Lippmann, who expressed a radical distrust of the ability of uneducated citizens to participate, even indirectly, in decision-making processes, did not leave without their followers. They see parliamentary democracy based on an ignorant electorate inadequate for both expressing the will of the people and exercising control over complex modern government. Apparently, the problem of incompetent citizens could only be resolved by strong political parties, as suggested already by V. O. Key, who associated public opinion in the last instance with the political party in opposition.

Regardless of whether the technologically driven contemporary advocacy of participatory and deliberative democracy is entirely utopian or only (too) optimistic for the present time, recent practical and conceptual developments in reference to public opinion stimulate a reflection on the fundamentals of public opinion process to find new answers and solutions to the enduring questions of political representation, participation, and public opinion, and identify new questions that may radically shape our future ideas of political democracy. If we agree that public opinion is, or should be, essential for any democratic social system, the first matter at issue is the concept of public opinion itself. What is the essence of defining public opinion—is it the consideration of "public," or of "opinion," or both? Is the political dimension fundamental to any definition of public opinion, or should we understand it in a much broader, anthropological sense?

There is a degree of consensus among public opinion theorists that public opinion is a *communication* phenomenon *par excellence*. For those who believe that public opinion is, at the same time, a *political* phenomenon on which modern democracy is grounded, one of the key issues is the definition and development of forms of communication through which public opinion can be (re)presented adequately to the theoretical demands of democratic life. As John D. Peters argues, "As long as political life is not centered on a single place where the people can assemble as a single body, the expression of the people's voice(s) will always be inseparable from various techniques of representation" (see Chapter 3). Another reason for the assumed necessity of political representation is that most of the social "facts" (at the same time, socially produced facts) are not directly accessible to all citizens, but only through "techniques of representation." Parliaments, newspapers, and polls are the most distinctive institutionalized forms of such "techniques." This problem relates to the questions of both *how* and *who* (or *what*) is (re)presented in/by public opinion, that is, to the nature of *publicity* and to the nature of *the public*.

Early (normative-political) public opinion theories, in which the concept of opinion is defined as correlative to *the public*, may be defined as *substantive* which—in contrast to what Francis G. Wilson named *adjective theories*, in which the term "public" is used as an adjective to describe the specificity or *quality* of an *opinion*. The former stress a tight, authoritative singleness: "the public" as the object of a quest for a universal collective subject or a privileged arena of struggle. The latter refer to a more relaxed, decentered pluralism: publicness as something spread liberally through many irreducibly different collectivities. Although eighteenth-century rationalism saw the development of a great faith in the possibility of an enlightened public opinion, the shift from substantive toward adjective theories in the twentieth century indicates the loss of (a hope for) a rational-critical nature of public opinion. Instead, the questions of social control and public representation became central in theories of public opinion.

Not only in theoretical, but also (and perhaps particularly) in practical and empirical terms, both conceptualizations entail severe controversies. In the broadest sense, public opinion in the sense of a single opinion held by the public, or a distribution of opinions among the members of the public, refers to the *mass* public, that is, to all voting-age citizens. This is "the public" typically referred to in public opinion *polls*. Such a broad conceptualization of public opinion disregards the communicative nature of public opinion; it is neither the interaction nor coorientation among individuals and groups that bring about public opinion, and there is no action involved in it. Polling is an accurate "operationalization" of Key's definition of public opinion, according to which public opinion "may simply be taken to mean those opinions held by private persons which governments (or any other client) find it prudent to heed" (1961/1967: 14). Defining polling as a (or even *the*) form of public opinion liberates the concept from any democratic principles and makes it even compatible with manipulation and oppression; it reduces Kant's principle of publicity to Habermas's "representative publicness."

Yet the "adjective" alternative is not free of grave controversies either. They primarily relate to the nature and, indeed, the definition of, opinion. Ever since Plato "opinion" has been understood more as a conviction not based on a firm philosophical procedure of cognition (*doxa* in Greek *opinio* in Latin), in contrast to factual knowledge that is based on scientific procedures and thus accessible to only a few (*episteme* or *scientia*). "Opining" lacks of certainty; it is, as Kant argued, subjectively and objectively an insufficient form of "holding for true," unlike believing and knowing. In contrast to Kant, Tönnies closely linked opinion with human reason and placed rational opining superior to affective believing. Later, with Habermas, public opinion was conceived of as a result of rational, critical discourse in the (liberal bourgeois) public. Yet, as Habermas argues, in the twentieth century the public was transformed into "the court before whose public prestige can be displayed—rather than in which public critical debate is carried on" (1962/1995: 201); in other words, the publicness was "refeudalized." In fact, these developments prove that Habermas's conception of the impartiality of discussants in a public debate was a utopian ideal that was *never* materialized, even not in the "golden age" of the liberal bourgeois public.

Social roots of public opinion in the eighteenth century and the subsequent theoretical developments and controversies on the nature and definition of public opinion characterize also the four introductory theoretically oriented contributions to this volume. They are centered around the key theorists who significantly contributed to the history of the concept of public opinion, but for different purposes and from different perspectives. Splichal's chapter is an introduction to the intellectual history of the concept that reveals a variety of diverse ways of thinking about public opinion, ranging from an instrumental reasoning by the Scottish utilitarians, disciplinarian conceptualizations in Jeremy Bentham or Noelle-Neumann more recently, to Kant's transcendent moral principle and Habermas's communicative-rational principle of publicity based on the public of educated people who reason and enjoy art. On the one hand, and despite fundamental differences, all theorizations have substantiated the legitimacy that publicity and public opinion confer to laws, politics, even wars. Yet on the other hand, the most significant historically institutionalized forms of public opinion—parliaments, mass media, and polls—largely withdraw the legitimization basis from public opinion inasmuch as they suppress a free public expression of opinions and reduce Kant's moral maxim of a "free public use of reason" to the maxim of representation of the will of the (majority or even minority of) citizenry.

All the introductory chapters at least loosely lean on Habermas, among other theorists, but only Beaud and Kaufmann get to grips with details of his theory. They bring into focus social and cultural history of public opinion in France to confront the preponderance of the bourgeois public over all other forms of public life in Habermas's theory. Different sociohistorical conceptualizations of the emergence of public opinion in the eighteenth century, which have given rise to the work of Habermas, stimulate them to question the actual social referent of the public opinion phenomenon. They revise Habermas's conceptualization of "public opinion" in which the "public" constitutes a veritable collective actor that has succeeded in imposing its own vision of the world in the name of the general interest, and in opposing monarchical and ecclesiastical privileges. The classical "conceptual approach," which emphasizes pre-Revolutionary, enlightened public opinion and the hypothetical causal effects of the Enlightenment, seems to conceal the anthropological regularities of opining as a procedure of sharing differences and individual interests, which speaks in favor of a "sociological approach." Baker's distinction between rumors, extra-institutional, and institutional channels of opinion production and expression, on which Beaud and Kaufmann's criticism of the idealization of a single public (the public) of reasoned men is based, is reminiscent of Tönnies's differentiation between published opinion, public opinion, and the public's opinion. The three historical social practices typical of different social classes are competing, but also coexisting. Thus, there is no justification to be obsessed with "king's gestures and the words of educated" while neglecting the "changes of world-view of ordinary people"; the public sphere should be conceptually pluralized by taking into account the plurality of subjects publicly expressing opinions from the very beginning. As also Peters indicates with Hölscher and Habermas, and particularly Kantorowicz's doctrine of the "king's two bodies," the idea of a sociological aggregate, "the public," did not exist until the eighteenth century when the bourgeoisie replaced the body as a model of political society with the communicative practice of critical debate and the print. Public opinion as "common opinion" or "mentality," proposed by Beaud and Kaufmann, takes into account the actual historical development and the social context of opinion formation, in contrast to normative conceptualizations, where it is grounded on a disinterested communicative action. In this perspective, opinion polling that developed in the twentieth century could be seen as a "natural" continuation of the domestication of public opinion based on the isolation of individuals, as a part of the broader process of "disciplining the masses."

John D. Peters takes another perspective on historical developments—that of specific forms of communication in the public sphere considered adequate to the theoretical demands of democratic life. The forms of communication postulated by normative democratic theories as fundamental to enlightened public opinion—dialogue, interaction, information-gathering, and participation—are in dissonance with the spread of communication and representation in modern nation-states. Peters uses some of the key points in the intellectual history of public opinion to explore the problem of realism and, by implication, fiction in public opinion. He confronts the notion of public opinion as "the voice of the people," as if the people could speak in one voice, with the absence of the public sphere in the sense of a single place where the people can assemble. As a consequence, the expression of the people's voices can only be based on different forms of representation. All different theoretical solutions to the problem of representation in public opinion or "giving form to the public body" during the last three centuries involve "the claim to transport a body across space or time, to bring to presence something invisible or inaudible."

The problem of representation relates with that of externalization. Park (1904/1972) and Blumer (1948) emphasized that public opinion is not a unanimous opinion with which everyone in the public agrees, but rather it should be considered an opinion which is external to every individual and viewed as something objective. As Park suggested, precisely because public opinion is a product of individual critical attitudes, it is expressed differently in different individuals. The process of externalization is not specific to public opinion. Similarly, an artistic performance is expected to enable each spectator to watch his "own" performance, or to create in his head his unique performance, thus making the "objective" performance "external" to the author's scenario.

As Peters argues, the dream of political presence remains present until the end of this century, particularly in diverse "apparatuses" from the mass media to survey procedures that register popular will and reduce the obscure complexity of facts into comprehensible images, and in the belief of progressive political theory that face-to-face participation is the best setting for democratic communication. If the public is fictitious or only "a mode of imagining," it does not mean that it is fabricated or false; it is as genuine as all other "imagined communities" or "fictionalized social groups" because, in Anderson's words, "all communities larger than primordial villages of face-to-face contact (and perhaps even these) are imagined" and individuals can "experience" them only through representations (1983/1991: 6). Unique to modern (empirical) representations is the claim of realism: they ought to be "accurate" and "verifiable"; society ought to be visible not as "an allegory like the king's body," but as a "fact."

The communal dimension of public opinion is the gist of Sinikka Sassi's contribution. She returns to the lost face-to-face community as an enduring normative ideal and the locus of "local opinion," which she defines in an analogy with (national) public opinion as shared views that emerge in a locality. The former is associated with abstract, imagined nation-bound citizenship and the latter with citizenship with its rights and duties springing from locality, where the claims of accuracy and verifiability of representations and facts seems much more feasible. Following Ferdinand Tönnies's ideas developed in *Kritik der ˜offentlichen Meinung*, she extends his concept of the opinion of the public beyond the nation-state to imply the local context. One of the reasons allowing such a revision is that the meaning of "local" in Tönnies's times differed substantially from its present meaning, when due to new communication technologies the local does not necessarily imply particularity, self-sufficiency, and customs and tradition in contrast to urban agglomerations. In many ways, localities are interrelated rather than independent, and foster relations of exchange and cooperation; thus, they cannot be considered a *Gemeinschaft*-type social structure. In addition, Sassi argues, the formation of "local opinion" is at present backed by democratic procedures and a representative system of higher-level organizations—municipal, regional, national, and international. In contrast to "public opinion," "local opinion" emerges in direct interaction and is highly social by nature; Sassi defines it in terms of shared experiences among individuals rather than their isolated considerations. The idea of local opinion associated with the *social sphere* does not pertain to Hannah Arendt's concept of "the social" as opposed to "the private," typically exemplified with "the absorption of family unit into corresponding social group" and simultaneously swelling conformism (1958/1989: 40). Rather, sociality is conceived of in Lii's (1998) terms as the essence of human life and, thus, also the foundation of the public: through the societal self-organization private individuals are brought together, which makes public life possible. The social sphere is "opposed" to the public rather than the private: it denotes "a cultural landscape on which various forms of performance and public drama are staged, and through which social bonds are created and collective experiences articulated." It is similar to the public sphere in form, but differs from it in substance: if the public sphere is essentially organized to enable rational discourse, the social sphere emphasizes sense, body, and performance in creating a shared living context for individual members.

Individuals and their local context are also in the forefront of the subsequent theoretical considerations by Andrew Calabrese, Gerard A. Hauser, and Tom Hoffman. In different ways, they all relate to political learning and the differences between the two broad classes of citizens in contemporary societies—informed and politically involved elites and disengaged, disinterested, and potentially irrational masses.

Hoffman confronts the instrumental understanding of rationality as a strictly economic model favoring the efficiency of the use of available means with a broader, more traditional notions of *political* reason, which implies a moral content, and suggests some points of tension between the two views of political rationality. Since early U.S. surveys on voting behavior, when liberal democratic theory was confronted with the typical American citizen's political ignorance and inattention, attempts in different directions strove for the vindication of the mass electorate. Most recently, some researchers have attempted to reconceptualize the political reasoning process by viewing it in the aggregate, and others describe individuals as effective—albeit inarticulate—employers of cognitive short-cuts. But both "aggregate" and "shortcut rationality" conceptions of political reasoning assume the existence of an intellectual division of labor that contributes to the normatively problematic nature of these responses. As Hoffman suggests, political reason should involve not only means-ends calculation, but the consideration of how preferences come to be held and a weighing of those preferences' compatibility with broader normative requirements. Because politics is an inherently collective, cooperative phenomena, it excludes by definition coercion, manipulation, and indoctrination, relying instead on compliance with modes of persuasion and bargaining. In such conceptions, rationality is related to some larger good and not reduced to the individual's resource efficiency. Thus, whereas mass publics may, in these ways, be described as rational, they fail to meet the requirements of democratic theory.

Nonetheless, the new conceptions of political reasoning are important in questioning the postulates of democratic theory, particularly the Kantian demand for the public use of reason by the individual. Democratic theories must confront the division of labor in modern mass societies that separates the electorate into two broad groups—informed and politically sophisticated elites and disengaged, potentially irrational masses. Since the time that Walter Lippmann published his classic book, *Public Opinion*, there has been fundamental disagreement among intellectuals and political leaders about what role citizens can and should play in public debate in a democratic society. Whereas Lippmann argued that the "omnicompetent citizen" is a myth, and that public debate should be left to the control of experts and executive actors with experience and intrinsic knowledge about the problem who are acting "from inside," John Dewey vigorously defended the opposite stance and considered the average citizen as one whose civic competence is worthy of cultivation and trust rather than of suspicion and underestimation. In Dewey's argument, the ability to participate as listener and speaker in public debate, both literally and figuratively, is essential to competent citizenship. Using the Lippmann-Dewey "debate" as a starting point, and with an emphasis on the idea of media institutions as political institutions, Calabrese's contribution reviews the key arguments about civic competence and its relationship to communication technology in the modern world. He argues that media literacy should serve as a means not only of generating discerning consumers and skilled workers, but also citizens who are capable of serving both as "authors" and "addressees" of the rules that govern their political lives.

Pedagogical foundations for the vitalization of civil society and its members are also at the forefront of the contribution on political learning and vernacular rhetoric by Gerard A. Hauser. By participating in civil society's culture of rhetoric, citizens could learn modes of understanding and interaction, and sustain relations of collaboration on the basis of mutual respect, which makes civic community possible. Hauser emphasizes that the model of public opinion as derived from the vernacular rhetoric of civic conversation does not require returning to the *civitas* of civic virtue or reproaching negative consequences of an evil individualism. The model of civil society is based on the transactions that occur within its network of associations where "strangers encounter difference, learn of the other's interests, develop understanding of where there are common goals, and where they may develop the social capital of trust necessary for them to function in world of mutual dependency."

The dominant Western tradition(s) in theorizing public opinion are challenged not only because of thorough theoretical developments, but also, and even primarily, because of "alternative" cultural and political processes in which public opinion is embedded. The three typical "alternatives" discussed in the second part of the volume—postmodernism, Islam, and socialism—have in common a radical historical or cultural *difference* from the dominant Western democratic culture originating in the Enlightenment. These deviations from the dominant paradigm clearly reflect how important is for the social sciences, as John Dewey once emphasized, not to neglect the fundamental distinction between facts that are what they are independent of human action and will, and facts that are what they are basically because of human interest and purpose, that is, a fundamental difference between physical and social sciences. Public opinion theories are not an exception. This is well illustrated by Barrie Axford and Richard Huggins in the discussion of how the conceptualization of Public Opinion is influenced by "postmodern populism." They examine some salient features of the structuration of public opinion often discussed as symptomatic of a crisis in democratic institutions and practices. In contemporary societies characterized by the disintegration of the "rational public" of the Enlightenment, it is perhaps sensible to speak, instead of about public opinion, about some kind of opinion temper or climate in which there are no longer opinions but rather attitudes that are shaped and changed in the processes that derive from the human tendency for cognitive consistency—in short, harmonizing attitudes and behavioral patterns in the organization of the "inner world." Instead of rational discourse, the mechanisms for assuring attention and achieving internal and external consistency come to the fore, "a sociopsychological calculation of supplies" by the media, as Jürgen Habermas names them. As stated for example by Walter Lippmann and Harold Lasswell, this particularly includes the supply of *stereotypes* and *symbols of identification*. Using these symbols, political actors try through the media to become attractive to the citizens without arousing their critical capacities and stimulating their awareness. As Axford and Huggins argue, "governing more than ever becomes a massive public relations exercise." Mass media, particularly television, act in a way that is calculated to mobilize the public, which inducts a "perverse form of direct democracy," as Bourdieu would say, that is, actions that resemble riots of a mob more than the expression of opinion by an "imagined" public. However, Axford and Huggins suggest a more nuanced reading of the potential threats to and opportunities for democratic governance that lie in different ways of structuring public talk, mainly by using recent evidence from changes in United Kingdom politics and making some mention of developments elsewhere. They place the debates about political communication and public opinion in the context of a putative transformation of political modernity, where that refers both to the institutional forms and discursive practices of liberal democracies and to the cultural and philosophical baggage that attends these.

Basyouni Hamada's contribution offers another divergent view on the formation and expression of public opinion based on the Islamic cultural theory. It is based on the argument that the cultural and political environment determines the nature and quality of public opinion. Its impact is evident in the introduction of highly centralized communication systems geared exclusively toward nation-building goals. Characterized by pervasive government ownership and control of the mass media, these systems are justified as necessary to achieve political stability and social harmony. Whereas in the European culture, religion was clearly separated from public opinion (most notably in Tönnies's theory), the opposite is the case of the Islamic world. As Hamada argues, the main reason lies in the fact that Islam is not only a religion in the traditional Western or Christian sense, but it is much more: a social order, philosophy of life, a system of economic principles, and a rule of government. The fundamental difference between the two cultural currents is in their conceptualizations of human rights. If the Western perspective may be called anthropocentric because the individual is in the center of the legal and moral concerns, Islam is clearly theocentric: the Absolute, God, is paramount and man exists only to serve His Creator. The *Qur'an* assures everyone of the right to read, write, and to know, and also freedom to express opinions. Yet, these rights remain limited in scope and hampered by several factors. Hamada specifically deals with a "democracy by decree," experienced by many Arab countries, that did not challenge the conservative social structure and brought about no independent political institutions, but rather severely limited the democratization process by harsh regulations and laws.

The pattern of democracy established "by decree" and politically fabricated public opinion was also typical of the former socialist countries. Ten years after the fall of the Iron Curtain, France Vreg's contribution sounds like an unbelievable, demonic tale; at the same time, however, it addresses the future of socialism based on political pluralism as a necessity for any developed complex society that wishes to be rational, democratic, and just. Socialism is not to be equated with the East-European systems of one-party politocracy, as Vreg argues, because socialism was congruent with democracy ever since its beginnings in the European political thought. The soviet model of socialism was actually a deformation of the potentials of socialism as a humanistic, pluralist democracy; thus, the socialist ideas are still in the process of ripening and waiting for the historical momentum—"the dramatic search for a more democratic organization of social and political life will continue."

Among a large number of conceptual disputes on public opinion during the last half of the century, one of the most salient issues is polling. Critical examinations of public opinion polling are part of the development of communication and public opinion theories and research that are marked by the deepening of critical consciousness among researchers that the discipline they are developing, research they are undertaking, and scientific instruments they are using are much more than merely a result of their individual mental production. There is no consensus on whether or not the polls have any validity as a measure of public opinion and what are their consequences for democratic life. James B. Lemert proceeds from Blumer's seminal critique of polling's assumptions, where he took for granted that polls could indeed predict election outcomes, but that was not to justify the validity of polling, that is, that polls would actually poll public opinion. In contrast to Blumer's objections to conceptualizing elections as a form of public opinion, Lemert argues that elections as legitimized expressions of collective opinion or the "will of the people" have a long history in democratic theory. There is also considerable evidence that what past elections "mean" and what future elections might produce can figure prominently when politicians consider their options in the "influence framework," one of the two political arenas in which, according to Lemert, issue opinions become visible and are processed. Whereas "election framework" occurs only on the day the votes are counted, the "influence framework" occurs the rest of the time, including the campaign preceding an election. Both frameworks emphasize participation-based opinion information. Despite all discordances, Lemert sees polls as, at least in principle, becoming part of effective public opinion, if or when poll results are made visible to decision-makers, and if decision-makers are inclined to use polls as an indicator of public opinion.

The controversial nature of polling is also reflected in disagreements between Lemert and Steven Barnett, who is questioning polling because of its potentially distorting implications for democracy. Barnett found within the governing classes and the body politic in Britain a growing belief in the role and legitimacy of opinion polls which are, together with focus groups, increasingly popularized as a positive step towards creating an "inclusive" and consultative democratic political environment. Although he agrees to some degree that public opinion generally, or as addressed in polling at least, does not exist but is manufactured, he also argues that this is a too simplistic observation. It does not make sense to dismiss the notion of a "general will" and, thus, public opinion simply because the measuring instruments are prone to distortion or manipulation by elite opinion formers. An additional important reason for not simply casting off "public opinion polls" is their increased presence in the media. Results of polling published in the media (re)initiate the process of opinion formation, which in one way or another may influence opinions published by the media and the policy-making and legislative processes. Thus, polls in many ways fulfill some of the functions traditionally considered the domain of political parties, pressure groups, elections, and other political institutions.

Pertti Suhonen would clearly endorse this idea on which his case study on the public presentation of polling results in the Finnish media is based. As he argues, polling and journalism together fulfill the same representational function as elections and referendums, and they also ought to compensate for the functions of civil society based on people's active participation and organization. Polls are not just another story in the media; they are increasingly used in overall journalism and foster the development of "precision journalism," which in addition to polls uses different ways of "scientific" gathering, analyzing, and reporting data in news stories. Suhonen analyzes five specific roles of journalism based on polling in the production of public opinion: (1) commissioning the polls and selecting research questions; (2) the selection of news items from other poll material available; (3) the evaluation of the results with means of news visibility; (4) supply of an interpretation to the audience with headlines and other linguistic strategies of the text; (5) a critical evaluation of the research methods, results, and their social significance. Content analysis of Finnish mainstream media reveal several linguistic strategies used by the journalists to make polling news attractive to the readers, which usually imply a biased picture of the findings. Another characteristic of poll journalism found in Finland is the lack of criticism in the presentation of data. Whereas polling and its social functions are constantly a matter of dispute among social scientists, a public debate on the reliability and social role of opinion polling takes place only seldom, for example, when the survey results show a clear contradiction between the public opinion and government policies or when different surveys produce contradictory results.

Poll journalism brings us to a more general relationship between public opinion and the media. At least since the mid-1800s the communicative nature of public opinion is inseparable from the operation of mass media, particularly their functions of making (controversial) issues more salient and appropriate for public discussion than others, and determining the limits of legitimate public discussion in society. In contemporary democracies, the idea of publicity primarily refers to the media where the "public use of reason" or "public discussion" supposedly could take place. Mass media are constitutive of any adequate contemporary theory of democracy and public opinion, despite their contradictory nature: On the one hand, mass media are at the very heart of the theorizations of, and practical endeavors directed towards, the "enthronement" of public opinion; on the other hand, the media are also used as the most powerful argument against the possible existence of a rational public opinion. Already in Tönnies', Dewey's and Lippmann's discussions of public opinion at the beginning of the century, newspapers were considered more important than other forms of political organization of society or the public. With the development of radio and television, the importance of the media became even more obvious. Although for a couple of decades, public opinion polls perhaps took the lead in the public opinion debates, with the development of computer mediated communication the primacy was returned to the media. Some recent ideas of public opinion as primarily a form of social control are even built upon a (highly questionable) assumption of a direct causal connection between media contents and individuals' behavior and attitudes. Indeed, the media have played and still play the central role in the processes of theorization and political institutionalization of public opinion.

Winfried Schulz looks at the empirical evidence of the characteristics of "the modern publicity process," a formula that Jay Blumler used to summarize the fundamental changes that political systems are undergoing in our time. In his discussion of the changes in the postmodern public sphere (or, as he names it, "a media-constructed public sphere") and the processes of its fragmentation supposedly caused by the increased availability of media (television) channels, Schulz presents the case of Germany, which suggests that the people expand their attention and accommodate to an expanding media system (though obviously with different speed in different segments of the population), rather than concentrate on certain media or channels and neglect others, as is often assumed in the literature. These empirical findings lead Schulz to the conclusion that one of the assumptions of the model of a media-constructed public sphere—that people concentrate on certain media or channels and neglect others—can be called in question. If indeed there were only little or no overlap of the audiences, different segments of the society would be "adjusted" to different streams of information and opinion, and the public sphere would dissolve into a large number of publics without any "common denominator." However, there is some empirical evidence that a high channel repertoire and high attention to TV information programs contribute to political cynicism, which makes the prospects of future developments rather annoying.

The concluding chapters by Christiane Eilders on the role of media opinion in "policy-agenda-setting" and Sandra Moog on American political communication in the information age further discuss how the mass media have developed into the primary arena for political communication. Moog deals with the dynamic that characterizes the electronic public sphere due to the increasing dominance of television and mass opinion polling since the 1960s. Eilders's contribution focuses on the role of the consonance in public opinion in the process of policy-agenda-setting. Similarly to Schulz's "media-constructed public sphere," media are not seen as neutral information agencies, but as actors in the political discourse influencing the agendas and decisions of the political system. Mass media are not considered, and not expected to be, the representatives of public opinion. Eilders's discussion of the media's contribution to the political discourse focuses on editorials that present the "collective opinion" of a media outlet and supposedly allow for an assessment of its specific contribution to the political discourse. Whereas Moog explores the role that new media technologies and new formats for media use may be expected to play in intensifying or pacifying trends towards more superficial communication in the public sphere, Eilders examines explicit and implicit expressions of editorial opinion (as a "significant part of public opinion") in the media that may have a significant impact on the political system.

To some extent, the contributions collected in this volume return us to the famous controversy between Dewey and Lippmann, whose divergent visions of the public and public opinion were based on the fact that the growth of complexity, which is paradoxically brought about by the very same technological developments that were invented to reduce it, implies that more and more of the world that we have to deal with is out of the individual's reach, out of sight, out of mind, so it can only be imagined, as Lippmann would say. Even the newest developments of computer-mediated communication do not lead by themselves into Dewey's *Great Community*. Paradoxically, they also enable the development of those nonpolitical forms of community life and scientific, religious, artistic, educational, industrial, and commercial groupings that should be, according to Dewey, strictly demarcated from the organized public. The greater the number of transactions among people, the smaller the proportion of transactions in which an individual can participate either directly or indirectly in the regulation of indirect consequences, and the greater the need for the (political) representation. The amount of information available is growing, information access is becoming easier—but at the same time, the gap between the amounts of produced and used information is deepening. The media supply is also growing, yet it often does not imply a greater diversity but, rather, the homogenization of the supply seems to be a consequence of media concentration and competition for the audiences.

The contemporary extension of political democracy and the development of the new mass media do not necessarily imply the refeudalization of publicness, as Habermas argued, but could also extend the public sphere to a wider layer of society, for example, along the lines of thought explicated by Beaud and Kaufmann, Peters, Axford and Huggins, or Sassi. In contrast to the forms of the public that existed before the twentieth century, the modern "large public" is neither spatially not temporally bound. The new media both create a new kind of publicness that does not refer to the sharing of a common locale, but is rather despatialized and nondialogical, and largely linked to the type of *representational visibility* produced mainly by television, and—in principle at least—enable *interaction* and make possible (although they do not assure) the rise of the "virtual public" as a materialization of formerly only abstract intellectual connection between individuals denoted by Tönnies as the foundation of the public. New technological communication possibilities rightly provoke an intellectual excitement. Yet, the question about the emancipatory and authoritarian power of communication technologies raised by Raymond Williams decades ago is still in place.

REFERENCES

Anderson, Benedict. 1983/1991. *Imagined Communities: Reflections on the Origins and Spread of Nationalism*. London: Verso.

Arendt, Hannah. 1958/1989. *The Human Condition*. Chicago: University of Chicago Press.

Blumer, Herbert. 1948. Public Opinion and Public Opinion Polling. *American Sociological Review* 13, 542-554.

Bogart, Leo. 1995. Media and Democracy. *Media Studies Journal*, Summer 1995, 1-10.

Bryce, James. 1888/1995. *The American Commonwealth*. Indianapolis: Liberty Fund.

Habermas, Jürgen. 1962/1995. *The Structural Transformation of the Public Sphere. An Inquiry into a Category of Bourgeois Society*. Trans. T. Burger. Cambridge, MA: MIT Press.

Key, V.O., Jr. 1961/1967. *Public Opinion and American Democracy*. New York: Knopf.

Lii, Ding-Tzann. 1998. Social Spheres and Public Life. A Structural Origin. *Theory, Culture & Society* 15(2): 115-135.

Park, Robert E. 1904/1972. *The Crowd and the Public*. Ed. by H. Elsner, Jr. Chicago: University of Chicago Press.

I

THEORIZING PUBLIC OPINION

1

Publicity, Democracy, and Public Opinion

Slavko Splichal

FROM THE PRINCIPLE OF PUBLICITY TO PUBLIC OPINION

Modern democracy is usually thought of as a product of the intellectual movement of Enlightenment, when the idea of publicity was raised to the fundamental moral principle. Although it had an instrumental function for the Scottish utilitarians, and even a disciplinarian role for Jeremy Bentham, Immanuel Kant exalted it to a transcendent principle mediating between politics and morals in public law, and maintaining harmony between them. In his treatise on *Perpetual Peace* (1795/1983), Kant developed the transcendental formula of public justice according to which all actions that affect the rights of other men are wrong if they are not public. Kant's principle of publicity was not directly connected to public opinion but rather to the reconciliation of politics with morals; yet his notion of publicity came very close to the idea of public opinion when he related it to the mutual "agreement of all judgments with each other." Bentham should be credited for the first in-depth discussion of the relationship between public opinion and the principle of publicity, and the definition of the latter as the foundation of public opinion and people's sovereignty. According to Bentham, publicity is a necessary precondition "for putting the *tribunal of the public* in a condition for forming an *enlightened judgement*" (Bentham, 1791/1994: 590; emphases added). He saw in the principle of publicity a safeguard for public confidence in the assembly and an assurance that it would perform its duties. Bentham emphasized the importance of general visibility and accessibility, which ought to enable efficient control over power elites. Similarly to the disciplinary technology that he elaborated in *Panopticon* (1787/1995), Bentham related the principle of publicity to a "system of distrust" and argued that "every good political institution is founded upon this base." In Bentham's understanding of publicity, the aspect of rational debate had only secondary importance—in sharp contrast to Jean Jacques Rousseau and later democratic theories, Bentham did not proclaim the view that all individuals have the ability to use reason— and the critical character of publicity was entirely absent.

The early theorizations of publicity and public opinion were concluded with the first monograph entirely devoted to the "rise, progress, and present state of public opinion," as the author William A. MacKinnon (1828) subtitled the book. Similarly to Bentham, MacKinnon differentiated between three social classes based on wealth, of which only the middle class actually generates public opinion. Whereas, according to MacKinnon, "popular clamour is powerful in proportion as the lower class is ignorant and numerous" and relies on the ignorance and prejudice of the uneducated, the fundamental characteristic of public opinion is that it is well-informed and intelligent:

> Public opinion may be said to be, that sentiment on any given subject which is entertained by the best informed, most intelligent, and most moral persons in the community, which is gradually spread and adopted by nearly all persons of any education or proper feeling in a civilized state. (MacKinnon, 1828/1971: 15)

The increase in power of public opinion was, according to MacKinnon, closely related to the development of liberal government: "public opinion secures a liberal form of government, not that a government secures public opinion" (MacKinnon, 1828/1971: 9). And similar to what Edmund Burke (1769/1967: 106) had written before him, MacKinnon emphasized—in striking contrast to Bentham, Kant, or Hegel—that the government must be governed by public opinion and must follow its dictates. Rousseau went even further by arguing for the idea of the absolute sovereignty of the people as a community of equal citizens (irrespective of their status, property, etc.) within the nation-state, although this idea was even at that time clearly utopian. He considered public opinion a form of general will that is based on the debate and decisions of "appropriately educated people" (whereas those less educated may need to be enlightened) and expresses itself through laws. However, public opinion is specific in that it is a guarantee for the execution of all other laws and thus superior to them, and that it is the judgment of the people that is expressed in *censorship*[1]—"the kind of law of which the censor is the minister, and which he only causes to be applied to particular cases, after the example of the prince" (Rousseau, 1762/1947: 113).

Whereas the theories of the rule of public opinion from Edmund Burke to Jürgen Habermas—in spite of abundant theoretical (e.g., Hegel) and empirical critiques (e.g., Lippmann)—attributed sovereignty to public opinion and to the public itself,[2] the public, as the materialized form of the principle of publicity, has always been either implicitly or explicitly limited by the competence and status of individuals. As a matter of contradiction, all effective forms of institutionalization of public opinion in the bourgeois legal state (parliament, mass media, polling) reflected and/or initiated gradual disintegration of the liberal public, and finally "The principle of publicity based on the public of educated people who reason and enjoy art and the medium of bourgeois press—has been refunctioned for demonstrative and manipulative purposes" (Habermas, 1965/1980:10). This transformation was paralleled by severe criticism of the rule of public opinion. The period of confidence in public opinion, based on the belief in the moral judgment of the common (middle-class) man proclaimed in the Age of Enlightenment, was followed by a period of distrust in his capabilities and competence.

Doubts were first clearly expressed by G. W. F. Hegel and, since the mid-1800s, followed by the political-philosophical and social-psychological critiques of "the tyranny of majority" (Alexis de Tocqueville, John Stuart Mill, James Bryce, Gustave LeBon, Gabriel Tarde) that continued to dominate up to the rise of positivism and empiricism emerging in social sciences in the early 1900s. However, the inherent limitations, theoretical assumptions, and "external" (social) conditions of public opinion were not systematically studied before the period of the "sociologization" of public opinion theories in the beginning of the twentieth century, particularly in the treatises of Robert E. Park, Ferdinand Tönnies, John Dewey, and Walter Lippmann.

Although early liberal understanding of public opinion emerged from the doctrine of sovereignty of the people, Hegel was the first to clearly voice the ambiguous and inherently contradictory role of public opinion. He defended the publicity of the Estates' debates in Germany only on the grounds of expanding knowledge about public affairs among the general population. Publicizing debates should enable public opinion to gain insight into problems as well as reliable information needed to make rational judgments (but not decisions concerning the state). In contrast to the early liberal belief that the government has to follow public opinion, Hegel (1821/1971: 197, §302) considered the Estates as mediators and reductors of the power of the crown as well as particular interests of individuals and associations, and the bulwark against "an unorganized opinion and volition . . . in opposition to the organized state." For Hegel, public opinion was but "the unorganized way in which a people's *opinions and wishes are made known*" (Add. §316; emphases added). Within public opinion, two different strands are ceaselessly interwoven: (1) public use and authority of reason and (2) contingency, ignorance and faulty reasoning. Thus, public opinion should be thought of both in the sense of *vox populi, vox dei*[3] and—as Hegel quoted the Italian Renaissance poet, Lodovico Ariosto—of an ignorant vulgar who reproves everyone and talks most of what he understands least.

Nevertheless, ever since Enlightenment, public opinion bestows an aura of legitimacy upon laws, policies, decisions, convictions, or even wars, but often for manipulative purposes: they all appear justified or valid if they are in accordance with "public opinion." Whereas premodern states legitimized their origin and development with the divine will, in modern democracies this function is largely assumed by public opinion. It is indispensable to the legitimacy of governments that claim their power is based on the consent of the governed. In this sense, public opinion is functionally equivalent with religion, as Ferdinand Tönnies (1922) argued. Such a "legitimization pressure" can partly explain why "the public" and "public opinion" are so differently, even controversially, interpreted and defined, constantly appealed to but, at the same time, so often ignored in practice.

Since early modern times, public opinion was typically institutionalized in three distinct nationwide[4] forms, but none of them genuinely represented an ideally defined public:[5]

1. *Parliament*. If anything, parliament may generally be called an "organ of opinion of the public," although even this is not always completely justified. This belief reflects a widely held assumption, advocated by normative political theories and early sociological theorizing of public opinion, notably by American pragmatists (Park and Dewey) and Tönnies. However, representative government has never been a system in which parliamentary representatives had to regard opin-

ions of the electorate; it has never been a direct form of popular sovereignty. Rather, since its foundation, representative government, even if based on the principle of universal suffrage, has been a rule by elites, distinguished from the majority of citizens by their social status, education, particularistic interests, and way of life.

2. *Newspapers and the media.* Since its very beginning, the press played an important role in conceptualizations of public opinion. It delivered not only information to the public and, thus, was an important element in the process of public opinion formation, but it was also the main means of expression of the public, constituting a virtual public. In addition, the press was a general medium for more restricted means of expression, such as associations, meetings, or demonstrations, whereas the public was always, and nearly exclusively, a newspaper-reading public. However, newspapers not only express the opinion of the public, but also influence public opinion. In reality, newspapers are neither organs of public opinion nor are they identical with it; rather, they are primarily organs of political parties and commercial corporations. In Tönnies', Dewey's, and Lippmann's discussions of public opinion, newspapers already were considered more important than other forms of political organization of the public.

3. *Polling.* Public opinion polling developed during the decline of the critical (reading) public. During the last fifty years, it was largely considered the first "scientific mastering" of public opinion and generally institutionalized in Western democracies. Although formerly social sciences rather unsuccessfully attempted a scientific operationalization of normative concepts of public opinion, with polling, as its prophets believed, they seemed to finally achieve a satisfactory degree of empirical validity. Moreover, media owners and newsworkers soon became aware of the importance of polling as a competitive form of institutionalization of public opinion and largely adopted "scientific polls." Yet similarly to the press and parliament, polling was soon criticized for its negative effects on public opinion and democratic life, and accused of antidemocratic manipulation and control over public opinion.

Regardless of whether public opinion was considered as originating from rational discussion or merely as a widespread diffusion of elite opinion, even by coercion; or whether "public opinion" presupposed the public either as a corporate social entity or merely a (statistical) aggregation of individuals; or it was even conceived without any specific actor—it was always assumed that public opinion is (at least) publicly expressed opinion that in some way represents the will of the (majority of) people or citizenry. Yet, even this least common denominator was dissolved by the rise of polling in the 1930s.

ENDURING CONTROVERSIES IN CONCEPTUALIZATIONS OF PUBLIC OPINION

Despite, or perhaps because of, an extremely fast development of social sciences, the controversies about public opinion intensified during the last century of the millennium. With the rise of empirical research, normative theories of public opinion waned progressively, and a gap occurred between traditional normative-philosophic and new operational conceptualizations. Sociologization of public opinion theories and research brought about, or intensified, two types of dissents: (1) In contrast to political theories, the positivist stream steadily depoliticized the notion of public opinion, drawing it near to a universal, transhistorical concept. (2) Within sociological theorizations that retained the political character of public opinion as their prime qualifier, the conflict between advocates of an active role of the public (e.g., Tönnies, Blumer) and those restricting members of the public to mere observers (e.g., Lippmann, Noelle-Neumann) was intensified. Paradoxically, the former grounded their argument for an active role of public opinion more on the historical and cultural processes, whereas the opponents considered primarily political functions of public opinion. The institutionalization of public opinion polling in political systems raised the question of (non)equivalence of different forms of expression of public opinion, particularly between institutionalized and noninstitutionalized manifestations. By the end of the century, postmodernism radicalized the question of *consensus* and *homogeneity* as the primary purpose of public opinion— either as a consequence of rational deliberations or an effect of the individual's almost psychotic fears—arguing that consensus could only represent a local optimization, whereas heterogeneity or heteromorphism would prevail nationally and globally.

   None of these controversies can be limited to the twentieth century. Essentially, they are all closely linked with the two fundamental contradictions that marked the idea of public opinion since its earliest conceptualizations: (1) The *internal*, or *semantic*, contradiction is a consequence of connecting two contrasting concepts, "public" and "opinion": public refers to the universal, objective, and rational; and opinion to individual, subjective, and unstable. (2) The *external* contradiction results from the relationship between the actors forming and expressing public opinion and the actors to whom it is addressed, or between the expression and realization of public opinion. With the rise of mass media, an additional dimension of opinion *reception* aggravate the contradictions— (3) the relationship between those forming and expressing, and those receiving "ready-made" public opinion. The three fundamental contradictions are "responsible" for the oscillations in conceptualizations of public opinion between holistic endeavors to place public opinion in the sphere of collective, and reductionist endeavors to attribute it exclusively to the individual.

Internal contradiction. "Public opinion" is a poetical compound word, as only in poetry may the incompatible become united. Such an idea is to link "opinion" and "public," which is actually an attempt to unite in reality the absolutely incompatible—"one" with "many," individual rights (proclaimed in liberal state) with public interest (emphasized in social welfare state). The concept of "opinion" implies *unity* (*the* opinion), whereas its specific characterization ("public") denotes *many* individuals and, thus, opinions (Jordan, 1918 in Tönnies, 1922: 132). Opinion is distinctively individual and lacks of certainty. As Kant argued, it represents subjectively and objectively insufficient form of "holding for true" (unlike believing and knowing). In contrast, Tönnies (1922) explicitly linked opinion with human reason and placed rational *opining* superior to affective *believing*. Nevertheless, as Allport (1937: 13) argued, "opinion" is always an instance of "behavior of human individuals."

The notion "public" has just the opposite sign than "opinion": it refers to participation of many people, which fundamentally questions the character of individuality of the "opinion." Whereas *opinion* is marked by the variable, subjective and uncertain, *public* aspires to achieve the universal, objective, and rational. The controversial nature of "public issues" is based on the separation of the "being" and the "value"of things discussed, as Park (1904/1972: 61) maintained: their meaning can be accepted as identical by all members of the public, but the value (e.g., importance, evaluation, salience) is different. At the end of the process, public opinion can never result in a complete *agreement*, because, at the very least, differences in degree, intensity or firmness of opinions always exist. In the strict sense, public opinion cannot be conceived as a single, unified opinion, or a perfect agreement of a relatively large group of people (crowd, mass, public, audience, or even population, people, or nation). It can only be a conglomerate of different, often conflicting, opinions.

Nevertheless, at least a vague idea of *the opinion* connecting many individuals and/or spreading through many collectivities usually appeared as a fundamental element of its definition.[6] In *The Social Contract*, Rousseau (1762/1947) related *volonté générale* to the agreement upon the common benefit, which arose from the resistance to the benefit of each individual, in contrast to *volonté de tous* that was merely the sum of all individual wills. In *Critique of Public Opinion*, Tönnies (1922: 301) emphasized that the power of public opinion is "the greater, the higher is the level of its firmness and energy, which make it to move: both together, the mass with the speed factor, make the *momentum* of the public opinion." Whereas the "power" of public opinion is based on the level of *consensus*, the process of public opinion formation and expression is fundamentally characterized by *controversy* and *dissensus*. According to Tönnies, public opinion differs from other forms of complex social will by the *nature* of "consensus and rational agreement" (Tönnies, 1922: 53). He insisted that commonness does not mean merely what people or objects "have in common," that is, the *properties* of agents, but rather the *relations* between them: "we think of feelings etc. which already are an expression of the boundness among people, and which condition this boundness" (Tönnies, 1922: 44).

In public opinion process, consensus could be considered a counterfactual ideal and presupposition which all participants anticipate in that they strive not merely for empirical agreement but for a consensus motivated by the general interest. In practice, it can only denote commonly the most acceptable opinion so that the distances between it and all individual opinions are minimized. Yet a certain *degree* of mutual agreement is a necessary condition for public opinion to influence institutions of decision-making, or, as Dewey would say, for the public to secure, through its officers, the regulation of long-term consequences of transactions among individuals and groups for society. This specific *regulative power* defines the difference between the public, which is always directly related to the state, and civil society, which is a network of organizations and movements independent from the state. In civil society, which links together a variety of groups that develop as self-governing spheres, regulation is aimed at internal or intragroup transactions among individuals rather than indirect and long-term external consequences of in-group transactions; the latter lead to the formation of the public. Through public opinion, civil society can act on the basis of its *moral power*, in contrast to *economy*, whose regulative power is enforced by money, and *the state* (political society), which acts directively through the legislature.

External contradiction. The second, *external*, contradiction of the concept "public opinion" originates from its political dimension: since early theorizations, public opinion was supposed not only to *express* but also to *materialize* the will of the people. As argued by Key (1961/1967: 547): "If a democracy is to exist, the belief must be widespread that public opinion, at least in the long run, *affects the course of public action*" (emphases added), although many theorists and, particularly, empiricists would strongly disagree. The idea of public opinion has been ever since Rousseau linked to the ideals of people's sovereignty, the principle of rule by majority, political representation, and formal, constitutionally established ways of participation in the decision-making process. But that relationship is also contradictory in nature. Firstly because, as emphasized by Wilson (1962: 5), "Historically, formal participation has run far ahead of the idea of free opinion, and free opinion is logically perfect only when there is no mechanism of political censorship or coercion. . . . In support of public decisions, the majority is ready to deny the right of expression to certain opinions, especially when it is believed they contradict the principle of the continued existence of the community itself." Secondly, public opinion has never been understood as *directly participating* in the execution of state power, but rather as a *critique* of state power. This contradiction was only *supposedly* "resolved" in behavioristic conceptions (where public opinion is only an aggregation of individual opinions) and in the constitutionalistic conceptualization of Carl Schmitt, who saw the unique function of public opinion in affecting "state life" through the *acclamation* of physically aggregated people (Schmitt, 1928/1954: 242-247).

The changing role of media. Public opinion is inherently based on communication. "In politics communication makes possible public opinion, which, when organized, is democracy" (Cooley, 1909/1971: 650). It is not surprising, then, that the development of a new form of communication—*mass media*—brought about an additional contradiction with regard to the subject of public opinion. Whereas formerly "the public" has been predominantly understood as a normative foundation of democracy, as public forum shaped in critical discussions about public affairs by constantly interacting, educated, and informed individuals, modern mass media have created a new type of "public," which is largely depoliticized and does not participate in political deliberations and decision-making. Changes in the communication sphere are homologous to what happened in the sphere of politics where representative democracy *has replaced* participatory democracy as known in antique Athens. In the same way, the dominant forms of communication became far more effective in public representation before the people than involving them in public discussions as active participants—communicators. Early newspapers with very limited circulation helped spread revolutionary ideas that delegitimized the authoritarian political order and extended the arena of public debate essential to representative government. On the other hand, the history abounds with examples of the abuse of the media for the worst forms of tyrannical suppression of society and the media themselves, or for commercial interests. The period of state socialism in Eastern and Central Europe[7] is only one of too many historic examples of the former. Critical publicity characteristic of early political newspapers was largely substituted by "manipulative publicity" that, similarly to feudal "representative publicness," could only serve the manipulation of the public and legitimization of political authorities before it, but remedies prescribed for the recovery were quite different.

Commercial obstacles to the formation and expression of public opinion are no less critical. In the age of Enlightenment, the principle of publicity and the public use of reason were not subordinate but, on the contrary, *opposed* to the sphere of economy and its dominant right of private ownership. The idea to conceive of the freedom of public expression as a "special form" of the right of ownership has been born later, in the mid-1800s, though related to the earlier liberal free market model, where independent producers and consumers were supposed to reach an agreement about the type, quality, and price of products to be exchanged. For the representative of bourgeois class in Karl Marx's *Debatten über Pressfreiheit* (1842/1974) it was a "classic inconsistency" if the press were exempted from the general rules of economy, as it was for Walter Lippmann eighty years later an "anomaly of our civilization" that "community applies one ethical measure to the press and another to trade or manufacture," instead of treating the press as "a business pure and simple" (1922/1960: 321).

Tönnies and Dewey were perhaps the last vigorous defenders of the normative concept of "opinion of *the public*" in the sense of a common judgment formed and expressed by those who constitute the public, "the public" being expressly singularized. Later on, plurality and diversity of *opinions* typical of democratic societies preponderated over the unity of *the public* in conceptualizations of public opinion. The scholarly attention was redirected from the final *state* and *normative goal* (consensus) to the everyday *processes* of opinion formation and expression. Even in political theories, *the* public opinion was understood in the sense of V. O. Key's *consensus on fundamentals* that *permits* and *limits* rather than *directs* certain governmental actions. In other words, public opinion is not seen as an organized, active opinion resulting from (political) discussions, but a judgment—formed and entertained by those who constitute a public, and about public affairs—which may be activated if organized by a specific (political) actor, for example, an interest group, political party, the media, or even pollsters.

REINVENTING SOCIAL CONTROL: FROM THE TYRANNY OF MAJORITY TO THE FEAR OF ALL

As the concept of public opinion always referred to the political sphere, it was also always caught in ideological confrontations. Luhmann had a right to state that "the theory of 'public opinion' . . . has always had a problematic (not lastly an ideological) relation to reality" (Luhmann, 1969: 104). In the eighteenth and early nineteenth century, public opinion was the expression of economic and political emancipation of bourgeoisie and its particularistic (class) interests, although in the early phase of the struggle for a legal state, the difference between bourgeois and "general" interests was only latent. In the struggle for the affirmation of its interests (first against the domestic aristocracy and then against the bourgeoisie of foreign countries), the bourgeoisie was forced to present its particular interests as general, "higher" national interests in order to get support of lower classes and mobilize them. When the principal political goals were achieved, public opinion became "ambivalent" and split because of the profound difference between the normative (individual, political) equality and actual (structural, particularly economic) inequality of citizens. Prioritization of the rationality of discourse generating public opinion in theories reflects both the tendencies to preserve the Enlightenment idea of public opinion and to protect the bourgeois ideology of public opinion from demands originating in lower classes. Critiques of the "tyranny of the majority," which multiplied since the mid-nineteenth century and probably reached the peak with Lippmann's *Phantom Public* (1925), clearly exemplify this tendency. Hence Adorno's and Horkheimer's critique of "instrumental rationality" that in capitalism superseded rationality based on autonomous and critical use of reason promoted by the Enlightenment. As opposed to this "tyrannical perspective," opinion polling that expanded the base of public opinion to *all* citizens was not entirely falsely considered an impetus to the democratization of society and rejuvenation of public opinion.

In the twentieth century, the bourgeois idea of publicness was essentially refeudalized both in practice and theory. Passivizing and depoliticizing of the public resulted in the abolition of the public as a specific social category, as the subject of public opinion. Mills and Habermas saw the main reason for the fall of the public in the increasing interventionism of the state that penetrated the public and limited its autonomy in forming opinions through discussions, so that it finally disintegrated into the mass. However, this theory of the fall of the bourgeois public overlooked the possibility that, historically, this process proceeded in the opposite direction, that is, that the bourgeois public transformed itself into the subject of the public representation of power.

Namely, a way out of the double "freedom" from the ruling power—
that is, (1) not being subject to power and (2) not being in power—is
also to achieve power, not only to achieve autonomy from power.
When the public is transformed into a power actor, it disappears as the
public, but not as a historical subject. In a way, we may recognize this
idea already in Tönnies's *Kritik der öffentlichen Meinung*, in which he
claimed that with the rise and strengthening of the middle classes their
ideas were also rising and strengthening; and the new classes succeeded in turning their particular ideas into a common good of the political
public. The struggle for freedom of thought and press and the fight for
other rights of citizens was "in its essence an expression of the fight of
the new-bourgeois, the national-bourgeois class that positions itself as a
'public'—. . . for power, i.e., first for participation in the power of old
classes and the monarchy which it restrains, and later increasingly for
independent power" (Tönnies, 1922: 128). In the aftermath of the bourgeois revolutions of the eighteenth and nineteenth centuries, the actual
reduction of the public to the bourgeois class effectively meant the narrowing of the social base of the public and its immuring against the
emerging working class, and thus the loss of its critical stance. Hence,
on the one hand a sphere of quasi-public opinion—opinions (speeches,
statements, etc.) publicly presented by the authoritative institutions—
was constituted; on the other hand, a sphere of informal, nonpublic,
individual opinions developed, which was no longer associated with
the political institutions. Concentration of capital and monopolization
rapidly increased the power of private entrepreneurs, the public transformed itself into a state institution, and a large class of citizens without
economic and political power was taking rise: "the mass" was born. As
the liberal press helped constitute the liberal public a century earlier,
now the development of *mass* press substantially contributed to the
refeudalization of publicness.

This was the kind of transition at the end of the nineteenth century when the first *social-psychological* conceptualizations of public opinion appeared. The most prominent sociological theorists of public opinion of the time (e.g., Tönnies and Bauer in Germany, Tarde in France,
and Dewey, Park, and Lippmann in the United States) explicitly referred
to psychological research as a source as valuable as normative political
theories of the eighteenth and nineteenth centuries. The emerging social-
psychological tradition "emancipated" public opinion from its enlight-
ened-rational character and from its "dependence" on freedom of the
press. Public opinion increasingly meant reactions of masses and manipulated or imitating behavior of individuals. The public lost its rational,
strictly political character and reference to a "national people." With his
book *Psychologie des foules* (1895/1930), Gustave LeBon is regarded as the

founder of the new tradition, which also heavily influenced Park's dissertation on *The Crowd and the Public* (1904/1972).

Objections against rationality and legitimacy of public opinion gained the momentum in the mid-nineteenth century, essentially following the arguments put forward already by Burke, MacKinnon, and Hegel. Arguments of Tocqueville (1840/1969), Mill (1859/1985), and Bryce (1888/1995) legitimized the narrowing of "the public" to the representatives of the educated and wealthy middle class. Whereas the liberal-democratic concept of public opinion was critically oriented against the absolutist authority, the revised theory of public opinion in the period of the consolidation of the rule of law attempted to legitimize and conserve the economic and political power of the bourgeois class against the working-class *mass*. In *Liberty*, Mill—based on Tocqueville's analysis of *Democracy in America*, a destructive critique of the majoritarian principle—even advocated despotism as a legitimate mode of government in dealing with "barbarians," and in public opinion he saw a great danger to democracy: "The modern régime of public opinion is, in an unorganized form, what the Chinese educational and political systems are in an organized; and unless individuality shall be able successfully to assert itself against the yoke, Europe, notwithstanding its noble antecedents and its professed Christianity, will tend to become another China" (Mill, 1859/1985: 138).

In the sociological and socio-psychological traditions of the twentieth century, some authors (e.g., Tönnies, 1922; Hennis, 1957) tried to resolve the perplexity of the "tyranny of majority" with a distinction between the norm-generating, accountable and sovereign public opinion, and "common" or "mass opinion." The "solution" is basically an actualization of the difference between the pre-Enlightenment (enlightenment, social control) and Enlightenment concepts (participation) of public opinion. In the new dualization, "public opinion" largely refers to opinions presented in/by mass media:

> Public opinion is, what the majority of the learned think. . . . Thus, what is politically thought, opined, talked, "whispered" (why not also grumbled?) outside the press, parties, universities and other institutions of the "social representation," is not public opinion but "common" opinion (die "gemeine" Meinung). . . . While "public opinion" ought to be rational or at least rationalized, "mass opinion" ought to be superficial. (Schmidtchen, 1959: 237)

The difference between "public" and "mass" opinion points to the significance and controversial nature of *professional communication* and the importance of *knowledge* and information in decision making which increased enormously since Rousseau's times, along with the exponential growth of the quantity of disposable knowledge produced and the discrepancy between *experts* and "ordinary" citizens or, as some scholars conceptualized the difference, between leaders and followers.

V. O. Key asserted that the interaction between leaders and followers might be best understood if public opinion was conceptualized "as a system of dikes which *channel* public action or which fix a range of discretion within which government may act or within which debate at official levels may proceed" (Key, 1961/1967: 552). He argued that the opinion-action relation in the relationship between followers and leaders is relatively loose, in contrast to Francis G. Wilson, who was interested in mechanisms and agencies that "should *represent* popular opinion"—the monarch, the parliament, civil service, some kind of trained ruling class, and judiciary—and claimed that "the representative system is the highest agency for the *effective expression* of the popular mind" (Wilson, 1962: 64-65).[8] According to Key (1961/1967: 76), neither does public opinion rule, nor it is ruled: "The hypotheses about interactions within the political elites and about interactions between the political elites and mass opinion . . . seem far more plausible than the alternative simplistic views of the role of public opinion." Key emphasizes the role of *mass opinion*[9] as a part of a complex system of interactions within the circles of influence and leadership, and between them and mass opinion. However, he ultimately relates this channeling process to the institutional system of political parties. Public opinion is not institutionalized itself, but it has its "referent" in the party system, so that "the ultimate weapon of public opinion is the minority party."

The difference between Wilson and Key in the 1960s in their conceptualizing of the relationship between the public and the government is almost a mirror image of the Dewey-Lippmann controversy in the 1920s. Dewey argued, as did Wilson forty years later, that "representative government must at least seem to be founded on public interests as they are revealed to public belief. The days are passed when government can be carried on without any pretense of ascertaining the wishes of the governed" (Dewey, 1927/1991: 181). Yet, Dewey knew very well that popular judgments and political conduct might be effectively muddied and controlled, and so did Lippmann who ascertained, in contrast to Dewey, that the "creation of consent" did not die out with the appearance of democracy. On the contrary, it extended and improved enormously, so that "persuasion has become a self-conscious art and a regular organ of popular government. . . . Under the impact of propaganda . . . the old constants of our thinking have become variables. It is no longer possible . . . to believe in the original dogma of democracy" (Lippmann, 1922/1960: 248). He regarded public opinion as too ignorant, intuitive, uncertain, and fallible to influence decisions or direct executive actions that should be in the hands of those who possess an insider's knowledge of events and are able to act effectively upon highly complex affairs. According to Lippmann, the need of the top-down creation of consent has definitely outrooted the need of the formation of consensus—if it ever existed at all.

Tönnies' was probably the first conceiving a dynamic theory of public opinion as a minority-majority interaction.[10] According to Tönnies, the formation of public opinion is in a continual state of flux from its gaseous to the solid state. The intellectual core of the opinion of the public, its *Gelehrtenrepublik*, is always constituted by the *minority* of the most educated individuals who represent the most solid (firm) and reliable part of the opinion of the public. For Tönnies, public opinion is formed through a process in which a single published opinion is progressively becoming the opinion of many, of the majority and, eventually, even the opinion of all. The opinion of the public represents an agreement of the majority or even all citizens; yet, for the majority, this agreement can be only a passive, tacit consent or acceptance of the opinion considered to be rational, whereas only the educated elite effectively participates in an active formation and expression of opinion. In a way that resembles the views of Tönnies, Herbert Blumer conceived the public as consisting of two parts: (1) the active part composed primarily of interest groups and (2) "a more detached and disinterested spectator-like body." Public opinion formed and expressed by the public is "a collective product formed through public discussion and is not a unanimous opinion with which everyone in the public agrees, nor is it necessarily the opinion of the majority. Being a collective opinion it may be (it usually is) different from the opinion of any of the groups in the public" (Blumer, 1946/1966: 48).

Yet Tönnies' theory reached almost no responsiveness, and Blumer's interactionist ideas were heavily criticized by behaviorists. A large part of public opinion theories was marked by the "learned minority-unlettered majority" *dichotomy*. Within the new dominant paradigm established in psychology, sociology, and communication research, public opinion was progressively depoliticized, although early sociological theorizations still emphasized the political dimension of public opinion. Unfortunately, the most frequent scientific reaction to the growing complexity of political and public opinion processes was reductionism, typically expressed in the psychologization of public opinion research, the reduction of public opinion to characteristics and effects of group (and later mass) communications, and the development of public opinion polling, which reduces public opinion to an aggregate of anonymous answers of isolated individuals to a set of arbitrarily defined questions. All the fundamental dimensions of conceptualizations of public opinion that developed since the eighteenth century were completely excluded from newly emerging models: the formation of citizen consensus through public discussion (or with acclamation), the role of the state and authoritative institutions in the formation and realization of public opinion, the importance of political and economic organizations and associations within the (nation-)state and international relations, the effects of the professionalization of political and communication processes, and, last but not least, the importance and specific functions of the mass media. The definition of public opinion proposed by Wilhelm Bauer in 1930 clearly marked the deviation from normative political theories:

> Public opinion represents the formation of a defined group will which imparts a certain equable color to the judgments and will expressions of the majority of individuals, without being rationally deliberated in each single case. We may say that the frame of mind (*Stimmungsgehalt*) of a temporally bounded group is condensed in it, since the social willing receives a more or less solid form (*Gestalt*) in it. (Bauer, 1930: 19)

Paradoxically, however, the new social-psychological paradigm (re)introduced the questions of power and social control as the central, but presumably nonpolitical issues. As Wilson (1962: 108, 109) stated, "Public opinion, to the sociologist, is one of the means by which social behavior is directed. . . . The view of public opinion as a phase of social control has . . . led the sociologist to the study of propaganda." The emerging positivist paradigm treated public opinion as an organic social process and linked it to the social-psychological findings about group interaction rather than democratic theory. The new empirical, social-psychological stream apotheosized in polling developed into the dominant paradigm after the Second World War both in the United States and Europe, and progressively in all countries with parliamentary political systems. One of its most outstanding peaks is represented by the model of the spiral of silence which Noelle-Neumann developed in the 1970s.

Noelle-Neumann (1980/1993: 229-234) brought up the pre-Enlightenment dichotomy of *popular* versus *public* opinion, which she labeled as a difference between the "social control" and "rationalist" functions of public opinion. According to Noelle-Neumann, the latter concept denotes a rational human activity instrumental in the process of opinion formation and decision-making in democracy, but a more "realistic" concept is that denoting a form of social control with the main function to promote social integration and to insure a sufficient level of consent on which actions and decisions may be based and, thus, legitimized. She draws a parallel between these two concepts and Robert

Merton's distinction between *manifest* and *latent* functions: a rational process of opinion formation represents the manifest function of public opinion, and social control represents its latent function (Noelle-Neumann, 1980/1993: 220). The distinction between manifest and latent functions in Merton's terms implies not only the distinction between the functions in terms of objective consequences for a specified entity, but also in terms of their validity and, thus, relevance for research. According to Merton's conceptualization(1949/1993: 333), the function of social control, because it is a latent function, represents the potentially more fruitful object of study than the classical "common-sense" manifest function of public opinion. As Noelle-Neumann claims, the "rational" concept of public opinion "does not explain the pressure that public opinion must exert if it is to have any influence on the government and the citizens. *Raisonnement* is enlightening, stimulating, and interesting, but it is not able to exert the kind of pressure from which—as John Locke said—not one in ten thousand remains invulnerable" (Noelle-Neumann, 1980/1993: 227). However, she believes that the power of public opinion is easy to explain if public opinion is conceptualized in terms of social control. Noelle-Neumann refers here to her "spiral of silence" theory, which predicts that individuals will tend not to deviate from majority opinion in society in order to avoid isolation and negative sanctions. By doing so, they generate integration and cohesion in a society—which is exactly the latent function of public opinion, according to Noelle-Neumann.[11]

Noelle-Neumann resumed, and radically passivized and individualized, the postwar German behavioral tradition initiated by Gerhard Schmidtchen. He grounded his public opinion theory "on the empirical knowledge of social and social-psychological group processes in the population at large and their relationship to politics" and thus articulated a "realistic-typical definition of the concept of public opinion." According to Schmidtchen's definition, "all those *forms of behavior of any groups of people* ought to be considered 'public opinion,' which are capable to modify or conserve the structures, practices, and goals of government" (Schmidtchen, 1959: 257; emphases added). Schmidtchen's definition suggests that the concept of public opinion should refer to a very wide (indeed, practically, an all-inclusive) sphere of human activity. Public opinion should include not only political, but also economic and cultural activities of people and all ideas and habits that direct or shape behavior, such as religion, custom, and ideology. Under the umbrella of public opinion every kind of human behavior ought to belong: verbal and nonverbal; opinions, forms of behavior, even the "material facts as remnants of past activities"; rational and irrational; interested and disinterested; knowledge and ignorance; conscious and unconscious; manifest and latent (Schmidtchen, 1959: 261). The only restriction on all of these different kinds of activities and behavior is that they should concern political power. With the advent of electoral democracy, the traditionally adversarial relationship between the people and their government has been supplanted by one of dependence (Ginsberg, 1986: 58). In this new relationship, public opinion breaks free of its critical-oppositional role and become the correlate of power. "Public opinion is the correlate of power. Public opinion is the aggregate of related phenomena—something which politically exists only in a given relationship between authority and the people" (Schmidtchen, 1959: 255). Habermas had praised this idea as an important step toward the required synthesis between the classical concept of public opinion and its social-psychological surrogate. However, he sharply rejected Schmidtchen's understanding of public opinion on the ground that it completely ignored the intention of a politically active public (Habermas, 1962/1995: 243).

Schmidtchen, following the earlier social-psychological tradition and under the influence of Robert K. Merton, consistently neutralized and universalized the notion of public opinion. Public opinion conceptualized as a "correlate of power" presumably exists in all social systems—in "monarchic, aristocratic and totalitarian" systems just as it does in "democratic" ones (Otto, 1966: 120). It should not be related to any specific form of government; what is important is only the enduring tension between the governing and the governed, which is present, in manifest or latent form, in any form of government (Otto, 1996: 101; see Wilson, 1962: ix). According to Otto, with public opinion as a mode of behavior (*Verhaltensweise*), those who are governed can always express consent, rejection, or desire for change to the power system. In this, the most important are the possibilities for public opinion to problematize the goals and existence of the government. Such possibilities are available not only in elections, but range from total disinterest and passive opposition to sabotage and armed resistance (Otto, 1966: 119). Because various tendencies in public opinion may undermine the goals and the very existence of power, it must be able to scan and control public opinion and direct it toward the support of power. To achieve this, the authorities use a wide variety of psychological methods of persuasion. In their efforts, the power structure must be supported by sustained social, economic, international-political, and military conditions and must continually demonstrate its own success if it wants to assure a long-term favorable climate of opinions and the willingness of a population for co-operation.

As Schmidtchen himself pointed out, and after him Otto, this understanding of public opinion sharply diverged from the liberal-classical, the conservative-liberal, and the traditional sociological concepts principally in the absence of the assumption that "the eschatologically good orientation of reason and its pure emanation, public opinion, provides for a satisfactory course of events" (Schmidtchen, 1959: 263; similarly Otto, 1966: 120). Schmidtchen, Otto, and Noelle-Neumann are convinced that only a wide (transhistorical) concept of public opinion is suited to cognitive goals of sociology of politics as an "empirical social science," which should be based on empirical recognition of social and social-psychological group processes of an entire population (Otto, 1966: 119-120). In their view, empirical import must be expressed in the universality of concept, that is, in the fact that forms of public opinion can be empirically identified in every type of society. However, they do not draw their attention to the necessity that a theoretical concept must be (ultimately) tied to the phenomenal world. What Otto is suggesting is rather an openness of the concept of public opinion that allows it to relate to any type of society. In this sense, for example, Otto stresses that her conceptualization "leaves enough space to place numerous aspects of public opinion" (Otto, 1966: 120). As this example clearly illustrates, although openness may promote a desirable objectivity in concept formation and/or definition, it can easily lead to a mere vagueness. "The concept that means all things to all people—like the sayings in the fortune cookies—generates more relationships to other similarly vague ideas than is possible with any precisely defined, constrained concept" (Cohen, 1980: 138). Schmidtchen's definition that "public opinion is a correlate of power and the aggregate of related phenomena—something which politically exists only in certain specific relationships between the government and the people" (Schmidtchen, 1959: 255) is very loose and comes close to being a tautology, because the subject being defined— public opinion—also appears in the predicate itself as "something." "Something" is, in fact, public opinion itself. The definition therefore tells us only where we can find public opinion ("in certain specific relationships between the government and the people") and not what public opinion actually is—a renewed evidence of the validity of Tönnies' assertion in his *Kritik* that it is rather easy to find out in what form public opinion appears, but much more difficult to ascertain what it is.

For decades, the universalization and depoliticization of the concept of public opinion in the behavioral tradition was often, and with sound objections, challenged by the "normativists":

> The modern sociological tradition in the discussion of public opinion shows an impressive diversity. But one of the most incisive of the differences is the *conflict* between those who consider process and believe in scientific study alone, and those who would see in the opinion process some advancement toward the attainment of *humanitarian and rational goals*. . . . The empirical approach, quite nat-

urally, proclaims its intention of not considering the normative aspects of the opinion process, but such a result has hardly been achieved, since the empirical method is based quite often on the sheer avoidance of moral, ethical, and other evaluative issues. (Wilson, 1962: 103; emphases added)

Following Blumer's critique of public opinion polling, Wilson radicalized the critique of the empirical paradigm and was among the first to warn of the hidden ideological character of so-called "neutral" public opinion polls. He argued that pollsters could not be merely "objective inquirers into public opinion." Rather, "The pollster has an ideology just as does the person who is interviewed and correlated" (Wilson, 1962: 170). On the other hand, there is a symmetrical relation between the pollsters and the people: not only social scientists and pollsters are interested in political views of the people, but the latter also have interest in what political views of the former may be. Very soon, the partiality of pollsters was quite openly "admitted" by Childs when he demanded that researchers must at least make an effort to ask the "right" questions, because "To ask the masses the wrong questions, questions for which they have little or no competence, may be as disastrous to the cause of democracy as not asking any questions at all" (Childs, 1965: 358).

Particularly with Bourdieu's (1972/1979) thesis that "public opinion does not exist," questions about the ideological nature of empirical opinion research intensified, leaving little hope for the reawakening of ideas about the convergence of different interpretations and understandings of public opinion. In his critical statement, Wilson in some ways anticipated such a development when he warned that, in a mass society that is likely to become a totalitarian society, it does not suffice to claim that there is no public opinion. With this remark, Wilson problematized not only the results of empirical public opinion polling, but a more general conclusion about the absence of public opinion in nondemocratic societies or in societies where the masses are not involved in the operations of the state: "It seems best to admit that the mass man represents a kind of public opinion, but that in the light of Western philosophy the corrupted reality of this opinion denies it the capacity to create political obligation. And, implicitly, obligation may then arise from some source which is not public opinion" (Wilson, 1962: 281). Yet, if we merely concluded that public opinion does not exist (any longer) without attempting to "reconstruct" it in the changed social circumstances, then we would consent to the nondemocratic conditions in which "the mass man" would find himself.

PUBLIC OPINION POLLS-SAVIORS OR HANGMEN OF DEMOCRACY?

Long ago the notion of public opinion in empirical research has ceased to mean in reality existing unity. "Political opinion polls provide a certain reflection of 'public opinion' only if they have been preceded by a focused public debate and a corresponding opinion-formation in a mobilized public sphere" (Habermas, 1992/1995: 362). On that account one could speak only about "mass opinions" (a collection of individual opinions), but definitely not about the "unified public opinion." It is not only that the true object of public opinion research is not *public* opinion and not even *opinion*, but rather, that *private attitudes*[12] are the object of research. Empirical research of public opinion has emerged as the result of the equation of the spheres of politics and consumption, and the decline of a critical public. Politics has begun to be sold just like any other commodity. As Zolo (1992: 129) claims, "The political market owes its democratic functionality to the existence of a 'public opinion' which is in a position to evaluate the market's offerings and to control its procedures." Yet consumers of political goods are in a worse position than the consumers of economic goods because they cannot directly control or immediately sanction the quality of the good or service. Nor is the media plurality characterized by such a high level of competition among producers and the consequent differentiation of goods (contents diversity) that might characterize the economic market. Within this framework, empirical opinion research (polling) has been implemented as an institutional actor in the political sphere. Up to a point, public opinion polling should diminish the asymmetry in the relationship between political "consumers" and political elite. Indeed, public opinion become the object of empirical research in the period when the process of commodification of politics was already accomplished. Empirical research has only improved the reliability and efficiency of, rather than caused, the harmonization of mass consciousness (public opinion) with the dominant opinions and interests.[13] The role played by public opinion polling can be compared to the role of the mass media, which Dewey and Lippmann, and Mills and Habermas later on, described as one that did not provide the public with the kind of information and opinions that could provoke discussion and connect people in a conversational community.

In public opinion theories, opinion is considered public in three different senses: (1) as an opinion which is publicly expressed or published; (2) as any individual, private or public, opinion on public affairs; (3) as opinion expressed by the public. Operationalization of public opinion in survey research usually effectuates the second meaning (of public affairs) and rejects the others. In other words, the sum of individual private opinions is taken as if they were *the* actual public opinion, not one of possible models of it. Opinion polling is not aimed at publicly expressed opinions; moreover, respondents in survey interviews are always guaranteed *the anonymity of their opinions*. The object is not the opinion(s) of the public in the nonoperational sense, that is, in the sense implying anything more than the legal age and the legal capacity of the persons surveyed. Proceeding from the ideas of American pragmatism and symbolic interactionism, Herbert Blumer pioneered in questioning the validity of public opinion polling, that is, whether it actually deals with public opinion (Blumer, 1948: 542). As he observed half a century ago, in polling "the findings resulting from an operation, or use of an instrument, are regarded as constituting the object of study . . . the operation determines intrinsically its own objective" (Blumer, 1948: 543).[14] Such research has completely omitted any endeavor to empirically capture a fluid and complex public, but decided instead for an operational conception of the public as an aggregate of individuals. Blumer was among the first to severely criticize the transformation of public opinion from "a property of groups" to an "attribute of individuals," explicitly carried out by those who justified polling as an instrument of measuring public opinion and, strictly speaking, made public opinion equal to what public opinion polls polled. In addition, even the notion of public affairs, on which the operational understanding of public opinion is built, was problematized. As Bourdieu (1972/1979: 124) established, empirical research of public opinion falsely presupposes that there is a consensus in society about which questions are relevant and should be asked by researchers. In reality, no such consensus exists, because it could only be formed as a result of a really existing public opinion, which, as Bourdieu points out, does not exist.

To some extent, *instrumentalization* of public opinion through *commodification* and *political institutionalization* could have diminished the scientific relevance of public opinion in its genuine sense. Polling helped transform autonomous public opinion(s) into much more manageable mass opinions that could be created and shaped to suit particular commercial or political interests. However, since at the same time public opinion polling has gained political importance, public opinion has not lost its scientific relevance. Controversies over value and function of opinion polls for democratic political processes are as old as polling itself, and they largely reflect much older efforts at theorizing public opinion and democratic government. The first eminent "representatives" of fundamental disagreements concerning the political function of polling were George Gallup and Lindsay Rogers; their strife in the 1940s reflected ideas presented by Dewey and Lippmann during the 1920s.

Gallup (1940) claimed that polling results were a "mandate from the people" to the government; that is, in a society in which direct democracy is impossible, polling ought to compensate for the limitations of electing political representatives. Public opinion revealed through polling was believed to provide a democratic counterweight to the growing independence of political representatives and, therefore, a separation of representation from popular rule. From that perspective, as Albig later argued, public opinion polls may be an indication of democratic developments. In predemocratic societies, customs, beliefs, and convictions are subjects of early indoctrination and remain very stable over a person's lifetime, so that "(p)eriods of limited opinion do not have need for the recorders of opinion, for the straw-vote takers and pollers, for the study of opinions as important phenomena" (Albig, 1956: 175). In much more complex and changeable democratic societies, recording of opinion changes became existentially fundamental to governments. Similarly, V. O. Key related the interest of governments in the distribution of public opinion among their citizenry to "the ethical imperative that government heed the opinion of the public (which) has its origins in democratic ideology as well as in the practical necessity that governments obtain support of influential elements in society" (Key, 1961/1967: 4).

In contrast, Rogers (1949) grounded his criticism of polling on the criticism of the tyranny of public (that is, majority) opinion professed earlier by Burke, Bryce, and Lippmann, according to which political representatives should be responsible to the general rather than any particularistic public, thus they should not follow the dictates of the public. Rogers considered "completely false" Gallup's ideas that in societies with representative political systems, polling might help reestablish town meetings of the antique Greece on a national scale, because polling prevents the discussion and agreement that are essential to an effective (democratic) government, and even substitutes for them. "*Vox populi* cannot help democratic governments to decide what they ought to do. Political and intellectual leaders must propose alternative policies. They must educate the electorate, and if the leadership and education are effective, then the people will demonstrate their 'essential wisdom'" (Rogers, 1949: 235). For this process, polling is dysfunctional: the contribution of polling to the improvement of democratic government is limited to "debunking the claims of a pressure group as to the amount of strength behind it" (p. 188) and inquiring locally into "matters of community needs and preferences." Only on questions of local (in contrast to national) concern, "while *Vox populi* may not be *Vox dei*, *Vox pollsteri* may be considered the equivalent of *Vox populi*" (194, 196).

POSTMODERN DISPERSION OF PUBLIC OPINION?

When referring to practical processes of opining in contemporary societies characterized by the disintegration of the public in the Habermasian sense, it is perhaps more sensible to speak, instead of public opinion, of mass opinion or a kind of opinion temper or climate, or simply of social distribution of opinions, as Beaud and Kaufmann suggest in their chapter. Here, individual private attitudes rather than publicly discussed opinions are shaped and changed in the processes that derive from the human tendency for cognitive consistency—in short, harmonizing attitudes and behavioral patterns in the organization of the "inner world." Instead of rational discourse and striving after consensus, the mechanisms for assuring attention and achieving internal and external consistency come to the fore: selective perception and remembering, identity construction, partial perception and identification with "public" personalities—generally, a tendency to receive information that gratifies the use of the media and to avoid information and opinions that could cause cognitive dissonance (Festinger, 1957/1962). This leads to the need for a constant supply of symbols of identification by the media (Lasswell, 1981) and "social-psychologically calculated offers" (Habermas, 1962/1995: 217) on the media side. By using symbols, political actors try, through the media, to attract the attention of the population and avoid a commitment to "rational arguments which could arouse the critical capacities of the recipient of the message and stimulate his awareness" (Zolo, 1992: 146). As a consequence, "governing more than ever becomes a massive public relations exercise," as Axford and Huggins argue in their chapter in this book. Mass media, particularly television, "act in a way that is calculated to mobilize the public," which inducts a "perverse form of direct democracy" (Bourdieu, 1998: 64)—actions that more resemble riots of a mob than the expression of opinion by an "imagined" public.

Yet opposite theorizations of publicness and public opinion (e.g., Mayhew, 1997; Peters, 1995; Thompson, 1990) emphasize the many-sided "narrowness" of "rationalistic conceptions" of public opinion. They proceed from changes in economy, politics, and culture brought about by the development and massive use of new information and communication technologies, which ought to revolutionize earlier processes and conceptions of public opinion. Rationalistic theories are blamed for the historically incorrect neglect of the actual exclusion of large social groupings (e.g., women, workers) from the public. In addition, they putatively do not realize that the contemporary developments of communication technologies and publicity changed communication and political processes to such a degree that the general accessibility and active participation of citizens in the formation and expression of public opinion have been invalidated even as normative ideals. These processes have been supposedly replaced by the "mediatization of politics" (Thompson, 1990) and the "rhetoric of representation" (Mayhew, 1997). Thompson argues against Habermas' refeudalization theory that "the development of mass communication has created new opportunities for the production and diffusion of images and messages, opportunities which exist on a scale and are executed in a manner that precludes any serious comparison with the theatrical practices of feudal courts" (Thompson, 1990: 115). Rather, new communication technologies, primarily television, increase the visibility of political leaders and limit their control of information flow, which moves the audiences away from passive consumers. From a different perspective, Jean-François Lyotard argues against Habermas' early discursive conceptualization of the public that there are no universally valid pragmatic rules in language as the necessary condition to reach "consensus" in a rational discourse; neither can consensus be the purpose of dialogue (Lyotard, 1979: 106).

In spite of the changed circumstances and new controversies, public opinion is still much more than a fiction, mystery, or blind alley—as Habermas, Lippmann, or Allport would say. As Peters (1995) argues, public opinion since its eighteenth-century origins always had a significant "symbolically constructed component" and never existed apart from mediated representations, in the sense of Benedict Anderson's "imagined community" whose most representative example is "the nation." A typical process in which imagined communities originate is the ceremony of "almost precisely simultaneous consumption ('imagining') of the newspaper-as-fiction" that individuals perform in private, but they are aware that the same "ceremony" is performed simultaneously by thousands of other anonymous, private persons (Anderson, 1983/1991: 35).[15] One can see the roots of Anderson's idea in Tönnies' conception of "the large public" consisting of "spiritually connected" members, although Tönnies understood the public as an essentially political and moral phenomenon in contrast to postmodern largely depoliticized conceptualizations. For Peters, public opinion is generated by a sort of "imagined public" formed by symbols. Instead of a direct interaction among individuals, symbolic representations of the social whole are circulated before them, primarily through the media, that may stimulate them to act as a social entity. The formation of a postmodern or, as Mayhew names it, "New" public, is much more affected by mass media, television in particular, than by contiguous interactions among members of the public. Yet, such an imagined public is nonetheless as "real" as any other imagined community in the sense that "in acting upon symbolic representations of 'the public' the public can come to exist as a real actor. . . . Fictions, if persuasive, become material, political reality" (Peters, 1995: 18, 19).

Habermas became aware of the fundamental importance of global economic, political, and technological changes for (the conceptualization of) the public sphere only much after the publication of *The Structural Transformation*, and in 1990 he added three revisions to the 1962 original edition.[16] He justified the revisions as resulting from developmental changes in the self-regulation of society in the period between the early 1960s and late 1980s, which significantly affected (1) the private sphere and the social foundations of private autonomy; (2) the structure of the public (sphere) and the composition and behavior of the publics; and (3) the legitimization processes of mass democracies. He revised his earlier theory of the "linear development" from a reasoning to a consuming public (what he termed "refeudalization of publicness") with the idea of the "ambivalence of the public," which he first developed in his theory of communicative action as the idea of the ambivalent— authoritarian and emancipatory—potential of communication (Habermas, 1981: 574). This shift was believed to be the consequence of objective, empirical social changes that also transformed the nature of the public and public opinion. Although Habermas stressed that this revision did not mean the withdrawal from the original intentions that guided him in the writing of *Structural Transformation*, he did confess that his revised model was now closer to the liberalist concept of public opinion and the "tyranny of the majority" found in Tocqueville and J. S. Mill than to the classical liberal theories of the rule of public opinion.

With the revision, Habermas created an ambivalent relation to the research tradition shaped by Paul Lazarsfeld. In his early period, Habermas accepted Lazarsfeld's ideas (not that he knew them well, as he would later admit) as a possible path toward the resolution of the contradictions found in normative theories of public opinion. Later, when he became better acquainted with Lazarsfeld's approach, he "denounced" it. In fact, however, Habermas' revision can be seen as a "correction" of his earlier theory using just the results of the empirical sociological studies advanced by Lazarsfeld. In light of the results of these studies, the individual "rationality," one of the key assumptions of classical theories of public opinion, takes on a different meaning and in contemporary society becomes "nonproblematic." Individuals selectively and rationally pay attention to what political actors in their environment say and how they act and search out relevant political information. The homogenization of their opinions is not a consequence of manipulation; rather, it originates from "rational" reconsideration of one's own beliefs, when individuals interactively discover they disagree with others, as for example in the "spiral of silence."

Habermas' concluded the original edition of *Structural Transformation* with a pessimistic quote from Mills' *Power Elite* about the decline of the public and the emergence of "a society of the masses." The pessimism clearly implied also Habermas' agreement with Mills who, unlike Lazarsfeld, critically emphasized the importance of the values that shape, or should shape, the selection of (research) problems and policies. Conversely, Habermas' revision concludes with "reasons for a less pessimistic evaluation, and for a less obstinate and declarative view on the public sphere than before." The new introduction concludes with Joshua Meyrowitz's ideas (1985: 315-317) about a curious similarity between the information society and the pre-class society of hunters and gatherers expressed in (1) the lack of boundaries and territorial loyalty; and (2) egalitarian tendencies that reduce differences between males and females, children and adults, and leaders and followers. However, his revision is lacking in a more explicit and conclusive validation.

All the changes we have experienced in the late twentieth century do not justify in themselves the rebuff of the idea of an "enlightened" public opinion. As Dewey argued in the controversy with Lippmann, "Until secrecy, prejudice, bias, misrepresentation, and propaganda as well as sheer ignorance are replaced by inquiry and publicity, we have no way of telling how apt for judgment of social policies the existing intelligence of the masses may be" (Dewey, 1927/1991: 209). Danilo Zolo, for example, argues similarly to Habermas that the neo-classical doctrine of democracy remains without satisfactory explanatory power and calls for an entire reconstruction of democratic theory. Such a theory must take into account the fundamental changes in (the relationship between) the private and public sphere, and changes in the legitimization processes of mass democracies as suggested by Habermas, but in a much more critical way. The reasons for such a critical reassessment are: (1) The asymmetrical, noninteractive nature of mass-political communication is developed to such a degree that the idea of "electronic democracy" has definitely become a utopia. (2) By its further dispersion and primarily as a consequence of the "narcotizing dysfunction" of the mass media, the public sphere transformed itself into "a reflexive area, a timeless metadimension in which the 'real' public passively assists, as if in a sort of permanent television broadcast carried out in real time, in the exploits of an 'electronic' public" (Zolo, 1992: 166). These two tendencies are taking on worldwide proportions and are bringing about "a second structural transformation of the public sphere" which is global and more radical than the one analyzed by Habermas in the 1960s, because "the sovereignty of the political consumer—i. e. the autonomy, rationality and moral responsibility of the citizen called upon to pass sovereign judgement on the competition between parties—can now hardly amount to more than empty verbiage in the context of the massive spectacularisation of teledemocracy to which pluralistic competition between the parties . . . is being reduced" (Zolo, 1992: 170).

New procedures of mediatization and representation that dominate in postmodernity, and their social consequences, suggest that we should diverge from classical conceptions of public opinion based on the principle of publicity. Yet this turn is so radical that the question is in place as to whether all these communication procedures—greatly diversified opportunities and practices of reception and consumption in the first place—still help form and express public opinion. The answer to this question is essentially determined by the definition of public opinion— and clearly negative if public opinion is conceptualized as opinion of the public which makes political claims that authoritative institutions must take into account. The core of the problem is in the question of what does constitute the material substance of the postmodern, dispersed "imagined public": paradoxically, it is not the public, but the *mass*.

ENDNOTES

1. According to Rousseau, the role of the censor is not to judge "the opinion of the people" but only to express it.
2. In a clearly historically incorrect assessment, Wilson (1962: 34) even generalized the liberal belief that public opinion obliges public servants to follow as "one of the converging ideas in the theory of public opinion."
3. "The voice of the people is the voice of God."
4. Modern public opinion is, as a matter of fact, conceptualized as a phenomenon closely linked with the nation-state. This "matter of fact" was particularly emphasized by public opinion polling in which respondents are randomly selected from the population of citizens. Thus, citizens represent a sort of "natural" population despite the fact that modern states at best exist for no more than a few centuries (but often only a few decades or even a few years). Regardless of whether such equalization is justified or not, there obviously exist other forms of expression and representation of (public) opinion that are less (or not at all) institutionalized and involve relatively small numbers of individuals and/or groups.
5. Bryce (1888/1995) defines as the three fundamental forms of popular government (1) government by the plenary assembly of citizens; (2) representative system; and (3) government by public opinion. According to Bryce, government by public opinion could be considered an attempt at the application of the first form on a numerous population, or as a modification of the second form. Cf. Tönnies, 1922: 323.

6. A further step away from this "least common denominator" established in normative theories of public opinion is represented by blurring out the difference between public and private opinions brought about by Lippmann's concept of "public opinions" (in plural) as "the pictures of public affairs inside the heads" of individuals (Lippmann, 1922/1960: 29).

7. See Vreg's contribution in this volume.

8. Wilson does not make a clear distinction between popular opinion, public opinion, and popular mind (1962: 64-65).

9. Key considers "mass opinion" as "opinion of the mass of the people" and relates it largely, though not exclusively, to the survey data. The "mass of the people" constitutes the "*inattentive* public," which mostly does not pay attention to political issues, whereas the "*attentive* public/s" manifest high and continuing interest on governmental policy.

10. My reading of Tönnies' theory of public opinion is presented in Splichal, 1998 and 1999, and Hardt and Splichal, 2000. See also Sassi's contribution in this book.

11. An exhaustive analysis of the Noelle-Neumann model of public opinion is presented in Splichal, 1999.

12. There is no commonly accepted distinction between "opinion" and "attitude," and the terms are often used as synonymous, although social psychologists avoid using the term "opinion" in favor of "attitude." Thus, Theodore Newcomb (1950: 176) suggested replacing the term "public opinion" with a more accurate one, which should be "group attitudes." Even Park (1904/1972) wrote interchangeably of the public's attitudes and public opinion. Attitude is usually defined as "an individual's disposition to react with a certain degree of favorableness or unfavorableness to an object, behavior, institution, or event—or to any other discriminable aspect of the individual's world" (Ajzen, 1993: 41). As English and English (1972: 293) argue, opinion is "intellectual," whereas attitude is "evaluative" (pro-con, positive-negative). In contrast to opinion, attitude is considered a hypothetical and operational construct: because it is not directly observable, it can be only inferred from measurable cognitive, affective and conative reactions to the attitude object. Cognitive reactions are defined as "expressions of beliefs." Although in social psychology, at least to my knowledge, believing is not contrasted with opining and knowing as distinct forms of "holding for true," as conceptualized in the Kantian tradition (e.g., Tönnies), it is at least interesting to note that "attitude" is related to "belief" but not to "opinion." In my view, opinion is more complex than attitude, and it is objectively a more certain form of holding for true than belief (i.e., it is a more rational concept), although the latter might be more certain in subjective terms. According to *Oxford Dictionary*, "attitude" came into English about 1710, thus later than "opinion" (but in the same way: from Latin

via Italian and French), and at the time when the term "public opinion" had been already coined. For the history of the concept "attitude," see Fleming, 1967.

13. Beaud and Kaufmann in their contribution to this book disagree with this view, arguing that historically, survey methods were part of the process of domestication of public opinion since before the bourgeois revolution. There is no doubt about it, but at the same time, survey response data were gathered and used for reformative and even revolutionary aims, as well as pure entertainment. In *Public Opinion* (Splichal, 1999) I published a comprehensive analysis of social and theoretical implications of polling.

14. From this perspective, Lemert's and Hauser's contributions in this book are particularly illustrative.

15. Modern computer mediated communication significantly increased possibilities of symbolic construction of events and actors. A good example of the power of simultaneous consumption of a symbolically constructed actor is the fictitious rock singer Joanna Zychovicz, constructed in the virtual world of the Internet by a Swedish advertising agent. She is promoted as "Poland's Number 1 country and western singing star." On her web site one can find pictures of Joanna as a child in Poland, pictures from her singing career, her boyfriend, latest releases, tour details and personal appearances, and download a sample of her famous hit "Dirty Country Girl." <http://www.joannafanclub.com>

16. The revisions first appeared in the introduction to the German Suhrkamp edition published in 1990.

REFERENCES

Ajzen, Icek. 1993. Attitude Theory and the Attitude-Behavior Relation. In D. Krebs and P. Schmidt (eds.), *New Directions in Attitude Measurement*, 41-57. Berlin: Walter de Gruyter.

Albig, William. 1956. *Modern Public Opinion*. New York: McGraw Hill.

Anderson, Benedict. 1983/1991. *Imagined Communities: Reflections on the Origins and Spread of Nationalism*. London: Verso.

Allport, Floyd H. 1937. Toward a Science of Public Opinion. *Public Opinion Quarterly* 1, 1, 7-23.

Bauer, Wilhelm. 1930. *Die öffentliche Meinung in der Weltgeschichte*. Wildpark-Potsdam: Athenaion.

Bentham, Jeremy. 1787/1995. *The Panopticon Writings*. Edited and introduced by M. Bozovic. London: Verso.

Bentham, Jeremy. 1791/1994. Of Publicity. *Public Culture* 6, 3, 581-595.

Blumer, Herbert. 1946/1966. The Mass, The Public, and Public Opinion. In B. Berelson and M. Janowitz (eds.), *Reader in Public Opinion and Mass Communication*, 43-50. New York: The Free Press.

Blumer, Herbert. 1948. Public Opinion and Public Opinion Polling. *American Sociological Review* 13, 542-554.

Bourdieu, Pierre. 1972/1979. Public Opinion Does Not Exist. In A. Mattelart and S. Siegelaub (eds.), *Communication and Class Struggle: 1. Capitalism, Imperialism*, 124-130. New York: International General.

Bourdieu, Pierre. 1998. *On Television*. New York: The New Press.

Bryce, James. 1888/1995. *The American Commonwealth*. 2 vols. Indianapolis: Liberty Fund.

Burke, Edmund. 1769/1967. The British Empire and American Revolution. *Selected Writings and Speeches of Edmund Burke on Reform, Revolution, and War*, 46-112. Ed. by Ross J. S. Hoffman and Paul Levack. New York: Alfred Knopf.

Childs, Harwood L. 1965. *Public Opinion: Nature, Formation, and Role*. Princeton, NJ: D. van Nostrand.

Cohen, Bernard P. 1980. *Developing Sociological Knowledge: Theory and Method*. Englewood Cliffs, NJ: Prentice-Hall.

Cooley, Charles H. 1909/1971. The Significance of Communication. In W. Schramm and D. F. Roberts (ed.), *The Process and Effects of Mass Communication*, 643-654. Urbana: University of Illinois Press.

Dewey, John. 1927/1991. *The Public and Its Problems*. Athens: Swallow Press.

English, Horace B. and Ava C. English. 1958/1972. *Obuhvatni recnik psiholoskih i psihoanalitickih pojmova [A Comprehensive Dictionary of Psychological and Psychoanalytical Terms]*. Beograd: Savremena administracija.

Festinger, Leon. 1957/1962. *A Theory of Cognitive Dissonance*. Stanford, CA: Stanford University Press.

Fleming, Donald. 1967. Attitude: The History of a Concept. In D. Flemming and B. Bailyn (eds.), *Perspectives in American History*, Vol. 1, 287-368. Cambridge, MA: Charles Warren Center for Studies in American History.

Gallup, George H. and Saul F. Rae. 1940. *The Pulse of Democracy*. New York: Simon and Schuster.

Ginsberg, Benjamin. 1986. *The Captive Public: How Mass Opinion Promotes State Power*. New York: Basic Books.

Habermas, Jürgen. 1962/1995. *The Structural Transformation of the Public Sphere. An Inquiry into a Category of Bourgeois Society*. Trans. T. Burger. Cambridge, MA: MIT Press.

Habermas, Jürgen. 1965/1980. *Teorija i praksa* [Theorie und Praxis]. Beograd: Kultura.

Habermas, Jürgen. 1981. *Theorie des kommunikativen Handelns*. Frankfurt: Suhrkamp.

Habermas, Jürgen. 1992/1995. *Between Facts and Norms. Contributions to a Discourse Theory of Law and Democracy*. Trans. W. Rehg. Cambridge: Polity Press.

Hardt, Hanno and Slavko Splichal. (2000). *Ferdinand Tönnies on Public Opinion*. Boulder, CO: Rowman & Littlefield.

Hegel, Georg Wilhelm Friedrich. 1821/1971. *Philosophy of Right*. Translated with notes by T. M. Knox. London: Oxford University Press.

Hennis, Wilhelm. 1957. *Meinungsforschung und repräsentative Demokratie. Zur Kritik politischen Umfragen*. Tübingen: J. C. B. Mohr (Paul Siebeck).

Kant, Immanuel. 1795/1983. To Perpetual Peace. In *Immanuel Kant: Perpetual Peace and Other Essays*, 107-144. Cambridge, IN: Hacket.

Key, V. O., Jr. 1961/1967. *Public Opinion and American Democracy*. New York: Alfred A. Knopf.

Lasswell, Harold D. 1981. Nations and Classes: The Symbols of Identification. In M. Janowitz and P. Hirsch (eds.), *Reader in Public Opinion and Mass Communication*, 17-28, 3rd edition. New York: The Free Press.

Le Bon, Gustave. 1895/1930. *The Crowd. A Study of the Popular Mind*. London: Ernest Benn.

Lippmann, Walter. 1922/1960. *Public Opinion*. New York: MacMillan.

Lippmann, Walter. 1925. *The Phantom Public*. New York: Harcourt, Brace and Co.

Luhmann, Niklas. 1969. *Legitimation durch Verfahren*. Neuwied: Luchterhand.

Lyotard, Jean-François. 1979. *La condition postmoderne*. Paris: Editions de Minuit.

MacKinnon, William A. 1828/1971. *On the Rise, Progress, and Present State of Public Opinion, in Great Britain, and Other Parts of the World*. Shannon: Irish University Press.

Marx, Karl. 1842/1974. Debatten über Pressfreiheit und Publikation der Landständischen Verhandlungen. *Marx-Engels Werke*, Vol. 1, 28-77. Berlin: Dietz Verlag.

Mayhew, Leon H. 1997. *The New Public. Professional Communication and the Means of Social Influence*. Cambridge: Cambridge University Press.

Merton, Robert K. 1949/1993. Manifest and Latent Functions. In C. Lemert (ed.), *Social Theory*, 328-334. Boulder, CO: Westview Press.

Meyrowitz, Joshua. 1985. *No Sense of Place. The Impact of Electronic Media on Social Behavior*. New York: Oxford University Press.

Mill, John Stuart. 1859/1985. *On Liberty*. London: Penguin.

Mills, C. Wright. 1956/1968. *The Power Elite*. London: Oxford University Press.

Newcomb, Theodore M. 1950. *Social Psychology*. New York: Dryden Press.

Noelle-Neumann, Elisabeth. 1980/1993. *The Spiral of Silence. Public Opinion—Our Social Skin*. Chicago: University of Chicago Press.

Otto, Ulla. 1966. Die Problematik des Begriffs der öffentlichen Meinung. *Publizistik* 2, 99-130.

Park, Robert E. 1904/1972. *The Crowd and the Public*. Ed. H. Elsner, Jr. Chicago: University of Chicago Press.

Peters, John D. 1995. Historical Tensions in the Concept of Public Opinion. In T. L. Glasser and C. T. Salmon (eds.), *Public Opinion and the Communication of Consent*, 3-32. New York: Guilford.

Rogers, Lindsay. 1949. *The Pollsters. Public Opinion, Politics, and Democratic Leadership*. New York: Alfred A. Knopf.

Rousseau, Jean Jacques. 1762/1947. *The Social Contract*. Trans. C. Frankel. New York: Hafner.

Schmidtchen, Gerhard. 1959. *Die befragte Nation. Über den Einfluss der Meinungsforschung auf die Politik*. Freiburg: Romabach.

Schmitt, Carl. 1928/1954. *Verfassungslehre*. Berlin: Duncker & Humblot.

Splichal, Slavko. 1998. Public Opinion as a Form of Social Will: Ferdinand Tönnies' *Critique of Public Opinion*. *Communications* 23, 1, 99-126.

Splichal, Slavko. 1999. *Public Opinion. Theoretical Developments and Controversies in the Twentieth Century*. Lanham, MD: Rowman & Littlefield.

Thompson, John B. 1990. *Ideology and Modern Culture*. Stanford: Stanford University Press.

Tocqueville, Alexis de. 1840/1969. *Democracy in America*. 2 vols. Trans. G. Lawrence. New York: Doubleday.

Tönnies, Ferdinand. 1922. *Kritik der öffentlichen Meinung*. Berlin: Julius Springer.

Wilson, Francis Graham. 1962. *A Theory of Public Opinion*. Chicago: Henry Regnery.

Zolo, Danilo. 1992. *Democracy and Complexity. A Realist Approach*. University Park: Pennsylvania State University Press.

2

Policing Opinions: Elites, Science, and Popular Opinion

Paul Beaud
Laurence Kaufmann

> Only isolated individuals can be dominated.
> —Hannah Arendt

Choosing public opinion as a subject of study inevitably entails pondering its true "nature," but, to say the least, its ontological status is far from garnering a consensus amongst sociologists. For some, "public opinion doesn't exist": it's only an artifact constructed for the purpose of political legitimation (cf. Bourdieu, 1993). For others, public opinion is what polls measure: the result of adding up individual opinions through recording and statistical processing methods (see, e.g., Boudon, Bourricaud, and Girard, 1981). Endless disputes pit the "artificialist" sense of public opinion for a sociology of suspicion that denounces it as a collective illusion serving the reproduction of the status quo against its "referentialist" sense for an empirical sociology that considers it a real and quantifiable entity.

Translated from French by Matthew Lazen.

In order to get beyond this opposition, we need to reinscribe public opinion in the sociohistorical space of the practices, representations, and interests that presided over its emergence in the eighteenth century, then link it to the process of scientific and political objectification, elaborated in the nineteenth century and reinforced in the twentieth, which made it seem increasingly self-evident. This return to the origins allows us to render the concept and object "public opinion" eminently problematic, while avoiding reducing it a priori to any one of its senses. Grasping public opinion as the current state of an historic production allows us to expose the social labor of definition and unification that has obscured its successive sedimentations and to deconstruct the "black box" that its largely unquestioned use has allowed to be put in place. From this point of view, Habermas' work on public sphere makes an essential contribution, less for its historical precision, sometimes criticized, than for the new kind of interrogation and investigation it has given rise to.

For Habermas, it is necessary to elaborate a concept of public opinion that is at once "historically meaningful, . . . normatively meets the requirements of the constitution of a social-welfare state, and . . . is theoretically clear and empirically identifiable" (Habermas, 1991: 244). However, let it be said right off, the articulation, which sometimes borders on fusion, between these different levels doesn't make the task easy; one can, in fact, distinguish between at least three different conceptions of public opinion in his work: a sociologico-descriptive conception that defines it by its subject (the eighteenth century bourgeois public), an ideologico-political conception that conceives of it as a new legitimating authority whose symbolic power has managed to supplant that of the absolute monarchy, and an ethico-normative conception that deems it the only truly democratic procedure for making decisions about the course of collective living via the rational and open weighing of arguments. Because the historians who have examined the invention of public opinion have primarily positioned themselves with respect to the first two conceptions that we have just mentioned, we will begin by focusing on them.

THE HISTORICAL GENESIS OF PUBLIC OPINION

According to Habermas, public opinion must be understood in its beginnings as the public's opinion, that is, the opinion expressed by private persons who gather in relatively informal civil institutions (salons, coffee houses, curio cabinets [cabinets de curiosité]) to discuss the regulation of trade and, above all, art and literature. This public is essentially bourgeois because, even if it encompasses a large part of the urban aristocracy, unproductive and devoid of any political function, its true social base is made up of *owners* of the means of production. Only they enjoy enough freedom of thought and action to contribute to the regulation of commercial exchanges and the stabilization of a system of property that contributes, historically, to the development of civil society. But this public is, therefore, also *literary*, as it is composed of readers, spectators, and listeners of art who will claim the right to express lay aesthetic judgments without necessarily bending to the expert opinions of the "arbiters of the arts." The increase in literary and artistic spaces and the enlarged access to cultural goods enabled by their growing commercialization progressively modifies the status of culture, which loses the symbolic function of representation, of staging authority, to become an object of discussion and publicly formed judgment. The bourgeois public, symbolically unified by a subversive label, "the Republic of Letters," lays claim to cultural criticism in the name of free thought, thereby contesting the censure of the state academies' monopolies of interpretation (see Merlin, 1994).

The psychological emancipation permitted by the private sphere which, removed from the demands of survival, favors both experiments with affective relations within the nuclear family and introspection through silent incorporation of the printed work in closed spaces is added to economic emancipation that places property owners above material circumstance and the cultural emancipation that the exchange of ideas ensures them. The intimacy of his rapport with the text predisposes the bourgeois to psychological and moral self-determination whose validity he can later test in face-to-face comparison with his peers. Thus, for Habermas, the private sphere becomes the place for the unrestrained blossoming of "the feeling of humanity," universalizing by definition, that modifies the self-interpretation of private individuals. For, marked by the literary stamp of reflective intimacy, they think of themselves above all under the aegis of the abstract individuality of a natural person as "pure and simple human being." The *ideal* of the public sphere appears as the logical extension of this private sphere; the private salon's egalitarian communication and humanist introspection is extended to literary salons where the public use of reason places the honest man's moral value and his arguments' intrinsic validity above the privileges of his class. The public literary sphere thus opens up a communicative space founded on the impersonality and rationality of argument in order to transcend the particularisms that constitute the rights and privileges of birth.

The Politicization of the Literary Public Sphere

The political orientation of the public literary sphere, at first implicit because drenched with culture and morality, becomes more and more explicit when it extends its sphere of expertise to "the general" and aspires to debate everything, including the political. In the name of the enlightened authority of a "court of opinion" that rests on the necessity of transparency proper to "the publicity principle," free discussion of art and literature turns into a critique of secrecy, the monopoly of decision-making, and the arbitrariness of state decrees. The transformation of the literary sphere into a politically oriented public sphere is still more accelerated, according to Habermas, by the imbalance between the economic power of the bourgeoisie, productive and holding the greater part of the realm's wealth, and its political impotence due to the fact that it has no institutional means of collective action. Torn between expansion of "a far-reaching network of horizontal economic [and cultural] dependencies," in which it actively participates, and the persistence of "the vertical axis" of political dependencies that prevents it from venturing outside its sole recognized field of expertise, commercial exchange, the bourgeoisie attempts to assert itself as a full-fledged social force (Habermas, 1991: 15). Public opinion, the regulated expression of judgments of taste about Belles Lettres, then becomes the means for an eminently political action, consisting in denouncing the unjust foundations of the monarchical order.

Public opinion, henceforth conceived as "the enlightened outcome of [common and] public reflection [on the] foundations of the social order," counters the opacity of political exchanges with the transparency of communicative exchanges that is supposed to allow the collectivity to determine, in concert, the reasons that might justify the advent of a new world (Habermas, 1991: 96). Once turned into *action* and, what's more, revolutionary action, public opinion inaugurates the fundamentally modern political project—even if, as Habermas says, it remains unfinished—of the self-institution of society by itself.

Thus, if we follow Habermas, the "public" in "public opinion" constitutes a veritable collective, historically original actor that has succeeded, in the face of a monarchical and religious order founded on the defense of particular privileges, in imposing its own vision of the world in the name of the general interest. The composition of this collective actor, despite its pretensions of universality, is certainly limited, as it extends only to private individuals of bourgeois station. However, insofar as the narrow educated public incessantly refers to a broader, indeed unlimited, public it tends to conceive of itself as the spokesperson for a general humankind that could one day, thanks to education and decent living conditions, accede to the public sphere of enlightened men. Thus, according to Habermas, even if the expansion of the public hits up against the objective social and intellectual limits of illiteracy and poverty, its pretension to universality can't be reduced to a mere ideology in the service of cultivated property owners' class interest. For, this interest, insofar as it explicitly disregards social hierarchies in favor of general norms, both rational and valid, in principle, for *anyone*, takes on the appearance of universality that makes it coincide objectively with the general interest.

Nonetheless, if the propensity towards universalism contained, essentially, in an enlightened public's humanist ideology might justify the emancipatory potential that Habermas attributes to it, it is no less the case that its basic postulate links public opinion's historical genesis to the existence of a subject, the public, that is to say, a relatively homogeneous group of individuals in terms of their social status and education. As this point has been widely challenged by historians, we will now tackle these criticisms, without overlooking the recent revisions that Habermas himself has made to this model.

THE HISTORIANS' POINT OF VIEW

Like contemporary sociology, historical research oscillates between an artificialist and a referentialist approach to public opinion. The proponents of a conceptual approach understand it as a "political invention," a figure of speech that made it possible for the people excluded from power to claim a network of authority parallel to that of the crown (cf. Baker, 1990). On the other side, the followers of a sociological approach attribute it to real social practices that Baker suggests classifying in three categories (cf. Baker and Chartier, 1994). According to him, public opinion refers, on the one hand, to rumors, to vicious talk, "to the murmurs of daily life" that manifest an "already-there of public opinion" whose existence didn't depend on being thematized as a juridical and political entity that might oppose the monarchy (Baker, in Baker and Chartier, 1994: 12-14). This informal speech is juxtaposed with the institutional channels of production of opinion (the Parliament, the Estates General and Provincial Estates, the royal or provincial academies) that experiment with new forms of democratic sociability and a new kind of official discourse (cf. Furet, 1981 and Roche, 1993). To this, we must also add the extra-institutional circulation of opinion by traditional actors, such as parliaments, which reveal, through pamphlets and improperly published remonstrances, the internal stakes of the political system.

From an analytical point of view, the inscription of public opinion in the reality of everyday life, the intelligentsia's forms of sociability, and the emancipatory writings of the cultivated public are in no way mutually exclusive, these three dimensions being perfectly capable of coexisting. On the other hand, from an historical point of view, its inscription in a specific social domain is the stake of struggles between competing social groups that attempt to decide, by mechanisms of mutual exclusion, which of the different potential "publics" has the right to constitute public opinion (Chartier, in Baker and Chartier, 1994: 15). The attempt by certain social formations to appropriate and monopolize public opinion, along with the unequal means at their disposal for establishing it as their realm of political expression, shows the close interrelationship between social strategies and discursive strategies, social facts and concepts, that the aforementioned approaches aim precisely to separate. Consequently, classifying the different currents that make up, each in its own way, the history of public opinion, seems risky; for the sake of clarity, we will take this path nonetheless, even if it means sacrificing some of the analytical complexity of the cited authors, in order to better highlight the major axes of their investigations, an approach all the more justified in that they themselves have had to adopt it over the years.

From Ideology of the Public to Mentality of the People

A number of historians of the eighteenth century have attacked the idealization of a single public of great minds who somehow manage to disseminate, via the circulation of the press and contestatory philosophical writings, a liberal and egalitarian ideology in the heart of "a plebeian public sphere" incapable of thinking for itself. This description, even if it excessively caricatures Habermas' model, highlights its direct affiliation with a history of ideas that supports a vertical model of contagion through representations, the narrow circle of the intellectual elite contaminating, by the effectiveness of its writings, the mass of indigents whose new convictions, acquired by revelation in the course of reading or overhearing something, will supposedly be immediately translated into political action.

The characteristic approach of French "New History" refutes this intellectualist conception that revives endless causal imputations ("it's Voltaire's fault, it's Rousseau's fault") that sacrifice sociohistorical complexity to the a posteriori intelligibility generally instituted by the retrospective and "intello-centric" gaze of today's historians (see Chartier, 1991). For the analysis of the literary genesis of public opinion, by conferring on it the status of a coherent system of representations that defines ideologies and their "vertical" mode of transmission, is far from exhausting all the practices and representations that characterize mentalities and their "horizontal" mode of development.

Certainly, swinging between an elitist historiography that denigrates it as a simplified, indeed distorted, derivative of ideology of which it only retains a few "crumbs," and a populist historiography that consecrates it as the only authentic expression of collective temperaments, the notion of "mentality" has long been a more normative than analytical term (cf. Vovelle, 1990). However, it makes it possible to underline the determinant role that implicit meanings, "common sense," plays in everyone's cognitive economy. Unlike ideologies, which designate disembodied and invariant concepts linked to a small group of individuals interested in their propagation, mentalities designate representations "in action" that take on meaning within the framework of ordinary experience. In this pragmatic sense, mentalities aren't reducible to ideological remnants bastardized by the rough thinking of the common classes; they refer to social practices, forms of communication that mobilize a "savoir-faire," a practical intelligence distinct from, if not incompatible with, the rhetorical art characteristic of the elites (cf. de Certeau, 1984). Thus, the notion of mentality allows us to shift the analysis from the circumscribed culture of educated people onto the broader culture of common people, in the anthropological sense of ordinary life, cultural practices, and the symbolic system that gives them meaning. It likewise allows us to move from the peripheral production of cultural goods to "mass production" formed, well before its time, by the proliferation of speech characteristic of oral culture (see Ginzburg, 1980a). Far from the pejorative connotations associating it with cultural backwardness, mentality recovers its legitimacy; it even becomes a strategic theoretical concept because it constitutes the "meeting point . . . [between] the individual and the collective, the long term and the everyday, the unconscious and the intentional, the structural and the conjunctural, the marginal and the general" (Le Goff, 1985: 169).

Rehabilitating the People Without Opinion

Contrary to the traditional historiography obsessed with the kings' gestures and the words of the educated, sociocultural history proposes to look "in the farmyards and streets, everywhere where ordinary people have changed their world-view," to see what their dreams, prejudices, and practices have been (Darnton, 1993: 19). For, as Duby says, if "lower class ideologies" haven't had access to the discursive tools which would have allowed them to formalize their worldview in durable cultural productions, their silence shouldn't be interpreted as "an absence" (cf. Duby, 1985). The history of ideas has nonetheless led to just this negationist interpretation, adding retrospective symbolic violence to the political violence that succeeded in muzzling them in the past. By inferring the mentality of an entire period based on the opinion of those who had the ability to make their opinions known, it commits a double error. On the one hand, it replaces the logic of appropriation and the second-hand (*l'occasion*), characteristic of popular practices in accordance with the "invention of the everyday" that de Certeau speaks of, with a discursive logic that is fundamentally foreign to it (cf. de Certeau, 1984, 1997). On the other hand, it deduces ideas' real influence on the lower classes' opinion directly from their objective dissemination. This double translation arbitrarily privileges educated thought as "generic"; however, the particular, no matter how exemplary, can never reach the collective without mediations (cf. Boureau, 1989). In order to avoid these difficulties, the "new historian" starts with the principle that only practices allow us to reliably infer, like "the indexical paradigm" of which Ginzburg speaks, what are the operative beliefs, conscious or not, that are logically associated with them (cf. Ginzburg, 1980b). By hypothesizing that collective representations are only explanatory when they are translated into acts, it thus gives itself the means to skirt a "history from above" that makes the error of prejudging a priori the influence of enlightened discourses on everyday ways of acting. In the same way, it also gives itself the possibility of exploring "from below" the "structured and structuring mediations" that have enabled the progressive transformation of a period's dreams and ideas into a reality principal, and then a revolutionary action (cf. Chartier, 1989).

For the historian of mentalities, this notion refers to "mental nebula" whose distribution is sufficiently transversal to go beyond the dichotomies, often homological, that split society in two, whether between the educated public and the uncultured public, innovation and tradition, conscious representations and archaic habits (cf. Le Goff, 1985). It replaces the linear and deterministic causality that takes popular culture for the mere receptacle of enlightened culture's exogenous discourses with relations based on reciprocal exchanges, which integrates them into the same cultural continuum. Immediately, the logic of exclusion that treated popular culture as the dominated by-product of the dominant high culture or, inversely, as the incommensurable emanation of a completely "other" way of life, becomes a logic of mutual inclusion (cf. Grignon and Passeron, 1989). Rather than opposing the public's culture, linked to the dynamic and prospective history of literature, ideas, and taste to the people's culture, frozen in a priori permanent structures like spontaneity, irrationality, and superstition, it becomes a question of analyzing the circulation of significations that integrates them into one and the same kind of "mental apparatus."[1] Only this integrative approach allows us to understand how the opinion of "have-nots" could, at a given moment, resonate with the opinion of the "intelligentsia" so as to generate a social and political movement on such a scale.

In this framework, the privileged object of sociocultural history becomes the cultural circulation that enabled the public opinion that is reflexive and objectivized in specific spaces of enunciation and the one manifested in practices, spontaneous and "unthought," to jointly construct a new political culture. To account for this communication, which goes beyond class membership, it is still necessary to explore the content of these so-called "nonpublic" opinions that the privileging of "true" public opinion has relegated to the shadows of obscurantism and the refuse of history. For the "new history," the reality of the past resides less in the first-hand testimony of authorized opinions than in the "terra incognita of common opinion" revealed by "indirect discourses" reconstituted from sources such as judicial archives and clandestine literature (Ozouf, 1974: 295).

THE MICRO HISTORY OF PUBLIC OPINION

When analyzing popular opinions, one is struck by a form of categorizing the public and private that hardly corresponds to the juridical division that Habermas speaks of which governs the bourgeois arena. The practice of *lettres de cachet*, widespread up until 1750, shows that the "people of modest means," contrary to what the grand narrative of people dazzled by the light of reason leads one to believe, are far from being unconditional proponents of the publicity principle. Requests for *lettres de cachet* imploring the king to arbitrate family conflicts—by imprisoning an irreligious father, a woman of little virtue, or an excessively dissipated spouse—plead rather for a politics of secrecy which alone can hide "family disorder" from the eyes of the vast majority (cf. Farge and Foucault, 1982). For the common people, unusual justice of the king allows the guilty parties and their relatives and friends to avoid the opprobrium that goes along with a trial in good and due form. Consequently, contrary to the clear division of private and public that the public of the Enlightenment aims to institute, the mysteries of royal justice are not necessarily what distress the popular imagination. To the contrary, ordinary justice is considered not a system guaranteeing equal application of the law but an institution that is defamatory because it is public. By inflicting on the guilty a spectacular sentence, openly and publicly, it transforms a private scandal into a public scandal that brings dishonor. *Lettres de cachet* are the sole recourse for keeping the secret "in the family." Paradoxically, the private, in fact, remains private even while it is made public at the apex of power, thus testifying to the supremely personalizing relation that binds subjects to their sovereign and weaves familial micro-history together with the macro-history of the state. This symbolic alliance, in and through the act of repression, testifies to the paradoxical emotional connection that links the people to its monarch in a mix of quasi-private closeness of "subject to subject" that allows a family to share its pain and suffering with him, and of distance, the king transforming a private conflict into a problem of public dimensions that only he can resolve.

But if the common people fear publicity, which they associate a priori with the mutual surveillance imposed by the unavoidable over-crowding of their quarters, when it affects them, they know how to use it quite well against the private life of the aristocracy (cf. Farge, 1992: 252-253). That is what their hearty endorsement of harsh satire of the depraved mores of the court indicates, its success being inversely pro-portional to that of the great works of the philosophical party (cf. Darnton, 1991). If "public curiosity was not a character trait, but an act which brought each and every individual into politics," this initiation into the obscure mechanisms of power seems to pass, then, not through the big door of the Parliaments or the Councils that harbor the reason of state, but through the small door of the royal palace's alcoves (Farge, 1995: 197).

In fact, in the seditious writings that circulate around Paris, it is not the parliamentary debates or the state of finances that are gibed at but the personal intrigues, the private animosities, the sexual caprices that distract the king from his duties to the nation and bankrupt the public treasury. Moreover, by abandoning the thaumaturgic ritual that consisted of laying hands on the sick or the major religious ceremonies that his adulterous affairs with mistresses of lowly condition prevented him from observing, Louis XV seemed to have lost "the sense of majesty" well before his people (Darnton, 1993: 22). To this objective desacralization of a king who forgets the duties attendant on his rank is joined the subjective desacralization engendered by the "disrespectful discourses" of the pamphleteers who people the "mythological land" of royal politics with lascivious duchesses, homosexual priests, impotent princes, and shameless ministers (Darnton, 1991: 175). Political folklore, which spreads stories of moral depravity and abuse of power through public rumors, gradually transforms the "two bodies" of the king—the physical body and the sacred, political body that is his responsibility to incarnate—into a single, banal body that is no longer anything more than a toy in the hands of his "whores," a grotesque body suspected of an impotence that the people mock.[2] The ontological alterity and inaccessibility of the world "on high" is severely compromised by the stories of the court's salacious and unscrupulous behavior. The anonymous speech of public rumors, thus established as judge of the shameful mores of the aristocracy, makes it possible to demystify the symbolism of a power that claimed the mystery of transcendence. However, without mystery the king is nothing, for his claims to the throne rest on another claim, that of an interior illumination that must necessarily be obscure and incomprehensible to his subjects (Walzer, 1992: 35, 42).

By bringing the emptiness of this pretension to light, the rumors of decadence and despotism symbolized by the royal orgies, the unjustified imprisonment, necessarily have political public effects.[3] But, contrary to the diffusionist hypothesis, they don't take root in the secular critical reason of the philosophers. Plebeian opinion, where social rancor and attachment to the king intermingle, invents its own mode of desacralization that partakes more of an emotional break-up with a monarch guilty of bad behavior than of intellectual argument. Nevertheless, this emotional distancing is more than anecdotal; actually it marks the deterioration of the "ontological model" of the collectivity that absorbed the particular into the mystical body of the realm, symbolized by the sovereign (cf. Merlin, 1994). By dissociating the "mere body of the king" from the symbolic body of the collectivity, it empties the royal word of its substance, that is, of the people itself, which it could stand for with a "we, France" with the force of law (cf. Boureau, 1988).

FOR A TRANSVERSAL SOCIAL MODEL OF OPINIONS

It appears, then, that the a posteriori synthesis of enlightened opinion and popular opinion into a single counter-power that the great minds of the time are supposed to have led to victory is an error. The social distribution of opinions, too often concealed by the unitary figure of public opinion, is as relevant a fact in the eighteenth century as in ours, their heterogeneity manifesting the existence of interpretive communities as different in the form of their speech as in "the formality" of their practices (cf. de Certeau, 1988). Nevertheless, if the level and impact of the demystification that these opinions impose on the established order needs to be differentiated, it is not necessary to empty the analysis of the basic points that partially justify their integration into the same "critical modes of thinking" (*mentalité critique*; Chartier, 1991: 134). The enlightened public's repeated staging of contestation is not without consequence; it enables the commoners' loss of faith, still kept in check by fatalism, to be embodied by giving them the words to express it. In this way, placing a new repertory of contestation at their disposal gives form to a latent subversion that the progressive separation of the common people from the "institutions of belief," as de Certeau calls them, already made possible (cf. de Certeau, 1981). More concretely, subversive statements, far from being confined to the sociocultural milieu that produced them, circulate in a network of polymorphous communication that imposes, at the moment of their "passage" into a determinate social sphere, its characteristic form of expression (cf. Darnton, 1993). Thus, the gossip sustained by indiscrete courtiers is transformed into public gossip that is spread in the coffee houses and streets, then crystallized into a printed work taken to be exemplary thanks to the fame of the characters concerned and clever plotting. In prerevolutionary France, orality and writing seem to function in unison.

The social and cultural differences between spheres of production, modes of interpretation, and means of expressing opinions evident in the spontaneous form of rumors, the hybrid form of written work, or even the sophisticated form of philosophical writings, testifies to the progressive materialization of a not monolithic but rather composite court of opinion. Nevertheless, this heterogeneity can't be frozen, contrary to what the model of public sphere of the "first" Habermas suggests, into a radical split that opposes term for term particular differences of opinion and general principals, the great ideas and lowly works, the public and the private, enlightened opinion and vulgar opinion. Certainly, popular culture, which we have less understood here through its social base, be it peasant or urban, than by the "repertory of themes and acts" that characterizes it, maintains an ambiguous relationship to the publicity principle (Chartier, 1991: 142). For the actors of ordinary life, public opinion, in its semantic usage as in the social reality that it is supposed to designate, seems to retain the traditional sense of reputation that the enlightened public will later denounce as a mass of prejudices and "hearsay" incompatible with the fate slated for it by its noble identification with the exercise of critical reason. But this preliterary sense takes nothing away from its potentially political scope. If the plebeian public opinion constituted by reputation has the power to make and unmake the common people's honor, it can also erode the prestige of the monarchy by revealing the king's escapades.

This point is fundamental because it allows us to revise Habermas' model. The analysis of "nonpublic" opinions shows that the subversive impact of the publicity that they make use of doesn't reside in the intrinsically political content of their object, like the government's "affairs." It is found in the very movement of making visible and accessible on the public square what the people itself considers to be worthy of interest. The object of publicity itself matters less, therefore, than the circulation of "opinions about" that the commoners dare display, whether they be about their own existence, everyday events, or the behavior of the king and his court. By expressing an opinion, they already de facto contest their predestined role: that of giving their consent to the "acts of authority" (*la chose publique*) that official, religious, and punitive ceremonies have the responsibility of deciding once and for all (Farge, 1995: viii). However, once the publicity principle is primarily referred to the publicizing process that makes it possible to collectively define what "counts as" an object of opinion, the analysis of public opinion must change focus.[4] It needs to bear on the procedures that govern this pooling together, even if it is founded on referents with as little apparently emancipatory value as conjugal disputes and the sexual mores of the dominant class. Otherwise said, the truly public nature of public opinion is certified neither by the substantial nature of its subject, the "public," nor by the intrinsic content of the object on which it bears, a petty news item or a matter of State; it is certified by the adoption of a common, and thus potentially universalizing, point of view, that places in question, by its mere existence, the universality supposedly embodied by the political and moral authorities. This universalizing movement is what necessarily sets public communication in motion, whether it be critical discussion or conversation or gossip that ensures, as Tarde says, "the communion of minds" (see Tarde, 1901/1989). The communication of opinions, regardless of their content, thus marks "the unanimous and contagious effort of harmonization," the shared quest for "accord" that constitutes the very principle of the social bond (Tarde, 1901/1989: 129). In this framework, public opinion, scholarly or popular, is not an innocent social phenomenon; to the contrary, it shows, in its form and not in its contents, that "the social act *par excellence* is to make [individual opinions] public," and thus capable of being shared, if they are not actually shared (Dupront, 1965: 225).

From this more descriptive than normative perspective, the a priori epistemic division between the public's opinion and that of the people, just like the a priori juridical division between the private and the public, risks compromising understanding of the sociohistorical reality of the eighteenth century (cf. Olivesi, 1995). It obscures the convergence of these opinions in one and the same direction, the one that makes public confidence the ultimate source of moral law. In fact, once private opinions appear in the public sphere of gossip or deliberation in order to sanction the actions of those in power by praise or blame, they assert themselves as supreme judge of good and evil. They counter "divine law," which decides through revelation what is sin or duty, and "the civil law" of the state, which regulates "crime and innocence," through coercion, with "the law of opinion or reputation" which distinguishes, through approbation, between "vice and virtue."[5] To the extent that the law of opinion aspires to be purely moral, its jurisdiction has no limit. Another's respect makes for as absolute and inviolable a law in the social world as that of the prince in the political world. Thus, the actual content of this law matters little; what matters is that it counters the mysteries of the Church and the political secrecy of the state with "a third power" that makes it possible to try anyone, including the sovereign, "before the moral court of society" (Koselleck, 1979: 122). Within this analytical framework, the apparently incidental actions of the court that raise the wrath of the common people become essential stakes; public opprobrium makes it possible to designate the sphere of power as the very sphere of negation of the moral position henceforth represented by civil society.

Immediately, the "law of reputation," particular to plebeian opinion, and the "philosophical law," particular to enlightened opinion, which already designated, for Locke, one and the same law, that of public opinion, must be treated together. And the introduction of moral legitimacy is fundamentally revolutionary in its very principle: no one can escape another's opinion or control it, whether it be based on the abstract and rational rules that are supposed to govern man in general or on the concrete and everyday rules that must run the social life of men in particular. This convergent politicization of public opinions, via the moralization of power, compromises the overly strict epistemic hierarchy that separates, in Habermas, opinions that are "well informed" by rational procedures and potentially emancipatory cultural resources, and opinions that are "poorly informed" by prejudices and the self-evidence of *doxa*. For, from the sociohistorical point of view, the differences that separate public opinions, grasped here from the point of view of processes of heterogeneous interaction that link men to each other, are more a matter of degree than of kind. For this reason, as Habermas will later recognize, it is appropriate to "pluralize" the public sphere in its formative phase and take into account the multiplicity of subjects uttering public words and the "centers of opinion" that correspond to them.[6]

From Ignorant People to Ignorance of the People

The retrospective rejection of the tutelage of literary opinions, if it enables us to rehabilitate "public curiosity" as one means among others to break the secrecy of politics, risks bringing out another bias almost as significant as intello-centrism: a "populist" bias that consists of immediately attributing to popular speech a reflective and performative ability that justifies its inscription on the horizon of autonomous and politically effective action.[7] This way of proceeding has a major drawback; in the desire to give, at all costs, a voice to people who have never been asked what they thought, the historian risks obscuring the objective social and epistemological differences that separate the informal organization of popular rumor and the formal organization of reasonable argumentation (cf. Ozouf, 1974). In fact, this approach is not content to do justice to the social complexity of the reality of a period by placing the stress on the multiplicity of public opinions; it likewise attempts to do justice to popular "cunning intelligence" by endowing it with the same communicative power as the intelligence of intellectuals.[8] By doing this, it short-circuits the intrinsic semantic value of the enlightened public's opinions as well as the level of objectification that is characteristic of them, which Habermas uses to found his ideal model of rationality. But above all, by shifting the seat of political action to the opinion of common people, this approach risks obscuring the social classification—which pretends, moreover, to be purely epistemic—that refuses to give public rumor the status of opinion. Finally, by focusing the analysis of public opinion on reputation and the circulation of vicious remarks, it tends to turn it into a transhistorical category that makes it impossible to take into account the immense normative labor that ideological discourses accomplished in order to assert it, between politics and philosophy, Revolution and Enlightenment, as the generic principle of government. And it thus forgets the symbolic and technical apparatuses that managed to individuate and then assert, within the jumble of social occurrences that constitute the multitude of opinions, a single politico-ideological sense for public opinion.

For popular movements hit up against a bourgeois social class, armed with economic power and symbolic capital, that managed to appropriate for itself the ideological superstructure of public opinion (see especially Eley, 1992 and Fraser, 1992). Certainly, the constitution of the bourgeois state, democratic in principle, had to compromise with the hardly "literary" protean forms by which all those who were practically barred from the civilized forms (*formes policées*) of criticism forced the doors of "publicity" and thus won political existence (Colliot-Thélène, 1998: 36). But *the stake* of this "negotiation" seems scarcely democratic insofar as the mental tools (concepts, symbols) and the concrete systems (statistical and scientific techniques) that it deploys attempt to thwart the rise to power of the "low-lives" (Duprat, 1998: 10). Thus, in order to avoid spontaneously conferring on the people the status of political actor that the very individuals who claim this status fight tooth and nail to deny, we must analyze the ingenious alchemy that enabled the government of opinion to preserve the illusion of participation by all in political action, even while holding at arms length a people that proves, in fact, to be singularly "unpopular" (Ozouf, 1989, 65).

VOX POPULI, VOX SCIENTIAE

In 1745, Louis XV's general comptroller of finances, Philibert Orry, sent the provincial administrators a questionnaire whose principle purpose was the census of individuals and their property. Nothing too original—the practice had been known for a century. What is more original is the last instruction given to the "investigators:" "You will plant rumors in the cities . . . of your département about a one-third increase in import duties. You will also spread rumors . . . about a levying of two men per parish for a militia to be formed in the future. . . . You will carefully record what the inhabitants say about this and you will mention it in the report that the King has requested of you" (cited by Lecuyer, 1981: 173).

Orry just invented experimental social psychology and the art of governing with polls two centuries ahead of time. One can even praise him in the terms used by the historian Lynn Case to qualify the work of the French judicial and police authorities of the nineteenth century—in this case, at the time of the Second Empire: their reports, he said, are a much better source for understanding opinion than the methods of Mr. Gallup! (cited by Blondiaux, 1998: 57n.). These days still, the state authorities, here and elsewhere, wisely divide their orders for opinion surveys between institutes in the public eye and more discrete administrative dispensaries specializing in information just for the state. Even if one hardly discusses the latest philosophical work there any more, coffee houses are still privileged sites for the expression of public opinion that a practiced police ear will know how to pick up better than a survey questionnaire, even if its methodology resembles other, more routine, police methods, such as those by which one induces suspects, plaintiffs, or witnesses to make a statement ("where, when, how, how many times?").

It's not surprising, then, to find legal experts and criminologists in the forefront of modern theorists of opinion. This is the case of Gabriel Tarde, author of *Criminalité comparée* (1886), *The Laws of Imitation* (1890), and *L'opinion et la foule* (1901), whose works, quickly translated into English, exerted great influence on American social psychology, like those of his Italian colleague Sighele whose work *La Folla delinquente* (1891) was translated the following year into French and in the five years following into all the major European languages. This meeting of the scholarly and the political is not coincidental: one century after a revolution that supposedly placed opinion in power, members of the political and scientific elite still interrogated the limits of this great principle about which the philosophers of the eighteenth century made a barrage of solemn declarations.

In his *Principles of Politics Applicable to All Representative Governments*, Benjamin Constant wrote that "a man condemned to death by laws to which he consented is politically more free than someone who lives tranquilly under laws instituted without recourse to his will" (Constant, 1980: 363). But how was it possible to imagine, not long after the Revolution, that these laws could emanate from an uncultured people that Taine, an extremely illustrious historian, described as follows in 1875 in *The Origins of Contemporary France*:

> Take the still rude brain of one of our peasants and deprive it of the ideas which, for 80 years past, have entered it by so many channels, through the primary school established of each village, through the return of the conscript after his seven years' service, through the prodigious multiplication of books, newspapers, roads, railroads, foreign travel, and every species of communication. Try to imagine the peasant of that epoch, penned and shut up from father to son in his hamlet, without parish highways, deprived of news, with no instruction but the Sunday sermon, solicitous only for his daily bread and the imposts . . . not daring to repair his house, always persecuted, distrustful, his mind contracted and stinted, so to say, by misery. His condition is almost that of his ox or his ass, while his ideas are those of his condition. (Taine, 1896: 374-375)

Venerated by his contemporaries in both Europe and the United States, Taine gives them a history of the French Revolution to make the bourgeoisie quake, without sparing its great figures: Robespierre, Danton, Marat are qualified as madmen and barbarians, manipulating a bloodthirsty mob prey to alcoholic delirium.

Wiser than Taine said, the victorious revolutionaries showed themselves to be, at first, partisans of stalling and only giving property-owners—males, of course—access to political rights, just as the Greeks had already done, reserving access to citizenship for *oikosdespotès* alone, the masters of the house, owners of the means of production (slaves) that allowed them to live without having to work with their hands. Nothing new, in this advent of a new era: in 1802, the Count Roederer, advisor to the government, writes as much, without mincing words, to the Premier Consul, the future Napoleon I: public opinion is that of the public, "that is to say, of that part of the nation which shares common interests with the entire people, but which has, more than the people, a comfortable living, leisure, good upbringing, conversational facility, and finally an opinion and the influence to make it win out, that is to say, the property owners" (cited by Blondiaux, 1998: 55).

If another proof were necessary that one could only reasonably entrust the governance of the nation to the elites, Tocqueville will provide it, in another form, when he returns disenchanted from America, convinced that giving power to the opinion of the majority amounts to instituting a new despotism. Because "the majority lives in the perpetual utterance of self-applause," he writes, "I know of no country in which there is so little independence of mind and real freedom of discussion as in America. . . . The Inquisition has never been able to prevent a vast number of anti-religious books from circulating in Spain. The empire of the majority succeeds much better in the United States since it actually removes any wish to publish them" (Tocqueville, 1990: 263, 265).

THE FANTASY OF DECADENCE

But there's even more behind these doubts about the ability of the masses to manifest this spontaneous Cartesian rationalism that Tocqueville nevertheless continued to give the people credit for. For the nineteenth century bourgeois, laboring classes meant dangerous classes[9] and the people's opinion meant rumors (rumeurs), fickleness, folly, prejudice, vicious gossip (ragot), and, when all is said and done, disorder, violence. The imagination of the class come to power through the revolution is fed by stories in which it glimpses the possibility of its destruction through the fury of the revolutionary crowds, those "excrements of the Nation" as Taine called them.

Already, in the preceding century, Edward Gibbon set the tone in his The History of the Decline and Fall of the Roman Empire, inspired by a daydream amid the ruins of classical Rome.[10] There's no doubt that history must repeat itself and the barbaric plebes will once again overwhelm civilization. The nineteenth-century bourgeois sees the barbarian at his gate, as promised. He discovers their traits and disquieting mores in newspaper serials, notably those of Eugène Sue: his Mysteries of Paris, a raging success, draws its readers into "fearful curiosity"[11] about the seedy districts of the capital, the world, so near to the ritzy neighborhoods, of the proletariat, the "hoodlums" (apaches), crime, and prostitution.

But bourgeois fantasies will also feed off another literature besides these novels paid by the line. This century's analysis of political and philosophical ideas sometimes takes after psychoanalysis, even scientific production, when it ventures into the sociological and anthropological. As Blondiaux (1998: 61) writes, "The birth of the social sciences coincides with the scientific confirmation of the doxa model's presuppositions, inferring, in the name of reason itself, the public's absence of rationality, its extreme malleability, and its always latent dangerousness."

Well before Gallup then, one will undertake to poll the unpollable, the masses, the multitudes (le nombre). A science of the state—as its etymology indicates—early statistics places itself in the service of a form of social science that will lend support to the convictions of the bourgeois about himself and the other, as well as to his fears. In England, Galton confirms in his way, by calculation, the evolutionary theories of his illustrious cousin Darwin. By tracing the genealogies of the scholars, artists, writers, and men of State of his era, and applying to them the probability methods developed by Quételet, he establishes beyond a shadow of a doubt that genius is hereditary, an observation confirmed by Pearson at the beginning of the twentieth century: comparing the fathers' professions to their sons', he easily deduces that the reproduction of the elites is a function of innate aptitudes.[12] It goes without saying that the reverse is necessarily true: criminologists, craniologists, and physionomists alike locate atavistic traits that contradict the belief that the man of the people could be turned into a good citizen. Doesn't he have the face of a criminal or a potential revolutionary? And what can be proven individually is even easier to prove when considering groups, as the first social psychologists of crowds will demonstrate. In opposition to the Italian Lombroso, the author of the notorious *L'uomo delinquente* (1876) who studied the configuration and weight of the brain of born criminals to find their links to "the primitive savage," Lacassagne, another illustrious criminologist, advances this "sociological" argument: the criminal is a microbe but he needs a "culture," the social milieu (see Darmon, 1989).

This time, vocabulary is borrowed from medicine, chemistry, to account for the gregariousness of the masses, the reactions that are unleashed there, the effects that they can have. Scientism feeds off of metaphors: Tarde sees the urban population as a milieu favoring feverish eruptions, moral epidemics. A doctor converted to sociology whose work will be translated into a dozen languages during his lifetime, Le Bon, in his *The Crowd, a Study of the Popular Mind* (1895) appeals to hygienics to describe how crowds are the seat of all contagious diseases. In Charcot's courses, attended by a certain person named Sigmund Freud, our explorers of lower class group behavior find an answer to the infantile irrationality of the ferment that they observe: all of that is a matter of hypnosis but also hysteria, which causes Le Bon to write that the crowd is "feminine."

For Le Bon, the collective mechanisms observable in the crowd are the very negation of what is presupposed by democratic political activity. The group exerts powers of suggestion on the individual that make him abandon all reason in favor of his instincts alone, even if it means sacrificing his personal interest. Freud himself, even while distancing himself from Le Bon's explanation, will later applaud this description in his *Group Psychology and the Analysis of the Ego*: "one must take into consideration the fact that when individuals come together in a group all their individual inhibitions fall away and all the cruel, brutal and destructive instincts, which lie dormant in individuals as relics of a primitive epoch, are stirred up to find free gratification" (Freud, 1959: 15).

THE DOMESTICATION OF OPINION

One could endlessly multiply the examples of these thematic affinities visible in the works of the founders of the new social sciences as well as in political thinkers or literature: themata[13] that organize representations as well as a set of scientific problems, even though the responses to the problems posed differ, unless, more simply, the difference lies in the eventual interpretations made of them and whose oppositions can help mask the original similarities.

Nevertheless, in two apparently very different domains, the organization of production and political organization, an almost identical remedy that will be found this time to the problem that, in final analysis, forms the substratum of the elites' representations of lower class behavior and that Le Bon had identified as the ultimate explanation of their irrationality—the leader, as according to him, a herd can't do without a master. Never at a loss when it comes to metaphors, Tarde, for his part, will speak in his *Laws of Imitation* of the power of the chief as being like that of the hypnotist, the medium, who knows how to put the crowd into a somnambulistic state, a "cataleptic state," recalling the collective trances of primitive societies.[14]

In order to discipline the savage, to domesticate him, it is necessary to isolate him. In his very political *Principles of Scientific Management*, Frederick W. Taylor writes in 1911 that the issue of the organization of work rests on an understanding of psychology. The average worker, on whom he will attempt his first experiments and whom he places in the category of "oxen" just like Taine, is certainly, "physically and mentally thick," but by nature "uncomplicated," "like young girls or kids": a good word, a little attention from his supervisor suffice to make him produce. But put him in a group, let him "chatter" and problems begin, because in a group "men are pulled downwards, imitate the weakest," conspire to contest authority, to "deliberately trick the boss." At the heart of the techniques that he invented to fight these natural penchants, there is, even more than what's normally associated with his name (time-keeping, the study of movements, separation of conceptualization and execution, etc.), a political principle of acting on the individual: dividing the group is the goal of the division of labor.

Even if the comparison might seem incongruous, we will take the liberty of comparing Taylor's writings and the minutes of contemporaneous French parliamentary debates on the question of whether it is necessary to change the electoral laws in order to better ensure the secrecy of the ballot, debates that will end in 1913 with the adoption of the voting booth. Studying the arguments of its partisans and adversaries, beyond what strangeness it reveals of political divisions, will lead us back to Tarde and Le Bon, as far as the majoritarian conception of opinion goes, and to all those, like Taylor, who have thought about ways of disciplining the masses, to borrow this time from Foucault.[15]

Let's see then what the right and left think about it.[16] Surprisingly, in final analysis, it is for the same reasons ultimately that one will fight for the voting booth and the other against it. For the aristocracy, which doesn't fail to make ironic remarks about the resemblance between a voting booth (*isoloir*) and a urinal (*urinoir*), hiding oneself in order to vote amounts to demeaning oneself, sinking to the level of people who have no opinion of their own, who vote in fear, in a fit of passion, in short, under another's influence. The left is in perfect agreement with this last point, on which it bases its campaign for the voting booth, knowing that its electorate votes under others' influence when it votes with a more or less open ballot under the gaze of the local worthies in their presence and thus, in most cases, under the gaze of the employer, the factory or land owner, which often means the mayor or right-wing representative, as under the *ancien régime*.

Not knowing how to make its acts fall in line with its principles, which should have inclined them more towards publicity, the left will win a Pyrrhean victory, having given the right what the latter logically should have claimed itself—a mechanism, which will be used by many others, suited to exorcising its dread of the masses. The voting booth will reinforce the grand principles (universal and equal suffrage) but adds to the list of technologies of enclosure and serialization of individuals analyzed by Foucault by limiting opinion to the individual: imposed in the name of the fight against domination, the voting booth turns out to be one disciplinary technique among others, "a technology for severing social bonds" (Garigou, 1988: 44). Beyond that, it symbolizes an evolution in the political field's functioning that exorcises the fears that the whole political class has always manifested towards the "sovereign people." The voting booth reconfigures the political landscape on the basis of a dissociation and a recreation "of new ad hoc groupings—electorates—produced by the specific activity of political entrepreneurs. . . . At first, this dissociation is the artifice by which the act of voting is separated from other social activities, and in a way, emptied of its social content. In this sense, the voting booth . . . releases the voter from the straitjacket of the multiple bonds that define him socially." It concretizes the institution of a new conception of the citizen-voter, "not that of processions and the reality of social groups, but that of the individual defined by his function and his relation to the entrepreneurs who offer their wares in the marketplace of political goods" (Garigou, 1988: 45). The path is clear for Gallup and his European epigones, what was just said about the voting booth applying word for word to polls.

In retrospect, one might be astonished that it took so long to arrive at this solution. In fact, it is useful to remember that it is necessary to search in classical political economy for the origins of public opinion, which will be institutionalized in the first decades of this century by an electoral reform, then by its means of empirical display, the poll, which completes the mechanism. This new pacified political space is none other than the marketplace as surface of exchange theorized by Adam Smith[17]: "The eighteenth-century idea of public opinion parallels the economic idea of the free market economy. Here is the public composed of discussing circles of opinion, peers crowned by parliament; there is the market composed of freely competing entrepreneurs. As price is the result of anonymous, equally-weighted bargaining individuals, so is the public of public opinion the result of each man having thought out things for himself and contributing his weight to the great formation" (Mills, 1963: 354). Is it necessary to recall that the great polling institutes often are nothing more than departments of organizations studying the market; that the old relation between homo politicus and homo oeconomicus finds itself theoretically and methodologically justified by the predominant practice of these institutes who have adopted the principles of methodological individualism and the definition that flows from it of what public opinion is: "The aggregate of similar public opinions about problems of public interest" (in Boudon et al., 1989: 142).

But let there be no mistake. Giving in to the rite of critiquing polls and the biased questions through which they suggest responses to the interviewees would mean missing the real problem. The heart of the matter lies elsewhere: in the effects that they produce in the functioning of the political system and in the place that public opinion occupies there. Fixating on criticizing polls on a methodological level amounts to forgetting that behind the methods there are always theories that have all the more chance of producing effects on reality in that they coincide with the dominant lines of force of an epoch. That is what we wanted to illustrate in bringing together some scientific paradigms and some ideas that have structured political thought in the nineteenth and early twentieth centuries, in order to highlight their common substructure: what Max Weber has called "elective affinities" and Georges Duby "the intellectual equipment" of a period, that by which one attempts to explain the specificity of modern apparatuses for the domestication of opinion (the voting booth, polls, but also the bureaucratization of party apparatuses) in a process of co-construction, alloying, that has joined together political elites and scientific elites. It is because an entire scientific current shared the same presuppositions as almost the entire political class that administrative methods for grasping reality could easily find the necessary allies in the latter for their spread. It is necessary to recall here what Foucault wrote about the relationship between power and knowledge (and not only favoring it because it serves us or applying it because it is useful); "there is no power relation without the correlative constitution of a field of knowledge, nor any knowledge that does not presuppose and constitute at the same time power relations . . . the subject who knows, the objects to be known, and the modalities of knowledge must be regarded as so many effects of these fundamental implications of power-knowledge and their historical transformations" (Foucault, 1977: 27-28).

CONCLUSION

If the concept of public opinion is indeed, from a normative point of view, the result of the disinterested communicative action recommended by Habermas, it comes across, from a sociohistorical point of view, as a strategic tool in the service of instrumental action by individuals and groups associated with the exercise of power. As for the ideal fiction of the sovereign people, it is at odds with the "realist" political conception of the people, a people reduced to a raw material whose form and unity can only depend on those who are worthy of handling affairs of state and who are disdained as an antipublic against whom the "true public" must erect the safeguards of reason (cf. Merlin, 1994). Within this framework, public opinion is the consequence of a disciplinary process that attempts to educate the people in citizenship by substituting the codified, individualized, and intermittent forms of polls and elections for spontaneous and collective forms of popular action. Certainly, the nineteenth century also contributed to the development of new forms of expression, such as petitions, committees, resolutions, strikes, and so forth, that signal the construction of a politicized plebeian public sphere for which subversive publicity constitutes an alternative to the liberal organization of civil society on which Habermas focuses.[18] But the twentieth century, by ascribing public opinion to an apparently asocial collection of individual states of mind, snatches from the concept of general will any reference to action and transforms, via mechanisms for recording opinions, the inorganic crowd that is impenetrable to governmental action into a carefully dispersed public (cf. Olivesi, 1995; Stourdzé, 1972). The politics of transparency implied by the publicity principle and that made it possible, ideally, to place the reasons behind the state's actions in plain view prove to be, in point of fact, an organized method for foreseeing the citizens' reasons for action. The more or less developed communicative reason that guided extra-institutional exchanges thus degenerates into a statistical reason that only gives the people "the illusion of politics" and favors a classed "us" that the politically administered narcissism of the bourgeoisie has managed progressively to assert as universal (Furet, 1981).

Against this pessimistic observation, sociology can only bank on the normative point of view of "the ethics of discussion" that the "second" Habermas adopts, on condition that it be revised (cf. Habermas, 1993). For Habermas, the seat of social and political emancipation is no longer the monopoly of elite culture, but rather its everyday communicative practice, rooted in "the lived world" of shared cultural conviction and mutual presumptions of truth, that constitutes the experimental laboratory of truly public opinion. However, once the public use of reason is widened to "communicative action" with respect to which every human being is competent, normative, moral and practical orientations of social life are no longer linked to bourgeois ideals that were rendered necessarily precarious by their inscription in a specific period and specific institutions. From then on, public opinion manifests, at least normatively, the presence of an anthropological invariant: social man's potential to reasonably establish, starting from openly competing individual opinions, a freely agreed upon consensus that enables political judgements at the "base" of society. In this perspective, it is clear that the "publicization" of individual opinion can't be obtained by either its fusion into a general will or a public spirit that would unify the part and the whole, nor by its quantitative accumulation as a "nonpublic opinion" that makes a whole with parts. The form of totalization that characterizes public opinion, far from being statistical or "collectivist," is procedural, the horizon of its construction being the realization, in the end, of a rational agreement in accordance with general interest.

All that remains, then, is to define the term "procedural" in a way that isn't satisfied with an ideal of consensus, necessarily damaging for minorities, but which is capable, to the contrary, of integrating the dissensus with which heterogeneous publics, with necessarily divergent interests and identities, are inevitably confronted (cf. McCarthy, 1992). In the same gesture, the "procedural" constitution of public opinion must integrate different types of communities, not only the argumentative community made up of scholars and politicians, but also the community of "common knowledge" that ordinary agents hold, or think they hold, about each other (see Lewis, 1969). In fact, the ideal public opinion that Habermas speaks of, although founded on objective facts, is not necessarily shared, the intrinsic validity of an argument not allowing one to conclude that it will garner another's agreement. On the other hand, "common opinion" is a mutual opinion that each person adopts in the belief that everyone shares it (cf. Livet, 1990); it is thus taken for truth less because of its intrinsic content than because of the dynamic of agreement that it solicits, every one being "naturally" disposed to endorse an opinion that he believes to be common.

This definition of public opinion as common opinion has the advantage, compared to its ethico-normative model, of taking into account its actual historical status by reconceptualizing it as the emergent effect of interwoven interindividual references, simultaneously descriptive—but what do other people think?— and prescriptive—what should the majority think? Furthermore, it allows us to recover the notion of mentality that sociocultural history proposes saving, at least partially; for mentality can be defined not as an opinion that is, in fact, common, which risks ratifying the illusion of oneness of an unlikely "spirit of society," but as the set of possible points of view about the world. "A mentality is not only the fact that several individuals think the same thing: this thought, in each of them, is, in various ways, marked by the fact that the others think it also" (Veyne, 1974: 113). For Arendt, its this propensity for "a broadened mentality" that makes men capable of raising a particular case to the rank of common problem, thus actualizing the sum of possible opinions that they potentially carry in themselves (cf. Arendt, 1968). In this analytical framework, all opinions, even developed in solitude, are public; for they are, more or less, representative of position-takings of those who, even when empirically absent, remain present in mind, no one being able to escape "this world of universal interdependence, where I can make myself the representative of everybody else" (Arendt, 1968: 242; see the elaboration in Quéré, 1993). This movement of universalization can rest on the mutual opinion that enables minorities to keep silent what they can't say without risking the blame of the majority. But they can also depart from this logic of conformity and bank on the communicative rationality that allows anyone to go beyond his place in order to join the universal community that the revolutionary ideal was able to glimpse.

ENDNOTES

1. The expression is from Febvre, 1953.
2. On the subject of the two bodies of the king, see the pioneering work of Kantorowicz, 1997.
3. On the importance of rumors and the effects that public declarations, be they informal, can have on the social order, cf. Kaplan, 1982.

4. The use of this expression "counts as" is far from being innocent. The philosopher John Searle uses it, in fact, to describe the process of institutionalization that enables a group of individuals to endow brute facts, which are meaningless a priori, with a social value that is totally meaningful—see Searle, 1995.

5. The very famous distinction between these three laws comes from John Locke, *An Essay Concerning Human Understanding*, § 7-10. Cited by Koselleck, 1979: 58. [Chapter 28, "Of Other Relations," 352-354 of Locke, John. *An Essay Concerning Human Understanding*. Ed. Peter H. Nidditch. Oxford: Clarendon Press, 1975.]

6. On the exhibition of centers of opinion, notably during the revolutionary period, see Monnier, 1994.

7. This criticism, particularly aimed at the work of Arlette Farge, is found in Guilhaumou, 1992: 279.

8. On this nice notion of cunning intelligence, see Detienne and Vernant, 1991.

9. We borrow this expression from the title of the work by Chevalier, 1981.

10. This same Italy inspires this pessimistic musing by Taine: "What a cemetery of history!"

11. The term, invented by Eugène Sue himself, is repeated by Marx and Engels in *The Holy Family*, dedicated to this serial writer.

12. On Galton and Pearson, see especially Desrosières, 1998.

13. We borrow this term, changing it slightly, from Holton, 1982. [This French work cited by the authors is a translation of selections from two English works where Holton discusses themata, *The Scientific Imagination: Case Studies* and *Thematic Origins of Scientific Thought: Kepler to Einstein*.]

14. On this aspect of Tarde's thought, see Mucchielli, 1998.

15. It is worth recalling that the first work published by Tarde begins with a critical reading of the works of Jeremy Bentham, who is at the heart of the analyses developed by Foucault in *Discipline and Punish* (1977).

16. We take the essence of this analysis from Garigou, 1988.

17. On this subject, cf. Mairet, in Smith, 1976.

18. Eley, 1992: 329. It is easier to understand then the importance that the democrats assign to the existence of spontaneous public spaces and their "enlightenment praxis," as Eley says, intermittent and preformatted vote-casting obviously not sufficing for there to be popular participation in government.

REFERENCES:

Arendt, Hannah. 1968. *Between Past and Future: Eight Exercises in Political Thought*. New York: Penguin Books.

Baker, Keith M. 1990. *Inventing the French Revolution: Essays on French Political Culture in the Eighteenth Century.* Cambridge: Cambridge University Press.

Baker, Keith M. and Roger Chartier. 1994. Dialogue sur l'espace public. *Politix* 26, 5-22.

Blondiaux, Loïc. 1998. *La fabrique de l'opinion: Une histoire sociale des sondages.* Paris: Seuil.

Boudon, Raymond, Philippe Besnard, Mohammed Cherkaoui, and Bernard-Pierre Lécuyer. 1989. *Dictionnaire de la sociologie.* Paris: Larousse.

Boudon, Raymond, François Bourricaud, and Alain Girard. 1981. *Science et théorie de l'opinion publique: Hommage à Jean Stoetzel.* Paris: Retz.

Bourdieu, Pierre. 1993. Public Opinion Does Not Exist. *Sociology in Question*, 149-157. London: Sage.

Boureau, Alain. 1989. Propositions pour une histoire restreinte des mentalités. *Annales ESC* 6, 1491-1504.

Boureau, Alain. 1988. *Le simple corps du roi: l'impossible sacralité des souverains français, XVe-XVIIIe siècles.* Paris: Editions de Paris.

Chartier, Roger. 1989, November-December. Le monde comme représentation. *Annales ESC* 6, 1505-1520.

Chartier, Roger. 1991. *The Cultural Origins of the French Revolution.* Trans. L. G. Cochrane. Durham: Duke University Press.

Chevalier, Louis. 1981. *Laboring Classes and Dangerous Classes in Paris During the First Half of the Nineteenth Century.* Princeton, NJ: Princeton University Press.

Colliot-Thélène, Catherine. 1998. L'ignorance du peuple. In G. Duprat (ed.), *L'ignorance du peuple: Essais sur la démocratie*, 17-40. Paris: Presses Universitaires de France.

Constant, Benjamin. 1980. *Principes de politique applicables à tous les gouvernements.* Texte établi par Etienne Hofmann, Tome II. Genève: Librairie Droz S.A.

Darmon, Pierre. 1989. *Médecins et assassins à la belle époque.* Paris: Seuil.

Darnton, Robert. 1991. *Edition et sédition: L'univers de la littérature clandestine du XVIIIème siècle.* Paris: Gallimard.

Darnton, Robert. 1993. La France, ton café fout le camp! De l'histoire du livre à l'histoire de la communication. *Actes de la Recherche en Sciences Sociales* 100, 16-26.

de Certeau, Michel. 1997. *Culture in the Plural.* Ed. Luce Giard. Trans. T. Conley. Minneapolis: University of Minnesota Press.

de Certeau, Michel. 1984. *The Practice of Everyday Life.* Trans. S. F. Rendall. Berkeley: University of California Press.

de Certeau, Michel. 1981. Une pratique sociale de la différence: croire. In *Faire croire: Modalités de la diffusion et de la réception des messages religieux du XIIe au XVe siècle*, 363-383. Rome: Ecole Française de Rome.

de Certeau, Michel. 1988. *The Writing of History.* Trans. T. Conley. New York: Columbia University Press.

Desrosières, Alain. 1998. *The Politics of Large Numbers: A History of Statistical Reasoning.* Cambridge, MA: Harvard University Press.

Detienne, Marcel and Jean-Pierre Vernant. 1991. *Cunning Intelligence in Greek Culture and Society.* Chicago and London: Chicago University Press.

Duby, Georges. 1985. Ideologies in Social History. In J. Le Goff and P. Nora (eds.), *Constructing the Past : Essays in Historical Methodology,* 151-165. Cambridge: Cambridge University Press.

Duprat, Gérard. 1998. Introduction. In G. Duprat (ed.), *L'ignorance du peuple: Essais sur la démocratie,* 1-16. Paris: Presses Universitaires de France.

Dupront, Alphonse. 1965. Livre et culture dans la société française du XVIIIe siècle. In F. Furet (ed.), *Livre et société dans la France du XVIIIe siècle.* Vol. 1, 185-238. Paris: La Haye, Mouton et Cie.

Eley, Geoff. 1992. Nations, Publics, and Political Cultures: Placing Habermas in the Nineteenth Century. In C. Calhoun (ed.), *Habermas and the Public Sphere,* 289-339. Cambridge, MA: MIT.

Farge, Arlette. 1995. *Subversive Words: Public Opinion in Eighteenth-Century France.* University Park: Pennsylvania State University Press.

Farge, Arlette. 1992. *Vivre dans la rue à Paris au XVIIIème siècle.* Paris: Gallimard.

Farge, Arlette and Michel Foucault. 1982. *Le désordre des familles: Lettres de cachet des Archives de la Bastille au XVIIIème siècle.* Paris: Gallimard.

Febvre, Lucien. 1953. *Combats pour l'histoire.* Paris: Armand Colin.

Foucault, Michel. 1977. *Discipline and Punish: The Birth of the Prison.* New York: Pantheon Books.

Fraser, Nancy. 1992. Rethinking the Public Sphere: A Contribution to the Critique of Actually Existing Democracy. In C. Calhoun (ed.), *Habermas and the Public Sphere,* 109-142. Cambridge, MA: MIT.

Freud, Sigmund. 1959. *Group Psychology and the Analysis of the Ego.* Ed. and Trans. J. Strachey. New York: Norton.

Furet, François. 1981. *Interpreting the French Revolution.* Trans. E. Forster. Cambridge: Cambridge University Press.

Garigou, Alain. 1988, March. Le secret de l'isoloir. *Actes de la Recherche en Sciences Sociales* 71/72, 22-45.

Ginzburg, Carlo. 1980a. *The Cheese and the Worms: The Cosmos of a Sixteenth-Century Miller.* Trans. J. and A. Tedeschi. Baltimore: Johns Hopkins University Press.

Ginzburg, Carlo. 1980b. Signes, traces, pistes: Racines d'un paradigme de l'indice. *Le Débat* 8, 3-44.

Grignon, Claude and Jean-Claude Passeron. 1989. *Le savant et le populaire: misérabilisme et populisme en sociologie et en littérature.* Paris: Gallimard/Le Seuil.

Guilhaumou, Jacques. 1992. Espace public et Révolution française: Autour d'Habermas. In A. Cottereau and P. Ladrière (eds.),

Pouvoirs et légitimité: Figures de l'espace public. Raisons Pratiques 3, 275-290.

Habermas, Jürgen. 1991. *The Structural Transformation of the Public Sphere: An Inquiry into a Category of Bourgeois Society.* Cambridge, MA: MIT.

Habermas, Jürgen. 1993. *Justification and Application: Remarks on Discourse Ethics.* Cambridge, MA: MIT.

Holton, Gerald. 1982. *L'invention scientifique.* Paris: Presses Universitaires de France.

Kantorowicz, Ernst H. 1997. *The King's Two Bodies: A Study in Mediaeval Political Theology.* Princeton, NJ: Princeton University Press.

Kaplan, Steven L. 1982. *The Famine Plot Persuasion in Eighteenth-Century France.* Philadelphia: American Philosophical Society.

Koselleck, Reinhart. 1979. *Le règne de la critique.* Paris: Editions de Minuit.

Le Goff, Jacques. 1985. Mentalities: A History of Ambiguities. In J. Le Goff and P. Nora (eds.), *Constructing the Past: Essays in Historical Methodology,* 166-180. Cambridge: Cambridge University Press.

Lecuyer, Bernard-Pierre. 1981. Une quasi-expérimentation sur les rumeurs au XVIIIe siècle: l'enquête proto-scientifique du contrôleur général Orry (1745). In R. Boudon, F. Bourricaud, and A. Girard (eds.), *Science et théorie de l'opinion publique: Hommage à Jean Stoetzel,* 170-187. Paris: Retz.

Lewis, David K. 1969. *Convention.* Cambridge, MA: Harvard University Press.

Livet, Pierre. 1990. Structure de l'opinion collective. In L. Sfez and G. Coutlée (eds.), *Technologies et symboliques de la communication,* 113-122. Grenoble: Presses Universitaires de Grenoble.

McCarthy, Thomas. 1992. Practical Discourse: On the Relation of Morality to Politics. In C. Calhoun (ed.), *Habermas and the Public Sphere,* 51-72. Cambridge, MA: MIT.

Merlin, Hélène. 1994. *Public et littérature en France au XVIIème siècle.* Paris: Les Belles Lettres.

Mills, C. Wright. 1963. *Power, Politics, People: The Collected Essays of C. Wright Mills.* Ed. I. L. Horowitz. New York: Oxford University Press.

Monnier, Raymonde. 1994. *L'espace public démocratique: Essai sur l'opinion à Paris de la Révolution au Directoire.* Paris: Kimé.

Mucchielli, Laurent. 1998. *La découverte du social: Naissance de la sociologie en France.* Paris: La Découverte.

Olivesi, Stéphane. 1995. Histoire de l'opinion publique. *La Pensée* 302, 41-53.

Ozouf, Jacques. 1974. L'opinion publique: Apologie pour les sondages. In J. Le Goff and P. Nora (eds.), *Faire de l'histoire. Volume 3: Nouveaux objets,* 294-314. Paris: Gallimard.

Ozouf, Mona. 1989. *L'homme régénéré: Essais sur la Révolution française.* Paris: Gallimard.

Quéré, Louis. 1993. Opinion: The Economy of Likelihood. An Introduction to a Praxeological Approach to Public Opinion. *Réseaux: The French Journal of Communication* 1(1), 139-162.

Roche, Denis. 1993. *La France des Lumières*. Paris: Fayard.

Searle, John. 1995. *The Construction of Social Reality*. London: Allen Lane.

Smith, Adam. 1976. *Recherches sur la nature et les causes de la richesse des nations*. Ed. and Pref. Gérard Mairet. Paris: Gallimard.

Stourdzé, Yves. 1972. Le désir désamorcé. *Epistémologie Sociologique* 13, 47-59.

Taine, Hippolyte. 1896. *The Ancient Régime*. Trans. J. Durand. New York: Henry Holt and Company.

Tarde, Gabriel. 1901/1989. *L'opinion et la foule*. Paris: Presses Universitaires de France.

Tocqueville, Alexis de. 1990. *Democracy in America*. Trans. H. Reeve. Ed. and Intro. P. Bradley. New Intro. D. J. Boorstin. New York: Vintage Classics.

Veyne, Paul. 1974. L'histoire conceptualisante. In J. Le Goff and P. Nora (eds.), *Faire de l'histoire. Volume 3: Nouveaux objets*, 94-133. Paris: Gallimard.

Vovelle, Michel. 1990. *Ideologies and Mentalities*. Cambridge: Polity Press.

Walzer, Michael, ed. 1992. *Regicide and Revolution: Speeches at the Trial of Louis XVI*. Intro. M. Walzer. Trans. M. Rothstein. New York: Columbia University Press.

3

Realism in Social Representation and the Fate of the Public

John Durham Peters

One of the chief problems in theorizing the public sphere is finding forms of communication that are adequate to the theoretical demands of democratic life. As long as political life is not centered on a single place where the people can assemble as a single body, the expression of the people's voice(s) will always be inseparable from various techniques of representation. In this essay, I examine a variety of solutions to the problem of representation: the pomp of the king's two bodies; the print-based chatter of the bourgeois public sphere as theorized by Habermas; representative government as theorized by John Stuart Mill; the dream of a revolutionary newspaper among the American Progressives; and the debate between Walter Lippmann and John Dewey about the proper forms of communication for democracy, among others. Realism is the dream of accessing the facts without any apparatus of representation, and it is fundamentally tied to the bourgeois dream of casting off the king's body and its associated pomp and stultification. And yet, I will argue, something very like the king's body—the need for condensational symbols of complex totalities—is still very much with us and occurs, ironically enough, at the heart of all projects of realistic representation.

THE KING'S BODY

Medieval Europe did not know institutional spheres of public and private as the Greeks and Romans did, but it did contribute one crucial trope to the enduring repertoire of conceptions of public life. The king's body served as the first of many devices of symbolic condensation for social affairs. The idea of a public realm of citizens or a sociological aggregate—"the public"—did not exist until the eighteenth century (Hölscher, 1979). In medieval political thought, only one person was public, in the sense of being worthy of visibility: the feudal lord. Likewise, the trappings of office and "symbols of sovereignty, for instance the princely seal, were deemed 'public'" (Habermas, 1964/1974: 50). Habermas calls this form of publicity "representative," a somewhat confusing term in English The German word *Repräsentation*, in contrast, carries such connotations as prestige, ceremony, and imposingness. Representative publicity makes no reference to an open social site where citizens (a notion arguably quite lost from Augustine till perhaps Rousseau) participate in politics through discussion. It is rather the glory of power created by the personal presence of the rulers (Habermas, 1964/1974: 51; Habermas, 1962/1989: 12-14). In contrast to the bourgeois public sphere, the medieval public sphere involved the display of prestige, not criticism; spectacle, not debate; appearance before the people, not on their behalf (Habermas, 1962/1989: 8). The logic of a representative public sphere is succinctly stated by Prospero at the beginning of a performance within Shakespeare's *The Tempest*: "No tongue! all eyes! be silent" (IV.i.59).

The doctrine of the king's two bodies is the most articulate theorization of a representative public realm (Kantorowicz, 1957; cf. Hariman, 1995, ch. 3). The king, as it was stated by Queen Elizabeth's lawyers, has both a "body natural" and a "body politic," the one being his physical, mortal body, the other being the state as a metaphysical, immortal corporation. The natural body of the king thus represented the body politic, as in the instructive if apocryphal statement of Louis XIV: *l'état, c'est moi*. Again, the sense of representation here is not that of a statistically representative sample or of representatives to a political assembly. Rather, the king is as an allegory of the body politic. The body has long served as a microcosm of society, from antiquity through Herbert Spencer, but the monarch stood as a real presence of the cosmopolitical order, not a pale reflection of some elusive but deeper reality. This fusion of body, will, and polity was, of course, a central target of modern political theory and agitation from the seventeenth century on, culminating in the spectacular beheadings of Charles I and Louis XVI that symbolically sought to sever this linkage. The successor public sphere, the bourgeois, sought to replace the body with the word, specifically the word of critical debate and print culture.

But the executioner and the guillotine did not banish the royal ghost. The longing for political presence lingers today, both in the practice of the mass media, which often serve to reduce messes of empirical fact into comprehensible images, and in the undying dream in progressive political theory of face-to-face participation as the best setting for democratic communication. The dream of participatory democracy insists that democracy goes best when the bodies of citizens are present to each other; it rests on a principle of presence no less than the doctrine of the king's two bodies.

MODERN MEDIA AND REALISTIC REPRESENTATION OF THE PUBLIC

Giving form to the public body has become, in many ways, the stewardship of the media of representation over the past two and a half centuries. Given a sufficiently broad definition, mass media arise in a wide variety of social orders, not only modern, electrified ones. Coins, cathedrals, statuary, stained glass, and pilgrimages are all, for instance, historically important mass media of communication (Curran, 1982; Menache, 1990). All social orders have perhaps prepared large pictures of the world that surpass any individual's experience or sensation to fill their media. What is unique to modernity is the portrayal of actualities and the claim of realism. The notions of society and the public are coeval with new techniques for representing social wholes in such forms as novels, newspapers, encyclopedias, and social statistics, which all emerge in the eighteenth century in Western and Northern Europe and are inseparable from the more general modernization processes of that era. All attempt to portray a world in which first-hand acquaintance of the social order is no longer sufficient. The novel, as Georg Lukács (1915/1965) and Raymond Williams (1973) have shown, is a genre socially and historically tied to the disappearance of "knowable communities." Such forms of representation offer panoramic surveys of the social horizon; newspapers, novels, encyclopedias, dictionaries, statistics and demography, scatterplots and pie charts, zoos, museums, the census, and visual panoramas all fabricate representable totalities beyond the direct acquaintance of any mortal. The king's body symbolically condensed the social macrocosm into a microcosm, but new forms did so by empirical representation. Entire populations became knowable as bodies of knowledge. Uniquely modern is the claim of accuracy and verifiability, that is, of realism.

With the disputed term realism, I intend something vaguer than specific political, metaphysical, literary, or scientific doctrines; I refer to that long revolution in social representation and self-knowledge, beginning in eighteenth-century Europe, which links the early impetus of the newspaper and the novel with more recent statistical sample and polling research. The project is the making visible of society, not as an allegory like the king's body, but as a fact. The famous lines from Stendhal's novel *The Red and the Black* (1830) capture much of what I have in mind: "A novel, sir, is a mirror carried along a great road. It reflects to your eyes the blue of the sky as well as the puddles in the road" (1830/1964: 361). Realism in literary and social representation broke through ancient taboos about low or vulgar style and content, with the profound social consequence that ordinary life could be made an object of public knowledge. Things that no one had ever thought to study systematically— births, marriages, deaths, diseases, incomes, opinions—became amenable to analysis only thanks to a large, and quite revolutionary, loosening of older inhibitions about the representation of the world in all its elegance and its vulgarity (Auerbach, 1953; Watt, 1957). Because of its realism, ancient Greek and Roman literary theorists would have undoubtedly found social science among the low forms of culture.

Key to realism is the claim to factuality. One might say that ancient myth or medieval statecraft (stagecraft) performed what the news does for us today: to give a sense of the forces that order—and disorder—our universe. But a qualitative shift lies in the claim that the news can be verified. The stock market reports do not belong to the same order of truth as Greek myths. We have learned to understand news reports as possessing a currency of verifiable reference that myths lack. The claim that verbal or numerical representations of social forces can be cashed in for the hard currency of observation continues to inform the diverse practices of the nonfiction side of the media, which we should not conceive only as newspapers, magazines, cinema, radio, and television, nor even the more diverse forms of information and entertainment, but as all practices of social envisioning and documentation, including statistics, accounting, insurance, census-taking, polling, social services and social sciences. These techniques enable society and the public in a world in which they are invisible to the naked eye.

Though the twentieth century goes much further in portraying invisible social totalities than any other so far, practices of graphically representing large numbers have a longer ancestry reaching at least to the eighteenth century (Ludes, 1992; Tufte, 1983). The novel and statistics are each an answer to the problem of how to display a cross-section of a quantitative complexity. One uses narrative, the other aggregation. Both enact—and depend on—a new apprehension of space and time: the possibility of a snapshot of spatially dispersed events (Anderson, 1991). A novel might weave several strands of plot together with the device of "meanwhile"; a statistical report could do so with a "cross-section." Letters, a term that once meant the whole of literature and now only means correspondence, were also a central narrative structuring device. The shuttling of letters in the epistolary novel, such as Richardson's *Pamela*, Rousseau's *Julie*, or Goethe's *Werther*, arguably the dominant novels of their time, was an apt metaphor for the shuttling of point of view from one character, place, time, or line of plot to another, a traveling in imagination across an emergent social totality (just as the telephone was later a key device motivating cinematic cross-cutting; Kessler, 1991). Not only factuality, but also actuality, is key to modern realism in social representation.

Statistics, as mentioned, provided another means of imagining social wholes as simultaneities. Statistics, a term translated from the German term *Statistik* in the eighteenth century, originally signified the comparative (and often competitive) study of states and their climates, geography, and demography. Statistics are an emblem of the shift from the king's body to the realistic representation of the body politic. Statistical techniques are devices of what Foucaultians calls "biopower," providing elites and administrators with the aggregate intelligence needed to control populations, tax incomes, or raise armies. By the early nineteenth century, what Ian Hacking (1990) calls "the avalanche of printed numbers" was set in motion by the liberal utilitarian reformers staffing western European bureaucracies. Statistical data accumulated about marriage and divorce, birth and death, class, income, crime, suicide, and other kinds of deviancy. That population remains the technical term for any statistical aggregate attests to the biopolitical origins of the practice. Like newspapers, novels, and encyclopedias, the objects represented by statistics defy immediate acquaintance. These forms give a panoramic *tour d'horizon* of a vast social collective, often nationally defined. They are means of condensing intelligence of otherwise intangible totalities. More emphatically, biopolitical practices such as statistics are not only documentary but creative: they serve to constitute what they study. These data not only counted social life: they created categories for people to act on and in, thus, in the striking phrase of Hacking (1986), "making up people" (such as "working-class," "split personality," or "kleptomaniac"). Realistic practices such as statistics are possible only once their object is imagined; once the object is imagined and measured, it can take on a new life of its own. The line between fiction and nonfiction is always thin in social representation; as Hacking would insist, it is a dynamic border, always shifting as new categories turn into facts of behavior and identity.

A newspaper is likewise an instrument of data-reduction, organizing, as Anderson notes, its diverse material by date. Like the encyclopedia, the chief principles of narrative organization in the daily press are miscellaneity and comprehensiveness. In a daily, articles find themselves juxtaposed to others with which they share no obvious relation except occurrence on the same day; in an encyclopedia, they are arranged by initial letters of the alphabet. As with all social interaction in the city, the newspaper and encyclopedia juxtapose unacquainted subjects in a common space. One genre treats the variables, the other the constants (Sloterdijk, 1981). The newspaper, as a vernacular form, is both novelistic and statistical in its modes of social reportage (Davis, 1983). The tension between story and information, as Michael Schudson (1978), borrowing a page from Walter Benjamin (1936/1968), has argued, structures twentieth-century journalistic genres generally: human interest stories and stock market reports, sports stories and box scores. The polarity of narrative and data marks the twin extremities of realistic social description since the eighteenth century, with many hybrid forms between. Academic battles between quantitative and qualitative approaches in the social sciences—including the debate between the advocates of polling and the advocates of deliberative groups for measuring public opinion—are only a late and local variant on this larger theme.

THE PROSTHETIC BODY POLITIC

The bourgeois public sphere is inseparable from realistic techniques of representation. Yet it tends to legitimate itself with images drawn from political assemblies, leading to a tension in its chief product and raison d'être, public opinion. Public opinion claims to be the voice of the people, as if the *populus* really could speak in one *vox*. Keith Baker (1990: 172) argues that the modern notion of the public originates in "the transfer of ultimate authority from the public person of the sovereign to the sovereign person of the public" that took place in late eighteenth-century France. The public is a sort of corporate personality, a successor of sorts to the monarch. For the ancients up to the eighteenth century, the constitution of this body in various kinds of face-to-face assembly was generally taken for granted. Today the Athenian agora, the Roman forum, the London coffeehouse, the New England town meeting, or the

African-American church still captivate the imagination of democratic thinkers. The problem is that the forms of communication that many versions of normative democratic theory posit as necessary for enlightened public opinion—dialogue, interaction, information-gathering, and participation—are out of phase with the scale of communication and representation in modern nation-states.

Even though it favored tropes of discussion and debate, the bourgeois public sphere from its beginnings was textual, anchored in nascent print culture (Warner, 1990). As Habermas (1962/1989: 43) notes of readers of the *Spectator* and *Tatler*, two famous pioneers in English literary journalism, "the public [*das Publikum*] that read and debated this sort of thing read and debated about itself." The "public" was thus a reflexive creature of moral weeklies and other institutions of vernacular literature; discussion about it created the spaces for discussion in it. Since its eighteenth-century birth the bourgeois public sphere has always been at least partly a virtual community, a symbolic diaspora anchored by sites appointed for conversation. The claim to realistic representation thus depends on some kind of symbolic constitution of the object to be represented in the first place. How to reconcile the longing for presence in assembly—the roar, hisses, and cheers of the crowd, the festive rubbing of shoulders with fellow-citizens—with the necessity of representation is a problem in modern democratic theory that has received a number of answers.

PARLIAMENT PLUS CONVERSATION: A TWO-STEP FLOW

One answer is wide-ranging public discussion on a national scale, anchored in Parliament. This compromise with scale is well exemplified in J. S. Mill, who exemplifies both the nobility and the contradictions of the liberal tradition, being both an advocate of the extension of the franchise and political participation and a critic of democratized culture. He calls for a combination of mediated and face-to-face discourse. A key passage from Mill's *Representative Government* (1861/1952:, 330) reads:

> In the ancient world, though there might be, and often was, great individual or local independence, there could be nothing like a regulated popular government beyond the bounds of a single city-community; because there did not exist the physical conditions for the formation and propagation of a public opinion, except among those who could be brought together to discuss public matters in the same agora. This obstacle is generally thought to have ceased by the adoption of a representative system. But to surmount it completely,

required the press, and even the newspaper press, the real equivalent, though not in all respects an adequate one, of the Pnyx and the
Forum.

This quote beautifully captures the notion of the newspaper as a surrogate for assembly, a surrogate that reaches across distances. Popular
government, he argues, must have "utmost possible publicity and liberty of discussion, whereby not merely a few individuals in succession,
but the whole public, are made, to a certain extent, participants in the
government, and sharers in the instruction and mental exercise deriv-
able from it" (Mill: 363). Yet the hub of the national conversation he
locates in Parliament, an institution that inherits the tasks of the most
diffuse bourgeois public sphere. Parliament is "to be at once the nation's
Committee of Grievances, and its Congress of Opinions" (Mill: 361). It
ought "to indicate wants, to be an organ for popular demands, and a
place of adverse discussion for all opinions relating to public matters,
both great and small" (Mill: 362). *Representative Government* institutional-
izes the debate and discussion Mill called for in *On Liberty*. Though Mill
assumes that the actual work of government will be done by a cadre of
elites specially trained for public service—the many talk but the few
administer—he believes public discussion not only to be a school of
moral and intellectual virtue but also the chief avenue of political participation, along with such forms of political engagement as voting, jury
duty, running for or holding office. Parliament is the hub that sends
spokes of enlightenment into the nation at large: "and it is from political
discussion, and collective political action, that one whose daily occupa-
tions concentrate his interests in a small circle round himself, learns to
feel for and with his fellow-citizens, and becomes consciously a member
of a great community" (Mill: 382).

THE PROGRESSIVE QUEST FOR PARTICIPATION

Mill, as we see in that key phrase, "great community," was something
like a Deweyan *avant la lettre*. (Mill saw the public sphere as a school;
Dewey wanted to make the school into a public sphere.) American
Progressive intellectuals sought a forum that was able to collect the geographically scattered character of democratic life in the United States.
Not impressed as Mill by the potential of legislative assemblies as the
central theater of public discussion, Dewey, Park, and Cooley, among
others, turned to the other side of Mill's analysis of modern, dispersed
democracy: the newspaper. Mill, as we have seen, thought the newspaper a kind of prosthetic replacement for the Athenian Pnyx or Roman

Forum. Its chief lack was its inability to involve the entire electorate as speaking (writing) as well as a hearing (reading) body. The forms of communication it sustained were, in the view of the Progressives, insufficiently interactive or participatory. They explored the newspaper as a solution to both the problems of social scale and the defects of American democracy.

Charles Horton Cooley, for instance, announced to his journal in 1892 that he had found the social sensorium in the newspaper (Quandt, 1970). How so, the social sensorium? Herbert Spencer, the looming presence for all American social thinkers in Cooley's generation, discovered anatomical analogies in society, worked out in tedious detail. There were societal digestive and muscular systems, but there was no societal nervous system, no central place of coordination and control. A social brain would, after all, blend uneasily with Spencer's laissez-faire political and moral economy. The Progressives thought that his vision of coordination without community, aggregation without unanimity, a social body without a social mind, was a correct description of modern society, but a terrible ideal. Spencer sounded an inadvertent call to arms. In Cooley's view, Spencer's mistake was to take as natural what was an outrageous social deficit. Cooley's discovery of the social sensorium at the same time John Dewey, his teacher at the University of Michigan, was contemplating a revolutionary newspaper, *Thought News*, a sort of daily encyclopedia for the people, foreshadows a characteristic theme in Progressive thinking about mass communication: what society lacks (such as a sense of community or spiritual unity) new forms of communication will supply. They thought the losses in face-to-face communication in the great society could be compensated by new mechanisms of distance communication.

The Progressives had a higher standard of participatory communication than Mill. For him, the dispersed talk of mechanics and tradesman was a sufficient piece of the national conversation. For the Progressives, in contrast, the task was the overcoming of political dislocation, alienation, and drift, of the political and spiritual effects of speed, bulk, and disorder in late nineteenth-century urbanization and industrialization. The communal dimension in American life was not simply an object of nostalgia but an enduring normative ideal of how people ought to communicate with one another. Social relations of give and take, acquaintance, and cooperation, together with the intellectual skills of recognizing and debating the social forces that shaped one's world, were, they thought, not antiquated dreams doomed to disappear with agrarian America, but a moral code fit for any just democratic polity, in whatever conditions. Robert Park, who with Franklin Ford was part of the *Thought News* misadventure, and later one of the key consolidators of sociology as an academic discipline with the University of Chicago as its center, later described the natural history of the American newspaper as an attempt to restore what the village once provided: familiarity with everything that is going on, acquaintance with the people who live around one (Park, 1923). For the Progressives, like Mill, the newspaper was a means to initiate people into a great community. Mill thought the great community was already there, waiting (perhaps reluctantly) to welcome the newly enfranchised classes. The Progressives thought the great community was in eclipse, but revivable through instruments of communication at a distance. If lack of community was the problem, communication was the answer. The problem was their blindness to the contrast between interaction and imparting. Interaction always requires limits on participation, whether of members or chances to speak, whereas imparting has no natural upper limit.

Centralized staging and dispersed talk: the configuration remains central to both liberal political theory and to the intellectual history of studies of the social and political meaning of mass communication. The tradition of mass communication research associated with Paul Lazarsfeld and his students centers on the intertwining of face-to-face and mediated messages in what they called variously supplementation, personal influence, or the two-step flow. This tradition, until recently, has, like the Progressives, tended to think that conversation is not importantly out of step with the requisites of social scale (Simonson, 1996). The dangers of visual representation (the spectacles of the media universe) can be held in check by the chatter of political representation (the interchange among neighbors and between ordinary folks and their representatives). The recent argument sees spectacular representation as a precondition for political discussion, the framer or informer of civic debate. As Elihu Katz has quipped, "no conversation without representation." The effects tradition has thus made explicit its Millian picture of communication at the societal level: a central theater of political discourse links and triggers scattered conversations through the land. But the central theater today is television, not Parliament, which ominously suggests to some thinkers a return of the display politics of the feudal era rather than the talkative politics of the bourgeois republics. Katz's gamble is to think that the two can coexist and stimulate each other. The question is whether that is the best we can do for democracy in current conditions.

LIPPMANN'S STRANGE REALISM

The assault on the Progressive dream of a popular newspaper serving as a participatory public sphere was made with singular force by Walter

Lippmann, whose skepticism about an informed public supported by a newspaper prosthesis paralleled the 1920s skepticism about face-to-face presence in writers such as Franz Kafka, T. S. Eliot, or Virginia Woolf. Both modernists and "democratic realists" such as Lippmann saw the other side of mediation. Lippmann saw the obstacles in media forms; the modernists saw the face-to-face as itself mediated. His *Public Opinion* (1922) assessed the damage. His distrust was directed against media claiming to represent the world outside; his target was not audiovisual media, but the press, specifically the news media. The hearing and seeing aid of journalistic representation was not a representation of society but an obstacle. The best-known chapter from the book, "The World Outside and the Pictures in Our Heads," set up the classic contrast between reality (the world outside) and the images and symbols we make about it (the pictures in our heads; the epigraph for the book is from Plato's story of the captives in the cave). Lippmann's book is sometimes taken as a critique of the ideal of objectivity in journalism, but the virulence of his nostalgia for an immediate access to the facts only restates the dream of an unvarnished social truth delivered by realistic representation.

The arguments of *Public Opinion* reveal, largely inadvertently, the connection between fact and fiction in social representation. Lippmann criticizes social fictions while he depends on them. Consider the often-read but rarely analyzed opening of the book—the story of an imaginary Atlantic island on which people of English, French, and German nationality have resided for a long time. Due to long intervals in the delivery of mail, these people got the news of the outbreak of World War I six weeks late. "For six strange weeks they had acted as friends," Lippmann concludes, "when in fact they were enemies" (1922: 3). This fable is intended to illustrate the ways that all citizens everywhere can be out of touch with the environment in which they live— persisting in their own little pictures, when in fact the world outside has changed. It serves Lippmann as an allegory of the fate of philosophical democrats in the early twentieth century, "acting as if" when their reality has vanished. Lippmann points to the islanders' folly, caught in a time warp, going through the motions as if all were well, when "in fact" it was not. But he does not notice the strangeness of this "in fact" or the even more bizarre fact that a community of friends could be turned inside out when bundles of processed wood pulp covered with inky markings arrived in their midst. All the magical thinking that Lippmann imputes to the psychology of the common people appears at the heart of what he wants to take as "fact." Lippmann wants realistic representation to cure the public of superstition, but he fails to note that the world outside consists of such wildly symbolic representations such as declarations of war. It is curious that he calls for fidelity to reality when he sees so lucidly just how much of "reality" (World War I, for instance) was spun by insiders in ways that really did win or lose battles, consent, and lives. Lippmann sees social construction everywhere, but he wants to transcend it, as did his disciples who saw in public opinion polling a cleaner way to get at the pulse of democracy. He forgot that realism is not only a dream of accessing the truth but a set of conventions of representation. Yesterday's realism is today's mannerism. Nothing quite looks so stylized as the "realistic" journalism, literature, or social science of a century ago. Upton Sinclair's reporting, Dreiser's novels, or Durkheim's study *Suicide*, for instance, all show the brilliance and limits of their time. They do deliver social truth, but not of the realistic kind their authors wanted to provide.

Lippmann counts the island's communal life as defectively out of step; he has already pulled us into a regime in which governmental speech acts take priority over lived social worlds. Lippmann has no trust in the face-to-face, and much of the book's most withering critique is directed against the idea that twentieth-century people could live in a self-contained community or have the epistemological powers to envision the complexity of the world's transactions. His answer to the crisis of a knowable world and an informed public is statistical totalities, one of the abiding options in realist social representation since the eighteenth century. Like the literary modernists, in Lippmann face-to-face talk has become the special case, an island in a larger universe of communication flows. This makes the task of communication with the public elusive indeed. While arguing that knowledge must not settle for mere images, he described a world in which "facts" are increasingly alien to the experience of concrete individuals. His plea for journalism—like all other agencies of social representation—to grasp nothing but the facts ironically appears at a moment when the classic priority of reality over symbols is superceded. When Lippmann (1922: 14) writes, "For it is clear enough that under certain conditions, men respond as powerfully to fictions as they do to realities, and that they in many cases help to create the very fictions to which they respond," he thinks he is diagnosing a characteristic feature and potential defect of the human psyche, but we can see that he is also laying bare the logic of postmodern political action.

Lippmann is quite explicit about the surpassing of the old organs of sensation and the need for modern supplements. Like Sigmund Freud (1930/1961) in *Civilization and its Discontents* seven years later, Lippmann argues that the need for the technological supplements, whether of media or polling information, stems from the fact that we are not gods. "The world that we have to deal with politically is out of reach, out of sight, out of mind. Man is no Aristotelian god contemplating all existence at one glance. . . . Yet this same creature has invented ways of seeing what no naked eye could see, of hearing what no ear could hear, of weighing immense masses and infinitesimal ones, of counting and separating more items than he can individually remember" (Lippmann, 1922: 29). Unlike Freud, Lippmann thinks the answer is a better prosthesis, more intelligence about social life. Such would allow vision at a distance and deception at a distance, because mediation always introduces ghosts who feed in the limbo between transmission and reception. (The term "cyberspace" was originally coined to describe the peculiarly liminal space along the telephone wires between the two voices.) Despite novel forms of knowledge and record, most citizens remain, in Lippmann's view, the victims of pseudo-environments and stereotypes. The body politic is not only out of reach: it never appears except as a fiction or abstraction.

Even Lippmann's philosophical antagonist John Dewey saw the public as an unwelcome intruder from the grave at times: "the public and its organizational ends is not only a ghost, but a ghost which walks and talks, and obscures, confuses, and misleads governmental action in a disastrous way" (Dewey, 1927: 125). For both Dewey and Lippmann, the crisis of democracy is a crisis of communication. Dewey sees the lack of participatory interaction as the most alienating feature of the age. The notion that interaction could cure the alienations of modernity is shared widely in the 1920s: Buber wants to turn I-It relationships into I-Thou ones; Heidegger calls for authentic confrontations instead of distraction; Hegelian Marxists such as Lukács, Marcuse, or Adorno are beginning to call for a joyful reconciliation of subject and object instead of pervasive reification, in the wake of the rediscovery of the early Marx. Dewey seeks to restore interaction as the principle of large-scale democracy. To his credit, Dewey did not see communication as the problem of putting private minds into perfect alignment. Rather, it was the problem of getting people to be full members in the public life of a community. Without this common partaking, society is a herd, not a human association. As Dewey (1916: 87) said, democracy is "primarily a mode of associated living, of conjoint communicated experience." Dewey never forget that fact comes from the Latin word for something made: all our representations enter into the world, not only picture it. Yet Dewey did not imagine the potential overtaxation of human energies in requiring each citizen to be a participant; he saw no discrepancy between the dynamics of face-to-face interaction and the dispersion of mass communication. To get everyone assembled in a national conversation would mean the silencing of everyone but the one speaker who happened to have the floor. In terms of his analysis of the political and communicative conditions in the twentieth century, Lippmann was surely on the right side of most of the key issues in this debate, a fact sometimes forgotten in recent recountings.

Lippmann, and even Dewey at moments, stands for a larger tradition in the twentieth century that has found the public a phantom, a being of whose presence one can never be sure. Social scientists, pollsters, marketers, activists, politicians, educational broadcasters, advertisers, reformers, evangelists, and political philosophers have all had occasion to lament the elusiveness or fickleness of "the public." From Lippmann and Carl Schmitt (1923) to Jean Baudrillard (1983) and Bruce Robbins (1993), conservative and radical thinkers alike have sought to expose the fictive character of this all-legitimating trope of democracy. From Dewey to Habermas to recent theorists of civil society, others, generally of a progressive bent, have bravely taken the bad news about the public's spectral character, still seeking to make notions of the public a lever to reform, normative imagination, or social criticism (for example, Carey, 1995; Garnham, 1992; Rosen, 1994; Scannell, 1989; Westbrook, 1991). Whatever the take on the public, all parties have to agree that popular will is today inseparable from the apparatuses that register it and make it an object of signification, whether broadcast or print news, government documents, the census, demographic research, the discourse of theorists, activists, and professionals who work "in the name of" the public, or the assemblies of those who protest or otherwise put their bodies on the line, duly televised to the rest of us. Contemporary conditions require us to part with the longing for presence in democracy—the affliction of Athens envy. That the public is a fiction, however, does not mean that it is only a fiction; as Lippmann saw, in spite of himself, fictions can be robust realities as well.

That all large-scale communities involve an element of fabrication does not mean, however, that all of these communities are equally robust or real. Indeed, the public is often a special effect within commercial and nationalist media practices that seek to conjure multitudes of fellow viewers and auditors. In early radio history in the United States, for instance, speakers before the microphone were often unnerved by the lack of an audience. This was also true of radio audiences, used to the effects of assembled compatriots on their listening experience. According to a public speaking text of 1928, a sense of the simultaneous audience was still rare on radio: "there is no mass-psychology on the part of the audience. The listeners are not aware of each other, get no support or stimulus from each other. Each one is listening alone" (Clapp and Kane, 1928: 410). But this generalization certainly did not hold for the mid 1930s, when commercialized radio culture was booming. Cantril and Allport (1935) noted how broadcasters used "social facilitation" to inculcate a sense of shared thought and feeling among a dispersed audience. Devices meant to give signs of a live assembly included studio audiences, sound effects (cheers, applause, clapping, canned laughter), practices such as "man in the street" interviews, genres of audience participation such as quiz shows, contestants called "at random" from the studio audience, contests, fan clubs, fan mail, promotional give-aways, telephone call-ins, direct address in radio talk, simulated interaction, and of course, applied research on the audience (ratings). Social science could be reflexively plowed back into radio material; Welles' "War of the Worlds" script even put a made-up rating of the evening's listening audience into the narrative (Cantril, 1940/1982: 5). The radio listener was hailed not as a lonely individual adrift among wayward signals (the position of the radio amateur), but as rubbing elbows with other listeners. Such authenticating details, "audience effects" as we might call them, were calculated to give listeners of a feeling membership in a larger imagined community (Peters, 1996).

The constitution of fictionalized social groups is not always innocent (this is precisely the unease Habermas has for the representative public sphere). The 1930s commercial radio audience was conjured as an assembly of consumers (not of citizens, voters, critics, students, or speakers, to name some other possibilities). From more recent examples of social movements, one can see social groupings that take shape in the fictional air of representation, only to assume force as they act as units. The radio audience was both a fact of power and an effect of representation, which is also the precise fate of the public. Of extreme importance for the market and state, the audience of commercial broadcasting was generally designed to experience itself as a diaspora of simultaneous intimacies. As both Bertolt Brecht and T. W. Adorno argued, the cozy aura of radio listening was not a natural fact but an ideological achievement that obscured the utopian potentials for public organization of the new medium. Such thoughts ought to be kept in mind for any other community constituted by far-flung representations (which are perhaps most of the communities in which many of us live). But neither should we, like Habermas, go too far in canceling all representation as such. The task is the discovery of just social representations, not only accurate ones; fictionality is not a criterion of critique, participation is.

THE REFLEXIVE PUBLIC

Ever since the public succeeded the king as the synecdoche for the body politic, it has been mixed up with representation, but twentieth-century mediations on the mediated sign allow us to explore the fate of the public acutely. Lippmann called the public a phantom in the 1920s, and by the 1930s, commercial broadcasters had found ways to call up the spirit of the public as an audible effect in radio material. At the same time,

public opinion pollsters were learning how to take representative samples. Even in several recent lines of social research on public opinion the
public is treated more or less frankly as an effect of representation
(Peters, 1995). Such examples make it clear that what is most unique
about the public in our century is its reflexive quality, its strange compound of live people and artifice, demographic variables and constitutive fictions, actual opinions and carefully crafted discourses. Realism is
both art and science.

Finally, the public is subject to all the same anxieties as the
"other" in twentieth-century communication theory more generally.
Dewey (1927: 117) put it well: "If a public exists, it is surely as uncertain
about its own whereabouts as philosophers since Hume have been about
the residence and make-up of the self." Whether figured as the masses,
the great unwashed, the audience invisible, the silent majority, the
implosion of the social, the voice of the people, a demographic segment,
or a phantom, the public partakes of all the chief troubles of communication in twentieth-century life: simulation, mediation, distance, self-
reflexivity, and representation. It may enrich our debates and our
inquiry to recognize that the lineage of these concerns go back at least to
the eighteenth-century newsletter, with its combination of public printed knowledge and personal scribblings, or even to the king's body, with
its mortal humanness on the one hand and metaphysical majesty on the
other. All representation involves the claim to transport a body across
space or time, to bring to presence something invisible or inaudible. The
phantoms that haunt the public are the phantoms that haunt communication itself (Peters, 1999).

REFERENCES

Anderson, Benedict. 1991. *Imagined Communities: Reflections on the
    Origins and Spread of Nationalism*. Second edition. London: Verso.
Auerbach, Erich. 1953. *Mimesis: The Representation of Reality in Western
    Literature*. Trans. Willard Trask. Princeton: Princeton University
    Press.
Baker, Keith Michael. 1990. *Inventing the French Revolution: Essays on
    French Political Culture in the Eighteenth Century*. Cambridge:
    Cambridge University Press.
Baudrillard, Jean. 1983. *In the Shadow of Silent Majorities*. New York:
    Semiotext(e).
Benjamin, Walter. 1936/1968. The Storyteller. In Hannah Arendt (ed.),
    Illuminations. Trans. Harry Zohn. New York: Schocken.
Cantril, Hadley and Gordon W. Allport. 1935. *The Psychology of Radio*.
    New York: Harper and Bros.

Cantril, Hadley. 1940/1982. *The Invasion from Mars: A Study in the Social Psychology of Panic.* Princeton, NJ: Princeton University Press.

Carey, James W. 1995. The Press, Public Opinion, and Public Discourse. In Theodore L. Glasser and Charles T. Salmon (eds.), *Public Opinion and the Communication of Consent*, 373-402. New York: Guilford.

Clapp, John Mantle and Edward A. Kane. 1928. *How to Talk*. New York: The Ronald Press.

Curran, James. 1982. Communications, Power, and the Social Order. In Michael Gurevitch et al (eds.), *Culture, Society, and the Media*. London: Methuen.

Davis, Lennard J. 1983. *Factual Fictions: The Origins of the English Novel.* New York: Columbia University Press.

Dewey, John. 1916. *Democracy and Education*. New York: Macmillan.

Dewey, John. 1927. *The Public and its Problems*. New York: Henry Holt.

Freud, Sigmund. 1930/1961. *Civilization and its Discontents*. New York: Norton.

Garnham, Nicholas. 1982. The Media and the Public Sphere. In Craig Calhoun (ed.), *Habermas and the Public Sphere*. Cambridge: MIT Press.

Habermas, Jürgen. 1964/1974. The Public Sphere: An Encyclopedia Article. Trans. Sara and Frank Lennox. *New German Critique* 3, 49-55.

Habermas, Jürgen. 1962/1989. *The Structural Transformation of the Public Sphere: An Inquiry into a Category of Bourgeois Society.* Trans. Thomas Burger & Frederick Lawrence. Cambridge, MA: MIT Press.

Hacking, Ian. 1986. Making up People. In Thomas C. Heller et al. (eds.), *Reconstructing Individualism: Autonomy, Individuality, and the Self in Western Thought.* Stanford: Stanford University Press.

Hacking, Ian. 1990. *The Taming of Chance*. Cambridge: Cambridge University Press.

Hariman, Robert D. 1995. *Political Style: The Artistry of Power*. Chicago: University of Chicago Press.

Hölscher, Lucian. 1979. *Öffentlichkeit und Geheimnis: Eine begriffsgeschichtliche Untersuchung zur Entstehung der Öffentlichkeit in der frühen Neuzeit.* Stuttgart: Klett-Cotta.

Kantorowicz, Ernst H. 1957. *The King's Two Bodies: A Study in Mediaeval Political Theology.* Princeton, NJ: Princeton University Press.

Kessler, Frank. 1991. "Bei Anruf Rettung!" In B. Debatin and H. J. Wulff (eds.), *Telefon und Kultur: Das Telefon im Spielfilm*, 167-173. Berlin: Volker Spiess.

Lippmann, Walter. 1922. *Public Opinion*. New York: Macmillan.

Ludes, Peter. 1992. Visualisierung als Teilprozess der Modernisierung der Moderne. In Knut Hickethier (ed.), *Institution, Technik, und Programm: Rahmaspekte der Programmgeschichte des Fernsehens*, 353-370. Munich: Wilhelm Fink.

Lukács, Georg. 1915/1965. *Die Theorie des Romans: Ein geschichtsphilosophischer Versuch über die Formen der grossen Epik.* Neuwied: Luchterhand.

Menache, Sophia. 1990. *The Vox Dei: Communication in the Middle Ages*. New York: Oxford University Press.

Mill, John Stuart. 1861/1952. Considerations on Representative Government. In Robert Maynard Hutchins (ed.), *Great Books of the Western World*, vol. 43, 325-442. Chicago: Encyclopedia Britannica.

Park, Robert Ezra. 1923. The Natural History of the Newspaper. *American Journal of Sociology*.

Peters, John Durham. 1995. Historical Tensions in the Concept of Public Opinion. In Theodore L. Glasser and Charles T. Salmon (eds.), *Public Opinion and the Communication of Consent*, 3-32. New York: Guilford.

Peters, John Durham. 1996. The Uncanniness of Mass Communication in Interwar Social Thought. *Journal of Communication* 46(3), 108-123.

Peters, John Durham. 1999. *Speaking into the Air: A History of the Idea of Communication*. Chicago: University of Chicago Press.

Quandt, Jean B. 1970. *From the Small Town to the Great Community: The Social Thought of Progressive Intellectuals*. New Brunswick: Rutgers University Press.

Robbins, Bruce. 1993. *The Phantom Public Sphere*. Minneapolis: University of Minnesota Press.

Rosen, Jay. 1994. On Making Things More Public: The Political Responsibilities of the Media Intellectual. *Critical Studies in Mass Communication* 11, 363-388.

Scannell, Paddy. 1989. Broadcasting and Modern Public Life. *Media, Culture, and Society*.

Schmitt, Carl. 1923/1985. *The Crisis of Parliamentary Democracy*. Trans. Ellen Kennedy. Cambridge: MIT Press.

Schudson, Michael. 1978. *Discovering the News: A Social History of American Newspapers*. New York: Basic Books.

Simonson, Peter. 1996, December. Dreams of Democratic Togetherness: Communication Hope from Cooley to Katz. *Critical Studies in Mass Communication* 13, 324-342.

Sloterdijk, Peter. 1981. *Kritik der zynischen Vernunft*. Frankfurt: Suhrkamp.

Stendhal. 1830/1964. *Le rouge et le noir: Chronique de 1830*. Paris: Flammarion.

Tufte, Edward R. 1983. *The Visual Display of Quantitative Information*. Cheshire, CT: Graphics Press.

Warner, Michael. 1990. *The Letters of the Republic: Publication and the Public Sphere in Eighteenth Century America*. Cambridge: Harvard University Press.

Watt, Ian P. 1957. *The Rise of the Novel: Studies in Defoe, Richardson, and Fielding*. Berkeley: University of California Press.

Westbrook, Robert Brett. 1991. *John Dewey and American Democracy*. Ithaca: Cornell University Press.

Williams, Raymond. 1973. *The Country and the City*. New York: Oxford University Press.

4

Public Opinion as Local Opinion

Sinikka Sassi

Ever since its emergence, the concept of public opinion has been problematic, not least today, but it still has its value and relevance at the nexus between political activism, media, and social power. In representative democracies, public opinion serves as a valuable tool for politicians to explore common understanding of and attitudes towards current social issues, but not only political elites make use of public opinion, because people themselves have a relation to it as well. In everyday life it is a means of relating to others and to the environment; it is characteristically human to generate a sense of belonging to a group through the notion of "what others think." Public opinion is part of the ideoscape or mental horizon, and most of the time we do not react to it consciously, taking it for granted like the air we breathe. It helps us to locate ourselves in relation to a larger community whether it be a social group, region, or nation. Only when we engage in action involving interests beyond our personal ones do we become aware of it and alert to it.

In a fragmented world the understanding of common reactions is not easily acquired and its relation to public opinion is not easily constituted. The new complexity is reflected in the Internet and its ability to collect and present a huge variety of opinions, some of which are most extreme and supported only by a tiny minority. The fear is often expressed that the Internet as a public sphere has the potential to give an unrepresentative minority power over a vast majority through its visibility. Network activists and members of cultural groupings, unlike the social movements of earlier periods, can foster a wholly indifferent attitude to majority opinions because of the decentered and more dispersed social world. However, movements claiming to respect democratic ideals are in principle not free from the viewpoints of the population at large, although they often foster opinions that exceed the usual ones or are not in accordance with them. This story begins precisely at the crossroads between network-based political action and public opinion—more broadly, environmental attitudes and the urban planning constituting its substance.[1]

MENTAL HORIZON OF OPINIONS

We may be interested in public opinion as such, its primary level if you wish, but may as well focus on its second level, the notion of public opinion in someone's mind. Here the observer is a network activist for whom a rather general horizon of opinion serves as a mental frame and provides, as intended, the right to enter claims in the name of a larger community. In this case the anticipated shared understanding concerns the insensitive manner of construction, the need for protection of the environment, and the local inhabitants' desire to be heard when their immediate neighborhood is at stake. The notion of a shared understanding is in essence a product of the media, which has an important, though often complicated, relation to values, attitudes, and opinions. As actors in the world we have to trust in the information we get because opinion-formation and decision-making would otherwise become impossible. To a great extent the picture in our heads thus originates in newspapers and television programs, which tend to mold our shared ideoscape, although only in broad outline and not in detail.

Surveys and Gallup polls are a valuable source of the details of political attitudes. They show, not surprisingly, that community respect for politics and political institutions is very low (Suhonen, 1997). It is so low that below the current point it may be difficult to proceed on the assumption that the political system still functions and has at least a minimum degree of legitimacy. Citizens' notions of their political participation and competence indicate a strong sense of disempowerment and, although interest in politics has fluctuated over the years, negative attitudes towards politicians have remained steady. For a network activist, these general opinions of the political system are not difficult to agree upon, but there are other, more controversial or conventional opinions, not as easily accepted. Moreover, when local political initiatives are at stake, awareness of national public opinion is not enough. When we believe we share a common conception with our neighborhood, we are not dealing with an abstract and average opinion but with an opinion that emerges in a particular locality. These opinions and attitudes may resemble the aggregate ones, but may differ from them in significant respects as well. Local context raises several questions: first, where do we seek public opinion where ecological planning, local environment, and people's relationship to nature are concerned? Second, how should one deal with the issue of entitlement when network activists in general do not represent the majority? Conversely, how much should public opinion be counted on and how far should it compromise one's own views?

Basically, we might seek local opinion in the same way as public opinion at the national level, by means of Gallup polls and surveys, which are actually an often-used method as far as local habits of consumption are concerned. When it comes to citizen contentment with city planning or local policy, there is neither much information gathered nor many polls conducted. Different methods also tend to produce different and perhaps controversial results, as was the case in Finland during the European Union membership process, when several research projects were carried out to assess public opinion, with somewhat contradictory outcomes. Whereas polls were able to show gradually decreasing numbers of the undecided category, in qualitative interviews the main sentiments were hesitancy, dissatisfaction with media performance, and suspicion of authorities (Kivikuru, 1995).

For analytic purposes it is possible to clarify the distinction between public opinion and local opinion by associating the former with abstract, nation-bound citizenship and the latter with citizenship with its rights and duties springing from locality. Local opinion could in effect be understood as the general will of local inhabitants. In the Finnish language the concept of public opinion also connotes the generality of the opinion more than its degree of publicity and sometimes this is made explicit by appropriate compounding. Thus, "general opinion" is used to refer to the majority opinion of citizens, whereas "public opinion" means the opinions prevailing in the publicity (Suhonen, 1998).

TWO TRADITIONS OF POLITICAL PHILOSOPHY

When the interest is not so much in the outcome of opinion polling as in the way local opinion is generated, the notion of civil society with its two different conceptualizations of opinion formation becomes essential. The idea of public space as a forum of public opinion formation and political participation is common to both the liberal Anglo-American school of political thought and the Hegelian German tradition. They also share political goals such as freedom of speech, association, and the press. The discrepancy between them resides not so much in the issues of public space and participation as in the profoundly different and sometimes opposing way they are conceptualized (Pulkkinen, 1996: 11-22). The concept of civil society in the Hegelian and the liberal traditions is related to the concepts of state and freedom in a genuinely contradictory way. The liberal school of thought associates civil society with liberty and the state with necessity, whereas the Hegelian school associates civil society with necessity and the state with freedom. Pulkkinen finds the difference in vocabularies so significant that she calls it a difference in political ontology.

In the Anglo-American tradition liberty is understood as freedom to act in accordance with one's own will, whereas other people and a community are seen as a potential threat to free individual action. Freedom as autonomy in the German tradition, however, means the ability to govern oneself, and to determine the laws of one's own action. It implies the subjugation of natural desires and interests under the governance of moral judgment. For Hegel (1852/1973), the state is a community and a subject legislating and regulating itself, and is consequently characterized by morality and freedom. The state is also the basis of public political space, whereas Hegelian civil society is based on the English doctrine of economic liberalism. It represented a system of economic relations where everyone was an end in himself but at the same time fully dependent on others because of the deep reciprocity involved in attaining goals. The establishment of reciprocal bonds does not, however, involve an intention to create a community or take care of others. Thus interdependence is not freedom but necessity.

Hegel uses the concept of the state to designate the sphere of freedom, that is, the morally motivated political action producing another kind of social bond. The state covers the morality of a community as well as the shared cognitive beliefs of the people and exists immediately in custom, and mediated in individual self-consciousness, knowledge, and activity. Although there is no way to learn the community's will except through individual consciousness, individual will should also carry out the general will. This is what political action is about; not guided by particular individual interest but by the approximation of general will.

Because conscious political action is intentional and moral, aiming at the good of the community, the highest purpose of an individual is public life.

According to Pulkkinen, the Anglo-American tradition retained the Greek connotation of civil society as a sphere of politics and political association. Civil society is created by the mutual contracts of equals, and thus represents the state of justice. It seeks to preserve everyone's life, liberty, and property and secure each individual's interests. The distinction between civil society and the government or state is clear-cut in this tradition, and whereas civil society is associated with freedom and equality, the state is identified with authority. The state power should constantly be monitored and suspected by civil society, and rebelled against and overthrown if it becomes too influential. Liberties of free speech apply to civil society, where a general and informed opinion would be achieved by free argument.

In summary, Pulkkinen defines the classical liberal civil society as an area of free individual action, functioning apart from, and often in opposition to, governmental power. The classical Hegelian civil society, by contrast, is conceived of as an area of private life and selfish motives, whereas the state is seen as an area of morally oriented political action, defined by self-regulating communal agency. In the Hegelian framework civil society is clearly not the sphere of political activism, which is dedicated to the realm of the state. In the contemporary Western world, popular understanding anchors civil society in the liberal tradition and, whereas civil society is the area of political initiatives, the state is often seen as a threat to its freedom.

DIVERGING POLITICAL CULTURES

After the French revolution and Napoleonic wars German, French, and English political thinking diverged in a way that still characterizes political vocabulary in these areas. Pulkkinen (1998) remarks how learned nineteenth-century Finns mostly followed German models, whereas liberalism was fairly insignificant in the political thinking. In considering political space, characteristic of the former is the constitution of community as a single subject. Whereas a strong demand for universal democratic participation appears as a positive consequence of this understanding, the presupposition of a unified will and one mind may result in heated conflicts about correct interpretations and the exclusion of "heretics," as in the case of rigorous European nationalism. Although traditions of political philosophy are mixed in Finland as elsewhere in Europe, the prevalent Hegelian conceptualization of political space and subjectivity resulted in the divergence of Finnish political culture from other Nordic countries. At the national level it has strengthened ethnic and linguistic homogeneity and created a need to merge political controversies into a unified national will. Pulkkinen suggests that the idea of a single subject joining varied groups to seek the realization of a collective mind has had a very strong political influence.

The liberal tradition is characterized by its understanding of political space as consisting in the first place of individuals and groups realizing their own interests, whereas politics in the Hegelian tradition is not defined by competing interests but by competing interpretations of the actual will of a nation. According to Pulkkinen, in all postcolonial situations this thinking has had a positive role, bringing justice to the people and breaking up inequitable structures suppressing the majority. The Czech Republic, Hungary, and Finland, former parts of empires, were among the small European nations taking advantage of the German ethnic-political concepts of people and nation.

In these countries both traditions are still effective, and although the liberal view today is largely prevailing, both the intellectual atmosphere and administrative practices alike may recall the Hegelian way of understanding politics and the political sphere. This heritage can give rise to two sorts of notion concerning public opinion. Conceptually, public opinion could, in effect, be understood as an expression of the general will of a community, as a processual and enduring phenomenon deeply rooted in the political life of the people, and not as something temporary and changing. Historically, the Hegelian heritage makes it easier to understand the dominant role of the political and administrative elites in opinion-formation processes. Even if general participation in political discussions and decisions was desired, it was not particularly alarming if the effort was actually left to the civil servants and politicians, because their task was the general good of the community.

Consequently, the relation between state and civil society has taken a more cooperative than controversial course in a country with a powerful Hegelian tradition. State officials came to be regarded as representatives of public good, and both state institutions and free associations were considered as organs of civil action and participation. Freedom of speech and the press could, however, be strongly promoted by such a political system as the case of Finland shows (Liikanen, 1997). Currently, the central position of the state permits it to lead in the development of the information society alongside the private sector. Civil society, which for some decades and in some aspects was superseded by universal welfare arrangements, has achieved new appeal among public officials and is now being reconstructed as an electronic infrastructure to which citizens are attached through a variety of institutions.

Although the major aim of the information society is to improve national competitiveness, and the civil aspect has emerged only recently, there are also real, although casual, intentions to develop it as a citizens' project. What is the appropriate response to government initiatives to recreate civil society—surely a paradox in itself? In a country with a liberal tradition like the Netherlands reactions to the prominent role of the state would undoubtedly be negative, strongly against both aid and intrusion. In order to be free, networked civil society should, in this view, not be subsidized by government, but should cooperate with the commercial sector to establish a firm economic basis. Although this argument is a nice illustration of the liberal tradition, in a country like Finland it is not sensible simply to ignore the assistance of the state. Because of its historical role, its active participation has at least to be considered, not forgetting its disciplinary potential and the aim of surveillance. Controversial as it may be, the state can be an asset from the perspective of civil society, provided that it is conceived of as a system of heterogeneous relations and not as an entity. This vision allows room for joint efforts every now and then instead of permanent opposition to the state apparatus.

TÖNNIES AND LOCAL OPINION

The Hegelian tradition has its continuation in Tönnies' work on public opinion, in particular in the way he constituted the subject and the nature of public opinion. He had a contribution to make to the issue of local opinion because he defined public opinion essentially as a social or collective will, and the public as a social category generating public opinion. His theory of public opinion was significantly different from the American mainstream approach at that time and, like most European analysts, he emphasized the traditional, religious, and cultural circumstances in which public opinion is formed (Splichal, 1998: 101). Tönnies' basic categories of public opinion are (Tönnies, 1922: 129-130; Splichal, 1998: 107-108):

1. Published opinion (*öffentliche Meinung*), which represents an individual's publicly expressed opinion, that is, an opinion meant for recipients in general.
2. Public opinion (*eine öffentliche Meinung*), which appears when published opinion becomes the opinion of many, of a majority of an open or closed "circle," particularly if it clearly expresses support or opposition. It represents a transition from published opinion to the opinion of the public.
3. The opinion of the public (*die öffentliche Meinung*), which is the real, articulated opinion in a strict sense. Its formation and

expression are related to a (great) public, which appears in various aggregate states. A physical bond is not essentially typical of the public, although it is possible for a short time, but it is rather a spiritual connection at the level of ideas. What distinguishes the public from an incidentally connected, dispersed, or present crowd is its capability to articulate opinions clearly.

It seems reasonable to assume that published opinion does not adequately represent social will because it is an individual opinion disseminated publicly. In the first place, it is not a representation of a collective goal and rarely has the power to guide the action of a community and its leaders. As an individual expression it is addressed to a public, and thus is not a creation of the public. The distinction is important here, because a theory of democracy should pay particular attention to the formation of opinion. Published individual opinions are important as part of the formation process but rather as signs of ongoing change, and not as shared judgements. Thus, in a neighborhood we might examine ecological and aesthetic attitudes and ask about the generality of discontent with a monotonous environment and large-scale construction. These opinions may still be largely diffuse and their convergence not complete enough to fuse them into a collective manifestation, although public discussion, especially letters-to the editor, might offer another picture.

Tönnies' two other categories, public opinion and the opinion of the public, are of special importance here. He also makes the distinction as a difference between *die unartikulierte* and *die artikulierte öffentlichen Meinung* (Tönnies, 1922: 131). The first is a conglomerate of various controversial views, desires, and intentions, whereas the second is a unified force, an expression of common will whose subject is a political entity. It presupposes a great public that is capable of making judgments and overcoming restricted and particular interests. The character of the public determines that the opinion of the public belongs to a specific form of social will and social structure, the reflexive and not the organic will, and to a society rather than to a community. Tönnies conceives the opinion of the public as a common way of thought, the corporate spirit of any group or association, insofar as its opinion formation is built upon reasoning and knowledge, rather than on unproven impressions, beliefs, or authority (Splichal, 1998: 108). The opinion of the public is a consensus, the unanimous opinion of citizens reached by their own, independent reasoning.

When it comes to local opinion there is an apparent need to understand it rather as the collective will of a community than as a conglomerate of different views, but is it justified to extend the concept to apply to locality? If only a large public can act as subject in the formation of an opinion of the public because of political nonpartisanship, absence of special interests, and support of the general good (Splichal, 1998: 112), what happens with more restricted publics? Tönnies (1922: 103) claims that it was characteristic of narrow publics to limit access, and he only speaks of publics as holders of public opinion. However, the opinion of the public is for him a concept of pure theory and an ideal (normative) type, whereas public opinion and publicly expressed opinion belong to an experiential (applied and empirical) world. Ideal types serve us with interpretation schemes and guide the formation of hypotheses, but they are also a frame of reference to the empirical world. As a pure abstraction the opinion of the public is open to discussion based on new knowledge and potential cultural change, and could thus be redefined. We can now assume that the formation of social will below the national level has become more important for several reasons, and that it justifies the conceptual reconstruction.

Tönnies considered the opinion of the public in the first place as a normative concept and an abstraction, but he also saw it as an ideal that can be largely enacted in a "human community" of the future (Splichal, 1998: 122). Moreover, it was not merely an ideal, because it existed in every society, at least in its ephemeral state. Tönnies understood it as a general way of thought, the corporate spirit of any group or association, insofar as its opinion formation was built upon reasoning and knowledge. In this sense, it was a "rationalized" or "reflected" form of religion. Tönnies emphasized the close relationship between religion and public opinion, which he regarded as sources of strength that could unite society internally. Hardt (1979: 141) points out that both of them, although binding on members of society, are often expressed as moral indignation and intolerance of those with different ideas. Finally, the concept of the opinion of the public can be characterized as dialectical (Splichal, 1998: 120), not only because it appears in different aggregate states but also because it can develop from public opinion. Thus, in favorable circumstances collective opinion can develop from partial opinion, but with time even the most solid opinion fades away, mostly because of insufficient action.

THE FEASIBILITY OF TÖNNIES' NOTIONS

Tönnies' conceptualization will probably meet with rejection in today's academic world because its tones differ from ours. Causes for objection spring from its emphasis on unity and rationality, which both seem to belong to the modern assets of thought, not to the period of late modernity. These dimensions point to a common ground of universalism that has now largely been replaced by the recognition and justification of difference and pluralism. The claim for unity of opinion is hard to meet because it is part of the Enlightenment spirit and burdened with the overtones of Western supremacy and patriarchy. However, it does not wipe away the significance of the aspiration to consensus reached by the majority of a community. In the democratic tradition the status of minority opinion has been much debated, often inconclusively, and it obviously will remain so in the future. It is an urgent issue that keeps the democracy debate alive. Moreover, the dichotomies of reason and emotion, universal and particular have existed for the last two thousand years and been the subjects of heated philosophical discussion. In the course of Western civilization either reason or emotion has gained by turns at the expense of the other. Consequently, when we emphasize one aspect we should remember that they coexist and that behind the one there is the other waiting to be rediscovered. Along with rationality, Tönnies himself underscored the significance of emotions and the understanding of human life as a wholeness. Splichal (1998: 123) points out that Tönnies' holistic theory also emphasized the unity of will and emotions that are expressed in reason, and the foundation of reason in human life processes. Thus, the rationality of opinion always implies the volitional and affective dimensions of opinion formation.

If local opinion is understood as an expression of social will, the problem of particular interests becomes urgent. We face the problem of the size of the community—how large should a community be to be able to advance the common good as against particular interests? Are local communities doomed, by definition, to be too small and bound to restricted interests? In what conditions could local communities create the opinion of the public? Provided that a variety of spaces and institutions exist for public conversation, something like local opinion could possibly emerge. In addition, we might offer some suggestions to help to overcome the problem of narrow interests and segregation of communities. First, localities are not independent but interrelated in many ways, and foster relations of exchange and cooperation, if only out of pure necessity. Bookchin (1987: 258) states that the concept of confederation is as old as the fact of municipal life itself. Initially more defensive than creative in character, it has, he asserts, provided us with extraordinary examples of freedom within localities and in the relationships between localities. Interdependence between communities is no less important than interdependence between individuals. In effect, the particular interests of a community are today squared with universal ecological concerns that meet them all, although with different consequences.

Second, the formation of local opinion is backed by democratic procedures and a representative system of higher-level organizations such as municipal, regional, national, and international. The autonomy of localities may be restricted by other forms of complex social will that

Tönnies called convention and legislation. The opinion of the public "competes" in *Gesellschaft* with these other forms of the complex social will. The subject of convention is society regulating general and economic life with recommendations and directives and the subject of legislation is the state giving orders (through mandate and indirection) in political life (Splichal, 1998: 123). It is just universal rights and formal democracy that give protection against particular interests. According to Heller (1988: 130) the persistence of modern democracies is due precisely to their formal character: civil liberties, pluralism, the system of contract, and the principle of representation.

Heller (1988: 144) is also convinced that in selection of values all human beings are equally competent and in deciding the problem of "what has to be done" no elite can play a crucial role. She further points out that although everyone is able to discuss and reflect on social goals and programs, citizens accustomed to political passivity are unlikely to be easily mobilized in defense of their democratic liberties. Tönnies, for his part, claimed that only an educated elite actively participate in forming and expressing the opinion of the public. In general, participation in opinion formation is determined by an individual's knowledge, reasoning, education, and political interests. Tönnies (1922: 91) stated that subjects and holders of public opinion are mostly the bourgeoisie and individuals of rank, men more than women, older people more than younger ones, and those who are personally affected by interests and certain problems more than those who are not. The opinion of the public could thus principally be defined as an opinion held by the educated, in contrast to masses of people. However, the subject of opinion is here considered rather as a historical category than as an ideal conceptualization, and Tönnies (1922: 229) himself expected ordinary people to become cocreators of the opinion of the public with the spread of general, particularly political education to lower social strata. In this way opinion becomes general and the potential reality of a unified opinion or consensus actually diminishes at the same time.

Tönnies' basic concept of the opinion of the public can with good reason be extended to imply the local context, although it was originally applied only nationally. As Tönnies himself stated that the phenomena described by the means of applied and pure concepts can be clearly distinguished from each other only in theory and that in the real world they exist intertwined, there is no reason why we could not apply the concept of the opinion of the public in a particular locality. In his day, the meaning of "local" also differed radically from what it is now when new communication technologies have occupied even the most remote corners of the world. The local is not necessarily characterized by being particularistic and self-contained, and based on customs and tradition in contrast to urban agglomerations.[2] We can also argue that the qualities of the public meet the prerequisites of articulated opinion. Societal development, in particular universal education and the impact of the media, has extended the scope of a knowledgeable and critical public, and strengthened its civic capabilities. Localities naturally differ in this sense and although some suffer from lack of active and critical citizens, some have them in abundance. Consequently, the historical heritage of Hegel's philosophy and Tönnies' ideas on public opinion seem to offer components of a valuable conceptual model, but how does the real fit into the ideal and what would their intercourse produce?

LOCALITY AND PUBLIC SPACE

Public space and public opinion are compatible in the sense that a homogenized and anonymous physical environment is not likely to produce a multiplicity of public discussion. Where occasions for grassroots political participation are largely missing and the local environment with all its physical, social, and cultural components is beyond the control of citizens, it will presumably result in indifference. Why care for something beyond your control? If the crude methods of modernization render parts of our intimate environment unpleasant or ugly, we soon learn to look the other way. However, the homogenizing landscape not only leads to indifference but also to demolition. If citizens cannot have any effect on everyday matters and on local surroundings, they are intentionally silenced but, if the disempowerment is intensified, for example, by unemployment and a deep sense of uselessness, the opinion may eventually make itself felt. Demolition regularly appear where the environment has already become rough and alienating. Such opinions are socially segregated, because there are groups that quite predictably become representatives of specific behavior.

In suburban or semi-urban neighborhoods social ties are created around families, because few other bonds exist and there seems to be little room for political life. In other words, ordinary social bonds are too weak to produce effective sociopolitical forms. A part of the current crisis in politics can be defined as a matter of community development and city planning, and be examined through the concept of *polis*. Bookchin (1987: 36-38), wishing to develop a definition of a community as a *polis*, outlines the essential aspects of the Athenian understanding of "good life." To go beyond mere survival, institutions are needed to constitute the means of human self-fulfillment. A body of ethics must exist that gives the required institutions substance as well as form, and a wealth of social activities must be cultivated in the civic center of the *polis*, and in the theater as well as the popular assembly and courts to nourish inter-actions and discourse. A mode of character development and education must be at work to enrich the interactions among men and women, thereby fostering the growth of ethical and intellectual insight. Underlying these various "means" is Aristotle's emphasis on human sol-idarity, which includes friendship but which is a word more far-reach-ing in its connotation of civic commonality. Aristotle (1932) states in the *Politics* that the *polis* is an end in itself, the realization of man's need for consociation apart from its material benefits.

As is known, Athenian politics was parochial by modern defini-tions of the term and limited to a minority of the population. Besides its inherent inequality, Aristotle's political theory is most severely criticized for its emphasis on the scale of the city-state. It is argued that the model is not applicable in our modern world where the importance of the mar-ket and the distinction between the state and the life-world constitutes a wholly different kind of social structure. Sihvola (1998) suggests that Aristotle's notion provokes interesting remarks precisely on the prob-lematic relationship between the power of the state and the freedoms of citizens. Accordingly, the state has to take care of the preconditions of the good life, whereas it is up to the citizens themselves to seize upon these opportunities. It is important that the subject of power be an autonomous citizen, whereas the division between the functions of state, civil society, and the market is a matter of appropriateness. The classical model, although being far from perfect, can help our thinking, because aspects of Tönnes' ideas are embodied in the institutions of *polis*.

In this movement between the ideal and real, the role of the state remains essential, because as an apparatus the modern state tends to pursue its own systemic interest along with its benevolent functions. Our societies are largely controlled by the state, and the operations of surveillance are being extended to cover the practices and areas of pub-lic life and constantly shrinking private terrain. Fiske (1998) sees alarm-ing tendencies in late modernity that are totalitarian by nature and oper-ate underneath the structures of democracy. Surveillance, as an agency of totalitarianism, is not readily opposed by democratic politics, working as it does through techniques rather than policy. Because a technique also has efficient and beneficent uses, it is much harder to combat than a political initiative. Fiske points out that it has only recently become so urgent to consider whether the freedoms of association and movement may be violated when both can be documented at will. Digitalized regis-ters combined with digitalized location systems make the monitoring of individuals and their political activities strikingly easy and seductive.

Present civil society may also become thoroughly controlled by its fellow members, as in the United States with neighborhoods increasingly guarding themselves by technological means against outside intrusions. The same technique—cheap video cameras—also allows neighbors to watch each other and to impose normality upon the community by exposing behavior that is inappropriate according to dominant codes. Technology, in this sense, is by no means socially neutral. Fiske notes that although surveillance is being extended throughout society, there is a differentiation in this penetration. Being white has the social power of defining itself as the norm, and surveillance externalizes this sense-making system into the spatial system of cities. This mechanism lends a material dimension to abstract or theoretical concepts of "social position" and "social space." Our imagination can push members of specific groups out of civil society by ignoring their existence or presence. Fiske suggests that the power to produce the normal is so important because normality discourages the cultural expression of difference. Plurality of opinion must be fostered just to oppose the normalizing effect of dominating cultural codes. Although Habermas' theory of the public sphere has been criticized for its implicit assumption of the public good as a singular, consensual concept, we should rethink the concept rather than withdraw it. Fiske sees an urgent need for a domain where opposition to totalitarian tendencies can be publicly organized, and Habermas himself has also lately reshaped his concept of public sphere into a more pluralized form (Habermas, 1992: 427).

THE CONTEMPORARY BODY POLITIC

If politics is taken to be a form of popular activity in administering public life, the constitution of the body politic becomes vital. Not only should the political elites be responsive and active but, as expressed in the Hegelian tradition, every individual is assumed to be a politically active part of the state. It also implies more than merely the right to express one's opinions. Bookchin (1987: 41) makes a clear distinction between democratic and republican procedures and argues that the ancient Roman republic had no democratic component in the Hellenic sense of the term. A face-to-face relationship between active citizens for the purpose of arriving at a consensus is alien to republican systems of government. A democracy is participatory; a republic representative. The first involves the exercise of power directly by the people; the second, its delegation to selected surrogates, who then reconstitute the political realm that initially existed at the base of the community into a distinctly separate and usually professional power at its summit. With the rise of the nation-state, larger institutions far beyond the reach of the ordinary citizen began to supplant the civic institutions within which some kind of face-to-face democracy was feasible. Bookchin (1987: 51-52) finds it hard to overstate the amount of intellectual mischief the extension of the word politics, basically rooted in the civic life of the *polis*, produced when it was permitted to encompass statecraft.

Classical politics always implied the existence of a body politic, and the notion was not a euphemism for an "electorate" or a "constituency." In ancient Athens it appeared as a real, physical, and clearly observable entity that could be seen daily in public squares where heated discussions over political issues intermingled with chitchat about personal and business problems. Modern civil society is sometimes understood as such a body politic, as a self-contained entity apart from state, government, and parties. Cohen and Arato (1992) include social movements, actually giving civil society a kind of avant-garde role in political change. However, in present-day democracies, in which the principle of representation is firmly rooted in political culture, citizens are not actually conceived as true equals to politicians and public officials. The idea of collective will and functioning local democracy is nevertheless hardly comprehensible without the notion of the classical body politic, which alone could give local political action its content. These days a strong demand also arises for the revival and reorganization of local democracy: first, weakening national structures give way to multiple local political organs, and second, the growing autonomy of citizens, although often forced, implies new rights and responsibilities. Thus, there are expectations of a more mature subject, capable of arguing and willing to participate in public life, and of new potential for this subject to take power. The utilization of these political options depends greatly on influential countertendencies, and the emergence of new political forms is often difficult to see because of the complex social transactions of the present world.

Tönnies' dichotomy between *Gemeinschaft* and *Gesellschaft* and the new forms of communalization might provide us here with some insights into future development. Although community and society are ideal types, various forms of communal and societal organizations may appear in different degrees simultaneously within the same structure (Splichal, 1998: 104). A case in point is neighborhoods where different types of organizational forms and social bonds coexist. Lash (1994: 211) describes social relations as a hierarchy in which they become more abstract in the transition from affinity groups to institutions. With each step upwards from posttraditional *Gemeinschaft* to late modern *Gesellschaft* the emotive and affective investment involved in trust thins out, as ethics becomes less and less linked to affect and increasingly linked to reason. Thus, neighborhood could be understood as a mixture of emotional and formal rational relationships that are involved in varied situations.

Lash (1994: 113-115) suggests that new forms of *Gemeinschaft* are emerging with the intensification of individualization. He maintains that the straightforward and dichotomous juxtaposition of tradition and modernity suggested by Tönnies and other classical sociologists is not at issue with the emergence of reflexive modernity. What is at issue is a three-stage conception of social change from tradition to (simple) modernity to reflexive modernity. Traditional society corresponds to *Gemeinschaft*, simple modernity to *Gesellschaft*, and its successor to a *Gesellschaft* that has to become fully reflexive. The motor of social change in this process is individualization. In Tönnies' view, the fact that the features of community are slowly disappearing while attributes of society prevail does not mean that historical development is inclined towards *Gesellschaft* (Splichal, 1998: 104). Instead, Tönnies anticipates the next stage in a "people's" or "new" community, which represents a synthesizing third stage of historical development. Consequently, Tönnies regards *Gemeinschaft* not just as a specific historical structure from which *Gesellschaft* develops, but also as a model signifying the future transformation of the latter.

Using the concept of posttraditional communalization Lash (1994: 209) points to new lifestyle groups that are a nexus of intensive semantic interchange. This *Gemeinschaft* orientation is individualized, already set free from traditional and early modern institutions, and the sensibility of these groups comprises not just knowledge but affect. Here Lash in effect comes close to Tönnies, whose theory represents a unification of will and emotion. The anticipated turn towards new communities makes it possible, in principle, to redefine the body politic, while at the same time new nonpolitical forms of politics and the changing basis of political activities may render the task difficult.

BEYOND THE POLITICAL: THE SOCIAL

Search for the expressions of collective will in today's society may seem fairly unproductive, because as a phenomenon it rather belongs to a premodern not a modern world and, because of pluralized individual interests, there is evidently no longer a solid ground for its growth. However, the very human need for acceptance and respect leads to creation of social ties and community formations in any society. If respect is not granted by our community we tend to create a subcommunity appreciating the skills we have at our disposal. The idea of democracy is necessary in order to avoid social segregation and the formation of deeply controversial communities, but democracy has to be accomplished through politics, presently a largely ignored area of popular activity. The procedures and issues of the political system should obviously be further discussed and questioned, and politics brought closer to everyday life. Interest in local politics could presumably be fairly easily aroused, but it would also soon make clear the lack of proper political fora necessary for its accomplishment. The way of proceeding is, in this context, to go beyond the political sphere into the social sphere, or sociality in Bauman's (1992) sense. Tönnies, in his critique and theory of public opinion, also prefers the complex processes in culture and society over their institutionalized forms in politics and the state (Splichal, 1998: 123).

The social sphere is here characterized as a domain opening up behind the political public terrain and appearing as a continuation from interior personal thought through interpersonal conversation to the exchange of ideas within a group. It is obvious that all societies, including previous ones, have had their specific ways of organizing themselves, notwithstanding the political sphere. Bookchin (1987: 39) discusses the distinction between the social and the political spheres in Aristotelean terms, which he finds fundamentally processual. The difference between the two is explained by the growth and development of the social into the political, not by their polarization and mere succession. Political life has developed out of social life to acquire a distinct identity of its own which itself presupposes social forms as its underpinnings.

Lii (1998) employs the term "social sphere" to deliberately distinguish this mode from the public sphere. It is through this societal self-organization that private individuals beyond families and close friends can be brought together, and public life is thereby made possible. For Lii, the social sphere means a cultural landscape on which various forms of performance and public drama are staged, and through which social bonds are created and collective experiences articulated. As with the public sphere, the social sphere represents a common space in which members of society are able to meet through a variety of media, to engage in public performance and thus to form collective sentiment. Although similar in form, Lii makes a fundamental distinction between the two. Whereas the public sphere emphasizes reason and language, the social sphere stresses sense, body, and performance. The public sphere strives to rationally negate any particularity and partiality associated with its members, and thus to rise above particular private views in order to achieve a supra-individual mind. The social sphere, in contrast, creates a shared living context in which the sensual perceptions of each individual member are articulated, and from which a social fabric among its members develops.

The postmodern social sphere centers around consumption and, Lii thinks, involves a different organizational principle than the previous ones. It is fragmented in the sense that consumers are organized around multiple product-related images. The social fabric in a society organized through "images" is not only abstract and unreal—magical in Lii's terms—but also transitory and simulatory. In these circumstances, individuals are not merely separated and divided from each other, but also share a common being, an image. The postmodern social sphere is thus simultaneously a process of disintegration and reintegration. Lii sees it most of all as a process of individuation: it is precisely when people are isolated from each other and the chance of external interaction is small that they start turning inward to their own selves. Leisurely recreation has greatly contributed to the process as it gradually became the artifact of electronic media and thus enabled people to be entertained in their private homes instead of in public places. Shopping malls and department stores have replaced coffee houses and theaters as the major places for public gatherings, making recreational consumption the prototypical social sphere of our time. Individuation is deeply interlocked with consumption, but consumption in the sense of imaginative pleasure-seeking rather than materialistic activity.

In all, the social sphere produces a form of societal self-organization and creates a cultural landscape in which private individuals can be brought together into a social collectivity. Different societies create different forms of social sphere and thus different forms of public life. Lii argues that public life can be maintained without necessarily resorting to external political forms, because the social fabric is established through various forms of performance in the social sphere. The relation between the current social sphere and public life, which is of special importance here, is left relatively open in Lii's discussion. The forms of sociality no doubt have effects, although often indirect, upon public discussions of collective goals and the common good, but what if an affluent social sphere exists without living connections with political institutions? Would it not cause further professionalization and centralization of politics?

A return to the Habermasean concept of the public sphere seems productive here, even at the risk of its presumed obsolescence. In the present world of media and mediation, it is the public sphere, of all the institutions of civil society, that is clearly growing in importance. A persistent doubt, however, lives in the minds of even the most determined proponents of democracy regarding whether ordinary people are competent to take the responsibilities involved at all. McGuigan (1998: 98) actually turns the presumption of a critical-rational subject around by arguing that the interaction between cognition and emotion be considered. He notes that if the opinions of the majority are to be included there is a need for a softer conception of the public sphere. The ideal subject has been that of a vigilant citizen who must be properly informed about what is going on and be extremely active politically. Because the public neither conducts rational communication nor is politically enlightened, he finds it a fictious construction. McGuigan (1998: 104) suggests that an exclusively cognitive conception of the public sphere is unsatisfactory, because distrust of the official system and formal democracy can also be expressed through affective communication and popular culture. Contributing to the decreasing interest in established politics may also be the trend toward social movements that function as media rather than as political influences (on social movements, see Melucci, 1996; on culturalization, see Lash, 1994). As we also know, there is no way to force people to participate in politics, however interesting the opportunities which emerge may be.

In these rather conflicting circumstances, dichotomies such as political and social could be replaced by the interplay between political action and sociocultural interaction. The social sphere is taken as the basis of public life and the source of the ethical relation essential for the maintenance of public life. Mediated and nonrealistic images account for a large part of the current social sphere which, thereby, is both divided and shared by nature. Although the collectivities created by this form of social interaction are typically cultural, interest in joined political efforts may rather be channeled through them than institutionalized politics. Both education and consumption, by producing new skills and civic competencies, can increase citizen participation. Environmental concerns are among the issues that may create an ethic of care and solidarity, but other social issues such as poverty and inequality may turn these sentiments towards hatred and distrust. In Bauman's view (1995, 1998), what is missing is not ethics itself, because it grows from sociality and thus precedes society, but institutions that could actualize it. Consequently, the problem of translating morality into justice is political in essence, concerned with procedures and practices.

TRACING LOCAL OPINION

Modernization is characterized by large-scale centralized hierarchical systems that have almost exhausted local initiative and responsibility, and although the trend has not been fully reversed, today some of these structures are disintegrating. Consequently, urban planning and living could become more localized and based on small-scale systems, having as their point of departure the needs of citizens and human sociality. Locality is important because everybody lives somewhere and, accordingly, develops a relationship with his or her immediate neighborhood, although much of this relation may remain unconscious or unconsidered. It is evident, however, that political institutions that could help to change moral impulses into societal influences or fuse local opinions into collective will are largely absent. If substantial opinions in a society remain silent or unheeded, they are expressed asocially, whether they be visible, such as damaging the environment, or appear as extreme bodily and mental reactions. To lead a good life, an individual should have the opportunity to exert an influence not only on his or her own life, but on the life of the community as well. In this sense, the Athenian ideal provides us with a sophisticated model because it was not confined to the conduct of discussion and decision-making only, but also comprehended the basic conditions of pursuing civil virtues.

Public opinion formation in Athens, as we can recall it, probably had not much in common with its aggregate form and the presumptions of a self-contained individual and a weak community, the latter components belonging essentially to modern political thought. Opinion produced by polling is a cross-section of notions on some current topic, a time-bound and transitory phenomenon that is nevertheless an influential tool in the games of power and politics. Public opinion can be used to create and strengthen consent but, being by no means neutral, can also express prevailing discontent. From the citizen's standpoint it can serve as a way of finding new undercurrents of social change, and as a means of producing new symbolic battlefields. However, the notion of an abstract public opinion will not suffice when issues of local environment and politics are considered because it does not meet the whole process of opinion formation. Its local counterpart, if understood more as the general will of a community, is a process instead of a momentary phenomenon and does not as easily surrender to being manipulated by the powers that be. This opinion is presumably not ephemeral because it grows from a soil of everyday experience and a way of living.

Tönnies' ideas, along with many contemporary commentaries, indicate that the sources of opinion formation can be found in sociality and in the sphere of culture. In principle, local opinion emerges through interaction and communication, that is, is highly social by nature, and should therefore be defined by shared experiences rather than by solitary considerations. Sociality is the essence of human life, which we do not need to invent or reinvent because it has existed and it will exist, even when all political institutions have collapsed. Instead of starting with the formal political organs we can begin to observe local life as such and try to discern action that is collective by nature, that is, transcends the individual sphere and emerges as something public. The local context offers occasions such as lectures, concerts, bazaars, excursions, voluntary work days, sport and gymnastic exercises, for tracing public opinion. The normative aspect emerges when, in order to change prevailing political practices, we start developing new forms of opinion formation and political activity. Although normative attitudes are not on a high tide in contemporary social studies, suggesting the development of locally active communities should not be avoided.

ENDNOTES

1. The web-site concerned, alt.espoo.kaapeli.fi, is part of a Finnish case study on local politics and ecological urban planning employing the Net as a tactical medium. Because this project aims at changes in the agendas and procedures of local democracy, how the role of public opinion is conceived and how the issue of representation is dealt with are significant factors. Although these web pages originally represented the particular interests of a few—the researcher and her husband—and were confined to a specific geographical area, they were meant to advance the public good more generally (Sassi, 1997, 1998).

2. I am grateful to Slavko Splichal for pointing out the very obvious fact that, with computer-mediated communication, for example, the Internet, the local is characterized by isolation and particularity to a much lesser degree than it used to be in Tönnies' days.

REFERENCES

Aristotle. 1932. *Politics*. London: Classical Library. Orig. Politica.

Bauman, Zygmunt. 1995. Morality Without Ethics. In *Life in Fragments: Essays in Postmodern Morality*. Cambridge: Blackwell.

Bauman, Zygmunt. 1992. A Sociological Theory of Postmodernity. In *Intimations of Postmodernity*. London: Routledge.

Bauman, Zygmunt. 1998. Postmodernisuuden ja etiikan epäpyhä allianssi. Zygmunt Baumanin haastattelu, haastattelijana Tuomas Nevanlinna [The unholy alliance of postmodernism and ethics. An interview with Zygmunt Bauman by Tuomas Nevanlinna]. *Aikuiskasvatus* 1(98), 4-11.

Bookchin, Murray. 1987. *The Rise of Urbanization and the Decline of Citizenship*. San Francisco: Sierra Club Books.

Cohen, Jean L. and Andrew Arato. 1992. *Civil Society and Political Theory*. Cambridge: MIT Press.

Fiske, John. 1998. Surveilling the City. Whiteness, the Black Man and Democratic Totalitarianism. *Theory, Culture & Society* 15(2), 67-88.

Habermas, Jurgen. 1992. Further Reflections on the Public Sphere. In C. Calhoun (ed.), *Habermas and the Public Sphere*. Cambridge, MA: Massachusetts Institute of Technology.

Hardt, Hanno. 1979. *Social Theories of the Press. Early German and American Perspectives*. London: Sage.

Hegel, G.W.F. 1852/1973. *Hegel's Philosophy of Right*. Translated with notes by T.M. Knox. Oxford: Oxford University Press.

Heller, Agnes. 1988. On Formal Democracy. In John Keane (ed.), *Society and the State*, 245-260. London: Verso.

Kivikuru, Ullamaija. 1995. From Public Opinion to Popular Sphere? Theme Interviews Tell a Different Story of Finnish EU Opinion. Paper presented at the IAMCR Conference, Portoroz, Slovenia.

Lash, Scott. 1994. Reflexivity and its Doubles: Structure, Aesthetics, Community. In Ulrich Beck, Anthony Giddens, and Scott Lash, *Reflexive Modernization*, 110-173. Cambridge: Polity Press.

Lii, Ding-Tzann. 1998. Social Spheres and Public Life. A Structural Origin. *Theory, Culture & Society* 15(2), 115-135.

Liikanen, Ilkka. 1997. Kansalaisen synty. Fennomania ja modernin politiikan synty [The Emergence of the Citizen. National Identity and Modern Politics]. *Tiede ja Edistys* 22(4), 343-351.

McGuigan, Jim. 1998. What Price the Public Sphere? In Daya Kishan Thussu (ed.), *Electronic Empires. Global Media and Local Resistance*, 91-107. London: Arnold.

Melucci, Alberto. 1996. *Challenging Codes. Collective Action in the Information Age*. Cambridge: Cambridge University Press.

Pulkkinen, Tuija. 1996. *The Postmodern and Political Agency*. University of Helsinki, Department of Philosophy. Helsinki: Hakapaino.

Pulkkinen, Tuija. 1998. *Kielen ja mielen ykseys—1800-luvun suomalaisen nationalismin erityispiirteistä ja perinnöstä poliittisessa ajattelussa*. [The Unity of Language and Mind—The Characteristics of Finnish Nationalism of the 19th Century and its Heritage in Political Thinking]. (To be published in English in *A Strange Northern Country* by SITRA.)

Sassi, Sinikka. 1997. The Internet and the Art of Conducting Politics: Considerations of Theory and Action. *Communication* 22(4), 451-469.

Sassi, Sinikka. 1998. Public Opinion as a Frame of Internet Activism. IAMCR conference, Glasgow, July 1998.

Sihvola, Juh. 1998. Yhteiskunta ja hyvä elämä. Aristoteles ja nykyajan etiikan haasteet [Society and Good Life. Aristotle and the Challenges of Modern Ethics]. *Aikuiskasvatus* 1, 12-21.

Splichal, Slavko. 1998. Public Opinion as a Form of Social Will: Ferdinand Tönnies' *Critique of Public Opinion. Communications* 23(1), 99-126.

Suhonen, Pertti. 1997. *Yleinen mielipide 1997* [Public Opinion 1997]. Helsinki: Tammi.

Suhonen, Pertti. 1998. Kansan tahto—siis minkä. Kamppailu yleisen mielipiteen käsitteestä [The Will of the People—Whose Will? The Contested Concept of Public Opinion]. In Ullamaija Kivikuru and Risto Kunelius (eds.), *Viestinnän Jäljillä* [Tracing Human Communication]. Helsinki: WSOY.

Tönnies, Ferdinand. 1922. *Kritik der Öffentlichen Meinung*. Berlin: Springer Verlag.

5

Democratic Theory and the Intellectual Division of Labor in Mass Electorates

Tom Hoffman

Survey research conducted in the United States since the 1950s has consistently indicated a profound lack of political sophistication (or political rationality[1]) among most members of the electorate. This evidence—although often simply ignored by theorists of democracy—seriously calls into question the ability of the majority to function in accord with the demands of democratic theory. But the evidence from the United States does more than merely call into question the realization of democratic ideals in America. It reinforces long-standing fears about the viability of "authentic" democratic governance in the context of any modern mass society. The widespread political ignorance and inattention found among the American electorate seems to confirm old worries about the political side effects of the thoroughgoing structural differentiation that distinguishes modern society. Mass democracies—organized on a huge scale and marked by significant information differentials corresponding to the individual's position within the system of divided labor—appear to suffer from deeply entrenched motivational and informational inequalities.

Still, the evidence that appears to confirm these fears about mass democracy has not gone unchallenged. Political theorists and public opinion researchers in the United States have pursued several distinct lines of response to the findings of political ignorance and inattention. Most recently—and perhaps ironically—some attempts to vindicate the democratic capabilities of mass publics have relied upon the very feature of modern mass society that seems to be the source of the inequalities of information and motivation in the first place: the division of labor.

By viewing political rationality as an aggregate or collective phenomena and, alternatively, by rejecting the view that political reasoning be fully deliberative or articulate, recent researchers[2] have accepted the evidence of widespread ignorance of basic political information while at the same time proclaiming the American public to be politically rational after all. These approaches not only reconceptualize the standards against which the electorate is assessed by redefining political rationality, they also ultimately rely upon an intellectual or ideological division of labor for their successful operation. It is, however, by no means clear that forms of political reasoning that have been reconceptualized in this way still satisfy the original demands of normative democratic theory. Proclaiming mass publics to be rational or reasoning after a manner is not the same as demonstrating that such publics display the kind of rationality demanded by the traditions of democratic theory. In this essay I point out some of the normative inadequacies of these approaches to vindicating mass democracy.

Contrary to the assumptions of some analysts,[3] there is no single "classical" or traditional democratic theory. Benjamin Page and Robert Shapiro are surely correct when they note that "Democratic theories of various sorts ask various things of the citizenry" (1993: 35). Despite this diversity, it can be argued that important and highly influential strands of democratic thought conflict with the new notions of political rationality. Here I will focus on a small number of democratic theories prominent in modern liberal social thought. (Because of the vast number of sometimes mutually contradictory theories of democracy, I leave aside those that are most distant from attempts to justify contemporary, liberal democracies.)[4] As it is, an exclusive focus on liberal democratic theory still leaves much to examine. After briefly sketching out several normative strands in liberal democratic thought, I will indicate how the reconceptualized notions of political reason pose problems for each. For instance, I suggest that from the perspective of one strand of theory, demands for electorate sophistication are motivated primarily by concerns for protecting the interests of each individual (and avoiding manipulation and social domination by elites), whereas from the view of another strand of democratic theory rationality is demanded because of a concern for individual development and expression. Finally, I turn to focus a bit more squarely on Kantian democratic thought, which represents—since the publication of John Rawls' *A Theory of Justice* in 1971—the dominant approach within Anglo-American political philosophy. The Kantian approach to democratic theory presents an especially interesting and problematic case because its very foundation resides in notions of rationality and of rights-holders distinguished by their exercise of individual reason. Thus, any change in the way we are to think about reasoning is likely to strike at the heart of theories in this tradition.

"Rationality" has been revised along two ultimately related lines. First, such public opinion researchers as Page and Shapiro (1992, 1993) and Erickson et al. (n.d.) have looked at political reason as an aggregate or collective characteristic. In this view, the electorate as a whole can be adjudged rational, regardless of the rational status of any of its individual members. Second, a large political psychology literature has emphasized the use by individual voters of cognitive shortcuts or rules of thumb in dealing with a political environment about which they are largely uninformed. Samuel Popkin's *The Reasoning Voter* is nicely representative of this literature because the book synthesizes much of the psychology research and overtly seeks to use it to vindicate the rational status of the electorate. This second revision essentially views political reason as an inarticulate or tacit phenomenon. People who use shortcuts in reasoning about the political world typically are unable to explain their reasons for acting one way or another. The two lines of revision are related, in that both imply an intellectual division of labor. In the first view, ignorant individuals cancel each other out in the aggregate, freeing public opinion for leadership by relatively well-informed elites. In the second view, many of the cognitive shortcuts used by individual voters rely upon signals from opinion leaders or (especially in Zaller, 1992) cues from party leaders among other information providers. The question is whether aggregate and forms of shortcut rationality meet the demands of democratic theory.

THE ANXIETIES OF MASS POLITICAL SOCIETY

Empirical studies that began in middle of the century used relatively new survey techniques and statistical methods to show that the typical American voter is largely uninformed about politics, inconsistent in his or her political values, unreflective about politics, and only weakly motivated to participate. This research, carried out at Columbia University (e.g., Berelson et al., 1954) and then at the University of Michigan (e.g.,

Campbell et al., 1960) seemed to confirm long-standing worries about the feasibility of authentic democratic governance in the context of modern, mass society. Although the normative ideals of democratic governance and democratic citizenship had achieved by mid-century a kind of worldwide hegemony,[5] the new evidence strengthened the hand of those who warned that these ideals were unrealistic at best, and it supported the view that democratic theory itself be revised to accommodate political reality.

Worries about the potential instability and irrationality of democratic publics, of course, were common long before "democracy" acquired a positive connotation. Although it is popular to characterize the American founders, for example, as motivated by self-interested elitism (e.g., Beard, 1913), it is probably fairer to say that their well-known suspicion of democracy was based at least as much on intuitions about large electorates that would only be empirically confirmed in our own century. Suspicions about the widespread tendency to view politics through unreflective and inflexible group-based identifications (termed "factions"before the advent of sociology) and a concern about the instability of public opinion and its susceptibility to manipulation animate many of the *Federalist Papers*. Like many Enlightenment-era thinkers, the American founders took an experimental approach to politics, but one experiment they stepped back from conducting—at least intentionally— was that of initiating the first mass democracy.

When the gradual expansion of suffrage in Great Britain and the United States threatened to bring about mass democracy anyway, theorists such as John Stuart Mill and Alexis De Tocqueville responded with institutional and cultural recommendations aimed at ensuring that public decision-making would be broadly consistent in its aims, realistic and informed in its choice of means, moderate and flexible. To these ends, Mill—the same theorist who inspires often radically egalitarian participatory or developmental democratic theorists—argued in his *Considerations on Representative Government* (1861), for an electoral system weighted in favor of the most highly educated voters. Meanwhile Tocqueville cast about for cultural and institutional mechanisms that would push citizens to remain engaged in decision-making processes and to practice their deliberative skills in a range of policy debates. Hence his identification of the importance of jury duty and engagement in local civic organizations.

Two commentators who more directly influenced postwar empirical researchers were Walter Lippmann and Joseph Schumpeter. Lippmann argued that the mass public understands political issues, which were necessarily remote from everyday experience, only in terms of "stereotypes." To Lippmann the decisions made on the basis of such stereotypes are irrational because they correspond only very crudely to reality (1922/1949, Part 3). Political rationality, essentially involves the acquisition of an accurate, fine-grained mental picture of the political world. An individual is more rational vis-à-vis some policy when his understanding captures enough of the complexity and nuance of the relevant circumstances to render accurate judgments about them.

Schumpeter anticipated many of the arguments of Anthony Downs (1957) and other rational-choice scholars. He also elaborated on Lippmann's basic insight about the individual's tendency to think in unrealistic terms about things distant from his or her daily experiences. Mass politics requires the members of the public to make decisions that they are ill equipped to make.

> Normally, the great political questions take their place in the psychic economy of the typical citizen with those leisure-hour interests that have not attained the rank of hobbies and with the subjects of irresponsible conversation. Things seem so far off. . . . One feels oneself to be moving in a fictitious world. (1942/1976: 261)

Because of the unreality of the political world and the typical citizen's correct perception that his vote has little or no ultimate effect on decision-making due to the sheer size of the electorate, he is likely to expend "less disciplined effort on mastering a political problem than he expends on a game of bridge" (1942/1976: 261).

Schumpeter's analysis was driven by his desire to demonstrate the compatibility of socialism—which he expected to prevail over liberal capitalism—with a realistic conception of democracy: one that relied on the public only to choose from among competing elites, and not to rule directly. But Schumpeter's reexamination of the capabilities of the mass electorate was also motivated by the rise of fascism in Europe. Because the typical democratic citizen has an unrealistic view of the distant political world, and because he or she lacks the motivation to expend cognitive energy on political matters even if these matters were more accessible, he or she is, Schumpeter argued, vulnerable to emotional—even infantile—appeals. Thus, he warned that due to the "weakness of the rational processes he applies to politics" the everyday citizen likely would suffer from a tendency to "relax his usual moral standards . . . and occasionally give in to dark urges which the conditions of private life help him repress" (1942/1976: 262).

Similarly, Philip E. Converse's classic essay on the lack of political sophistication among nonelites, "The Nature of Belief Systems in Mass Publics" (1964), concludes with a section examining the mass basis for the Nazi Party, as if to underline the possibly dire consequences of his empirical findings. The rise of Hitler's party, he notes, followed on the heels of a surge of new, unsophisticated individuals into the German electorate; the "mass base [of the Nazi party] was disproportionately recruited from among customary non-voters, the young and the peasantry" (ibid.: 253). But the overall theme of his essay is that—new entrants or not—the great bulk of any large electorate is likely to think in a quite rudimentary and inconsistent way (if at all) about politics. Only a thin crust of elites will seriously reflect on its political beliefs. This tiny sophisticated stratum is competent to make informed political decisions in a way that the bulk of the public is not.

Inspired by similar anxieties, the German emigre sociologist Theodor Adorno had—in the immediate postwar years—led a survey-based study of populations drawn from selected U.S. cities on which he and his colleagues based *The Authoritarian Personality*. This study was devised to identify "the *potentially fascistic* individual, one whose structure is such as to render him particularly susceptible to anti-democratic propaganda" (1950/1964: 1; emphasis in original). Although it had less impact on future empirical work, it illustrates the demanding nature of the Frankfurt school's view of rationality, despite an orientation toward autonomous decision-making that is quite different from the previously considered theorists' focus on well-informed decision-making.

The matter of rationality is addressed most directly (it is implicit in the entire work) in *The Authoritarian Personality*'s discussion of "cognitive personality organization" (ibid.: 461). A battery of questions intended to tap into cognitive personality are meant to track six dimensions that the authors take to delineate the irrational personality: (1) rigidity; (2) intolerance of ambiguity; (3) pseudoscientific or antiscientific (as vs. a scientific-naturalist) orientation; (4) anti-intraceptive (as vs. self-critical) thinking; (5) suggestibility or gullibility (as vs. autonomy); and (6) an unrealistic view of means-ends relationships. Those who are relatively less rigid in their thinking distinguish themselves by a "readiness to think over matters and to come to a solution through their own thinking as well as their unwillingness to take over traditional and fixed concepts and ideas without scrutiny" (1950/1964: 463). Thus, the first and fifth criteria relate political rationality to autonomous reasoning. On the other hand, criteria (2), (3), (4) and (6) have to do with well-informed reasoning. As for the second, the acceptance of ambiguity might be related to Lippmann's concern about the mass public's use of simplistic stereotypes. And intraceptivity, (criterion 4) is defined as a rational tendency "toward introspection, as well as a readiness toward gaining insights into psychological and social mechanisms" (ibid.: 466).

Adhering to the six elements of *The Authoritarian Personality*'s notion of "cognitive personality organization" is clearly a demanding—

that is, resource-costly—exercise. Like Mill, Tocqueville, Lippmann, and Schumpeter, Adorno et al. take "rationality" to mean more than just efficient decision-making. They require that an individual's political goals not be "infantile," that is motivated by pure passion and unsusceptible to critical examination and potential revision. By contrast, the rational-choice perspective inaugurated by Anthony Downs in *An Economic Theory of Democracy* (1957) takes the point of view of the individual actor and the maximization of his or her personal resources. This "instrumental" understanding of rationality is the classic economic view, which sets aside any concern about where the individual derives his or her ends or about the content of those ends and is, thus, essentially relativistic. It does not question the wisdom of the ends pursued, only the appropriateness or efficiency of the means.

Broader, more traditional notions of political reason, however, imply more than just an individual's consideration of available means and their compatibility with furthering a given set of preferences. They imply a thicker moral content. Political reason involves not only means-ends calculation, but the consideration of how preferences come to be held and a weighing of those preferences' compatibility with broader normative (i.e., social and cooperative) requirements. Politics is an inherently collective, cooperative phenomena. The political as process excludes—by definition—coercion, manipulation, and indoctrination, relying instead on compliance with modes of persuasion and bargaining. The implicit or explicit association of Nazism with political irrationality in the work of Schumpeter, Adorno, and Converse, suggests conceptions of political reason that involve judgments about how preferences, and policies intended to further those preferences, come to be held, as well as the effectiveness of those policies in furthering given goals. Such conceptions do not take the individual's resource efficiency as the sole benchmark; instead, they equate rationality with some larger good.

What such commentators as Lippmann and Schumpeter are worried about is that in a mass democracy, individual economic rationality may conflict with political rationality conceived of as effective decision-making consistent with the norms of politics. It may not, indeed probably will not, be "cost-effective" for any particular individual in a mass democracy to meet the demanding requirements of political reason. This is Downs's ultimate message as well. If Tocqueville, at the dawn of mass democracy, had sought out institutions by which the typical citizen might maintain adequate engagement with the political system, the Michigan-school researchers, from the vantage point of the mid-twentieth century, produced empirical evidence that such efforts had failed miserably.

According to Campbell et al. (1960, Ch. 10) less than 4 percent of American voters organized their thinking about politics in abstract ideological terms. A large proportion (45 percent) approached politics in a rigid manner, through identification of political issues in terms of simple group interests. Significant numbers of others seemed to have no real coherent organizing scheme for holding political information, let alone for reflecting on their political views in the self-critical way recommended by Adorno et al. Converse also showed that the typical (that is, nonelite) American held political values in an apparently ad-hoc way. He or she appeared to have no clear rank-ordering of political values or beliefs—no "centrality" to his or her belief systems—by which to systematically adjust to new information or events. With no real rhyme or reason to their understanding of the political world, Converse noted, it was no surprise that the same people who expressed support for "familiar principles of freedom, democracy and tolerance" (1964: 230) had been found by researchers (McClosky, 1964; Prothro and Grigg, 1960) to apply those values inconsistently when confronted with specific problem-scenarios.[6]

RESPONSES TO PESSIMISM

Since the 1960s several distinct[7] strategies have been adopted in an attempt to rescue the rationality of the American (and, by implication, the modern) electorate. Figure 5.1 is intended to show, in brief, how one might group the array of responses that followed on the heels of works like Converse's (1964).

Response 1 accepts the Columbia and Michigan findings as (to some degree) empirically valid, but holds that they are historically specific, not necessary features of mass democracy. Those normative political theorists who were even aware of them tended to brush aside the findings of the Michigan school, arguing that rigorous versions of citizen sophistication or rationality should be understood as prescriptive ideals, not descriptive claims. The fact that the mid-century American electorate did not live up to these ideals did not imply that democratic theory should be revised or made more "realistic"; it merely meant that efforts should be made to bring reality more in line with the ideals.

Unless a theorist is unabashedly utopian, the implication here is that, with the right reforms and institutions, most of the electorate could, in principle at least, hold sophisticated and realistic systems of belief about the political world in which they live. That does not mean that these reforms would be easy, or even likely, but simply that the opportunity existed. In this spirit, Carole Pateman (1970) called for institutions

Response 1: Empirical Evidence (Potentially) Time- or Context-Specific; Ideal Rationality Accepted.

1a: "Radical" or "Utopian" Variant: for example, Duncan and Lukes (1963); Pateman (1970). The ideal of rationality contained in democratic theory is a prescriptive ideal, not intended to be descriptive. Thus, descriptive, empirical findings say nothing to democratic theory. Implicit (unless unabashedly utopian): the ideal of democratic rationality could be at least approximated, given radical political reform.

1b: Nonradical Variant: for example, Key (1966); Nie, Verba, and Petrocik (1976). When the times or political context changes (and such changes have actually occurred or are likely), the electorate can display higher degrees of "ideal rationality." Empirical portrait of electorate as nonreasoning was true only for particular era. Examination of evidence from 1930s or 1960s would contradict the image of an nonreasoning electorate.

Response 2: Empirical Evidence Flawed; Ideal Rationality Accepted (Or Unquestioned).

The Empirical Methodological Response: for example, Achen (1975); Brown (1970); Pierce and Ross (1974). Measurement errors of some sort alleged.

Response 3: Empirical Evidence Accepted (Or Unquestioned); Ideal Rationality Rejected or Modified.

Democratic Theory has wrongly conceptualized political reason.

3a: Political Rationality Must Be Understood as a Collective Phenomena. The Individualistic Conception of Reasoning Is Flawed: for example, Page and Shapiro (1992); Erickson, Mackuen, and Stimson (n.d.)

3b: Individual Political Reasoning Does Not Display "Global" Coherence, Rather Follows Rules-Of-Thumb (Constraint or Ideology Not Necessary Elements of Political Reason): for example, Popkin (1991); Lodge et al. (1989, 1993, 1995)

Figure 5.1. Array of responses to the unsophisticated mass public thesis.

of workplace democracy (she held up as a model the Yugoslavian system of worker self-management) that would have meant a radical revision of the economic sphere's structural differentiation and, hence, a radical revision of the capitalist order.

Another variant of this response (1b in Figure 5.1) was less idealistic, but in a sense more optimistic about the potential of the existing political system. Nie, Verba, and Petrocik (1976), for example, argued that the Michigan school findings, though accurate to some degree, were based on surveys conducted during a particularly quiescent period of U.S. history and that by the 1960s, changing times had changed the American voter without the need for institutional reforms.

As well, a number of empirical studies (e.g., Achen, 1975; Brown, 1970; Pierce and Ross, 1974)[8] argued that measurement error was at the heart of the Michigan school's bleak findings. This is the most optimistic conceivable response (response 2 in Figure 5.1), but it applies only, if at all, to the most extreme formulation of these findings—Converse's characterization of public ignorance and disengagement as so extreme that much of the public could not be said to have "attitudes" about many political issues at all.

RECONCEPTUALIZED REASON

Interestingly, in Berelson et al. (1954) Schumpeter (1942/1976), and even Converse (1964) himself, we see hints of some ideas that, I believe, form the basis for the other main line of response to findings of public ignorance. This response (number 3 in Figure 5.1), on which I shall focus, tries to vindicate the mass electorate by reconceptualizing reason in ways that rely upon an ideological division of labor. In all three cases, though, the ideas are merely suggested, not followed up.

Schumpeter (1942/1976: 259), for example, muses in a footnote that

> Rationality of thought and rationality of action are two different things. Rationality of thought does not always guarantee rationality of action. And the latter may be present without any conscious deliberation and irrespective of any ability to formulate the rationale of one's action correctly. The observer, particularly the observer who uses interview and questionnaire methods, often overlooks this and hence acquires an exaggerated idea of the importance of irrationality in behavior.

This brief aside is the extent of Schumpeter's discussion of the matter, but his notion of a rationality of action seems to correspond to some subsequently developed ideas about individual citizens' use of on-line processing, opinion leaders (or "two-step information flows") and other techniques of the cognitive miser. The idea is that through the use of such techniques, citizens react in a complex and successful way within the political environment while appearing (to survey questioners) to be entirely ignorant because, as Schumpeter says, they are not able to "formulate the rationale" of their actions. Thus, their actions are rational and properly responsive, even though their minds are largely devoid of political content. Popkin (1991: 7) similarly argues for a kind of "rationality of action" of this type in which

> People use shortcuts which incorporate much political information; they triangulate and validate their opinions in conversations with people they trust and according to the opinions of national figures whose judgements and positions they have come to know. . . [in the process] learn[ing] to "read" politicians and their positions.

Because this kind of practical or "gut" reasoning is what voters really rely upon, "assessing voters by civics exams misses the many things that voters do know, and the many ways in which they can do without the facts that the civics tradition assumes they should know" (ibid.: 20).

Milton Lodge and his associates (Lodge, 1995; Lodge and Stroh, 1993; Lodge, McGraw, and Stroh, 1989; Lodge and Steenbergen, 1995) have elaborated and tested a psychological model—the "on-line processing" model—to account for this kind of inarticulate or tacit rationality of action. According to this model, citizens form evaluative impressions of candidates or other political entities as they encounter information about them. If they later encounter more information, this may be factored into the summary evaluation or "running tally" stored in their long-term memories, whereas the precise information that led to the impression or modification is forgotten. In other words, for purposes of cognitive efficiency, individuals retain only the end results of their on-the-spot reasoning efforts—the affect-based evaluations or impressions—and let go of the information or considerations that went into producing those evaluations.

Similarly, an anticipation of the aggregate or "collective rationality" approach is found in Berelson et al., who, on the heels of showing that "in any rigorous or narrow sense the voters are not highly rational" (1954: 310) make brief note of a "paradox":

Individual voters today seem unable to satisfy the requirements for a democratic system of government outlined by political theorists. But the system of democracy does meet certain requirements for a going political organization. The individual members may not meet all the standards, but the whole nevertheless survives and grows. This suggests that where the classic theory is defective is in its concentration on the individual citizen. What are undervalued are certain collective properties that reside in the electorate as a whole and in the political and social system in which it functions. (ibid.: 312)

Both Page and Shapiro (1992) and Erickson, MacKuen, and Stimson (n.d.) take an approach of this kind. The mechanism here is that of aggregation (often called the "magic of aggregation"), through which the random decisions of the majority—those uninformed by sophistication—"cancel each other out" effectively leaving the decisions of the minority of politically rational citizens to guide the electorate's responsiveness to objective events.[9]

According to this work, other associated mechanisms work to reinforce the positive effects of aggregation. Erickson, MacKuen, and Stimson (n.d.: 10.3) contend that not only does the aggregation process allow the informed to steer the whole, but that

the interactions between the ignorant and the knowledgeable—in both juries and electorate—make aggregation more exponential than additive. As thoughtful argument meets the vacuous, in daily conversation and in elite debate, the thoughtfulness gains weight with each repetition.

This auxiliary argument relies on the assumption that the "truth will out" or that the eventually victorious arguments in the so-called marketplace of ideas will be those that are most competent rather than merely most saleable to the mass public. In other words, it assumes the ultimate failure of demagoguery.

The parallel mechanism for Page and Shapiro (1993: 42)—one that they say may be "even more important" than the refining process of aggregation in producing rational political outcomes—is "the social formation of preference through collective deliberation." This process works through a division of labor between issue specialists (e.g., universities, research institutes, think-tanks); issue popularizers (e.g., pundits, other journalists, and politicians), and average citizens.

Converse (1964: 245) presents evidence for the existence of "issue publics" within mass electorates: subgroups that "specialize in"— that is, remain engaged in or well-informed about—particular issues. This idea seems to naturally lend itself to a division-of-labor conception, and highlights the overlap between the aggregation and short-cut or tacit rationality views, both of which ultimately rely on such issue specialists. On the pure aggregate view these issue publics are expected to be the informed voices that guide the electorate as a whole, whereas the random shifts of the uninformed cancel each other out. In the cognitive short-cut approach, they serve as the opinion leaders or trusted authorities who "cue" the otherwise uniformed and, thus, guide them directly at the individual level. In either case, the end products of some individuals' information-processing are seen to benefit others, either singly (and directly) or collectively (and indirectly). Some people do the cognitive work, and others pass on the fruits of that work to the masses who, in turn, emanate a responsive public opinion. All of these, as far as I can discern, are variations on the same basic theme.[10] "Political elites," Russell Hanson (1993: 285) writes,

> undoubtedly play a crucial role in this process [of preserving democracy through toleration], and there is a well-established line of empirical research on the different political interests and capacities of masses and elites as they bear on tolerance. The most interesting conclusion of this approach is that democracy does not depend on the existence of high levels of tolerance among the masses. So long as elites defend against intolerance, a democratic system may persist and even function smoothly in spite of intolerant attitudes among the masses.

Although it is less readily apparent, the on-line processing model articulated by Lodge and his colleagues also relies implicitly on a division of labor. Citizens must be "fed" the right information with which to make or update their on-line evaluations or tallies. Because the model tells us that citizens do not retain the information or the precise steps of reasoning that led to their "standing" judgements about candidates, these citizens will not be able to follow up in any meaningful way on past evaluations unless some information provider directs such follow-up efforts for them. To the extent that citizens use this kind of on-line reasoning, they forgo the ability to autonomously revisit their past evaluations, or for that matter, reasonably defend themselves against rhetorical efforts or argumentation intended to undercut their prior evaluations.

Only Page and Shapiro seriously entertain the idea that this kind of division of labor, in truth, leaves open the potential for manipulation (see especially Page and Shapiro, 1992: Ch. 9). "Our argument," as they frankly note, "is entirely consistent with the possibility that misinformation or misleading interpretations may be provided and the rational public deceived" (1993: 42). The problem of manipulation is acute because those aspects of political rationality that help insulate the individual from propaganda or demagoguery and that allow for critical feedback—functions emphasized in studies such as those of Adorno et al.—are no longer present when political rationality depends on a division of the intellectual labor.[11] How, then, can the division-of-labor conceptions be made compatible with normative democratic theory?

STRAINS OF LIBERAL DEMOCRATIC THEORY

My account of the various normative concerns expressed within the tradition of liberal democratic theory is inspired by Barry Holden's (1988) recent genealogical-conceptual study of liberal democracy. Some of Holden's terminology can unfortunately be a bit misleading, though, and so I have recast many of his labels for clarity's sake.[12]

Essentially, as Holden (1988: Ch. 2) tells it, Locke's double influence on liberal democracy takes the form of two "poles" or ends of a continuum that specify the proper role for the citizenry in a democracy. These two poles I call the "active view" and the "consent" view. The consent view of democracy is inspired by Locke's notion of the ultimate consent of the people. Holden (ibid.: 55) explains:

> Where consent is required for the performance of some action(s), those who give or withhold that consent can be seen as playing a decisive but negative role—"decisive" because their decision is necessary before the action(s) can be performed; "negative" because they merely respond to initiatives put to them by someone else.

This conception of the citizenry's role is likely to be much more congenial in general to the idea of a political division of labor, whether between government officials and all citizens, or between opinion leaders and nonelites. The "consent" view of democracy is less taxing than the other, "active" view of democracy also inspired by Locke. It demands less of any individual citizen's cognitive resources. Still, consent can be "manufactured" if informed subgroups share biases that influence (consciously or not) the way in which they present or frame initiatives to the mass public.

The "active" view of democracy carries with it a "richer" conception of the people's role. In this view, deficiencies in individual-level competence or political sophistication are an even more serious challenge to democratic legitimacy. "In effect," Holden says, "Locke's right of revolt is here developed into a positive initiating role for the people. Rather than the people merely responding to initiatives put to them by the governors (actual or potential) . . . it is the governors who respond to initiatives from the people" (1988: 576-578). It makes no difference that Locke himself expected this level of popular initiative only in rare circumstances—that is, after a citizenry had been subjected to "a long train of abuses." Locke's right to revolt was pregnant with an ideal of engagement that some later liberals would come to expect of citizens even in routine political times. A normatively legitimate "active" conception, it seems, must steer between two opposing dangers. On the one hand, as in the consent view, citizens might be prone to manipulation. Their activity—in a world of divided labor—might not be authentically self-initiated at all, but rather prompted externally. On the other hand, if the majority is uniformed on any particular issue, there is a danger that actions that are authentically initiated by the majority sentiment may be fundamentally misguided. In a democracy marked by a division of political labor, for example, the move to mass opinion polling as the basis for decision-making may short-circuit the rational process because the views of the informed sectors—or issue publics—will be lost amidst the views of the uninformed.

More specifically, these two different conceptions of the role of the electorate cross-cut the successive theories of democracy developed in the Anglo-American world. The three main theories—distinguished by their ultimate justifying views—include what might be termed "morally grounded," "protective," and "developmental" theories. "Morally grounded" theories are justified by the claim that some aspect of democracy is intrinsically necessary for the expression of a basic moral good, such as natural law, or moral (e.g., Kantian) law. What I have termed "protective" democratic theory argues for democracy as instrumental to the protection of some other moral good or principle—that is, some good not intrinsically bound up with the operation of democracy itself (e.g., utility or welfare). Finally, "developmental" theories see democracy as necessary for the proper development or "true-flowering" of the individual citizen. In truth, nearly all democratic theories are a complex mixture of elements of this crude typology. There are very few—if any—"pure" forms that match the scheme precisely.

Under the protective theory of democracy, the possibility of elite manipulation must be a major concern, depending on what a particular theory of this type identifies as a core interest and depending on what level of engagement in politics is required to protect those interests effectively. Idealized versions of Madisonian and Jeffersonian democratic theories might be included under the "protective" heading, as both these theories are concerned with (among other things) protecting against tyranny, although differing in the degree of direct citizen involvement they suppose this goal to require (i.e., Madisonian democratic theory would be more elitist and, thus, closer to the "consent" conception of citizen involvement, as opposed to Jefferson's more "active" notion). In terms of this protective strain, the problem with divided-labor understandings of mass rationality arises if any segment of the whole system perceives its core interests as divergent from the others'.

Reconceived notions of political rationality might also run into trouble with developmental theories of democracy if any degree of well-rounded political sophistication is considered a core part of the individual's developmental potential. It is true that if—as under so-called liberal privatist theories—the capacities of the individual to be developed are largely nonpolitical (e.g., personal expression or the capacity for fulfilling personal relationships), then public ignorance is not a crucial problem. Civic republican thought (e.g., Sandel, 1996), on the other hand, generally holds that the development of the individual's political capacities is central. Thus, to the extent that such civic republican ideas influence liberal democratic theory, normative concerns will be raised about conceptions of political rationality that allow some citizens to rely on others for political labor, leaving those political capacities un- or under-developed in themselves.

"Moral basis" theories include a wide range of views, so it is impossible to speak in the abstract about whether a theory of this sort will conflict with a notion of political rationality based on a division of labor. By the terms of one particularly prominent democratic theory of this sort today, however—Kantianism—the top-heavy distribution of political competence that emerges from the empirical studies of public opinion would almost certainly be found lacking. Even a moderate theory of democracy based on Kantian thought is likely to find reconceived notions of political rationality inadequate.

For example, in his *The Rule of the Many* (1996), Thomas Christiano explicitly sets out to reconcile the Kantian demand for equal recognition and respect of persons with the structural demands of modern mass society. Because he tries to keep the level of commitment demanded of individual citizens reasonable, and because he recognizes that a widespread division of labor is necessary to maintain or improve material living standards, Christiano retreats from the typically very demanding conception of citizen rationality implicit in most other Kantian theories such as that of Jürgen Habermas (1990), who envisions an ideal speech situation of universal and unlimited citizen deliberation.

Still, at the heart of Kantian moral philosophy is the argument that equal concern and respect are due to individuals because of their status as rational beings. The individual's reason—the fact that all reasoners share in a common "community" of the rational—entitles them to the most basic moral rights, and upon these the political rights of legal or political communities are founded.[13]

Christiano argues that a coherent Kantian view can accept a citizenry that delegates major political roles to specialists. Specifically, his theory allows citizens to relinquish the role of reasoning politically about the proper means to achieve policy goals. They can also step away from the tasks of deliberating over the political compromises that must be made in the course of the democratic policy-making process. In these respects, Christiano's view tracks the realities of mass politics, as revealed in the public-opinion literature. Christiano, however, argues that every citizen in a properly Kantian democracy must, at a minimum, be able and willing to engage in reasoning about the ultimate political ends[14] of the society, and that their reasoning—to be consistent with the values of Kantian universalism—must center around the interests of the whole society, not narrow self-interest. Reasoning about the political ends to be pursued (the basic political values) cannot be delegated by the individual because by doing so she is renouncing the very feature of herself which justifies her rights in the first place. On the terms of this prescriptive theory, then, divided-labor conceptions of political rationality remain insufficient to the extent that people's "preferences" (particularly about ends) originate externally—such as through the influence of elite-driven political discourse. For instance, John Zaller and others have suggested that the cumulative influence of elites might be responsible for the content of even the most stable of public preferences or predispositions (see especially Zaller, 1992: 310-311; and McClosky and Zaller, 1984), and because the public opinion literature does not clearly distinguish between preference formation of ends and means—certainly not in the way held as normatively significant in a Kantian democratic theory such as Christiano's—there is no reason to expect aggregate rationality notions to be satisfactory in regards specifically to preferences about ends.

Because of my concern to cover a breadth of considerations from the literature of democratic theory, I have merely suggested some of the likely points of tension between these views and the idea of aggregate or short-cut forms of political rationality. A more conclusive treatment would require instead of breadth, the juxtaposition of one particular democratic theory against the reconceptualizations of political reason that emanate from public-opinion research. The present analysis, though, leads to the tentative conclusion that the most obviously pressing normative concern raised by the picture of public "rationality" drawn by public opinion researchers is the possibility of elite influence in the establishment of the basic aims of the political system. As I have tried to show, this kind of elite influence may take many forms and results from the loss of cognitive "autonomy" that follows from reliance on divided intellectual labor. Thus far, besides Page and Shapiro's (1993) simple acknowledgment of the possibility, the political analysts who have rushed to vindicate the rationality of the electorate have not properly explored this potentially very troubling aspect of the evidence.

However, the new[15] conceptions of political reasoning may amount to an important corrective to those forms of democratic theory with which they conflict most deeply. In particular, Kantian or civic republican-developmental demands for the expression of political rationality by the individual might be scrutinized more thoroughly in light of the competing values that drive the division of labor in modern mass societies in the first place. This, more than anything, is what separates the electorate into two broad groups: informed and politically sophisticated elites and disengaged, potentially irrational masses.[16] Democratic theories suited to contemporary societies must confront this division of labor. To what degree such divisions should be accepted, however, is a large issue with which contemporary democratic theorists have only begun to wrestle.

ENDNOTES

1.   I will argue shortly that—contrary to some analysts (e.g., Smith, 1989)—the concept of the electorate's "sophistication" amounts to much the same thing as its capability to reason politically. For the moment, it should simply be understood that I am using reason and its cognates in a somewhat different sense than that used by Downs (1957). Downs is concerned with resource efficiency, or being economically rational. Political rationality in the sense that I use it in this paper stipulates that the end of the reasoning process be a satisfactory political decision, however that be defined.

2   Page and Shapiro (1992), Popkin (1991), and Erickson, MacKuen, and Stimson (n.d.) are just a few of the more prominent works that are part of this broader trend.

3.   See, for example, Schumpeter's (1942/1976: Ch. 21) discussion of "The Classical Doctrine of Democracy." Pateman (1970: Ch. 1) nicely analyzes the way Schumpeter and other so-called "elitist" theorists of democracy have propagated the idea of a monolithic "classical" or "traditional" democratic theory.

4.   One could easily bring into the discussion an overwhelming number of democratic theories by seeking to include a wider range, including Marxist theories (e.g., Macpherson, 1973; Harrington, 1972), nationalist-fascist ones (Schmitt, 1923/1992), or others in between.

5.   The widespread use of the designation "democratic" by political systems (both authoritarian and nonauthoritarian) in the twentieth century and its power to legitimize various practices and systems attests to its dominant position as a political ideal among modern populations.

6. Intolerance is not inherently inconsistent, of course, and is not even properly understood as undemocratic in a simple, straightforward way. Hanson (1993: 273-278) rightly points out that it is too often assumed to be so by social science researchers. At some level the philosophy of liberal democracy itself demands a refusal to tolerate some kinds of political acts. However, if respondents indicate a support for general principles of tolerance (of such things as basic minority rights) and then refuse to apply them in specific cases, there is a problem with logical consistency. Conover and Feldman (1980) term this kind of belief consistency "vertical" constraint: a consistency between general political orientations and more specific political beliefs.

7. By "distinct" I mean analytically so. In truth, some appraisals of electorate sophistication might combine more than one of these strategies. Thus my discussion here, depicted in Figure 5.1, should be understood as a representative simplification of sorts.

8. See also, Smith (1989) for a critical examination of many other studies taking this broad approach.

9. In an odd way, this may be the public opinion equivalent of the old classical economist's "invisible hand" argument for the marketplace. Both envision orderly outcomes resulting from a large number of unintended/unconscious actions. There are differences. In the economists' argument, each of the individual actors is conscious; the actors simply do not intend to promote the general welfare in the way that they are alleged to do so efficiently. And in the case of political aggregation, some people (the ultimately decisive set of informed citizens) are acting in a directly intentional way. It is just their less-informed peers who are "unconscious," so to speak.

10. As is, I think, the general picture of mass opinion formation presented in Zaller (1992).

11. In a concluding chapter, Zaller (1992) indicates how such a division of cognitive political labor can work without elite manipulation taking place, but this happy situation, as he notes, depends on the satisfaction of a set of preconditions, some of which seem unlikely to hold in many circumstances.

12. For instance, Holden describes one strain of liberal democratic theory as "radical theory." The term "radical," of course, typically denotes a perspective completely outside of liberal theory and in competition with it (typically on the Marxist left). Here, however, Holden means to denote a type of liberal democratic theory inspired by a notion in Locke's *Two Treatises of Government* (1689). I will redub this theory the "active" democratic theory. I will also redub its counterpart, which for obscure reasons he chooses to call "conventional." I shall call it the "consenting" theory of democracy. The reasons for these name choices should be clear shortly.

13. The Kantian notion of "personhood" identifies the rights-bearing individual and is based on that individual's capacity for reason. Although a large and controversial issue, on such theories, children and the mentally incapacitated are usually said to not be "persons" in this sense (i.e., they are not full rights-bearers), and are thus justly treated in a paternalistic way (see Meldon, 1980).

14. In truth, Christiano speaks of "aims" (and means) rather than "ends" in order to avoid implying that good Kantian citizens need reason only about policy outcomes. "Aims" more broadly refers to "those aspects of the society that are chosen for their own sakes" and may, thus, include some aspects of policy processes as well as outcomes (Christiano, 1996: 170).

15. These understandings of political reasoning—specifically understandings that move away from an individualistic and self-consciously rigorous (approximating deductive reasoning) models—may not, in fact, be so new. Recent revisionist interpretations of the thought of David Hume credit him with prescribing something similar in his moral and political philosophy (Baier, 1991; Norton, 1982).

16. Downs (1957) has argued that the means-end rationality of the individual leads to this kind of distinction (between rationally informed elites and rationally ignorant masses). However, much of this argument relies upon the more fundamental assumption of a division of labor in society, which creates a differential in the political information costs for differently positioned individuals. As Christiano (1996: Ch. 4) argues, one does not need to accept the narrow, economic understanding of individual rationality in order to be led to the conclusion that an elite-mass distinction will obtain (based on different information levels). The pervasiveness of the modern division of labor itself generates the problem.

REFERENCES:

Achen, Christopher. 1975. Mass Political Attitudes and the Survey Response. *American Political Science Review* 69(12), 18-31.

Adorno, Theodore, Else Frenkel-Brunswik, Daniel Levinson, and R. Nevitt Sanford. 1950/1964. *The Authoritarian Personality, Part I.* New York: John Wiley& Sons.

Baier, Annette. 1991. *A Progress of Sentiments: Reflections on Hume's Treatise.* Cambridge, MA: Harvard University Press.

Beard, Charles. 1913. *An Economic Interpretation of the Constitution of the United States.* New York: Macmillan.

Berelson, Bernard, Paul Lazarsfeld, and William McPhee. 1954. *Voting: A Study of Opinion Formation in a Presidential Campaign.* Chicago: University of Chicago Press.

Brown, Steven R. 1970. Consistency and the Persistence of Ideology: Some Experimental Results. *Public Opinion Quarterly* 14(1), 60-68.

Campbell, Angus et al. 1960. *The American Voter*. New York: Wiley.

Christiano, Thomas. 1996. *The Rule of the Many: Fundamental Issues in Democratic Theory*. Boulder, CO: Westview Press.

Conover, Pamela and Stanley Feldman. 1980. Belief System Organization in the American Electorate: An Alternative Approach. In J. Pierce and J. L. Sullivan (eds.), *The Electorate Reconsidered*. London: Sage Press.

Converse, Philip E. 1964. The Nature of Belief Systems in Mass Publics. In David Apter (ed.), *Ideology and Discontent*. New York: Free Press.

Downs, Anthony. 1957. *An Economic Theory of Democracy*. New York: Harper and Row.

Duncan, Graeme and Steven Lukes. 1963. The New Democracy. *Political Studies* 11, 156-77.

Erickson, Robert, Michael MacKuen, and James Stimson. forthcoming. *The Macro-Polity*. Cambridge: Cambridge University Press.

Habermas, Jürgen. 1990. *Moral Consciousness and Communicative Action*. Trans. Lenhardt and Nicholson. Cambridge, MA: MIT Press.

Hanson, Russell. 1993. Deliberation, Tolerance and Democracy. In Russell Hanson and George Marcus (eds.), *Reconsidering the Democratic Public*. University Park, PA: Penn State University Press.

Harrington, Michael. 1972. *Socialism*. New York: Saturday Review Press.

Holden, Barry. 1988. *Understanding Liberal Democracy*. Oxford: Phillip Allen.

Key, V. O., Jr. 1966. *The Responsible Electorate*. Cambridge, MA: Harvard University Press.

Lippmann, Walter. 1922/1949. *Public Opinion*. New York: Free Press.

Lodge, Milton. 1995. Toward a Procedural Model of Candidate Evaluation. In Milton Lodge and K. McGraw (eds.), *Political Judgement: Structure and Process*. Ann Arbor, MI: University of Michigan Press.

Lodge, Milton and P. Stroh. 1993. Inside the Mental Voting Booth. In Shanto Iynegar and William McGuire (eds.), *Explorations in Political Psychology*, 225-263, Durham, NC: Duke University Press.

Lodge, Milton, K. McGraw, and P. Stroh. 1989. An Impression-Driven Model of Candidate Evaluation *American Political Science Review* 83, 399-419.

Lodge, Milton and M. Steenbergen. 1995. The Responsive Voter: Campaign Information and the Dynamics of Candidate Evaluation. *American Political Science Review* 89, 309-326.

Macpherson, C.B. 1973. *Democratic Theory: Essays in Retrieval*. Oxford: Oxford University. Press.

McClosky, Herbert. 1964. Consensus and Ideology in American Politics. *American Political Science Review* 58(2), 361-382.

McClosky, Herbert and John Zaller. 1984. *The American Ethos: Public Attitudes Toward Capitalism and Democracy*. Cambridge, MA: Harvard University Press.

Meldon, A.I. 1980. *Rights and Persons.* Berkeley: University of California Press.

Nie, Norman, Sidney Verba, and John Petrocik. 1976. *The Changing American Voter.* Cambridge, MA: Harvard University Press.

Norton, David Fate. 1982. *David Hume: Common-Sense Moralist, Sceptical Metaphysician.* Princeton, NJ: Princeton University Press.

Page, Benjamin I. and Robert Y. Shapiro. 1992. *The Rational Public: Fifty Years of Trends in Americans' Policy Preferences.* Chicago: University of Chicago Press.

Page, Benjamin I. and Robert Y. Shapiro. 1993. The Rational Public and Democracy. In Russell Hanson and George Marcus (eds.), *Reconsidering the Democratic Public.* University Park: Penn State University Press.

Pateman, Carole. 1970. *Participation and Democratic Theory.* New York: Cambridge University Press.

Pierce, John C. and Douglas D. Ross. 1974. Nonattitudes and American Public Opinion: The Examination of a Thesis. *American Political Science Review* 68(2), 626-649.

Popkin, Samuel. 1991. *The Reasoning Voter.* Chicago: University of Chicago Press.

Prothro, James W. and C.W. Grigg. 1960. Fundamental Principles of Democracy: Bases of Agreement and Disagreement. *Journal of Politics* 22(2), 276-294.

Rawls, John. 1971. *A Theory of Justice.* Cambridge, MA: Harvard University Press.

Sandel, Michael. 1996. *Democracy's Discontent: America In Search of a Public Philosophy.* Cambridge, MA: Harvard Belknap Press.

Schmitt, Carl. 1923/1992. *The Crisis of Parliamentary Democracy.* Trans. Ellen Kennedy Cambridge, MA: MIT Press.

Schumpeter, Joseph. 1942/1976. *Capitalism, Socialism and Democracy.* London: Geo. Allen & Unwin.

Smith, Eric R.A.N. 1989. *The Unchanging American Voter.* Berkeley: University of California Press.

Zaller, John. 1992. *The Nature and Origins of Mass Opinion.* New York: Cambridge University Press.

6

Justifying Civic Competence in the Information Society

Andrew Calabrese

The subject of the loss and recovery of democratic community has been a recurring theme throughout twentieth-century social and political thought in the United States. John Dewey's (1927) account of the decline of local communities in the face of modernization and his prescriptions for a democratic state and a national community of communities—a "great community"—were premised on his assumption of our need for a foundation of a mediated network of localities. Dewey may not have been the most enthusiastic proselytizer for the press, and his ideas about the recovery of the spirit of community have not been highly influential in practice, but he did see the press as a means for linking a geographically dispersed society, and thus as a partial but necessary means for maintaining a national political community. It is useful to recognize Dewey among others who represent, for better and for worse, a long-standing American ideal aimed at the recovery of community through the use of advances in communications media. In the same tradition as Dewey's attempt to couple democratic and participatory ideals with the technological and economic imperatives of modern capitalism, the more recent subject of democratic communities in cyberspace has been of great interest to a growing number of scholars who desire to revitalize democracy and community locally, translocally, and transnationally (Abramson, Arterton, and Orren, 1988; Arterton, 1987; Barber, 1984; Rheingold, 1993).

Today, the idea of a multimedia superhighway is legitimated to a great degree by the rhetoric of expanding democratic participation. There is no denying the appeal of this rhetoric, or that it has some basis in the everyday life experiences of a small portion of the world's population, although what follows is a counterpoint scenario about the relationship between class structure in advanced capitalist society and the latest innovations in telecommunications. Although the scenario is not strictly hypothetical, its aim is to provoke discussion about the class structure of telecommunications infrastructure development, particularly in affluent countries. For it is in response to this context that I believe the meaning of civic competence must be defined in the information society.

CLASS DIVISION ON THE INFORMATION SUPERHIGHWAY

Two contradictory but ultimately compatible models of network activity will continue to emerge on the superhighway. One can be called the "consumer" model and the other the "civic" model. The two models have distinct characteristics, but they will be increasingly interdependent, particularly in the face of a declining ethos in the United States toward "public service" media and "public interest" policy-making, and due to the more general ideological backlash against welfare economics, which has been particularly misplaced with respect to telecommunications (Horwitz, 1989).

Although we are likely to see some uses of the superhighway become increasingly stratified along class lines, there will be some attributes in common across social strata. Based on patterns of the consumption of goods, services, and political ideas and representatives, all strata will be segmented, targeted, and mass-democratized in a further stage in the realization of Max Weber's (1946/1922) gloomy characterization of modern democracy not as a general uplifting of the civic virtue of the public, but as "the leveling of the governed" (226). New forms of entertainment and shopping will constitute the bulk of innovative new services available to consumers. Although ostensively "interactive" (*"Press now* to purchase, to select a story ending, to register your opinion, to vote. . . .") most patterns of mediated communication will be fairly characterized by their high degree of institutional and hierarchical control, and by their high-band-width downstream flows and low-bandwidth upstream flows.

The volume and nature of network interactivity will vary signifi-cantly on the basis of socioeconomic status. The information superhigh-way offers the prospect of broadband convergence and interactivity in such a way as to overlay class division upon market segmentation. The civic model will primarily occupy a stratum constituted by significant portions of the new class of technical and professional intelligentsia. Although the spending power of the new class as a whole makes its members prime targets within the consumer model, a portion of the new class—the portion that constitutes much of the "attentive public," that is, the audience for, and sometimes members of, policy elites—will engage proportionately more frequently in political deliberations than will mem-bers of lower strata. The "culture of critical discourse" described by Alvin Gouldner (1979) in his account of the rise of the new class will be inter-nally egalitarian and communitarian, and externally effective in exercis-ing political and economic power. For the new class, electronic democra-cy will facilitate and confirm its members' political franchise and their authentic access to the closest contemporary approximation of the early bourgeois public sphere. Finally, the cosmopolitanism of the new class will be enhanced by its activity on the superhighway. The high spatial mobility of its members will be mirrored by their high network mobility and activity in the formation and maintenance of political alliances and economic relations on a highly privatized, translocal, and increasingly transnational basis. The activities of the new class on the superhighway will be cosmopolitan and exclusionary, both by default and by design, as Christopher Lasch (1994) describes: "Their ties to an international culture of work and leisure—of business, entertainment, information, and 'infor-mation retrieval'—make many members of the elite deeply indifferent to the prospect of national decline" (Lasch, 1994: 47).

By contrast with patterns in the civic model, the information superhighway will be based almost exclusively on a consumer model for lower strata. Wage earners, the precariously employed, and the unem-ployed will interact infrequently on a horizontal dimension, except pri-marily in commercial modes that are institutionally and hierarchically structured and controlled for commercial purposes such as games and shopping, and to do more routine forms of telework. The low spatial mobility of lower strata will be mirrored by low network mobility and limited perceived prospects for using available network resources for creative expression or upward mobility, and by limited felt need for hor-izontal or upstream communication flows beyond those which are struc-tured for commercial purposes or for the accessing of social services where they are available.

The sense in which the consumer and civic models are interdependent is that the economic viability of the civic model will depend on the commercial success of the consumer model. Highly interactive and noncommercial horizontal communication activity, which will be engaged in primarily by members of the new class when they function not as consumers but as political actors, will be subsidized by revenue from high-bandwidth downstream flows, which will be consumed by all social strata. Although this may not be all that is in store on the information superhighway, it is aptly descriptive of the challenge facing any politically progressive vision of the emancipatory potential of these new forces of production, and of a vision of what the meaning of competent citizenship might need to include in such a context.

In sum, there is a widespread and growing tendency to develop and accept cyberspace primarily as a means of heteronomous relations of market exchange, and to ignore how the dominance of this tendency threatens the prospects for autonomous and democratic civic discourse. Writing many decades before the term *cyberspace* entered the popular lexicon of affluent societies, Walter Benjamin (1936/1969) attempted to reconcile hope for the emancipatory potential of using new communication technologies with the painful awareness of the realities of the uses of such technologies to mobilize masses of people to join in the most hateful of causes. Among the principal dangers of which Benjamin warned was that of "aestheticizing politics," that is, of making politics a spectacle in which expectations of ourselves as citizens would not exceed watching from the sidelines and cheering as charismatic leaders and emotionally appealing political agendas gain momentum and hold sway. Reflecting on the skillful use of the means of communication available to those who captured and held political power in Nazi and fascist Europe, Benjamin discussed how "mechanical reproduction" was being used to undermine the possibility of a critical public. If Benjamin were alive, his concerns about the aestheticization of politics, the depoliticization of political power, and the mobilization of hateful sentiments through modern means of communication would have persisted. Indeed, in light of new techniques that lend an even greater aura of authenticity to political discussions, he might conclude that things have changed mostly to remain the same. To put the matter more concretely in current terms, the idea of "electronic democracy" ought to go beyond platitudes about how "the digital citizen" of today has become a coveted target in terms of political marketing in modern democracies (Katz, 1997).

CITIZENSHIP AND COMMUNITY IN THE INFORMATION AGE

In Peter Riesenberg's (1992) account of the history of Western citizenship, he highlights two general concepts of the citizen—"active" and "passive"—the former prevailing from the time of the Greek city-state up through the French revolution, and the latter having lasted since that time. "Passive citizenship safeguarded everyone's person, property, and liberty. Active citizenship was reserved for the adult male who would contribute to the welfare of the state with his body and property" (1992: 271).[1] Riesenberg argues that although there has been a progressive expansion of equality in the enjoyment of basic human rights and dignity, "politics remained largely in the hands of traditional elites" (1992: 271). In that respect, he concludes that neither the French nor the American revolutions broke with the past, and that the model of active citizenship advanced by Rousseau, based on his image of the Geneva of his childhood, "proved an attractive, but illusory goal throughout modern history" (1992: 272; see also xviii).

We can see how, in modern terms, active and passive citizenship have parallels in the modern dichotomy between the *active citizen* and the *passive consumer*. Although the analogy is imperfect, similar connotations apply. In theory, dissatisfaction comes with the idea that citizenship can find meaningful expression in the reception of one-way, mass-mediated messages, and also with the fact that this system of mass communication is further structured by an intensely commodified culture. Such dissatisfaction leads some to hope that the "interactive" mode of ostensibly decommodified Internet communication will provide citizens with the greater capacity to resist passivity and become more actively engaged in political discourse and action, a view that I believe warrants healthy skepticism (Calabrese and Borchert, 1996; Masterman, 1995). For others, the very idea of *mass* communication is wrong in the first place because it underestimates the selective and critical capacities of the active audience. Yet another view, and one that I think has more reasonable and less polarizing potential, is to think of the system of mass communication as a system of representation (e.g., Dahlgren, 1995: 15-17; Keane, 1991: 44). As Peter Dahlgren writes, "We can safely assume that the mass media are not about to fade from the scene—and in fact they continue to grow—and that just as representation in democracy is unavoidable, so is representation in communication. Neither by itself necessarily means the demise of civilization, even though both generate special problems" (Dahlgren, 1995: 16). With this view in mind, I believe it is fair to say that the idea of passive citizenship, as defined by Riesenberg, is not something we can manage without. Nor is the idea of active citizenship—or civic competence—something we should reject as unattainable in all areas of our lives (Calabrese, 1999, in press).

To a degree, this view opposes the arguably simplistic dichotomy between *citizen* and *consumer*, which has parallels in the binary opposition of information and entertainment. Whereas such antinomies may be useful in terms of describing ideal types for analytical purposes, it makes no practical sense from an ethnographic viewpoint to normatively conceive of citizens as rational monads seeking only to be "informed," as if such an experience would necessarily negate the possibility of being "entertained." As to whether such a view puts us on a slippery slope to finding "the political" nowhere in cultural practices but in "oppositional" forms of consumption, I would disagree, although it is beyond my purpose to argue the point further at this time. More to the point of the remainder of this essay, I examine the basis of the hope that the modern means of communication can enhance the prospects of citizenship and expand the horizons of political community. What follows immediately below is a brief review of how the principles of citizenship are articulated in modern communitarian thought, and how communities are viewed as "seedbeds" of civic competence.

Communitarianism is a wide-ranging contemporary movement in the United States that distinguishes itself from liberalism, sometimes quite explicitly, by opposing the individualism, materialism, and greed that are seen to be underlying the liberal economic agenda. A commitment to spirituality, to shared values, and to a sense of communal obligation are characteristic themes advocated by intellectuals commonly associated with communitarianism. Among the most visible speakers on behalf of communitarian ideals are Amitai Etzioni, Robert Bellah, Mary Ann Glendon, and Michael Sandel. Among the intellectual legacies often cited by these authors is the work of Alexis de Tocqueville, who argued that what made democracy in America work was competent citizenship, cultivated through commitment and direct involvement in community affairs (Tocqueville, 1830/1945). Another, perhaps more fundamental, influence on communitarianism is Jean-Jacques Rousseau (1762/1968), whose notion of "the general will" is fundamental to the civic unity so prized among modern communitarians. The critique of the welfare state by communitarians, and visions of alternatives, bear directly on the compellingly persuasive political language of "empowerment," "virtue," "obligation," and "community" that are used widely by communitarians.

Communitarianism has been highly influential in both of the major political parties in the United States, with the current president being particularly attracted to some of its core propositions. The communitarian movement resonates with the popular and influential writings of William Bennett, who has managed to distinguish himself to some degree from the neoliberal positions of his own Republican party and even has managed to have considerable influence on the Clinton administration, including the president himself. The recovery of the idea of *virtue* in the contemporary lexicon of American politics has been nothing short of explosive, and Bennett, Ronald Reagan's Secretary of Education and George Bush's "drug czar," has become the most widely acclaimed self-styled expert on the subject. Aimed ostensibly at restoring the moral compass of American society, the rhetoric of virtue found its most popular, if not distorted and instrumentalized, expression in the 1992 "Republican Revolution" in the U.S. Congress, and it has been prevalent in much of the language used to justify the contemporary assault on the U.S. (and British) welfare state. Although Bennett is not alone among popular authors on the subject, his best-selling work has gained the most notoriety (Bennett, 1995, 1996). Among the targets that communitarians attack vigorously is the "culture of permissiveness" and the role they see it playing in the moral decay of American society, which they attribute to an undue sense of entitlement and consequent overdependency on government. In many ways, the communitarian agenda represents dissatisfaction with what Daniel Bell (1976) has referred to as "the cultural contradictions of capitalism." An economic agenda pushes us in one direction, and moral imperatives push us in another. Moral controversies about sex on television provide useful illustrations of such contradictions. Those who are absolutist in defending free enterprise, but who consider televised sex to be morally objectionable, find themselves locked in a paradox in which their economic priorities are in conflict with their moral judgment.

In some ways, modern communitarianism is seen to be an offshoot of the tradition of the classical tradition of civic republicanism, particularly with respect to their similar attachment to the idea of virtue as the essential normative element of good citizenship and a good society. In attempting to reconcile key aspects of modern communitarianism with civic republican thought in his critique of liberalism, Michael Sandel (1996) appeals to the idea of civic virtue. However, the degree to which there is an identity between communitarian and civic republican concepts of virtue is a matter of dispute. Modern communitarian thought stands firm on the position that a commitment to a prior, prepolitical conception of moral virtue is necessary in a good society. Although such a view fits within a republican tradition that originates with Rousseau, it is somewhat at odds with another strand of republicanism, namely that of the Roman republic, as revisited in the Italian renaissance by Niccolò Machiavelli. The concept of virtù discussed in the writings of Machiavelli carries with it the connotations of a stoic notion of strength of character—courage, ability, intelligence, even ruthlessness when deemed necessary—aimed toward achieving both a secure state and a citizenry committed to the common good. However, questions of justice, fairness, and individual suffering are not only less relevant to Machiavelli's concept of virtue, but rather it is a weak ruler who is preoccupied with them. Furthermore, Machiavelli paid only lip service to the moral authority of the Church, but in general he was more opposed to than supportive of the overweening power of the Church upon the state (Machiavelli 1961, 1970).

There are other unresolved tensions about the intellectual and moral foundations of communitarianism, such as those raised by Habermas, who suggests that modern communitarians overburden the proceduralist orientation of civic republicanism with an "ethical constriction of political discourse," making the republican model too idealistic to be workable (Habermas, 1994: 4). For Habermas, modern communitarians betray the republican ideal of a "praxis of civic self-legislation" when they seek to prepolitically settle upon a community's ethical convictions, and in the process preempt the possibility that political deliberation in a variety of forums can serve as the legitimate foundation of an ethical community. Such a position as this seems to deeply challenge the idea often underlying communitarian thought, that religious institutions—which are by most, if not all accounts, prepolitical institutions—should serve as the most fundamental and legitimate seedbeds of civic competence (Carter, 1998; Oldfield, 1990: 167-172). Such a view, Habermas suggests, undermines the republican ideal of public autonomy, or popular sovereignty, in which the citizen's rights to political participation and communication arise from and construct the ethical political community (Habermas, 1994, 1998b).[2] In contrast, he proposes a discourse-theoretic foundation for public autonomy that aims to overcome the differing limitations of communitarianism and liberalism by presupposing the possibility that citizens will be competent to deliberate democratically through the effective exercise of their rights of participation and communication. Furthermore, he argues, that is the only basis on which the democratic legitimacy of an ethical community can be sustained: "Indeed, the idea of citizens' legal autonomy demands that the addressees of law be able to understand themselves at the same time as its authors" (Habermas, 1998b: 260). Regardless of whether one accepts Habermas's procedural model of deliberative democracy, his critique of communitarianism's tendency to constrain the formation of the ethical foundations of political community is valuable. Not least of the reasons for this is that it highlights the need to concern ourselves with the preconditions for effective political participation and communication, a matter of growing complexity in the information age.

The localist orientation of much of communitarian theory and practice calls into question its power as a political movement. Ironically, communitarians are much less concerned about achieving a moratorium on rights claims by global corporations in areas of transnational trade, investment, and intellectual property—that is, of corporate welfare— than they are with questioning the virtuousness of welfare for the poor (Calabrese, 1999), evincing the fact that communitarianism generally accommodates, or at least fails to pose meaningful challenges to, the unjust structural conditions that neoliberal theory and practice create. In essence, communitarianism exerts its greatest leverage by moralizing in a manner that lays the greatest amount of blame before the most vulnerable victims of capitalism's failures. Despite these deep deficiencies, it seems unwise to polarize the discourse about communitarianism by concluding that it offers no progressive potential. As Jay Bernstein (1991) demonstrates in his exposition of Marx's "communitarian conception of right," communitarianism has powerful, if horribly underdeveloped and unrealized, potential to ground the articulation of unmet needs for competent participation in political community by way of a more forceful and honest engagement with the complex relationships between capital and communication. Truly progressive, democratic politics simply cannot survive by categorically rejecting this potential in communitarian thought.

Among the many attempts in the United States and a growing number of other countries to involve citizens more directly in their local communities through public deliberations are included "civic journalism," a movement that has resonated with communitarianism. Civic journalism attempts to make local newspapers play more of a leadership role in the fostering of constructive political debate over issues which concern a community. The idea behind this movement is for local media to spin more of a web of ties that bind a community together around common and important needs and interests. Consistent with communitarianism's lack of a materialist grounding, and perhaps civic journalism's greatest point of vulnerability, is that it inadequately confronts or explains the tension defining the production of news in a commercial media environment, namely, the tension between ideals of journalistic integrity and demands for commercial success. Advertising dollars, media conglomeration, interlocking media industry directorates, and the unexamined principle of consumer sovereignty all place an increasingly serious set of overlapping limitations on the willingness and ability of news organizations in any medium to bite the hands that feed them. Attacks on decadent journalism, combined with new proposals for responsible journalism that focus on the profession while paying no attention to the political-economic environment from which the professional ideologies of journalism arise, are myopic to say the least.

Communitarian views also influence contemporary developments in the "media access" and "community network" movements in many countries. Although there are many good reasons to support strong positive rights of access to the means of communication, the more general issue again is whether these locally oriented initiatives manage to address the large-scale political and economic constraints upon their efforts. Certainly there is more to the formation of civic competence and effective democratic participation than formal, minimal assurances of access to the means of communication can provide.

THE EDUCATION OF THE COMPETENT CITIZEN

The Roman orator Quintilian described the ideal citizen as "a good man skilled in speaking" (quoted in Golden, Berquist, and Coleman, 1976: 78). In other words, the citizen requires both ethical and critical-intellectual capacities to participate competently in the political community. However, in order to become "skilled in speaking," one must have means, and the complexity of those means has grown with the complexity of society. Discovering what the necessary means are, other than through the blind pursuit of technological fixes, and ensuring that they are foundations of a democratic education, is a project that has not been taken seriously in the breathtaking discourse about the information society. "Media literacy" should serve as a means not only of generating discerning consumers and skilled workers, but also citizens who are capable of serving both as "authors" and "addressees" (Habermas) of the rules that govern their political lives.

Since the time that Walter Lippmann published his classic book, *Public Opinion* (1922), there has been fundamental disagreement among intellectuals and political leaders about what role citizens can and should play in public debate in a democratic society. In this and a series of subsequent books, Lippmann argued that the "omnicompetent citizen" is a myth, and that public debate should be left to the control of more level-headed experts of various kinds. Among those who vigorously disagreed with Lippmann was John Dewey, whose *The Public and Its Problems* (1927) was written as a response that aimed to depict the average citizen as one whose civic competence is worthy of cultivation and trust rather than suspicion and underestimation. In Dewey's argument, the right and the ability to participate as listener and speaker in public debate, both literally and figuratively, is essential to competent citizenship.

Echoing Dewey, Carole Pateman (1970) begins with a critical explication of a position that challenges the assumptions that participation is impractical and unwarranted, and that it should be limited to voting for representatives. Drawing from Tocqueville's *Democracy in*

America (1830/1945), Pateman argues that the capacity for competent public judgment is derived experientially, and the feasible opportunity to participate in public life is a necessary precondition to that end. Tocqueville saw participation in local government as a means of enabling individuals to become effective participants in a national polity: "Town meetings are to liberty what primary schools are to science; they bring within it the people's reach, they teach men how to use and how to enjoy it" (Tocqueville, 1830/1945, Vol. 1: 63). Pateman's argument can be summarized as stating that participation in "political" and "nonpolitical" settings at local levels, where greater opportunities for participation are available, engenders a competent citizenry at representative levels. Her analysis emphasizes the value of local participation in the name of both participatory and representative democracy.[3]

Drawing more upon critical theory than the traditions of liberal and communitarian thought that influence Pateman's theory of civic competence, Jürgen Habermas has presented a theory of "communicative competence" that centers on the argument that communication can be systematically distorted by relations of power and domination, which necessitates that actors, listeners, and speakers develop the capacity to recognize when such forms of repression are happening (1970a, 1970b, 1979). Thus, as Thomas McCarthy (1973/1975) has noted, the pedagogical function of such a theory is to offer a guide for the critique of systematic ideological distortion and for the institutionalization of more democratic forms of discourse. Of course, Habermas has been taken to task for idealizing the conditions under which systematic distortion, assuming it can be identified, can be overcome (Holub, 1991). Despite this, his efforts to further develop a theory of communicative action continue to be based in part on the Kantian ideal of the free public use of reason rather than on instrumental rationality grounded in power relations (Habermas, 1984, 1987; see also Warnke, 1995). Most important about Habermas's view on communicative competence is its grounding in historical materialism, which he argues is essential if we are to be able to recognize how institutionalized forms of repression can cause deviations in discourse that impair democratic public communication (Habermas, 1970b).

Although Habermas's concept of communicative competence offers a valuable conceptual orientation to democratic education, its great deficiency as the foundation of a political project is its abstractness, which leaves much to the imagination as far as what sort of interventions are possible, both in terms of a critique of systematically distorted communication, and of the institutionalization of alternative forms of democratic communication. Although Habermas does not appear to have abandoned the general normative goal of a practical concept of communicative competence within a broader theory of communicative action, his more recent work is preoccupied with the legal preconditions of democratic deliberation, as noted above. However, even in his recent work, the pedagogical foundations for deliberative democracy remain unaddressed, except in very general terms.

In contrast, such preconditions are at the forefront of the work on democratic education by Amy Gutmann (1987, 1988), who has addressed in depth the relationship between political education and public deliberation. In her book, *Democratic Education* (1987), she presents two core principles, or limits, which she argues need to be placed on political and parental authority over education, namely, "nonrepression" and "nondiscrimination" (1987: 44-45). According to Gutmann, these limits aim to prevent the state, educational systems, and families from depriving children (and adults) from developing the capacities to deliberate rationally about conceptions of the good life.

For Gutmann, political education in the modern age necessitates state patronage, because in no other way can minimal guarantees be provided for creating a common basis of civic competence. In taking this position, she links welfare-state policies for universal public education to the politics of citizenship rights. Gutmann views education as a means to equip citizens with the capabilities to deliberate on what constitutes a good life and a good society. She defends the idea of a welfare state that is aimed at these capabilities through democratic education. Although this perspective does not dispute the contradictions of the welfare state, Gutmann reflects the liberal tradition that endorses such institutional forms as means to democratic citizenship. However, it may be idealistic for us to think that such a burden can realistically be placed on welfare states. On the other hand, it is difficult to think that citizens can develop such capacities to recognize and overcome the sorts of political and economic distortions described by Habermas, and the forms of repression and discrimination described by Gutmann, without having access to decommodified educational resources and experiences. In Gutmann's own work, she examines how the media are means of social learning, for better and for worse, and she makes a case for state support of media that can best serve to enlighten citizens rather than appeal to them simply as consumers (Gutmann, 1987: 232-255).[4] However, she neglects to delve into the importance, if not the necessity, of a system of formal education that can reinforce such values with respect to the citizens' use of the media. Clearly, the means of communication must be understood both as subject and object of political education.

Both Habermas and Gutmann have provided valuable criteria for gauging the degree to which there are impediments to the realization of civic competence. In the case of Habermas, his criteria are based on the cultivation of the ability to recognize systematic forms of distorted communication arising out of manipulation, deceit, and coercion. Gutmann's criteria are based on recognition of forms of repression and discrimination. In each case, the arguments are somewhat removed from the formation of a political project aimed at fostering civic competence.

Perhaps a more fruitful contribution to a political project of promoting civic competence is the work of Paulo Freire (1970, 1985, 1999). His approach to literacy education in the formation of a critical consciousness is not incompatible with the agenda Habermas has pursued. Indeed, Freire rightfully holds a more influential place than Habermas among educational researchers and activists who are engaged in political practice at a grassroots level. Although Freire's influence was realized first among the poor of the Third World, a growing number of educators, activists, and even policy-makers have recognized in recent years the value of his pedagogical methods and insights for liberation in advanced technological society. Perhaps it could be said that whereas Habermas and Gutmann offer critical-theoretical frameworks for identifying the conditions that impede the development of civic competence, Freire has done more to develop principles of effective intervention to achieve that goal. Although it is common, and not unreasonable, to hear social criticism being referred to as "intervention," the scope of intervention that Freire has sought and generated in others is one in which he has undertaken to cultivate and democratize the capacities of understanding and critique. In that sense, he has sought to deprofessionalize and demystify the act of critique, the ultimate aim being civic competence and democratic autonomy.

CONCLUSION

Since the time this chapter was originally written, the popular media in the United States have come under intensive scrutiny due to the killings that took place at a high school in Littleton, Colorado in April 1999. Television and newer media (particularly the Internet and video and computer games) were widely seen as causal factors in the immediate wake of the killings, although the quality of the evidence and arguments used to support the claims has been primitive. In reaction to the Littleton killings, and in recognition of the value of consensus about valid evidence in the process of policy-making, in May 1999 U.S. President Clinton ordered the Surgeon General to conduct a major study of the connection between violence in popular culture and real-life violence by young people. He also ordered the Justice Department and Federal Trade Commission to study advertising practices in the entertainment industry to promote the consumption of violent media among youth.

Along with gun manufacturers, the entertainment industry has been put on the defensive by outraged social critics, policy-makers, and citizens who blame these industries for creating images that are thought to inspire such killings. In response, entertainment executives (and gun industry executives) have begun to challenge this form of scrutiny, claiming that they are being treated as scapegoats for wider social problems (Broder, 1999).[5]

As mentioned at the conclusion of the previous section, a challenge to any efforts to cast media education and media literacy in terms of civic competence is to find the practical means for connecting high theories of citizenship and civic competence to the actual practices of media pedagogy. In addition, the nature of the controversy surrounding the events in Colorado brings recognition to another significant and somewhat neglected challenge. The prevailing tendency in critical discourse about media education and media literacy is to focus on how to educate children (and adults) to be more critical and discriminating users of television and other, newer media. However, critical media pedagogy's call for attention and support would carry far greater weight if it were more effectively grounded in empirically based arguments about media effects. Although there is a great deal evidence to support claims of the connections between media images and individual and social behavior, it is fair to say that media criticism and policy proposals related to this subject have generally been high-handed, but not well grounded as far as research findings are concerned. Ironically, although there is a substantial tradition of research that empirically examines how and what is learned, for better and for worse, through media use, this body of work generally is neglected in the theory and practice of critical media pedagogy, perhaps reflecting the more general persistence of unproductive methodological and epistemological divides that disconnect social science, critical social theory, and social practices. In sum, if the cause of civic competence is to be advanced by media education and media literacy, the context of intervention must be democratized by demystifying the goals and practices of media criticism. Finally, the state of knowledge about media effects should not be neglected by policy makers and media critics, nor should citizens be deprived of the democratic benefits of this knowledge.

ENDNOTES

1.   Stephen Macedo (1990) offers the following defense of passive, also sometimes termed "private," citizenship: "The benefits of private citizenship are not to be sneezed at: They place certain basic

human goods (security, prosperity, and freedom) within the grasp of nearly all, and that is nothing less than a fantastic achievement" (1990: 39). Of course, the "nearly all" to which Macedo refers only applies to the populations of affluent welfare societies, and even there only with some generous qualifications.

2. Although Habermas's essay, "Three Normative Models of Democracy," is published in the same volume as the above-cited essay from the 1998 volume (see Habermas, 1998a), I cite the 1994 version because of slight differences in the text. In the 1994 version, Habermas more strongly emphasizes the contrast between communitarianism and a procedural concept of civic republicanism. In the 1998 version Habermas is not as explicit about this contrast.

3. This view, which is a basis of the communitarian conception of civil society, is not without its critics. For example, in a critique of communitarianism, Kymlicka and Norman (1995) write that "The claim that civil society is the 'seedbed of civic virtue' is essentially an empirical claim, for which there is little hard evidence one way or the other" (295). I agree, although I place greater confidence in the anecdotal evidence supporting the hypothesis than in that which refutes it. More importantly, this hypothesis offers a valuable line of inquiry into the practical substance and value of the modern ideal of civil society and should not be so easily dismissed.

4. I am grateful to Alison Jaggar, a philosopher at the University of Colorado who works well outside the field of media studies, for provoking me, in the wake of the tragic high school killings in Littleton, Colorado in April 1999, to reflect on the general lack of attention to empirical findings regarding the social learning that takes place with respect to the uses of new media, particularly the Internet and video and computer games. I address this issue further in my conclusion.

5. There is no reason to doubt that there are wider problems at stake, and that there is a danger of their being neglected in the search for technological fixes, but none of this contradicts the value of systematic investigation about how deeply embedded particular industries may actually be in those problems. If media industry executives feel that the claims are unfair, they should seek vindication by challenging any findings that implicate their practices.

REFERENCES

Abramson, J., F. Arterton, and G. Orren. 1988. *The Electronic Commonwealth: The Impact of New Media Technologies on Democratic Politics*. New York: Basic Books.

Arterton, F. 1987. *Teledemocracy: Can Technology Protect Democracy?* Newbury Park, CA: Sage.

Barber, Benjamin. 1984. *Strong Democracy: Participatory Politics for a New Age*. Berkeley: University of California Press.

Bell, Daniel. 1976. *The Cultural Contradictions of Capitalism*. New York: Basic Books.

Benjamin, Walter. 1936/1969. The Work of Art in the Age of Mechanical Reproduction. In H. Arendt (ed.), *Illuminations*, 217-251. New York: Schocken.

Bennett, William J. 1995. *The Children's Book of Virtues*. New York: Simon & Schuster.

Bennett, William J. 1996. *The Book of Virtues: A Treasury Of Great Moral Stories*. New York: Simon & Schuster.

Bernstein, Jay. 1991. Right, Revolution, and Community: Marx's "On the Jewish Question". In Peter Osborne (ed.), *Socialism and the Limits of Liberalism*, 91-119. London: Verso.

Broder, John M. 1999, June 2. Clinton Orders Study on Selling of Violence. *New York Times* on the Web. Available at: <www.nytimes.com>

Calabrese, Andrew. 1999. The Welfare State, the Information Society, and the Ambivalence of Social Movements. In A. Calabrese and J.C. Burgelman (eds.), *Communication, Citizenship, and Social Policy: Rethinking the Limits of the Welfare State*. Lanham, MD: Rowman & Littlefield.

Calabrese, Andrew. In Press. Why Localism? Communication Technology and the Shifting Scale of Political Community. In G. Shepherd and E. Rothenbuhler (eds.), *Communication and Community*. Mahwah, NJ: Erlbaum.

Calabrese, Andrew, and Mark Borchert. 1996. Prospects for Electronic Democracy in the United States: Re-thinking Communication and Social Policy. *Media, Culture and Society* 18, 249-268.

Carter, Stephen L. 1998. *Civility: Manners, Morals, and the Etiquette of Democracy*. New York: Basic Books.

Dahlgren, Peter. 1995. *Television and the Public Sphere*. London: Sage.

Dewey, John. 1927. *The Public and its Problems*. New York: Holt.

Freire, Paulo. 1970. *Pedagogy of the Oppressed*. New York: Continuum.

Freire, Paulo. 1985. *The Politics of Education: Culture, Power, and Liberation*. Trans. Donaldo P. Macedo. New York: Bergin & Garvey.

Freire, Paulo. 1999. Education and Community Involvement. In M. Castells, R. Flecha, P. Freire, H. A. Giroux, D. Macedo, and P. Willis, *Critical Education in the New Information Age*, 83-91. Lanham, MD: Rowman & Littlefield.

Golden, James L., Goodwin F. Berquist, and William E. Coleman. 1976. The Education of the Citizen-Orator. In *The Rhetoric of Western Thought* (3rd ed.), 73-92. Dubuque, IA: Kendall-Hunt.

Gouldner, Alvin. 1979. *The Future of Intellectuals and the Rise of the New Class*. New York: Macmillan.

Gutmann, Amy. 1987. *Democratic Education*. Princeton, NJ: Princeton University Press.

Gutmann, Amy. 1988. Distributing Public Education in a Democracy. In A. Gutmann (ed.), *Democracy and the Welfare State*, 107-130. Princeton, NJ: Princeton University Press.

Habermas, Jürgen. 1970a. On Systematically Distorted Communication. *Inquiry* 13, 205-218

Habermas, Jürgen. 1970b. Toward a Theory of Communicative Competence. *Inquiry* 13, 360-365

Habermas, Jürgen. 1979. *Communication and the Evolution of Society*. Trans. Thomas McCarthy. Boston: Beacon Press.

Habermas, Jürgen. 1984. *The Theory of Communicative Action, Vol. 1: Reason and the Rationalization of Society*. Trans. Thomas McCarthy. Boston: Beacon Press.

Habermas, Jürgen. 1987. *The Theory of Communicative Action, Vol. 2: Lifeworld and System: A Critique of Functionalist Reason*. Trans. Thomas McCarthy. Boston: Beacon Press.

Habermas, Jürgen. 1994. Three Normative Models of Democracy. *Constellations* 1(1), 1-10.

Habermas, Jürgen. 1998a. Three Normative Models of Democracy. In J. Habermas, *The Inclusion of the Other*, 239-252. Ed. Ciaran Cronin and Pablo DeGreiff. Cambridge, MA: MIT Press.

Habermas, Jürgen. 1998b. On the Internal Relation Between the Rule of Law and Democracy. In J. Habermas, *The Inclusion of the Other*, 253-264. Ed. Ciaran Cronin and Pablo DeGreiff. Cambridge, MA: MIT Press.

Holub, Robert C. 1991. *Jürgen Habermas: Critic in the Public Sphere*. London: Routledge.

Horwitz, Robert B. 1989. *The Irony of Regulatory Reform: The Deregulation of American Telecommunications*. New York: Oxford University Press.

Katz, John. 1997, December. The Digital Citizen. *Wired*, 68-82, 274-275.

Keane, John. 1991. *The Media and Democracy*. Cambridge, UK: Polity Press.

Kymlicka, Will, and Wayne Norman. 1995. Return of the Citizen: A Survey of Recent Work on Citizenship Theory. In Ronald Beiner (ed.), *Theorizing Citizenship*, 283-322. Albany: State University of New York Press.

Lasch, Christopher. 1994, November. The Revolt of the Elites: Have They Canceled Their Allegiance to America? *Harper's*, 39-49.

Lippmann, Walter. 1922. *Public Opinion*. New York: Free Press.

Macedo, Stephen. 1990. *Liberal Virtues: Citizenship, Virtue, and Community in Liberal Constitutionalism*. Oxford, UK: Clarendon Press.

Machiavelli, Niccolò. 1961. *The Prince*. London: Penguin.

Machiavelli, Niccolò. 1970. *The Discourses*. London: Penguin.

Masterman, Len. 1995. Media Education Worldwide: Objectives, Values and Superhighways. *Media Development* XLII, 6-9.

McCarthy, Thomas. 1973/1975. Translator's Introduction. In Jürgen Habermas, *Legitimation Crisis*. Boston: Beacon Press.

Oldfield, Adrien. 1990. *Citizenship and Community: Civic Republicanism and the Modern World*. New York: Routledge.

Pateman, Carole. 1970. *Participation and Democratic Theory*. Cambridge: Cambridge University Press.

Rheingold, Howard. 1993. *The Virtual Community*. Reading, MA: Addison-Wesley.

Riesenberg, Peter. 1992. *Citizenship in the Western Tradition: Plato to Rousseau*. Chapel Hill: University of North Carolina Press.

Rousseau, Jean-Jacques. 1762/1968. *The Social Contract*. Trans. Maurice Cranston. New York: Penguin.

Sandel, Michael J. 1996. *Democracy's Discontents: America in Search of a Public Philosophy*. Cambridge, MA: Harvard University Press.

Tocqueville, Alexis de. 1830/1945. *Democracy in America* (Vols. 1-2, rev. ed.). Ed. and Trans. H. Reeve and F. Bowen. New York: Random House.

Warnke, Georgia. 1995. Communicative Rationality and Cultural Values. In S. K. White (ed.), *The Cambridge Companion to Habermas*, 120-142. Cambridge: Cambridge University Press.

Weber, Max. 1922/1946. Bureaucracy. In H. H. Gerth and C. W. Mills (eds.), *From Max Weber: Essays in Sociology*, 196-244. New York: Oxford.

7

Reading Public Opinion: Vernacular Rhetoric and Political Learning

Gerard A. Hauser

The public is not dead. With the victory by the United States in the cold war, and the collapse of authoritarian regimes in South American and in Eastern and Central Europe, and with the success of national movements in parts of Africa, and possibly soon in North America, there is growing optimism that democracy has emerged as the world's paradigmatic form of governance. A democracy relies on the will of the governed to certify and legitimate the decisions of the state, which means that reliance on majority rule as the basis for political decisions and official policies increasingly has become normal. Yet the rapidity with which majority rule and, therefore, public opinion have come to power should give pause.

The idea that the people reign has been a staple of Western political systems since Greek antiquity and is firmly embedded in Western political discourse. Although rhetorical appeals to "the people" may have considerable political cachet they nonetheless also reflect acknowledgment by lawmakers and leaders that their acts in some way require authorization (Bitzer, 1978). Democratic leaders especially rely on public discussion of the people's business to solicit and solidify their support. In this light the Athenian experience that linked the people to rhetorical discourse becomes more than a vestigial remnant of democracy's origin. Historically Western politics has sustained the connection between discourse on civic issues and setting public policy. It has regarded the people's interests as its rhetorical, if not theoretical, foundation and has narrated advancing their interests as a primary virtue of good governance.

On the other hand, the cry *"vox populi, vox dei"* has not been the sole preserve of democrats. Although it expresses the fundamental principle that lies at the heart of a democracy, it also signals what lies at the heart of political power. Consequently, monarchs and democrats alike have exploited the rhetorical capital of *"vox populi, vox dei,"* even though their definitions of "the people" and their interests have fluctuated to suit radically different ends and tastes (Boas, 1969; McGee, 1975). We need travel back in history no farther than a decade ago to find an apt and relevant illustration for this discussion in the "people's democracies" that emphasized giving form to the sovereignty of the people. These former soviet states were lacking in liberal content and, under a rubric that treated the people and the state as inseparable, subjected the masses to the will of the state (Touraine, 1997). This recent example of a most "undemocratic" political system by Western standards reminds us that the concept of governance responsive to the will of the people has a variety of meanings, each in some way requiring some means for representing official acts as a reflection of public opinion.

The diversity of constitutional forms in which the people's voice has been used as the authorizing agency for state action has particular salience today. During the last decade democracy's wave has broken across the planet and washed across the lives of peoples with no prior history of liberal democratic political participation. Popular participation in governance that seems normal to citizens of Western representative democracies took centuries to evolve. The United States, for example, which heralds its victory in the cold war as a mandate for exporting democracy to the former soviet states, took 150 years to learn how to live in a democracy. It was only after the English colonials had gone through a learning period of differentiation from living as subjects to the British monarchy that they were ready to separate from English rule. For those living in newly democratized parts of the world, the development of a new political consciousness and commitment to egalitarian traditions can hardly require less adjustment. The rise of *the public* as a voice to be taken seriously represents a sea change in political relations that requires political learning by leaders as well as the people.

In this chapter I wish to discuss the concept of public opinion in a sense that returns to its origins and that might provide a model useful for this learning process. I will begin with a consideration of the difference between two models of public participation—civic virtue and civil society—and argue that the latter is based in a different mode of communication than is usually associated with participatory democracies. Next I will discuss the prevailing understanding of public opinion as what opinion polls tell us and suggest that this view overlooks significant aspects of the political learning process whereby public opinion is formed. Then I will propose a more discursively oriented understanding of public opinion based on what I term "vernacular rhetoric" and argue that vernacular rhetoric is essential for redeeming the epistemological relevance of public opinion to public action. I will conclude by returning to the problem of political learning and argue that vernacular rhetoric is inherent to the learning process by which a civil society generates the "social capital" necessary for civic community to form and thrive.

PUBLIC OPINION AND CIVIL SOCIETY

Western societies undoubtedly have understood public opinion as a source of influence on collective action since the period of the Athenian democracy, even though the Athenians neither developed public opinion as a concept nor needed it to explain the vote of the *ekklesia*. Athenians participating in the political life of the polis recognized that their personal acts were more than representative; they were part of the collective whole that was the people's voice. Citizens in the culture of Athenian politics did not form a sense of majority tendencies by counting noses but by attending to the ongoing civic conversation that was as much in evidence in the agora as in the *ekklesia*.[1] Consequently, the idea that their personal acts somehow reflected the voice of the people would have been alien to their political experience. Their collective opinion as participants in the political process and the opinion of the people were one and the same, as the very citizens who interacted in the agora were the same men who trudged up to the pnyx to vote on public issues.

It would be naive to assume that ancient Athenian citizens were not influenced by the give and take of informal exchanges in the agora from which they could develop their personal sense of the trend in popular thought, or what we refer to as public opinion. But they understood their participation in the political process differently than we do today. It was a performance of public virtue we have come to call "civic virtue." Civic virtue grounded individual identity in citizenship and Athenian culture emphasized a citizen's public persona as the ground for that individual's meaning. As the inscription on Athens's ancient city wall announced: "The man with no public business has no business." In fact, the Greek word for the person who was mute on public affairs was *idiot*.

As a model of social organization, civic virtue invaded the private realm; the political organized the personal, leaving no buffer between political and social life. Some may romantically infuse Athenian democratic freedom with the spirit of individual accomplishment that expressed a man's[2] aretê, however civic virtue was a model of accomplishment organized by the state. An individual's virtue was not a personal trait but a public quality that had to conform to the ideals and standards inscribed in the laws and customs of the *demos*.[3] In his classic study exploring the startling terms of life in the ancient Greek *demos*, Fustel de Coulanges (1873/1956: 222) reminds us, "The human person counted for very little against the holy and almost divine authority which was called country or the state."[4] One achieved a reputation for exemplifying civic virtue by actions that served the country, or by activities that were entirely public in the arena of political activity.

The point I wish to stress is that, at its heart, the civic virtue tradition located public good by subjugating the private self to the public realm. Excellence, including moral virtue, was a quality of publicness, reflecting its understanding of moral virtue as a public rather than a private attribute. The citizen realized civic virtue by active and continual participation in public/political affairs. Civic virtue projected a moral vision of personal choice and action regulated by the sovereign authority of the political community, not by the sovereign or the individual actor. This vision was performed through conformity of the actor's particular will to the community's will. The community's political authority did not refer to the obvious fact that it was the source of morality but that the community existed as morality (Seligman, 1995: 202-204).

Within the Western tradition we embrace the model of civic life portrayed by civic virtue as part of our heritage. As heirs to the Greco-Roman traditions of democracy and republicanism, we tend to discuss public life in these same terms, looking for acts of civic virtue as the litmus test of the polity's health and the vibrancy of public life. However, this model is out of phase with the historical development of Western society and its changed conception of the individual. Modern democratic societies represent the people's voice differently than their Athenian ancestors. Since the seventeenth century *vox populi* has acquired the more technical meaning of *public opinion*, and the modern democratic state has transformed the legitimating invocation of *vox populi* from a rhetorical construct used to endorse predetermined actions to the political expression of the interested citizens as the basis for official action.

Enlightenment thinkers, such as Locke, Montesque, and Rousseau, maintained that humankind formed a community of sorts constituted under natural law and in existence prior to society, which was itself prior to the government. Their refutation of the Hobbesean identification of society with its political organization posited the idea of *civil society* as a third arena, independent of the family and the state, whose conscious acts of self-management were integrated with the state. This was a network of associations independent of the state whose members, through discursive exchanges that balance conflict and consensus, seek to regulate themselves in ways consistent with a valuation of difference. We are familiar with the development of this arena through Adam Smith's free market doctrine of economic cooperation. But more important than *laissez faire* for this discussion is the concomitant rise at this time of an autonomous public integrated with the state through expressions of its own opinion.

The Enlightenment concept of "public" represented a new understanding that went beyond what was objectively there and open to everyone's inspection. It designated a common concern that citizens, or at least literate ones, recognized as such. These common concerns, moreover, were expressed in new discursive spaces—newspapers, personal exchanges in coffee houses and salons, political clubs—that extended beyond the agora and the *ekklesia*. Jürgen Habermas's (1969/1989) *Structural Transformation of the Public Sphere* explores the development of these arenas as loci for open deliberation in which reasons for and against an idea were elaborated, tested, refuted, extended, and, ideally, resolved to the extent that it was recognized by everyone as held in common. This recognition was a new idea of public opinion as more than the sum of individual opinions. The dimension of common recognition that emerged from the conversations within civil society gave public opinion a strong sense. It also introduced the radical idea that such opinion formed outside the channels and public spaces of the political structure. Even more fundamentally, as Charles Taylor has observed, public opinion "developed outside the channels and public spaces of any authority whatever, since it is also independent of that second focus of European societies, the church. Governments were used to facing the independent power of religious opinion, articulated by churches. What was new was opinion, presented as that of society, elaborated through no official, established hierarchical organs of definition" (1995: 217).

The Enlightenment's new ideas about economy and public opinion altered society's expression of its own identity apart from the state and, moreover, established self-regulating domains for social coordination. Unlike the democratic polis or the monarch's court, the concept of civil society introduced a new arena independent of the state, existing between it and the family. The discursive spaces of government were no longer the only domain in which social will could be articulated and executed. Now there was a public sphere in which a public could form its own opinion that might challenge the state's primacy in setting social purposes and that might expect its understanding to bear weight on what the state did.

Our attention is directed to civil society, therefore, because it is the locus of opinion formation that asserts authority to guide the state. Whether civil society is colonized by the state and power elites, as Habermas depicts in his rendition of late capitalism, or remains open to the possibility of its own self-regulation, is itself subject to the rhetorical possibilities and performances it can sustain. In less theoretical terms, whether or not civil society embraces and lives in truth is fundamentally dependent on whether or not its members are informed and attentive to the truth.

Elsewhere (Hauser, 1998a) I have discussed in more detail how Enlightenment thinkers developed the economic, political, and moral relations they saw at civil society's core. Here I wish to underscore two points that bear on a rhetorically based public sphere: its milieu of strangers and its locus of agency in the individual.

The tradition of civil society arose in response to the diversity of interests and opinions that came into contact when national borders were thrown open to trade. Its roots are different from those of community, which values common beliefs and shared social practices. Civil society is concerned more with relationships among diverse groups and interests, which was a defining condition of Enlightenment society in Europe. The burgeoning populations of London and Paris, Europe's great cities, are illustrative of the transformation sweeping Europe. Both cities increased massively during this period. London's population in 1595 stood at 150,000; by 1632, 315,000; in 1700, about 700,000; around 1750, at 750,000. As Richard Sennett observes, these figures pale before the growth of London during the industrialization of the nineteenth century from 860,000 to 5 million. "But the people of the 18th Century didn't know what was to come. They could only see what had happened, and the city, especially after the great fire in the middle of the 17th Century, appeared to them to be becoming extraordinarily populous" (1978: 50). The growth of Paris seems less stark—1637 at 410,000; 1684, about 425,000; and 1750 at 500,000—but we must bear in mind that the population as a whole in France was stagnant, if not in real decline, during this period. Inspection of the birth to death ratio of this period suggests that the growth in both cities was fueled from outside by urban migration from rural areas. Sennett tells us the population of these cities, both of which were commercial and soon to be industrial hubs, was increasingly composed of strangers of a special sort: "alone, cut off from past associations, come to the city from a significant distance" (1978: 51), who were now part of its economic, political, and social fabric.

These conditions produced a milieu of strangers. Commercial, political, and social relations involved contact with an Other who did not share past alliances and customs and, moreover, due to society's increasing complexity, was a partner in shared dependency. Successful negotiation of the urban terrain did not require that you like those who were different, and there is ample evidence from references by Londoners and Parisians to these newly arrived outsiders in their cities as "motley," "amorphous," "questionable," "unformed" (Sennett, 1978: 51) that they were held in low esteem. But it did require that you were tolerant of them. Mutual dependency, after all, is not viable without mutual cooperation.

The importance of tolerance is nowhere better expressed than in Adam Smith's free market theory of economic cooperation. The doctrine of *laissez faire* advanced a model of economic behavior in which the open marketplace, freed from control by institutions of church or state, functioned in a self-regulating manner. Because consumers established value and wealth, those who entered the marketplace sought commercial alliances and adapted to marketplace conditions to secure profits. The passion of avarice was mitigated, he argued, by pursuit of interests, which required cooperation among economic partners with different interests and sensitivity to changing conditions for economic success (Hirschman, 1977/1997).

Still, civil society was not conceived as a model where anything goes. Here the moral philosophers of the Scottish Enlightenment, and Adam Smith in particular, set forth a new way of thinking about society that moved the locus of authority for right conduct from the community, as it is expressed in the civic virtue model, into the individual. In contrast to the civic virtue tradition, which subordinated the private self to the public realm, the eighteenth-century Scottish moralists saw the moral basis of society as a private ideal. A *civil* society was one in which individual responsibility for actions toward others could be counted on to exceed pure exchange value because, as Smith argued, humans are naturally inclined to benevolent sentiments toward one another. In a civil society social and cultural distance could be bridged if the complex web of human interactions were marked by tolerance and kindness (Seligman, 1995: 204). Unlike the tradition of civic virtue, in which merit was established by public conduct, the idea of civil society located the basis for moral relations with strangers in the individual self rather than a person's social being. *Virtuosity* receded as the criterion for judging individual actions, with *propriety* taking its place.

This same view of self-regulation among individuals who were marked by difference and interdependency carried over into political relations and continues today. In a most basic way, civil society is an ensemble of political relations constituted by its own rhetoricity. Historically, the discourse of clubs, societies, and other organizations of the day that deliberated questions of commerce, foreign trade, politics, family, culture, religion, and the like have produced civil society's self-organizing and regulating functions. These concrete manifestations of civil society engage in a rhetorical practice quite unlike that traditionally associated with the floor of parliament, however, though no less consequential. The idea of civil society entails the presence of public arenas in which issues are discussed and deliberated, with the understanding that the emerging consensus, or at least the prevailing tendency of opinion—a public opinion—will bear on future policies and conduct. These associations are sites of an ongoing conversation in which their participants negotiate how they shall act and interact. The structural and discursive features of civil society's network of associations suggest that rather than a single public sphere, in which social actors conduct their public deliberations, this society is composed of multiple spheres arrayed in a reticulate structure and whose borders have varying permeability to issues and participants. The social conversation within these spheres is the forming agency for public opinion.

DISCOURSE AND PUBLIC OPINION IN CIVIL SOCIETY

The concept of public opinion is fundamental to the modern understanding of a liberal democracy. Unlike an autocracy, a liberal democracy is predicated on interested members of society forming reasoned judgments that influence the course and direction of the state. It understands public opinion to be more than a nose count. A genuinely *public* opinion entails a prior process by which citizens arrive at an understanding of how public problems intersect with their lives, what their interests are and how they are at stake, and a reasoned judgment on how best to protect them.

This prior process can be summarized in terms of two fundamental principles: the principle of publicity and the principle of free speech. The principle of publicity holds that a society has the right to access all relevant information and viewpoints on public problems. As a corollary, it holds that a member of society has the right to call society's attention to matters s/he regards as public concerns. The principle of free speech holds that a person has the right to express his or her opinion without being subjected to legal penalties. From these two principles we can elaborate a more complete statement of basic rights protected by law and the necessary structures of public policy that guarantee a well-functioning liberal democratic state. But publicity and free speech are the *sine qua non* for these necessary guarantees to have effect and on which they ultimately rest.

Publicity and free speech are significant for public opinion laying claim to being more than an aggregate of raw, blind opinion. They disclose the centrality of rhetoric to a democracy because they imply that public opinion is the result of citizens participating in the conversation by which society arrives at a tendency of common understanding and judgment (Hauser, 1998b). A public of interested citizens forms and conveys that body of opinion necessary to certify the validity and legitimacy of conduct by bodies empowered to act. Consequently, publicity and free speech advance rhetorical communication—communication that urges a point of view—as the necessary condition for redeeming public opinion's claim to reflect, in some significant respect, public reasoning. The character of an antecedent rhetoric underwrites public opinion's claim to represent, in some significant respect, emergent tendencies of understanding among those who are aware of the issues entailed by a public problem and have reached a conclusion about them.

These principles set forth the basis for evidentiary claims that a public opinion exists as more than an aggregate response pattern, but as a civil judgment of sorts. Discourse provides the basis for understanding how public problems have been presented and to whom, how issues have been defined and by whom, who has engaged in public discussion of these issues and how their arguments have been supported or refuted, and how quotidian symbolic exchanges among members of a public constitute *vernacular* rhetorical transactions that express their views on the public issues to which they are tending. Conversely, the discursive requirements of publicity and free speech call into question assertions about public opinion that lack an empirical foundation in citizen discourse. As Pierre Bourdieu (1979) has argued, without a tether to the actual discursive practices of social actors, we lack *prima facie* evidence for membership in a public: that the opinion givers are even remotely engaged by the matters in question.

The type of political discourse implicit in the principles of publicity and free speech resonates with the ideals of public deliberation that are assumed to hold in a representative democracy. C. Wright Mills (1957, 300-301) summarizes these assumptions as including:

> that the individual conscience was the ultimate seat of judgment and hence the final court of appeal, . . . that among the individuals who composed [the public] there was a natural and peaceful harmony of

interests, . . . that before public action would be taken, there would be rational discussion between individuals which would determine action, and that, accordingly the public opinion that resulted would be the infallible voice of reason, . . . [and] that after determining what was true and right and just, the public would act accordingly or see that its representatives did so.

Whether such a public ever existed is doubtful. Nevertheless, these are the assumptions held by such proponents of classical liberal democratic theory as A. Lawrence Lowell. Writing in 1913, Lowell points to Rousseau's distinction between the freedom of humans in a state of nature to obey only their own will and the obligation of citizens in an organized state to privilege the common will: "A body of men are politically capable of a public opinion only so far as they are agreed upon the ends and aims of government and upon the principles by which those ends shall be attained" (1913: 23).[5] The theory holds that representative democracies form this opinion through the ebb and flow of reasoned discussion within a literate and informed *public*. On the other hand, even if such a public of "politically capable" citizens be entirely theoretical, the position accorded public *opinion* by Mills's summary remains a central tenet of representative democracies, thereby raising questions about the ways in which we may come to know what that opinion is and the status it should be accorded.

These are not questions that rest gently on the minds of citizens or scholars of democratic processes, due largely to what public opinion has come to mean: the results of opinion polls. By stating that, I do not question the value of survey research or the utility of opinion polls. Rather I wish to underscore the way opinion polls *disconnect* public opinion from discourse. Opinion polls conceptualize public opinion in scientific terms as a naturally occurring phenomenon that can be observed and described quantitatively.[6] They depict public opinion as an objective datum that can be detected without attention to the processes of personal interactions producing it. As opinion researcher Leo Bogart asserts (cited in Yankelovich, 1991: 39), "The world of public opinion in today's sense really began with the Gallup polls of the mid-1930s, and it is impossible for us to retreat to the meaning of public opinion as it was understood by Thomas Jefferson in the eighteenth century, by Alexis de Tocqueville and Lord Bryce in the nineteenth,—or even by Walter Lippman [sic] in 1922." Poller Daniel Yankelovich (1991: 39) declares the apparent victory of survey research as the barometer of public sentiment with the terse observation, "It is a practical advantage . . . to accept the steadily growing assumption that public opinion in America is largely what public opinion polls measure."

The seeming disjunction between the vanishing presence of informed public discussion as the basis from which a reliable public opinion is formed and the reliance on public opinion to legitimate the state's actions has produced a series of calls for interventions that might produce a more enlightened body of citizen opinion on public problems. Working in the tradition of liberal democratic political theory, James Fishkin (1995) expresses concern for unmotivated citizens subjected to public discussion reduced to television sound bites. He calls for *deliberative polling* in which a national random sample of citizens would be taken to the same location and immersed in the issues, with carefully prepared briefing materials and intensive discussions. After several days of working together, they would be polled in detail. Fishkin maintains that the results would reflect "the considered judgments of the public— the views the entire country would come to if it had the same experience of behaving more like ideal citizens immersed in the issues for an extended period" (Fishkin, 1995: 162). As Fishkin notes, this poll would be neither descriptive nor predictive of public opinion, but prescriptive of the conclusions people would come to if they had the opportunity and motivation to examine issues closely.

Fellow political scientist John Dryzek (1990: 173-189), after excoriating survey research in political science for its "mismeasure" of voters, calls for reform through implementation of *Q-sort technique*, a survey research method on which to base a program of discursive democracy. In Q-sort technique, the subject is asked to order a series of statements from those s/he most agrees with through those regarded with indifference to those found most objectionable. The set of rankings, called a sort, ascribes meaning to the items within it exclusively through reference to the rankings of the other items. The advantage of Q-sort technique for survey research, in Dryzek's view, is that the researcher does not impose a preconstructed meaning on the subject. "The ordering a subject produces represents his or her own construction of a particular reality. . . . "[7] This improvement notwithstanding, Dryzek's proposed agenda does not examine the subject's own discourse but her response to the discourse of the research instrument.

Similarly, Yankelovich, after indicting the culture of technological control for its embrace of instrumental rationality, urges replacing public opinion as reported by traditional polling with *public judgment*, a state of mind that evolves through three stages of understanding a public problem: "consciousness raising," "working through," and "resolution." The marks of public judgment are stability, coherence, and recognition (1991: 234), which Yankelovich maintains "depends on creating the circumstances under which representative thinking[8] can thrive: a public space, genuine debate, freedom from manipulation and coercion, the articulation of choices and their consequences, opportunities for working through, the coordination of consciousness raising and 'choice work,' responsive political leadership offering incentives for the public to do the choice work, and so on" (1991: 233). Having established a strong link between such public thinking and discourse, and having argued for a discourse-based consensus as the foundation for concerted action, Yankelovich completely abandons examining discourse by asserting that we deduce the presence of public judgment from surveys designed to test the stability, coherence, and recognition of opinions (1991: 234).

Each of these proposals posits a prescription for ideal citizens. Moreover, although they propose to redeem the *discursive* center of public opinion, when they project how to infer this discursively formed opinion, they rely on the discourse of surveys rather than the rhetorical give and take of those participating in actually formed publics. None have considered the alternative of examining the admittedly complex but nonetheless available dialogizing interchange (Bakhtin, 1981) between official and vernacular rhetorics that form and reflect public opinion.

Scholars working in the tradition of social psychology attempt to overcome the absence of discourse from public opinion surveys by seeking patterns of cognition that permit inferences from survey data to the reasoning processes of the typical citizen. They locate the reasoning problems confronting citizens along those lines set forth by Walter Lippmann (1922/1949), when he argued that public problems were too numerous and too complex for the average person to have command of the relevant information, much less to comprehend. Shanto Iyengar and Donald R. Kinder (1987) find an account for how the general public manages this task in the sway of television news on political thinking. They found that television news broadcasting has powerful consequences for how people perceive their society. Television's selective emphasis on issues strongly influences *what* people regard as important and sets their agenda for public problems most worthy of their attention. Iyengar and Kinder also point to the powerful influence of television news on *how* people think about public problems. Television editing has the inevitable consequence of emphasizing certain aspects of a public problem while deemphasizing others. In this way television news powerfully influences the factors that come to mind when people think about the issues of the day. It exercises a priming effect on how its attending public thinks about the issues. Agenda-setting and priming, according to Iyengar and Kinder, have a decisive influence on "the priorities people attach to various national problems, and the considerations they take into account as they evaluate political leaders or choose between candidates for public office" (1987: 117). Opinion poller Samuel Popkin (1991: 9-17), equally concerned with the Lippmann problem, argues that most people exercise "low-information rationality." People do not have incentives of good citizenship to gather information. Their information gathering is more pragmatically oriented toward dealing with the practical problems of everyday life, which they later apply to their political problems and choices. He contends that people need someone to make the connection between their daily lives and the public problems addressed by government. Usually political leaders or authoritative media news figures provide this link.

These social psychological approaches to opinion formation are typical in bypassing the communication that occurs among citizens on burning issues of the day. They contend, instead, that if a person is paying attention to the mass media, and if leaders present the right kinds of messages, it is likely that this individual will be influenced to think in particular way, and further that we can infer this reasoning on public problems from survey data.

Without gainsaying the valuable contributions of this line of research, reasoning from individual responses to a survey instrument to the character of public opinion decouples public opinion from citizen interaction that lies at its heart. Opinion polls measure a psychological phenomenon—the individual's attitude and possible influences on it as reflected by the types of responses s/he gives to a survey instrument. Public opinion is something other than that. It is public reasoning exhibited when individuals engage in and are engaged by the give and take of the political public sphere. A shared tendency of understanding and judgment is more a cultural than an individual expression. We err, in my view, when we confuse what is momentarily popular among a dispersed population—what polls are able to measure quite accurately—with a phenomenon that is embedded in and presupposes the cultural practice of rhetoric. Consequently, of the many possible political worlds that can be and are brought about through the discursive nature of political relations, survey research projects only one: a political world in which the individual must choose sides among contesting forces. Dryzek concludes that in this world, the only rational choice is to choose the side that best advances one's interests, thereby making rationality consist exclusively of instrumental action.

I wish to emphasize that the problem with this deflection from discourse does not lie in whether inferences about public opinion can be drawn on the basis of numerical count. The idea of public opinion inherently involves a sensed assessment of the common mind. Historically this sensed assessment has been conceived as a question of an idea's relative strength among community members, which in some way has always required gauging the comparative size and strength of commit-ment among those who held this or that view (Boas, 1969; Herbst, 1993; Noelle-Neumann, 1993; Speier, 1950). Rather, the basic problem lies in a confusion between a sociology of science, as reflected in Bogart's previ-ously noted view that public opinion means what opinion polls report, and a philosophy of science, in which the status of a claim is determined by its ontological fidelity to the phenomenon it purports to describe.

This relationship of claim to ontological fidelity has been a prob-lem for opinion polling as an applied methodology almost from its out-set. The contest between the social determinism of Lazersfeld's Columbia group and the social psychologism of Miller's Michigan group resulted in a general consensus in Miller's favor. However, as Miller himself acknowledged, "we did not have any theory which argued that political behavior was any different from social or economic behavior" (cited in Dryzek, 1990: 162). The absence of such a distinction remains today, according to Dryzek (1990), and is significant because a democratic society makes important assumptions about the role of dis-course in establishing political relations.

Democratic politics, by definition, involves discussion among those in a polity. Presumably, their political decisions are open to conver-sations with neighbors, coworkers, and friends, as well as public deliber-ations of a more formal sort. These informal conversations and more institutionalized discussions, speeches, essays, and debates involve the individual in an array of interactions focused on locating and clarifying interests, weighing alternatives, and advancing reasons addressed to how we will act and interact. They place participants in relationships that involve the future shape of their shared world. Dryzek (1990) has advanced the telling observation that survey research is problematic for studying this phenomenon because it fails to account for the discursive process by which publics and public opinion emerge. Instead, it measures beliefs, attitudes, and opinions an individual is capable of holding about politics outside of and independent of political discussion or action.

In addition to ignoring political discussion or action in the mea-sure of political behavior, political pollers disagree over the potentially distorting influence that discourse might have on poll results. Whether looking at panels sampled in waves or in focus groups, involving partic-ipants in discussion can encourage otherwise disengaged individuals to act as if they are interested (Clausen, 1968). Dryzek (1990: 160) makes the point that the survey instrument assumes "an individual's beliefs, opin-ions, and attitudes about politics are invariant across the degree of action or inaction involved in a situation (though of course survey researchers are interested in how attitudes change with time and politi-cal history, e.g., between two waves of a panel survey)."

These psychological assumptions about individual behavior, based on individual attributes of attitude, belief, and opinion, neither take into account nor account for the discursive character of political behavior. Consequently, of the many possible political worlds that can be and are brought about through the discursive nature of political relations, survey research projects only one: a political world in which the individual must choose sides among contesting forces. Dryzek concludes that in this world, the only rational choice is to choose the side that best advances one's interests, thereby making rationality consist exclusively of instrumental action.

VERNACULAR RHETORIC AND PUBLIC OPINION

Characterizing public rationality exclusively in terms of instrumental action has consequences for our understanding of the nature and place of public opinion as providing direction and evaluation for public policy. This characterization ignores the mediating influence exercised by our awareness of mutual dependency. Rhetorical exchanges between individuals and groups who reject the authority of the other's assumptions are inherently dialogical. At the same time, realities of interdependence require a mode of response with efficacy for addressing common problems. This condition challenges the rhetoric of common ground, on which political consensus has always rested. Since at least the end of World War II cooperation among social and political actors, as well as official action, have increasingly required a nonjustificatory rhetoric— one emphasizing mutually acceptable outcomes for disparate stakeholders without seeking justification in shared a priori commitments. This is another way of saying that when tradition has been shattered, we make sense of what has occurred and what we now confront by reconstructing the past in a new story that is subject to constant revision and reinterpretation as the conversational partners change. The primary challenge of the political public sphere has become the constitution of discursive spaces that encourage and nurture a multilogue across their respective borders and from which civil judgments sustainable in multiple perspectives can emerge.

   The visions of public opinion as a rational ideal or as an objective datum impose epistemological assumptions that are insensitive to this multilogue and the civil judgments it supports. Even when these visions have given discourse thematic priority, they have buried rhetorical norms amidst the rationalism of ideal communication or the instrumentalism of degenerate manipulation (Farrell, 1993; Ginsberg, 1986; Habermas, 1969/1989; Mills, 1957, 1963). Neither characterization bears satisfactory fidelity to the complex process wherein public opinion[9] is formed and communicated. Neither accounts for the dialogical engagements by which an active populace participates in an issue's development; the contours of the public sphere that color their levels of awareness, perception, and participation; the influence on opinion formation of sharing views with one another; or the terms of expression warranting the inference that a *public* has formed and has a dominant *opinion*.

A *public* is, after all, a construct we employ to discuss those individuals who are actively weighing and shaping the course of society. We do not confront a public in the flesh, as we can an audience. Often its members are geographically dispersed and always they are largely strangers. When reference to "the public" is more than an empty synonym for the general populace or an unreflective expression of liberal democratic ideology, it has specificity only because concrete expressions of civil judgment—expressions of common understanding among diverse social actors that emerge from formal and vernacular exchanges enacted in and across public spheres—provide palpable evidence that a public has formed: outpourings of letters, debate, commentary, and conversation as occurred in the United States concerning the role of radical right-wing "talk radio" programs in encouraging acts like the April 1995 bombing of the Federal Building in Oklahoma City, in which 167 adults and children were killed; massive demonstrations of disbelief and anger as those in Los Angeles following the jury verdict to acquit members of the LAPD of criminal assault charges resulting from the video-recorded police-beating of Rodney King; public displays of grief, as occurred when England's Lady Diana Spencer was killed in a high-speed flight from paparazzi, followed by the media-assembled montage of remonstrance directed at Great Britain's royal family for its seeming aloofness from the tragedy and failure to console its subjects; or voluntary cooperation with economic sanctions as occurred when American consumers reduced gasoline consumption in support of the Carter Administration's reprisals against Iran for holding fifty-two of its citizens hostage; or even unofficial but widespread boycotts, as occurred in the United States during the spring of 1995 when the new baseball season was played before largely empty stadiums, following a long and acrimonious strike in which millionaire owners and millionaire players appeared consumed with their own avariciousness by bickering over money.

As these examples suggest, the objects of attention susceptible to vernacular exchange range from affairs of state to cultural forms and icons. These exchanges are rarely of the type we associate with formal public address. More often they are vernacular expressions of opinion, uttered in conversations, written in letters to officials or the community, expressed by mass gatherings, economic boycotts, or other forms of symbolic inducement that indicate lived experience, preference, and degree of solidarity on the community's issues. Such expressions can coalesce to reflect a common judgment shared among disparate participants in society's dispersed public conversation.

A conceptual model based on actual discursive practice promises a different account of public opinion than do models that emphasize rational deliberation or opinion polling. Its differences suggest we can find valuable information for our understanding of the relationship between discourse and opinion by monitoring actual interactions on public problems, including the relationship between the quality of public opinion and the terms by which and under which members of a public discuss their interests. Such a model emphasizes a different rationality from the idealized mode of liberal democracy or the means-ends logic of instrumentalism and objectivism; it accentuates the practical reasoning (Farrell, 1993; Fisher, 1978, 1980; Gottlieb, 1968; Nussbaum, 1986; Wallace, 1963) endemic in the use of symbols to coordinate social action, or *rhetoric*. In addition, consonant with an understanding of complex societies as containing a plurality of publics and public spheres, it abandons conceptualizing *the* public as an entity with continuous existence whose function is to legitimize all public matters. Instead, a rhetorical model's sensitivity to the processual character of discursive formations shifts our conceptual focus to the formation of *publics* (Hauser, 1985). It stresses their organic cycles of emergence and decline mirrored in the particularized and processual developments of everyday rhetorical exchanges. These exchanges modulate as circumstances and issues engage the active attention of significant segments of society (Hauser and Blair, 1982). Further, it distinguishes publics from special interest groups. A vernacular rhetoric model italicizes the discursive endeavors of those whose symbolic formations authorize public acts and conduct taken in their name (Bitzer, 1978). Repositioning discourse at the center of public opinion promises rich possibilities for divulging *public* opinion, understanding its formation, and interpreting its meaning. Finally, centering society's ongoing conversation within the domain of forming and expressing public opinion refocuses attention on praxis, at once more complex, but more faithful to the practices of actors themselves. The vernacular rhetoric model of public opinion I am proposing encourages active analysis of this broader range of expression.

The conditions of emphasis I have outlined return to the origins of public opinion by locating it in civil society's discursive interactions. Civil society's network of associations constitutes a zone of interaction between the authority of the state and the privacy of the family. Public opinion emerges from these discursive exchanges that balance conflict and consensus in ways consistent with a valuation of difference and serves as a self-regulating mechanism on those who participate in civil society's public life.

To access and understand public opinion as a discursive formation requires greater attention to the social dialogue between official voices and everyday interactions of citizens engaged by a public problem. Certainly there is considerable evidence to suggest that leaders exert influence on what their followers think, such as in the studies by Iyengar and Kinder and by Popkin cited earlier. On the other hand, attending exclusively to the discourse of leaders focuses on reasons for acting that may not be shared by the people themselves. Free societies are alive with exhortations that appear in everyday symbolic exchanges on factory floors and in university lecture halls, in letters to the editor and to elected officials, in partisan exchanges of preferences through signs of affiliation, speeches in civic forums, economic actions of support or opposition, interviews disseminated through the media, and more. These expressions declare the range and intensity of civic conversation on the issues confronting a community. Within the associations of civil society, these expressions of preference become that society's means for political learning and political self-regulation. Recognizing and responding to differences is a self-monitoring discursive practice that goes beyond numerical weight. Vernacular social discourse is an index of political opinion; such popular reasoning embeds political opinion in narratives that intersect issues with people's lives.

CIVIC CONVERSATION AND POLITICAL LEARNING

I began this discussion by suggesting that a democracy requires public opinion for guidance and judgment, and that before citizens can engage in democratic practices they must acquire skills for living in a milieu of difference. I wish to return to this point to suggest that the exchanges of civil society are a significant source of such instruction. For this reason, these exchanges recommend themselves for critical inspection both as a resource for understanding discursive dimensions of public opinion and as a source of knowledge on how to achieve civic community.

By participating in civil society people acquire a sense of the range of difference and the mediating grounds of similarity that make it possible for them to form a civic community based on relations of collaboration. Civic community does not require that citizens think alike, or even that they subscribe to views that underwrite consensus. Consensus, in fact, is not to be expected when issues inflame partisan biases and alternative historicities (Taylor, 1971; Touraine, 1981). However, civic community does require citizens who are capable of participating in the deliberative interactions of civic conversation and who trust this conversation to prove consequential for policies eventually enacted in response to public problems.

Civic conversation contains empirical evidence of the political learning process inherent to a democracy and, thereby, redeems the epistemological relevance of public opinion. My observation is not entirely new. Nearly seventy-five years ago John Dewey (1927/1954) argued that majority rule merely for the sake of majority rule is foolish. More important than locating a majority is determining the means by which it became a majority (ibid.: 207). For Dewey, these were the means of political learning and they were grounded in communication. Political learning required something other than technical presentation. "The essential need," he wrote, "is the improvement of the methods and conditions of debate, discussion and persuasion. That is the problem of the public" (ibid.: 208).

Obviously full and accurate information is essential for competent public opinion to form. However, Dewey's insight that *political learning* rests less on increased information than on critical publicity underscores the instructive role of civic conversation in teaching us how to engage in acts of self-regulation without resorting to force or autocratic means for dealing with difference (McKeon, 1957). Attending to public arguments of leaders and participating in the vernacular exchanges of civic conversation is a democracy's mode of continuous political education.

Participating in civic conversation itself requires learning how to participate in the type of engagement called for in the works of Fishkin, Dryzek, and Yankelovich noted earlier. However, before we can have a productive conversation with difference we first must overcome the menace of difference that provokes distrust and the antidemocratic rhetoric of intolerance, or cynicism and withdrawal from the political process. For democracy to be a functional form of governance in a society of strangers, citizens must learn how to engage difference in a way that recognizes the individual and the group as a subject (Touraine, 1997).

Political learning is a form of *social capital*,[10] a mode of wealth, on analogy with physical property, that serves as a medium of exchange among social actors. Robert Putnam (1995: 67) defines it as "[the] features of social organization such as networks, norms, and social trust that facilitate coordination and cooperation for mutual benefit." Much as the health of an economy as a whole and the prosperity of its individual members are reciprocally related, with each enriching the other, social capital serves to vitalize civil society and its member. By participating in civil society's culture of rhetoric, citizens learn modes of understanding and interaction that make civic community possible. This culture teaches us how to engage difference performatively as other than threatening;

by enacting discursive transactions that establish trust among those with whom we are interdependent, we sustain relations of collaboration. These are exchanges that, in some fundamental way, must have a basis in mutual respect.

I wish to underscore, in this regard, that modeling public opinion as an inference extrapolated from the vernacular rhetoric of civic conversation does not require returning to the *civitas* of civic virtue or doom us to despair over the fracturing consequences of an invidious individualism. The model of civil society—a society that is self-regulating, a society that centers on the natural inclination of humans to pursue their interests, a society of strangers, a society with civility at its moral core—is predicated on the exchanges that occur within its network of associations. These places, these discursive spheres, these rhetorical arenas, are the sites where strangers encounter difference, learn of the other's interests, develop understanding of where there are common goals, and where they may develop the social capital of trust necessary for them to function in world of mutual dependency.

Robert Putnam's (1993a) investigation of regional governments in Italy, *Making Democracy Work*, provides an apt illustration of how such bonds are established. Putnam studied these regional governments from their inception in 1970. His data spans twenty years and shows patterns that conform to the ideals at the heart of civil society. Putnam found a positive correlation between participation in associations and civic involvement. People who belonged to sports clubs, singing societies, literary guilds, philanthropic groups, commercial associations, or clubs of any sort, also showed a greater tendency to participate in the civic affairs of the region. The relationship between joining groups and political participation had nothing to do with membership in a political party or participation in a political organization. Rather, the positive correlation was with participation in a community activity that gathers citizens who otherwise would had no reason to congregate.[11] As Putnam (1993a: 90) notes, a person who participates in secondary associations is more likely to develop skills in social cooperation as well as a sense of responsibility for collective enterprises.

Those with a sense of collective responsibility exhibited accompanying traits. They tended to read the newspaper more frequently. Their consequent higher levels of information on public problems encouraged them to enter into discussions of these problems more commonly than Italians living in regions with a low level of civic involvement. They also tended to vote in higher numbers on referenda. When deciding how to vote, they tended to confer with fellow citizens, rather than their representatives. They tended to organize themselves horizontally rather than vertically with respect to political representatives.

Citizens in civic communities did not contact their representatives as frequently as those in noncivic ones, and when they did make contact, it was to discuss policy rather than patronage. Equally, Putnam found that leaders in regions where there is a civic community tended to support grass roots participation, were relatively honest, and were predisposed to compromise with their political adversaries.

Putnam's study highlights how the associative bonds of citizens who constitute themselves as a civic community place confidence in fellow citizens rather than a political leader to assist in addressing their needs. They develop trust in their fellow citizens to obey laws, to act responsibly, and to exhibit sensitivity to legitimate needs, even in communities where economic, educational, social, and political differentiation are high. In sum, these communities value solidarity, civic engagement, cooperation, and honesty (Putnam, 1993a: 82-120).

Putnam's study illustrates how individuals participating in civil society's network of associations learn about strangers and, in the process, learn how to participate in a democracy. As strangers interact in a common context, although not necessarily tied to civic concerns, they acquire and spend social capital. They develop bonds of affiliation and levels of trust necessary for them to engage in the give and take of the community's public spheres. The give and take of this civic conversation is the caldron in which public opinion brews. Participation in it requires skill at producing and interpreting the vernacular rhetoric by which we conduct our public transactions with strangers: the everyday micropractices that reflect values, aspirations, concerns, affiliations, boundaries of acceptance, levels of tolerance, and the like that shape our civil judgments. These quotidian exchanges provide an understanding of those we are dealing with and where our interests coincide or diverge. Their *vernacular* quality reflects the possibilities for continuous exchange of social capital that can assure strangers that they share a common world. Vernacular rhetoric offers valuable lessons about participating in democracy's ongoing negotiation over how we shall act and interact (Bourdieu, 1990; Hauser, 1999). Vernacular rhetoric is the individual's method for monitoring public opinion and learning how to participate in its formation. Studying these exchanges promises insight into the character of public opinion beyond what the results of an opinion poll can offer.

ENDNOTES

1. During the democracy at Athens, the *ekklesia* was the Assembly of every male citizen who had been accepted as legitimate by his *deme* or a political division of ancient Attica. This Assembly would,

therefore, be a mass meeting of every enfranchised male. It was the sole legislative body and had authority, in many ways, over the Athenian administration and judicature.

2. I use the masculine pronoun when referring to political life in ancient Athens to reflect the fact that males alone were able to participate in its political processes. Apart from these references, use of masculine or feminine pronouns that do not refer to a specific person are random.

3. The *demos* refers to the people as a whole.

4. In this vein, de Coulanges (1956: 219) recounts the story of Nicias, who was celebrated as a brave and crafty general, but whose fleet was destroyed by the army of Syracuse after he failed to retreat on the advice of his diviner. Retreat by land also was impossible and neither he nor any of his soldiers was able to escape. When Athenians heard news of the disaster they did not blame Nicias for cowardice, knowing his bravery, nor for following the dictates of his religion in abiding by the advice of his diviner. They reproached him only for having taken with him an ignorant diviner who misread the eclipse of the moon and what it meant for military action. Their reading of this event was in keeping with their cultural belief in signs and the value they placed on acting with constancy based on their interpretation.

5. See Robert Nisbet (1975: 166-192), for a representative projection of Lowell's position into the context of late-twentieth-century challenges to liberal democratic theory.

6. This tradition received its impetus in the studies of the 1940 election by Lazarsfeld and his group (Lazarsfeld, Berelson, and Gaudet, 1944/1968). Its development from then until now has resulted in highly sophisticated techniques of survey measurement. What these measures mean is, however, a matter of considerable dispute, even within the polling community. See Bordieu (1979), Dryzek (1990), Ginsberg (1986), Habermas (1969/1989), Herbst (1993), Noelle-Neumann (1993), Popkin (1991), and D. G. Taylor (1986) for a sample of this range.

7. Dryzek (1990) offers this account of the difference between the generalizations generated by opinion research and by Q technique: "Opinion researchers make general statements such as 'vote choice in England is more affected by religion than by social class' or '50 percent of the population identifies with a political party.' Generalizations in Q take the form 'the environmental factor found in our Q study of Antarctica represents the orientation of a larger number of individuals concerned with Antarctica'; but we cannot determine the size of this larger group, in absolute terms or relative to the size of the other groups."

8. "Representative thinking" is a concept developed by Hannah Arendt to account for arriving at judgment. In representative thinking the individual attempts to think about the problem

through the perspective of a series of involved others. Through this mode of analysis, he arrives at a deeper understanding of the problem than would be possible from his own stance and is in a better position to arrive at an informed judgment. See Arendt, 1977: 241.

9. I am distinguishing public opinion from mass opinion (Mills, 1963) and popular opinion (Nisbet, 1975).

10. Primary development of the concept of *social capital* is credited to James S. Coleman (1988). See also Putnam (1993b, 1995, 1996).

11. The lone exception to this pattern was membership in Catholic church organizations which, given the church's traditional institutional authority in Italy, carries ideological meaning that tends to encourage a political stance with strong allegiance to the church's.

REFERENCES:

Arendt, Hannah. 1977. *Between Past and Future*. Baltimore: Penguin Books.

Bakhtin, Mikhail M. 1981. *The Dialogic Imagination: Four Essays*. Ed. M. Holquist, Trans. C. Emerson and M. Holquist. Austin: University of Texas Press.

Bitzer, Lloyd F. 1978. Rhetoric and Public Knowledge. In D. M. Burks (ed.), *Rhetoric, Philosophy and Literature: An Exploration*, 67-95. West Lafayette, IN: Purdue University Press.

Boas, George. 1969. *Vox Populi: Essays in the History of an Idea*. Baltimore: Johns Hopkins University Press.

Bourdieu, Pierre. 1979. Public Opinion Does Not Exist. In A. Mattelart and S. Siegelaub (eds.), *Communication and Class Struggle*, 124-30. New York: Bagnolet.

Bourdieu, Pierre. 1990. *The Logic of Practice*. Stanford, CA: Stanford University Press.

Clausen, Aage. 1968. Response Validity: Vote Report. *Public Opinion Quarterly* 32, 588-606.

Coleman, James S. 1988. Social Capital in the Creation of Human Capital. *American Journal of Sociology (Supplement)* 94, S95-S120.

de Coulanges, N. D. Fustel. 1873/1956. The Ancient City. Trans. W. Small. New York: Doubleday Anchor.

Dewey, John. 1927/1954. *The Public and its Problems*. Chicago: Swallow Press.

Dryzek, John S. 1990. *Discursive Democracy: Politics, Policy, and Political Science*. New York: Cambridge University Press.

Farrell, Thomas B. 1993. *Norms of Rhetorical Culture*. New Haven, CT: Yale University Press.

Fisher, Walter R. 1978. Toward a Logic of Good Reasons. *Quarterly Journal of Speech* 64, 376-84.

Fisher, Walter R. 1980. Rationality and the Logic of Good Reasons. *Philosophy and Rhetoric* 13, 122-25.

Fishkin, James. 1995. *The Voice of the People*. New Haven, CT: Yale University Press.

Ginsberg, Benjamin. 1986. *The Captive Public*. New York: Basic Books.

Gottlieb, Gidon. 1968. *The Logic of Choice*. New York: Macmillan Press.

Habermas, Jürgen. 1969/1989. *The Structural Transformation of the Public Sphere*. Trans. T. Burger, with the assistance of F. Lawrence. Cambridge, MA: MIT Press.

Hauser, Gerard A. 1985. Common Sense in the Public Sphere: A Rhetorical Grounding for Publics. *Informatologia Yugoslavica* 17, 67-75.

Hauser, Gerard A. 1998a. Civil Society and the Principle of the Public Sphere. *Philosophy and Rhetoric* 31, 19-40.

Hauser, Gerard A. 1998b. Vernacular Dialogue and the Rhetoricality of Public Opinion. *Communication Monographs* 65, 83-107.

Hauser, Gerard A. 1999. *Vernacular Voices: The Rhetoric of Publics and Public Spheres*. Columbia: University of South Carolina Press.

Hauser, Gerard A. and C. Blair. 1982. Rhetorical Antecedents to the Public. *Pre/Text* 3, 139-67.

Herbst, Susan. 1993. *Numbered Voices: How Opinion Polling Has Shaped American Politics*. Chicago: University of Chicago Press.

Hirschman, Albert O. 1977/1997. *The Passions and the Interests*. Princeton, NJ: Princeton University Press.

Iyengar, Shanto and Donald R. Kinder. 1987. *News That Matters*. Chicago: University of Chicago Press.

Lazarsfeld, Paul F., Bernard Berelson, and Hazel Gaudet. 1944/1968. *The People's Choice: How the Voter Makes up His Mind in a Presidential Election*. 3rd ed. New York: Columbia University Press.

Lippmann, Walter. 1922/1949. *Public Opinion*. New York: Free Press.

Lowell, A. Lawrence. 1913. *Public Opinion and Popular Government*. New York: Longmans Green.

McGee, Michale Calvin. 1975. In Search of "the People": A Rhetorical Alternative. *Quarterly Journal of Speech* 65, 235-49.

McKeon, Richard. 1957. Communication, Truth, and Society. *Ethics* 67, 89-99.

Mills, C. Wright. 1957. *The Power Elite*. New York: Oxford University Press.

Mills, C. Wright. 1963. *Power, Politics, and People*. I. Horowitz (ed.). New York: Oxford University Press.

Nisbet, Robert. 1975. Public Opinion Versus Popular Opinion. *Public Interest* 41, 166-192.

Noelle-Neumann, Elisabeth. 1993. *The Spiral of Silence: Public Opinion— Our Social Skin* (2nd ed.). Chicago: University of Chicago Press.

Nussbaum, Martha C. 1986. *The Fragility of Goodness*. New York: Cambridge University Press.

Popkin, Samuel. 1991. *The Reasoning Voter: Communication and Persuasion in Presidential Campaigns*. Chicago: University of Chicago Press.

Putnam, Robert D. 1993a. *Making Democracy Work*. Princeton: Princeton University Press.

Putnam, Robert D. 1993b. The Prosperous Community: Social Capital and Public Life. *American Prospect* 13, 35-42.

Putnam, Robert D. 1995. Bowling Alone: America's Declining Social Capital. *Journal of Democracy* 6, 65-78.

Putnam, Robert D. 1996. The Strange Disappearance of Civic America. [On-line]. *The American Prospect* 24. (Available: [http://epn.org/prospect/24/24putn.html]).

Seligman, Adam B. 1995. Animadversions Upon Civil Society and Civic Virtue in the Last Decade of the Twentieth Century. In J. A. Hall (ed.), *Civil Society: Theory, History, Comparison* (pp. 200-223). Cambridge: Polity.

Sennett, Richard. 1978. *The Fall of Public Man*. New York: Vintage.

Speier, Hans. 1950. Historical Development of Public Opinion. *American Journal of Sociology* 55, 376-388.

Taylor, Charles. 1971. Interpretation and the Sciences of Man. *Review of Metaphysics* 25, 3-51.

Taylor, Charles. 1995. *Philosophical Arguments*. Cambridge, MA: Harvard University Press.

Taylor, D. Garth. 1986. *Public Opinion and Collective Action: The Boston School Desegregation Conflict*. Chicago: University of Chicago Press.

Touraine, Alain. 1981. *The Voice and the Eye: An Analysis of Social Movements*. Trans. A. Duff. Cambridge: Cambridge University Press.

Touraine, Alain. 1997. *What is Democracy*. Trans. D. Macey. Boulder, CO: Westview.

Wallace, Carl. 1963. The Substance of Rhetoric: Good Reasons. *Quarterly Journal of Speech* 49, 239-49.

Yankelovich, Daniel. 1991. *Coming to Public Judgment: Making Democracy Work in a Complex World*. Syracuse, NY: Syracuse University Press.

II

NEW HISTORICAL EVIDENCES

8

Public Opinion and Postmodern Populism: A Crisis of Democracy or the Transformation of Democratic Governance?

Barrie Axford and Richard Huggins

In this chapter we will examine some salient features of the structuration of public opinion in political systems increasingly characterized by "postmodern populism" (Axford and Huggins, 1997). Although they are now modal, such features are often discussed only as symptomatic of a crisis in democratic institutions and practices. For example, it is a commonplace that governments rely increasingly upon public relations and the strategic monitoring of public opinion as part of a routine and technically sophisticated exercise in the management of their own visibility, and as a way of providing bespoke information for possible changes in demeanor and policy. For critics, the problem with this style of political communication is that it is highly self-referential and rhetorical. What used to reek of danger, because of the vagaries of the law of anticipated reaction, or at least held out the promise of accountability, has turned into a routine exercise in spinning, marketing, and demand management. Deluged with reports, figures and predictions, dazed by the welter of leaks, "prebuttals" and rebuttals, and romanced by vague promises of "empowerment," the public is either rendered supine, or capable only of playing back a mirror image of the official line. At best, even where some kind of deliberation is involved, the public are only "judicious spectators"; at worst, public opinion is just an "echo chamber," as V. O. Key, Jr., put it (1964: 557). In either case the democratic process and the quality of democratic life suffer as a result.

In what follows we will put forward a more nuanced reading of the potential threats to and opportunities for democratic governance that lie in different ways of structuring public talk, mainly by using recent evidence from changes in United Kingdom politics and making some mention of developments elsewhere. We will distinguish between mechanisms of "direct" democracy and more "deliberative" forms of public discourse, and also draw attention to the fashionable motif of "open government" with its apparent endorsement of a more informed and active citizenry. By distinguishing between these categories it may be possible to identify whether different practices are contributing to a reshaping of democratic governance and civic agency or are just part of a more elaborate exercise in symbolic politics and symptoms of a democratic malaise. But even this antinomy is too blunt for our purposes, because the messier truth is that both outcomes may subsist at the same time, because (1) in quotidian reality actions and processes have unintended as well as intended consequences, and (2) what many commentators dismiss as a marketing model of politics is an integral part of a transformation of political life in mediatized cultures. As Castells argues (1996: 476), all politics is now conducted in the frame of media and this "has profound consequences for the characteristics, organisation, and even the goals of the political process." At this point in the discussion it would be wrong to foreclose on the range of possible interpretations and outcomes. Thus the self-styled modernizing thrust of the Blair government in the United Kingdom, with its passion for announcing "great debates" on matters ranging from welfare reform to drug abuse; Bill Clinton's commitment to a trans-Atlantic "Third Way"; any number of experiments in civic innovation; even the sea change in the conduct of Italian elections and party politics inaugurated by Silvio Berlusconi in 1994 could be taken as paradigms for a transformation of modern politics, rather than just symbolic flourishes or cynical attempts at the manipulation of public opinion.

We will place the debates about political communication and public opinion in the context of a putative transformation of political modernity, where that refers both to the institutional forms and discursive practices of liberal democracies and to the cultural and philosophical baggage that attends these. In particular we will offer some thoughts on the extent to which more discursive forms of populism—whether "top-down" or "bottom-up"—which we take to be characteristic of this transformation, simply enlarge the public sphere by expanding the number of actors or are transforming it, and whether they can be seen as forces for emancipation (Dryzek, 1990: 22). Doing this allows us to evaluate the democratic potential of what we diagnose as postmodern populism, and it also serves to shift the terms of debate beyond questions of mere governing style, and the tendency to construe all developments in the complex structuration of public opinion as a sophisticated political display. This is a hard injunction to observe given the strong and enduring impression of the Blair government in particular as obsessed with image and with rebranding as part of new Labour's faux-chic and metropolitan vision of modernity. New Labour's message to the British electorate in the run-up to the general election in 1997 was that it would not be like previous governments, including those of its own party. Once in office Blair's vision "of a nation that is confident, creative, open and hungry to learn" was spun through mission statements and celebrity get-togethers at Downing Street, symbolized in a glut of official logos and slogans ("new" Labour, of course; "cool" Britannia; "the giving society") and pursued through an army of policy-review groups and people's panels. Without any sense of irony and with lamentably short memories, the Tory opposition was forced to remind Blair that "a government is not an advertising agency."

Political knockabout aside, this Tory reproof is at one with a pervasive, though often confusing interpretation of events, wherein the marketing model of governance is portrayed both as the leitmotif of modernization and as signifying the decline or even the end of (real) politics. There is also a further twist. For the most part the marketing model of politics is reduced to little more than an ensemble of techniques, including the clip-on tools of opinion-polling, "permanent" campaigning, and the systematic wooing of niche audiences. Having reduced political change to a matter of the implementation of smart technologies and the cynical use and misuse of different forms of media by politicians and their cohorts, it is easy to gloss over more sociologically astute questions about the role of cultural forces and new technologies in the transformation of politics and democracy. So the modernizing/declinist antinomy remains the dominant intellectual motif in discussions of political change and the putative crisis of democracy, but it is pure "a-priorism." In order to contextualize our argument we will outline the concept of postmodern populism and indicate why it is important not to foreclose on judgments about the nature of the transformations now in train.

POSTMODERN POPULISM AND THE TRANSFORMATION OF POLITICAL MODERNITY

To reiterate; much of the discussion of recent political trends paints a picture of modern institutions and practices being traduced by a politics in which the ideology of the market is pervasive, and in which promotional techniques are replacing more conventional forms of political brokerage and representation. To be sure, the public are invited to participate in the processes of debate and consultation—their input being trumpeted as more authentic than the machinations of politicians and parties or divers experts who are obsessed with power and interests—but in reality the populist feel of the new politics is vitiated by a more thoroughgoing commitment to control and to the tight management of change. In this milieu, governing more than ever becomes a massive public relations exercise, but a function that is often reactive because of its concern to be in sync with opinion it has already tried to gloss.

Marketing and the management of visibility are key aspects of postmodern populism. Other features include the appearance of what are now called "media" parties, which are leader-dominated; the conflation of public and private discourses and domains, and a profusion of seemingly populist devices/discursive procedures to enable more routine contact between citizens and government. At the same time, postmodern populism displays an increasingly robust vein of politics "from below" in the form of social movements, single-issue protest groups and protest "parties," and in the host of civic organizations concerned with democratic renewal, civic innovation, and forms of networking. Some of these features may not be compatible with others, nor with the standard model of liberal politics onto which they are grafted, but it is important to assess their transformative potential, and not to treat them simply as uncomfortable deviations from the democratic norm. To do this we must begin by situating the features of postmodern populism in broad social, political, and, above all, cultural currents.

To start with, all the developments noted above have either emerged or grown more pronounced in cultures that are thoroughly mediatized. Mediatized cultures are characterized by promotional discourses, the aestheticization of social and political life, and by the dominance of image. In media cultures, as Castells says (1996: 476), all cultural expressions and many of those involving power relations are now mediated by electronic communications, and politics operates in the "space of media." Promotion lies at the center of the political process, and image-making and breaking are key facets of the exercise of power. We should be wary of reducing these shifts simply to matters of style, treating them as "ephemera" that compare unfavorably with the visceral substance of politics and the meat of policy. In mediatized cultures the usual separation of form from content is increasingly meaningless. Style is not just a slick veneer buffed by the many p.r. and media professionals who bolster leaderships, but an expression of what all politics has become. Although it is all right to feel badly about this, it is no more than nostalgic to believe that it masks a more authentic or elemental discourse. This may be very postmodern, but the more pressing issue is whether a politics thus configured can supply sufficient resources and outlets for reflexivity and discursiveness, or, to borrow from Arendt (1998), anything resembling public spaces of appearance (though in postmodern populism the latter may perchance be virtual) in which speech and action are instantiated, and narrative enacts a world that is made and remade reflexively.

Second, for postmodern politics to be in any way emancipatory, it must promote reflexivity in the relationships between actors and the conditions for action; the problem is how? Modernizing processes augment the ability of agents to interpret and reinterpret the world around them in conditions of growing risk and uncertainty (Beck, 1996; Giddens, 1990). The greater contingency of lifestyles under postmodern conditions of irreducible pluralism carries with it the prospects both for greater reflexivity and for regression in the form of longing for a simpler lifestyle and the politics to match. In the world today there is no shortage of political formulas that promise security and/or redemption, but at the expense of reflexivity and of rationality. In principle, deliberative procedures hold out the promise of greater reflexivity and rationality achieved through the discursive process. The ideal deliberative forum prescribes "free and unconstrained public deliberation of all matters about common concern" (Benhabib, 1996: 68), but questions must remain as to whether such a prescription could be realized in any and all of the key institutions of a pluralistic, democratic system, and where, if at all, deliberative processes articulate with other means of collective decision-making and authoritative value allocation. One possible answer to these questions is to distinguish between types of deliberative procedures and between their extant functions, as being more-or-less reflexive, and we will take this up later in the chapter. There is also the question of what happens when support for deliberation as a procedural and strategic principle runs up against substantive principles or worldviews (of, for example party leaders or government ministers) that might be challenged in the process of deliberation itself (Guttman and Thompson, 1996).

Third, postmodern populism denotes a politics that is, in some respects, more anodyne, but also more complicated and frenetic than the previous categoric split between left and right. However, claims that the effective sealing of this divide at the putative "end of History" leaves only a single global geoculture do less than justice to the disordered and fragmented state of world politics and of politics within many national societies. Even within the "posthistorical" core of the global system, a politics based on identity, difference, and lifestyle—a new pluralism—is challenging assumptions about the fabric and the purpose of political action, the boundaries of the political (McLennan, 1995) and rationalist conceptions—grand narratives if you like—of society and politics (Guttman and Thompson, 1996). Now, this postmodern politics (nowhere fully realized) is certainly clamorous, but is it democratic? (Ridley and Jordan, 1998).

McLennan says that the anticategorical and antirepresentational flavor of postmodernism run up against the "imaginary presuppositions" of democracy itself (1995: 93). He means liberal, representative democracy, but the reasoning could be extended to include models that advocate a public life of deliberation, and that trade on the image of a consensual public sphere. The problem for both models is that the very idea of a demos, or of a collective identity known as "the people," is subverted by a postmodern politics and this must have consequences for the Blairite metanarrative of a progressive or new politics grounded in consensus, albeit a managed consensus. Of course in practice what we have labeled postmodern populism is bound to be an uneasy mix of philosophies and styles and a de facto accommodation between the universalist, individualist legacy of liberalism and the demands of a diverse and sometimes essentialist politics based on identity and difference (Benhabib, 1996). Attempts to supersede the dominant liberal paradigm in the shape of an institutionalized, radical pluralism and direct participatory and deliberative structures are often grafted on to the shards of older institutions in an attempt to marry the goals of difference, individuality, community, representation, and harmony to produce a workable public life. Of course, there may be no other way.

"NEW" LABOUR, MODERNIZATION, AND DEMOCRACY

Following the resignation of Peter Mandelson, the British Trade and Industry Secretary and sometime "Prince of Darkness," in the days before Christmas 1998, the style of government that he epitomized came under a good deal of scrutiny. For many observers and not a few Labour activists, the character of new Labour , and particularly the Blairite penchant for "modernization" as the means to symbolize and to realize "a new kind of politics" is conveniently, if somewhat contentiously, summarized as follows: a "modernised" politics shuns the rancorous conflict of left and right and seeks a mysterious middle course on all major issues (Giddens, 1994, 1998). A modernized politics means sidelining the apparatus and at least some of the functions performed by a mass party in a representative democracy, including the articulation of societal goals and values, elite recruitment, representation, and interest aggregation. It also involves downplaying the role of parliament, if not as a formally representative institution, then as a sounding board for mediated public opinion and the major forum in which government both communicates with and is held accountable to the public. Instead, this new style of government is said to rely heavily upon mechanisms that directly connect government to people: focus groups, road shows, citizens juries, people's panels, referendums, deliberative polling, and, of course, the Internet. In addition it is enamored of and, for the most part, well practiced in the arts of Doctor Spin and of public relations. In its commitment to the strategic monitoring of public opinion, both raw and—through the use of qualitative techniques—increasingly nuanced, new Labour has indeed fashioned a sophisticated marketing model of politics. Government looks to speak to citizens (conveniently amorphized as "the people") over the heads of narrow interests, party ideologues and hacks, and those nostalgic for one or other version of the socialist past. The realities, of course, are rather more inchoate.

As we have suggested there are different ways of looking at these developments or trends, each carrying its own normative burden. Writing in the recent, one-off issue of *Marxism Today* (November, 1998), Stuart Hall draws what some will find a sinister conclusion, namely that new Labour finds the rituals of indirect democracy tiresome, and that they would feel more untrammelled, better able to push forward with the vision of Blair's "Third Way," under a more direct, referendum style of governance. The same calumny attached to Silvio Berlusconi's flirtation with a videocracy in Italy after the 1994 general election, as a means of informing and communing with the Italian people, and there are some parallels between the two, not least their devotion to a "charismatic-managerialist" form of leadership. In this pathological version of the Blairite project, democracy commutes to a neoplebiscitary enterprise, but with a nice line in consultation. If this is too cynical, it might still leave the attempts to engage citizens directly in the processes of (limited) decision-making as no more than procedural, a convenient adjunct to liberal and "thinner" forms of citizenship, whose value has been reduced already by the erosion of representative institutions. The high-sounding rhetoric of the Blair government with the emphasis on "thicker," more collective forms of participation—through deliberative procedures and associative or stakeholder mechanisms—suggests otherwise, but, as always, the proof of the pudding is in the eating (Hirst, 1994; Hutton, 1998).

Although there is a great deal of concern with the inadequacies of the "thinner" conception of citizenship and democracy espoused by conventional liberal theory (Boyte and Kari, 1996), most critics who counsel the need for deliberative expressions of public opinion still remain cautious about the "near fatal attraction" with marginally "thicker" forms of direct democracy. This caution is born of designer anxieties about the allegedly depleted capacity of citizens for informed deliberation and choice, and about the populist simplification of decision-making though opinion polls, talk show democracy, and (in the United States) even direct primaries (Putnam, 1995). Interestingly, given our earlier references to the factors underlying the growth of postmodern populism, one strand of opposition reveals a continued Madisonian faith in the efficacy of deliberation by informed elites and an implicit challenge to the ascendancy of the direct-majoritarian version of democracy that has been dominant in the United States since the nineteenth century. Speaking in the first week of January 1999 about the impending trial of President Clinton by the U.S. Senate, the Director of Communications for the Republican Party was moved to condemn out of hand the dangers of government by public opinion. His mild polemic was occasioned by a piece of journalistic throw-away in which the awesome unfolding of the impeachment process and the breast-beating of many Washington politicians was contrasted with the ennui characteristic of public reaction to the spectacle and the generally high approval ratings that the beleaguered president continued to enjoy. On reflection this view may owe more to Walter Lippmann's strictures on the importance of keeping the public out of critical debates and decision-making than to Madison. Pandering to the masses, said Lippmann (1955: 20), created a "morbid derangement of government"; populists beware.

Constitutional proprieties apart, this argument has a certain ascetic appeal, especially if one can dispense with the feeling that at least some of the denizens of Capitol Hill were exercised by considerations of power and interest, or possibly prurience, rather than the public good, or, indeed, by a commitment to purposive deliberation. However, it does leave ordinary citizens as mere gazers at the feast, and by limiting the role of the public to that of spectators, separates public opinion—by this definition, fickle, uninformed, and easily manipulated—from that much rarer commodity, public judgment or practical wisdom, which remains the rightful province of accountable elites (Yankelovich and Destler, 1991). Whereas the separation of expressive, informed debate by citizens from purposive or policy-relevant action in deliberative forums is acceptable as an analytical distinction, it may have undesirable practical consequences. For example, Jürgen Habermas (1992, 1997) insists on a conceptual separation of purposive and communicative rationality, or system and lifeworld, with the aim of liberating the latter from the former. As a result he brackets reflexivity to the lifeworld and downplays the actual living agency of ordinary people that routinely crosses the border between the everyday and the systemic. In his version of the public sphere, the best citizens can hope for is to play the part of "judicious spectators," or "outside protestors" (Boyte and Kari, 1996) who seldom get their hands dirty on matters of account. Working within this model, deliberative forums always run the risk of subsisting in a political twilight world, having a status somewhere between a policy resource for governments and an exercise in group therapy. Clearly the notion of communicative action implies both the socialization of members of a community and the potential for purposive concerted action through discussion. But in a large-scale and complex polity, the trick is to bridge the two. Any pristine model of the public sphere still reproduces the pattern of usual politics, where representatives make formal decisions about public affairs and political authority is delegated, not practiced directly, or through deliberation, by the citizenry. Of course, even this state of affairs is a world away from, and by many would be deemed preferable to, the pathological version of Blairite modernization, where "the people" are "wooed rather than represented . . . spoken to, rather than speaking" (Hall, 1998), which smacks of honeyed words and offers only the veneer of democratic renewal. In what follows we look in greater detail at various ways of structuring public talk and consider how, if at all, they provide the basis for forging new relationships between citizens and government, perhaps bridging the conceptual divide between purposive and communicative action.

MODERNIZATION IN PRACTICE

The modernizing credo of the Blair administration has to be seen against the backdrop of rapid social, technological, and cultural change and of the perceived crisis in political representation and communication in Western political systems (Blumler and Gurevitch, 1995; Franklin, 1994). Falling participation levels and electoral turnouts and reportedly high levels of citizen disaffection and cynicism with political and public life, and a "dumbing down" of political communication and discussion have all been cited as evidence that such a crisis exists. How to address this putative crisis has given rise to a number of policy prescriptions. In Britain concern with differential levels of electoral participation resulted in the 1993 Plant Report, which advocated a range of innovation in democratic practice including voting at weekends, early morning voting, universal postal voting, and new forms of publicity to encourage greater levels of participation in the electoral process among certain groups.

Prescriptions about the reform of the political process are taking place in both "top-down" and "bottom-up" fashion, with the emphasis on the former. For example, the Green papers on modernizing local government (DETR, 1988a, 1988b, 1988c) are clear indications of the centrality of this agenda to the present administration. Policy prescriptions apart, the application of ICT technology has itself led to a proliferation of new avenues of communication between the state, politicians, and citizens. These avenues include the opening of websites for active public consultation on an increasing number of proposals; easier access to information and services under the *Direct.government* initiative; and a proliferation of other government websites. With varying degrees of sophistication and commitment Members of Parliament are using electronic mail to communicate with citizens and constituents. The future Scottish Parliament building is to be state of the art in its use of information technology and systems of public access (Coleman, 1997). Governmental interest in the potential impact of the developments in media technologies and their application to the political sphere occasioned a conference at the House of Commons in October 1997 entitled *Interactive Politics and the New Media,* at which the ways in which technologies are changing politics were discussed.

New "spaces" for political participation are also being opened up. In the last General Election a pilot project to allow voting in supermarkets was carried out to see if any noticeable increase in voter turnout occurred as a result. In addition to opportunities afforded by ICTs, other techniques more often associated with consumer market research are being employed to facilitate the strategic monitoring of public opinion. The use of citizens juries, deliberative opinion polls, consensus conferencing, and standing citizens panels is also on the increase. A number of local government authorities, police forces, and health authorities are experimenting with information technology and strategic monitoring techniques in attempts to increase levels of information exchange, participation, and deliberative involvement by citizens. The London Borough of Lewisham's *Dialogue* initiative, which consists of an extensive range of on- and off-line citizen's forums is one such example, which we explore in more detail below. "Bottom-up" developments such as UK Citizens Online Democracy, local community civic networks, cyberpolitical activism, and electronic discussion and information exchange networks among, for example, health-care user groups also constitute potentially significant developments here.

To pursue the argument we will break the discussion down into a consideration of plebiscitary and direct democracy, open government, and deliberative democracy. By doing this we hope to make typological and qualitative distinctions between different elements of the putative transformation.

PLEBISICITARY AND DIRECT DEMOCRACY

Concern with the quality of democratic practice and civic competence, coupled with unease at the emergence of a mediatized politics, is seminal for those who maintain that there is a crisis of representation and democracy. The argument runs as follows. The rise of the media-adept politician and the centrality of the media and media professional to the process of political communication and representation has led to a corruption of the political process in favor of individual leaders and image-based, personality-led politics. Furthermore, the ability of political leaders to use the media to bypass traditional institutions of government, such as legislative assemblies and organizations of political mobilization and aggregation, for example political parties, has strengthened the position of the leader at the expense of democratic accountability and the integrity of the political process. The increased use of strategic monitoring techniques, especially public opinion polling, creates an even stronger link between the personalized, charismatic leader and the public. The upshot is to raise the possibility for the creation of an "authoritarian pseudo-democracy based on plebisicitary opinion poll-ism and direct democracy-ism" (Poli, 1998). The proliferation of media and information technology applications (accompanied by concentration of cross-media ownership) has or is likely to enhance this marriage of technocratic and charismatic elements preparing the ground for a "listening dictatorship" (Donovan, 1998).

Developments in Italian politics in recent years, including the fragmentation of the party system, the rise of charismatic leaders such as Bossi and Di Pietro, and the emergence of *Forza Italia* as a vehicle for the political aspiration of Silvio Berlusconi exemplify the Western political crisis as we have characterized it above. Berlusconi and *Forza Italia*'s entry into Italian politics in 1994, accompanied as it was by a high reliance upon a slick, though hardly conventional, electoral machine, television promotion, market research, and a core of senior managers from Berlusconi's *Fininvest* business empire (McCarthy, 1996; Seisselberg, 1996), appears to be a clear example of the worst excesses of politics in media and promotional cultures leading to a "democratic czarism" (Donovan, 1998).

Parallels between Berlusconi and Blair are easy to make; for example, some have argued that the *New* Labour party is becoming a "light" or opinion party (Donovan, 1998) that has ditched its commitment to an authentic and consistent political program to become an opinion-reactive party whose ideological persona is unclear even if its media-glossed identity is not. Blair is said to demonstrate a "Napoleonic" tendency in his approach to leadership and Blackburn has argued that the current Prime Minister is "tempted by plebiscitary politics" (Blackburn, 1997: 16)

The shade of plebiscitary democracy often hangs over discussions about the direction of democratic change. The central concern of critics of this form of democracy is the perceived ease with which direct and popular democracy can lead to intolerance and demagogy. The potential for political leaders to court uninformed public opinion raises the spectacle of a Tocquevillian "tyranny of the majority" in which leader-dominated plebiscitary democracy is underpinned by a rabid media culture of talk radio and "scream" television (Barber, 1995) in which democratic values are displaced by populism and demagogy. But commenting on the emergence of Berlusconi's *Forza Italia*, Donovan argues that the growing prominence of political leaders in Italy (and elsewhere) does not confirm the alleged crisis of representative democracy. Rather, what may be taking place in various party systems is a process of remobilization and regeneration (Donovan, 1998).

Political parties are increasingly employing strategic monitoring techniques such as focus groups at both national and local level to refine their image and their policies, and the trend is not confined to parties, as the present government in Britain is doing the same. The most striking example to date has been the creation of a "People's Panel" in 1998. This panel consists of 5,000 people selected at random from across the United Kingdom who are consulted using telephone and other survey methods and is charged with the explicit task of generating ideas on how public services can be improved. Similar national surveys have been undertaken by the Local Government Association to canvass the "health" of local democracy, in terms of attitudes towards local government and methods for improving voter turnout and participation.

Attempts by local authorities in Britain and elsewhere to involve people in the political process are multiplying rapidly, partly under pressure from central government and partly from a perceived need for innovation within authorities themselves. The use of opinion research is increasing and a number of local authorities are using these approaches to increase participation and consultation amongst the local population. This opinion research can take various forms, including the use of focus group research, standing Citizens Panels, and opinion polling.

For example, in the City of Oxford the City Council, Thames Valley Police, County Council, and the Area Health Authority have established a large citizen body that is consulted through extensive postal questionnaires and telephone interviews on a regular basis about services, local information, policy, and legislative proposals. This system, called *Talkback*, involves nearly 1,000 participants who are representative of the City's general population and one-third of the group is rotated every year. The response rates to the surveys are high, around 65 percent, and the authorities involved use the information gathered in a number of strategic ways. Now, such a process can be seen as simply a matter of gaining feedback on the services provided by local authorities to the local taxpayer, but this may underestimate the possible reflexivity in the process. Furthermore the design of the instrument includes both direct and structured questions on services to more complex questions about the power and responsibilities of bodies within the local area and the institutional and political organization of the local authorities. Does this constitute mere consultation or a deliberative procedure in the making?

The recent announcement of a coordinated policy drive by central government, backed by forthcoming legislation, to modernize the political process at the local level has constrained local authorities to step up the consultative process (Blair, 1998; DETR, 1988a, 1988b, 1988c). The response of some local authorities has been to use systems of consultation to elicit responses on *how* local authorities should be organized, what services they should provide, and how local democracy should be run. Surveys have included questions on ways of increasing voter turnout, the perceived obstacles to participation in local political and civic activity, and ways of increasing public involvement in decision-making at a local level. In some cases these surveys are being augmented by the use of focus group research in which further, more detailed responses are sought on similar issues, but in a more interactive and discursive environment.

The use of consultative procedures like those detailed above raises three questions. First, are the authorities involved seeking to use this information to simply mandate policy plans and legislative proposals? Second, are local authorities utilizing aspects of a deliberative process to inform decision-making in a way that intentionally breaks free of classic liberal models of political representation; or, third, regardless of intention does the immanent dynamic of the deliberative process produce a transformation in practice.

OPEN OR DIRECT GOVERNMENT

On the face of it the same ambiguity is absent from discussions of open or direct government. The application of information technology to the day-to-day business of public administration and the state-citizen interface is clearly a paradigm for the modernization of government and may be a significant move to greater transparency in government. But, in contrast to the ambiguity of developments noted in the above discussion of direct democracy, the advent of an open government program seems to be a matter of the application of technology for administrative purposes rather than anything else. Since 1996, under the auspices of the Information Society Initiative, the British Government has been pursuing a policy of direct government via the World Wide Web and other information technologies. In 1997 the Direct Access Government service was created by the Better Regulation Unit to provide information about a range of government departments and provide access to forms commonly needed by business. The recent report of the Parliamentary Office of Science and Technology, *Electronic Democracy—Information Technologies and the Citizen*, provides a clear indication of how the further application of ICTs may be used to enhance delivery of government services. Open government means using ICT technology to allow citizens easier access information, services, and the submission of forms (Byrne, 1997). Under this project, evaluation of the performance of local authorities and government departments in meeting the commitments of the Citizens Charter is available on CD-ROM; The Driving and Vehicle Licensing Agency has made the first registration and licensing of vehicles an on-line service for car traders; the Patents Office has opened its databases to the public and the Ministry of Agriculture, Food, and Fisheries has computerized the tagging and registration system for cattle. Such a list could be extend extensively, but the direction and aim of policy is pretty much standard.

The rationale for open government differs from consultative and deliberative innovations (although there may be a connection between the two). The opening up of government departments and the creation of on-line access to government services can be incorporated into the strategy and rhetoric of modernization and democratization, but is driven by concerns about the cost and efficiency of public services and administration. So that although unintended consequences may flow from these innovations, such that informed consumers become more active citizens (Ilmonen and Sto, 1997), the main policy thrust of direct government is that of reducing costs, increased efficiency, and enhancing the public-government interface at the point of service delivery. This may change: future developments, for example the creation of virtual one-stop Welfare-to-Work-Shops (Byrne, 1997) or the use of a smart card to which benefits payments would be credited directly and which could be used to purchase goods and services, may make the impact of the open government program more ambiguous.

THE DELIBERATIVE PROCESS AND
DELIBERATIVE DEMOCRACY

Recently, interest in deliberative democracy has heightened partly as a strategic solution to the perceived crisis of democracy and partly as interest grows in the potential of ICTs to open new spaces and channels for political discussion, debate, and deliberation. As a consequence the concept is enjoying popular currency among democratic theorists, with a number arguing for the remodeling of politics along deliberative lines (Gutmann and Thompson, 1996; Habermas, 1996).

However, much of the discussion of deliberative democracy often appears to detach the deliberative process from the practice of everyday politics. In this respect the search for a set of deliberative practices that would ensure that political decision flowed from deliberation between members of a free, equal, and rational citizenry remain elusive and may be of limited practical value.

For Elster (1998) deliberative democracy contains two constituent elements. The first, the democratic element, is the participation in collective decision-making by those affected by the decision. The second, the deliberative element, refers to the inclusion in the decision-making process of deliberation over means and ends by participants "committed to the values of rationality and impartiality" (Elster, 1998: 8). For Fishkin (1991) there are three elements in the deliberative process: first, the exchange of political messages between individuals; second, opportunity to reflect on these messages; third, that messages can be processed interactively and tested against rival arguments.

These definitions may be overreliant on the notion of perfect speech and communication communities. The reality of including deliberation in the political process as it stands is likely to be less than ideal. Nevertheless, some of the developments identified above may be capable of meeting the stringent criteria of what constitutes a deliberative process. By joining citizens' panels and discussion groups and perhaps through some forms of panel surveys, the public may begin to cross the threshold that separates action from being acted upon.

However, even though the idea of deliberative democracy is attracting such attention, it does not enjoy universal approbation over what might constitute valid and useful deliberation and how deliberation can be included routinely within the political process (Sanders, 1997). Our intention is not to make the case for one particular form of deliberative practice over any other nor to argue that Britain is becoming a deliberative democracy. Rather, we suggest that certain developments (either by design or accident) constitute at least forms of proto-deliberation within systems of democratic representation. At the very least there is evidence that both national and local government intend that certain forms of deliberative practice may help in the renewal of representative democracy (DETR, 1998a, 1988b, 1988c; Stewart, 1996).

At a local level we can also identify shifts towards deliberative democracy in some purposive approaches. Whereas the example of citizen's panels, such as Oxford's experiment with *Talkback*, have been discussed as variations on the theme of direct democracy, they also possess synergies with deliberative processes. Although it does not conform to the ideal type of deliberative forum, *Talkback* and similar panels are channels through which informed opinion over key issues of local and national interest can be fed into the political decision-making process.

Other programs provide more advanced examples of a deliberative process. The London Borough of Lewisham, in a partnership involving Bologna, in Italy, and Ronneby, in Sweden, and the Information Society Project Office of the European Union, has embarked on a large scale program entitled *Dialogue* that is designed to involve local communities in decision-making. The project involves the use of a wide-range of techniques and strategies including on- and off-line citizens panels, a junior citizens technology project, "tellytalk," focus groups, and community forums. These various forums are used to increase citizen participation in local government and the data, views, and opinions generated by them are reported to Lewisham Council and other agencies with a view to inform subsequent decisions.

To a greater or lesser extent the examples given above are clearly "top-down" techniques that owe their development to regional, national, or local government. However, there are an increasing number of "bottom-up" deliberative projects that may be contributing to the transformation of the political process in Britain. One example is UK Citizens Online Democracy (UKCOD), a citizen-created service designed to promote on-line discussion and information dissemination. This project has been running since 1996 and has involved the creation of discussion forums at local and national levels on a range of issues. These have included local taxation rates for local councils, the European Monetary Union, and a major project for the 1997 General Election in Britain that involved discussion on constitutional reform and transport policy. Participation in the election project was high, from both public and politicians. The leaders of the three main parties and politicians from fourteen other parties competing in the elections were involved in on-line discussion with the public (Coleman, 1997). UKCOD aims to increase information and debate among the citizenry in a manner that it likens to a "bottom-up version of the BBC," stressing a commitment to public service and independence.

CONCLUSION

Much of the discussion of how far, if at all, the use of direct and deliberative procedures provides the basis of new relationships between citizens and government, and maybe even transforms democratic practice, is vitiated by the lack of empirical evidence on both the socializing effects of new communicative practice, and the policy impact of purposive rationality. Even in the United States, where there is now a voluminous literature on various sorts of citizens initiatives and not a little on those sponsored by governments at different levels, the tone of discussion is often hortatory, more action-research than analysis; or else consists of narrative, case-study accounts of particular interventions. From the point of view of manageable research, these lacunae are understandable, even if the dearth of longitudinal qualitative data and comparative evidence weakens the force of the claim to discern types of transformative practice. Our examination of developments in the United Kingdom underlines the need for systematic study, not least in the form of more refined classification and careful auditing, and also highlights the importance of seeing how changes reflect current preoccupations with modernizing government, but also how they map on to longer-term and deeper shifts in the cultural economies of core states and societies.

In this regard the idea of developments in the structuration of public opinion being part of a growing modality that we have called "postmodern populism" opens up fruitful areas of debate and not a few awkward questions. In the first place, postmodern populism seems an apposite designation because it captures the fluid quality of politics at the end of the twentieth century. Many of the forms and procedures we have examined have an obvious instrumentality, but they also express the tensions between "thinner" or liberal discourses of democracy and the "thicker" versions found in communitarian thought and applauded by various apologists for deliberative democracy. Such tensions are characteristic of polities now in transition.

Postmodern populism is a difficult concept to work with in discussions of democratic transformation because of the provenance of the terms. It may be that we have extracted only those aspects of both terms that support our case, but a treatment of democratic possibilities has to acknowledge the "radical sociopolitical pluralism" of late-modern or postmodern societies, and should try to rescue the idea of populism from its less savory associations. Populist measures can, and clearly do, carry a burden of bad publicity. As we have noted elsewhere (Axford and Huggins, 1997: 10), the literature is full of jeremiads on the potential for "video-populism" or for media-constructed saviors to market and manage a plebiscitary enterprise. Tony Blair has received a good deal of criticism in precisely these terms. It might even be argued that attempts to manufacture a consensus using populist devices is a smart way to manage postmodern polities, where politics is about the expression of differences which are themselves only convenient summaries of labile identities. At the same time it is easy to overlook the scope for reflexivity in the actual procedures involved and in the potential for spillover between types of public talk. Which is why it is, or may be, more than a simple exercise in classification to distinguish between direct and deliberative procedures and the seemingly neutral "resource category" of open government.

To some extent this argument rehearses the familiar point about there being unintended or unanticipated consequences that flow from a particular action. One need not support conspiracy theory to hold that governments often have only specific and pragmatic ends in mind when they canvass public opinion, in whatever form. However, it is not that much of a conceptual leap, and perhaps not too great a leap of faith, to acknowledge that what may start out instrumentally, as a convenient way of legitimating policy shifts, or even a procedure that consciously separates communicative discourse from purposive discourse, may become or contribute to a more robust discursive democracy. But in the absence of an appreciable body of evidence it is hard to be entirely convincing. Reflexivity is a feature of modern societies, and, we would argue, of postmodern ones too. One of the difficulties is whether, if at all, reflexivity, as practiced by individual agents, can become institutionalized reflexivity, that is, the culturally sanctioned expectation that individuals will perform a critical monitoring function, acting as both self-analysts and social critics (Axford, 1995). Facilitating a discursive postmodern populism "from above" would be one way of instantiating institutional reflexivity, but, as we have seen, the motivations of policy-makers are often more realist and mundane. There is little doubt that political elites prefer manageable forms of discursive populism, so that the question of where deliberative forums might subsist and flourish remains crucial. If the path to a more discursive democracy lies less in state-sponsored procedures and more "from below" in civil society, the old issue about the separation of expressive rationality from purposive rationality is still relevant, even in the case of manifestly oppositional "counterpublics" (Benhabib, 1996) which, though outsiders, are often policy-oriented.

Finally, there are the questions of whether postmodern populism is compatible with a more thoroughgoing deliberative democracy, and whether both are compatible with the more obviously nondeliberative features of actually existing democracy? Postmodern populism is a feature of societies that are marked by irreducible pluralism, so if deliberation is intended to achieve a substantive consensus, then not only is it unlikely in such milieus, but it does indeed smack of manipulation and control. If deliberation is understood to mean arriving at a procedural consensus, following active deliberation by various constituencies, then this goal is more realizable in systems still configured by majoritarian principles and representative structures. The nondeliberative features and traditions of real democracies still militate against free and open discussion among interested parties and have little room for the notion that deliberation is educative and emancipatory. Our brief excursion into the ways in which public talk is being structured in Britain leaves many of these questions unanswered, due to lack of empirical evidence over time. What it does suggest, however, is that notions of a crisis of democracy in postmodern, mediatized cultures may be overstated and that the roots of a piecemeal transformation of democratic practice may be found in a model of democracy that blends (albeit uneasily) aspects of a statist and aggregative model of representative politics with the prescriptions of more discursive models. In the nature of uneasy transformations, this one is still being played out, but the constraints of mediatized cultures and postmodern identity politics means that there is no going back to the pure-milk of liberal politics, nor, we would argue, no real chance of slippage into unreflexive and authoritarian or plebiscitary rule.

REFERENCES

Arendt, Hannah. 1998. *The Human Condition*. Chicago: Chicago University Press.

Axford, Barrie. 1995. *The Global System: Economics, Politics and Culture*. Cambridge: Polity Press.

Axford, Barrie and Richard Huggins. 1997. Anti-Politics or the Triumph of Postmodern Populism in Promotional Cultures? *Javnost—The Public* 4(3), 5-25.

Barber, Benjamin. (1995). *Jihad Versus McWorld*. New York: Times Books.

Beck, Ulrieh. 1996. World Risk Society as Cosmopolitan Society: Biological Questions in a Framework of Manufactured Uncertainties. *Theory Culture and Society* 13(4), 1-32.

Benhabib, Seyla. 1996. *Democracy and Difference*. Princeton, NJ: Princeton University Press.

Blackburn, Robin. 1997. Reflections on Blair's Velvet Revolution. *New Left Review* 22(3), 3-16.

Blair, Tony. 1998. *Leading the Way: A New Vision for Local Government*. London: IPPR.

Blumler, Jay and Michael Gurevitch. 1995. *The Crisis of Public Communication*. London: Routledge.

Boyte, Harry and Nancy Kari. 1996. *Building America: The Democratic Promise of Public Work*. Philadelphia: Temple University Press.

Byrne, Liam. 1997. *Information Age Government: Delivering the Blair Revolution*. London: Fabian Society.

Castells, Manuel. 1996. *The Rise of the Network Society*. Oxford: Blackwell.

Coleman, Stephen. 1997. UK Citizen Online Democracy: An Experiment in Government-Supported Online Public Space. In S. Clift and O. Ostberg (eds.), *Democracy and Government On-Line Services*, G7.

DETR. 1998a. *Modern Local Government: In Touch with the People*. London: DETR.

DETR. 1998b. *Modernising Local Government: A New Ethical Framework*. London: DETR

DETR. 1998c. *Modernising Local Government: Local Democracy and Community Leadership*. London: DETR.

Donovan, Mark. 1998. Political Leadership in Italy: Towards a Plebiscitary Democracy? *Modern Italy* 3(2), 281-293.

Dryzek, John. 1990. *Discursive Democracy: Politics, Policy, and Political Science*. Cambridge: Cambridge University Press.

Elster, John, ed. 1998. *Deliberative Democracy*. Cambridge: Cambridge University Press.

Fishkin, James. 1991. *Democracy and Deliberation*. New Haven, CT: Yale University Press.

Franklin, Bob. 1994. *Packaging Politics, Political Communication in Britain's Media Democracy*. London: Edward Arnold.

Giddens, Anthony. 1990. *The Consequences of Modernity*. Cambridge: Polity Press.

Giddens, Anthony. 1994. *Between Left and Right*. Cambridge: Polity Press.

Giddens, Anthony. 1998. *The Third Way*. Cambridge: Polity.

Guttman, Amy and Dennis Thompson. 1996. *Democracy and Disagreement*. Cambridge, MA: Belknap.

Habermas, Jürgen. 1992. *The Structural Transformation of the Public Sphere*. Oxford: Blackwell.

Habermas, Jürgen. 1996. *Between Facts and Norms*. Cambridge: Polity Press.

Hall, Stuart. 1989, November 20. Nowhere Man. *Marxism Today*, 3-8.

Hirst, Paul. 1994. *Associative Democracy*. Cambridge: Polity Press.

Hutton, Will. 1998. *The Stakeholding Society*. Cambridge: Polity Press.

Ilmonen, Kaj and Eivind Sto. 1997. The "Consumer" in Political Discourse: Consumer Policy in the Nordic Welfare States. In P. Sulkunen, J. Holmwood, H. Radner, and G. Schulze (eds), *Constructing the New Consumer Society*. Macmillan: London.

Key, V.O., Jr. 1964. *Public Opinion and American Democracy*. New York: Knopf.

Lippmann, Walter. 1955. *The Public Philosophy*. Boston: Little, Brown.

McCarthy, Patrick. 1996. Forza Italia: The New Politics and Old Values of a Changing Italy. In S. Gundle and S. Parker (eds.), *The New Italian Republic: From the Fall of the Berlin Wall to Berlusconi*. London: Routledge.

McLennan, Gregor. 1995. *Pluralism*. Buckingham: Open University Press.

Plant Report. 1993. *Report of the Working Party on Electoral Systems*. London: Labour Party.

Poli, Emanuela. 1998. Silvio Berlusconi and the Myth of the Creative Entrepreneur. *Modern Italy* 3(2), 271-279.

Putnam, Robert. 1995. Bowling Alone: America's Declining Social Capital. *Journal of Democracy* 6(1), 65-78.

Ridley, Fred and Grant Jordan, eds. 1998. *The Protest Business?* Manchester: Manchester University Press.

Sanders, Lynn. 1997. Against Deliberation. *Political Theory* 25(3), 347-376.

Seisselberg, Jorg. 1996. Conditions of Success and Political Problems of a "Media-Mediated Personality-Party": The Case of Forza Italia. *West European Politics* 19(4), 715-743.

Stewart, John. 1996. Innovation in Democratic Practice in Local Government. *Politics and Policy* 24(1), 29-41.

Yankelovich, Daniel and Ian Destler, eds. 1991. *Beyond the Beltway: Engaging the Public in U.S. Foreign Policy*. New York: W.W. Norton.

9

Islamic Cultural Theory, Arab Media Performance, and Public Opinion[1]

Basyouni Ibrahim Hamada

This chapter is based on the argument that it is not only the performance of Arab mass media that determines the quality of public opinion, but also the long-term political cultural environment in which both Arab mass media and public opinion operate. The impact of local social and cultural arrangements on modern media was evident in the introduction of highly centralized communication systems geared exclusively toward nation-building goals. Characterized by pervasive government ownership and operation of broadcast services and a close scrutiny of privately owned print media, those systems have been rationalized by invoking the need for political stability and social harmony. In addition, Arab cultural and political traditions dominant during the colonial and postindependence eras were also instrumental in setting early professional standards for modern Arab media practice and in defining their relationships with social and political institutions (Hamada, 1997: 250). It is clear also that indigenous traditions had a substantial bearing on the uses into which communications technologies were put. Newspapers turned into important outlets of literary expression by poets, novelists, and other men of letters (Ayish, 1998: 41).

It is inconceivable that any society would have attempted or achieved total and unrestrained rights to free speech, for a certain amount of restrictions goes hand in hand with the facts of life. Society's perception of the right to free speech is liable to change in accordance with changing conditions, for what we consider to be acceptable today may have been quite out of the question a century or even a generation ago.

A great deal of inhibitions and restrictions that are imposed on freedom of speech are extralegal. Public opinion determines, to a large extent, the acceptable limits of such freedom and rejects what is unacceptable or excessive. And yet, public opinion is not a free agent, as it reflects a combination of moral, religious, cultural, and legal influences. Legal rules provide a good indication of the vision of society and the standards by which it regulates the conduct of its members (Kamali, 1994: 15).

The idea that both media and public opinion are heavily affected by the cultural system is in line with what Ball-Rokeach and DeFleur conclude. They seem to agree, but not for the same reasons: classic sociology leads us to treat both media and audiences as integral parts of a larger social system. Media and audiences thus would respond to the same social forces and look to each other for a definition of those realities. Social realities portrayed by the media ensue both from their connection to social structures and from their interaction with audiences (Edelstein, 1988: 510).

In the light of the fact that both Arab media and public opinion are at least partly a product of the long-term cultural environment in which both perform, it is important to analyze the Islamic cultural theory. This analysis ought to help understand how the media and public opinion should together perform and interact. However, this kind of theoretical analysis has its own limitations, because it is well known that governments everywhere seek to preserve the political system as a whole by regulating the media and manipulating public opinion. Although control occurs in all societies, its nature and purposes vary. Therefore, it is necessary to investigate the Arab political reality, the communication constraints, and its effects on Arab media and public opinion.

FUNDAMENTAL PRINCIPLES IN ISLAMIC CULTURE

As expressed by one Arab scholar, the Prophet, peace and blessings of Allah be upon him, was an Arab, the *Qur'an* is written in Arabic, and the

Arabs were the matter of Islam [*maddat al Islam*], the human instrument through which it conquered the world. Islam is not only a religion in the traditional and relatively narrow Western sense: it is also a culture and state. As one Islamic scholar writes: "Islam, in its precise sense, is a social order, philosophy of life, a system of economic principles, and a rule of government" (Tessler, 1994: 75).

The liberal and revolutionary aspects of Islam and its Prophet Muhammad, which transformed society in the seventh century, are still today among the most potent forces at work for the betterment of humanity. They brought not only a new ideology, but inspired the energy and confidence that so radically altered man and the society in which he lived. They provided the impetus for a new age of culture and civilization, arts, learning material, and spiritual progress.

What was the nature of the service rendered to mankind? What were the gifts of the prophet that so profoundly affected man and society as he found it?

1. First and foremost he proclaimed belief in the Oneness of God. By submitting only to the will of one God, man was freed from servility to all other powers. He became aware of his worth and dignity (Ali Nadvi, 1978: 18).

2. Islam comprehends every aspects of the human soul because it is revealed for every single person living on this earth irrespective of his race, color, language, location, environment, historical or geographical circumstances, intellectual or cultural heritage, and his contribution to material civilization (Salem, 1982: 1).

3. The universality of Mohammed's mission has been clearly confirmed by the *Qur'an*; it is a logical consequence of the finality of his prophethood. A prophet after whom there was to be no other had to be a guide and leader for all men and for all ages. God has provided through him the complete code that man needs to follow the right path, and this in itself supports the concept of finality, because without completeness the need for other prophets would remain (Maududi, 1978: 4).

4. Islam comprehends and fulfills all the requirements of life, past and future until the end of human existence on the earth whether these requirements are spiritual, material, political, economic, social, moral, intellectual, or aesthetic (Salem, 1982: 1). In other words, Islam determines the rules that should form the basis of social, cultural relationship, economic, judicial, and political dealings, matters of war and peace, and international affairs. The Prophet brings with him a whole

system of thought and action, which in Islamic terminology is called *al Din* (a complete way of life) (Maududi, 1978: 6).

5. Islam confers the concept of the equality and brotherhood of all mankind. It was from Muhammad that the world first heard the revolutionary message of human equality. "O Mankind, your God is one and you have but one father" (Ali Nadvi, 1978: 18).

6. There is no distinction in Islam between private and public conduct. The same moral code that one observes at home applies to one's conduct in public. This is true of every institution of society and every department of government; all must conform the laws of Islam (Maududi, 1978: 14).

7. Islam does not recognize any division between the temporal and the spiritual, because man's desire to propitiate God and follow His commands permeates every fibre of human activity. Every one of man's actions, his behavior and morality, is guided by this motive, which, in the terminology of religion is known as *niyat* or intention. The intention or purpose with which any act is done is the criterion of its moral worth (Ali Nadvi, 1978: 27).

8. Islamic Shari'a differs from Westerns systems of law in two principal aspects. (1) The scope of the Shari'a is much wider, because it regulates man's relationships not only with his neighbors and with the state, which is the limit of most other legal systems, but also with his God and with his own conscience. (2) Unlike secular legal systems that grow out of society, Shari'a law was imposed upon society from above (*Britannica Online*, 1998).

9. Most philosophies have built their arguments on the idea that success is purely material, that life is an end in itself. This attitude is a result of the rejection of a transcendental meaning of life; life as a means to an end and not an end in itself (Shabeer, 1997: 41). A radical change brought about by Muhammad in the life of man was to make him conscious of the ultimate end of existence. Unaware of any ultimate purpose, man had for long fixed his eyes on trivial and ephemeral ends (Ali Nadvi, 1978: 30). Modern thought in Europe has developed in hostility to the church. In an anticlerical context, the concepts of secularism, humanism, nationalism, materialism, and rationalism, which are all based on partial truth, became responsible for the present Euro-American spiritual crisis. Islam can satisfy all the partial truth in all these powerful ideas (Al-Mehdi, 1978: 130).

10. Islam can solve the Euro-American civilization crisis through an intersected relationship between ontology, epistemology, and axiology: because the harmony and balance between sources of knowledge is the basic parameter of the Islamic epistemology. The basic principles of the value-based axiology are: (1) There must be a set of absolute values, because there is an objective absolute knowledge. (2) Neither this absolute knowledge nor its value reflections can be the subjects of the power structure because of their validity beyond time and space limitations. (3) None of the artificial mechanisms and institutions, which are time/space-bound, can produce ultimate values. In fact just the opposite is true. They can only gain legitimacy if they obey to this axiological foundation. (4) The time/space-bound relative values can have only functional legitimacy subservient to the ultimate value-system. Their functional validity should only aim to establish the social atmosphere for the realization of the Islamic normativism (Davutoglu, 1997: 73).

11. There is a fundamental difference in the perspective from which Islam and the West each view the matter of human rights. The Western perspective may by and large be called anthropocentric in the sense that man is regard as constituting the measure of everything, because he is the starting point of all thinking and actions. The perspective of Islam, on the other hand, is theocentric—God conscious. Here the Absolute is paramount and man exists only to serve His Maker (Brohi, 1978: 35). Needless to say that this Islamic vision of human rights should represent one of the most influential sources of news values and media ethics in the Islamic Arab World. Meanwhile, it has to direct the opinion formation toward the issues facing Arab public opinion.

ELEMENTS OF DEMOCRATIC LIFE IN MUSLIM CULTURAL THEORY

There is a misconception in the West and among the general public that Islam is only a religion and is not a democratic life system. But Islam brought about a radical democratic transformation in society because it is a total life system; only a small section of Islamic law deals with rituals and personal ethics, whereas the larger part concerns social order (Mowlana, 1993: 18). It is difficult to imagine either a more fundamental revolution or one whose dynamic has continued for so long. The forces that transformed men in the seventh century still have power to inspire him today. Muslims widely credit Islam as among the most powerful and pervasive cultural influence on their lives and in their societies, at least at the theoretical level.

The Right to Know

In Muslim cultural theory, knowledge is the key to the human condition and the power that drives human civilization. In the 6,291 or so verses of the *Qur'an*, there are about 791 references to the Arabic root *ilm* (to know)—roughly 12.7 percent—making it fourth after *Allah* (God), *Iman* (belief), and *Rabb* (Lord-Master). Knowledge links humans to God: only knowledgeable persons . . . fear God. *Ilm* (knowledge) constitutes the polar opposite to *Zann* (guesswork, speculation): they have no *ilm*; instead, they use *Zann* (45:24).[2] The basic commitment to truth is expressed in several places in the *Qur'an*: "this is Our Book that conveys the truth."

The following *Hadith* also tells us, for example, that truth must not be hindered by the prospect of invoking the disfavor of others, or even of causing discomfort to oneself: "tell the truth even if it be unpleasant." This robust attitude to the advocacy of truth is taken a step further by the *Hadith* that proclaims that the best form of *jihad* (holy struggle) is to tell a word of truth to a tyrannical ruler (Kamali, 1994: 12).

The Right to Choose Belief and Behavior

The people have a fundamental right to choice of belief and behavior. They also have a right to all the information required to make an educated and enlightened choice between alternatives (90:10) (Pasha, 1993: 95). One of the manifestations of personal liberty is the freedom of the individual to profess the religion of his or her choice without compulsion. Everyone must have the freedom to observe and to practice his or her faith without fear or interference from others. Freedom of religion in Islamic context implies that non-Muslims are not compelled to convert to Islam, nor are they hindered from practicing their own religious rites. The *Qur'anic* text declares that "there shall be no compulsion in religion"(Kamali, 1994: 87).

The people have a fundamental need for, and therefore right to, knowledge and education without coercion, deception, falsehood, manipulation, intimidation, or worse. Muhammad himself is forbidden to use coercion in the pursuit of his persuasive and educational objectives.

The Right to Read

The people not only have a general right to know, but also a specific right to read, which in Muslim cultural theory is not a mere right, but an all-important and universal duty (96:I).

The Right to Write

The right—and command—to read implies clearly and logically the concomitant right to write. This notion is further reinforced by the fact that the *Qur'an* specifically identifies the pen as God's chosen instrument in the process of teaching man (96:4).

The Right to Power

Power is a prerequisite for purposeful human existence and, consequently, power in Muslim cultural theory belongs to the people. The *Qur'an* strikes a powerful blow at all authoritarian and inherited power claims, hierarchies, and structures by placing power and its key correlates and components directly in the hands of the people. *Qur'an* also shifts the focus from brute force to negotiation, reconciliation, and rationality (8:61), and thus from the sword to the pen.

The Right to Choose Government

Muslim cultural theory makes all power use contingent on *Shura* (inclusion, consultation, representation, association, involvement, and participation in decision-making and power-sharing), which constitutes the basic requirement of collective human existence at all levels. As a result, one of the key corollaries to the people's right to power is the people's right to choose their government freely, openly, and fearlessly from among themselves at all levels from the lowest to the highest. Even Muhammad was commanded in the *Qur'an* to conduct Muslims affairs based on *Shura* (3:159) (Pasha, 1993: 65-71). However, the *Qur'anic* provisions on *shura* are primarily concerned with laying down the basic foundation of *shura* as a principle of public law, but the details as to its manner of implementation and subject matter on which consultation must take place are left out (Kamali, 1994: 41).

Freedom to Express an Opinion

Freedom to express an opinion is probably the most important aspect of freedom of speech in that the latter may comprise other verbal varieties such as a simple narration of facts, or comedy and fiction. Both Muhammad Asad and Abd Allah al Arabi have observed that the basic recognition of freedom of speech and opinion in the *Shari'a* requires that the people must also be accorded the freedom to group together, if they so wish, in pursuit of their common objectives.

The *Shari'a* thus entitles the people to organize themselves in parties, groups, and associations if they find this to be a more effective way of realizing their legitimate interests. Under the *Shari'a* people are also granted the freedom to criticize and monitor government activity by means of sincere advice, constructive criticism, and ultimately, by refusal to obey the government when it is guilty of violating the law (Kamli, 1994: 61). Muslim writers on the subject have consistently stated that Islam not only validates freedom of expression but it also urges Muslims not to remain silent nor indifferent when expressing an opinion that is likely to serve the cause of truth, justice, or be of benefit to society (Kamali, 1994: 16).

NEWS IN MUSLIM CULTURAL THEORY

News is based on "truth unmixed with willful falsehood" (2:42) about people, events, places, issues, and objects in the extended environment consisting of an endless space-time continuum. There are about 138 references in the *Qur'an* to the root word *naba'* meaning news. News, according to *Qur'an*-based cultural theory, has two origins: divine and other. If it is of divine origin, it is revealed through *Nabiy*—giver of the news (Prophet). Where news does not have a divine origin, it must still be based on firm and full evidence warranting a high degree of *Yaqeen*—certitude (27:22) and the *Qur'an* introduces several concepts and principles to help bring this about. First, news must be based on truth unmixed with willful falsehood: "do not mix *Haq* [truth] with *Baatil* [falsehood] and hide the *Haq* [truth] knowingly" (92:42). Second, the truth value of news is so paramount and overriding in Muslim cultural theory that the question of the character, competence, and integrity of journalists and their sources in the news-gathering and reporting process assumes critical importance. Third, news (and knowledge or information in general) has consequences that may adversely affect individuals, groups, or societies and as a result, it must carry a strong sense of responsibility and accountability on the part of journalists and their organization as well as the entire society: "O Believers, . . . verify it, lest you adversely impact some people unknowingly and then become embarrassed over what you did" (49:6). Fourth, mass media must not make mere suspicion the basis of their news reporting; nor should they mock nor deride other men and women or unjustly destroy their reputations (49:11,12). Finally, and very importantly, news must have a utility value to the extent that it is attainable; that is, it must provide *Nafa'* (benefit) to the people (13:17).

CENSORSHIP

At both individual and institutional levels, Muslim cultural theory seeks to balance the people's communication rights and freedoms with their communication duties, constraints, and responsibilities. On the side of freedom are such sweeping and powerful arguments as the people's fundamental rights to read, write, speak, know, and to power, which do not leave much room for arbitrary and authoritarian censorship of communication.

On the side of constraints are the equally powerful notions of the boundaries (*Hudood*) of good; of permissibility (*Halal*) and impressibility (*Haram*); of good (*Ma'roof*), and bad (*Munkar*). Moreover, communication in Muslim cultural theory is a fundamental and core activity defining, shaping, and directing human existence. On the other hand, communication in Islam, both spiritual and social, is a process of facilitating the individual's integration into the larger *Umma*. It is a process of harmonizing the believing inner self with the collective believing self of the community (Ayish, 1998: 41). It is interesting also to note that the word communication in its Latin usage does not exist in Islamic literature, and when it is used and translated in its contemporary context in the Arab Muslim countries, the term takes on a more technical rather than social connotation. Yet, when one considers the process of communication and interactions in an Islamic context, the term corresponds to such words as brotherhood, cohesion, unity, and understanding. Therefore, a distinction should be made between the Islamic term *tabligh* (propagation) and the general concepts of communication, propaganda, and agitation commonly used in contemporary literature. Propagation in an Islamic context is dissemination and diffusion of some principle, belief, or practice. The Islamic word for propagation, *tabligh*, means the increase or spread of a belief by natural reproduction; it is an extension in space and time. It is the action of branching out. *Tabligh*, in an Islamic context, has an ethical boundary and a set of guiding principles. In a broader sense, *Tabligh* is a theory of communication and ethics. This theory of communication and global integration is well stated by Ibn Khaldun in the *Muqaddimah* (an introduction to history) (Mowlana, 1996: 115).

PUBLIC OPINION IN THE POLITICAL REALITY OF THE ARAB MUSLIM WORLD

It has been argued by Huntington that the world is currently in a "third wave democratization" that has seen the widespread transformation of previously nondemocratic regimes toward democracy, especially in eastern Europe, Latin America, Asia, and sub-Saharan Africa. Only one major region—the Arab world—still lags behind in this worldwide movement of democratization (Goodson and Radwan, 1997: 1). However, some analysts have noted, correctly, that the drive for democratization in the Arab world was motivated by several factors: the increasing prominence of Islamic movements, the emergence of more autonomous associational and professional groups, the hardships associated with economic liberalization, and the fear of popular revolt. In the face of public discontent due to deteriorating living standards, some Arab regimes, particularly in poor countries, have opened up the system and allowed political contests in order to diffuse opposition to their policies and to allow other groups in the society to share the responsibility for solving chronic economic problems (American Political Science Association, 1991).

So far, this democratization process remains limited in scope and hampered by several factors. First, some Arab countries are experiencing what could be called "democracy by decree": political pluralism was granted from above and did not emerge as a result of change in social structure or the evolution of independent institutions. Second, the current democratization process is restricted greatly by regulations and laws that preclude its evolution and render it selective. The constitutions in several Arab countries stipulate that no political party can be legalized unless it recognizes the achievements of the regime, the revolution, and so forth. Third, psychological impediments often undermine the democratization process. There is a prevalent and conscious feeling among the people that their leaders did not assume power through a democratic process and free elections. Finally, the entire process is monitored closely by a vigilant army that is willing to step in if its privileges are challenged or to prevent any undesired forces from assuming power (Shahin, 1993: 496).

In his study on democratization in Egypt in the 1990s, Goodson states that "Perhaps no Arab country has made greater claims to democratization and is a more important test case of its possibilities than Egypt" (Goodson and Radwan, 1997: 15). Long considered a regional leader, Egypt has also been outspoken in its promise to democratize. Since Anwar Sadat opened Egyptian politics and society in the mid-1970s, and continuing in a more publicly explicit manner during the regime of Hosni Mubarak since 1981, the assessment of the progress in political process and culture shows some improvements, primarily in growing vibrancy of civil society. On the other hand, the continued absence of fair elections, which contributes to the continued weakness of the political opposition, coupled with the government's efforts to eliminate the Muslim Brotherhood's control of major syndicates, as well as the authoritarian political culture and ineffective political socialization, are major obstacles to effective democratization (Goodson and Radwan, 1997: 15).

Contrary to the theoretical model rooted in the *Qur'an*, most governments and power structures in the Arab and Muslim world are based on secrecy, exclusion, manipulation, coercion, authoritarianism, and tyranny, as many Muslim governments are absolute hereditary monarchies and many others are personal, military, or party dictatorships. In Muslim societies, including the Arab societies, the people may receive promises of freedom and democracy at the theoretical level, while being denied the same at the operational level (Pasha, 1993: 73-76).

In terms of freedom of expression, there is a significant absence of any institutionalized notion of free expression and dialogue. This situation is considered failure to uphold Islamic principles and is made more glaring by the inability to develop mass media capable of articulating to the Muslims masses the truth about themselves and the world.

Another issue that plagues all aspects of the Muslim world is that the restoration of an adequate system of consultation (*Shura*) among a body of elected leaders has yet to be implemented. Muslims domains for the past century have been ruled autocratically without clear representation by the people governed (Al Barzinji, 1998: 55).

In terms of mass media policy and control, Muslim reality being generally at odds with Muslim cultural theory, it is safe to predict that the mostly non-*Shura*-based and authoritarian power structures of the Muslim world would tend to be preoccupied with the imperative of self-preservation and, as a result, deny, diminish, dilute, or deflect the people's right to know, read, write, speak, and to power. As a result, the mass media in most parts of Muslim and Arab world would in general tend to be highly censored, elitist, mostly under government control, significantly disinformational, and primarily diversionary with low truth and utility value (Pasha, 1993: 76-78).

According to the cultural Islamic theory it is also safe to predict that Islam is not only a religion in the traditional and relatively narrow

Western sense. Instead, it is a culture and a state thanks to four concepts: *shura* (consultation), *ijithad* (independent reasoning), *ijma* (consensus), and *bay'a* (contractual acceptance of the ruler by tribes and urban corporations) (Leca, 1994: 60). The Prophet Muhammad and his four successors, the Guided Caliphs, presided over a society that strictly adhered to the spirit and letter of the *Qur'an* and *Sunna*. During that golden age, Muslims not only established a "perfect society" on earth but were also the master of the entire world. Politically, Islam emphasizes a participatory society through a system of *Shura*—the community's selection of a ruling council that must consult with others and be held accountable on the basis of *Shari'a*. Economically, Islam makes human labor the only legitimate basis of generating and accumulating wealth and recognizes and protects the sanctity of private property in all spheres, except where it touches upon vital interests relating to the community as a whole (such as water, energy, and other public utilities). Socially, Islam considers the family as the basic unit of society and recognizes that women are equal to, but different from, men. It accepts religious pluralism with differential rights and obligations for Muslims and "Peoples of the Book" (Christians and Jews) (Ibrahim, 1996: 54). As for communication, Islam guarantees the most professional performance of mass media in terms of its objectivity, its freedom, its ability to tell only the truth, uncover facts, and to criticize the governments to the fullest extent possible. Mass media from the Islamic perspective are devoted to form enlightened, informed, and active public opinion that can at any time contribute in decision-making process. But one can not say that this is the reality. A gap still exists between Islamic cultural theory and the practice. To make it clear, the mechanisms that govern the public opinion process according to the Islamic cultural theory are not completely different from that of the Western democratic theory. As such, Islam is consistent with a Western-type democracy—the Holy *Qur'an* being the functional equivalent of a divine democracy. There is no priesthood, and hence no theocracy under Islam. However, Islam differs from the Western democracy in the sense that the sovereignty of God in Islam is not just a supranational phenomenon. It covers all aspects of political and legal sovereignty also, and in these, too, no one other God has any share. To God alone belongs the rightful authority to exercise power on this earth over those whom God has created in it (Maududi, 1978: 8). Another major difference between Islamic and Western perspective is, basically, that in Islam the judge of the majority must govern and prevail except in one case—that is, when the will of public opinion contradicts with the Islamic *Shari'a*.

It is obviously evident that political reality in the Arab world hindered the democratic practice of both the media and public opinion. It is also safe to predict that what the people believe and hold as public opinion in the Arab World is to some important degree shaped by the conscious attempt done by the governments and media people to suppress information and manipulate public opinion for ideological and political reasons. Furthermore, public opinion does not exist and the media do not function properly if the Arab governments have a culture that is authoritarian, manipulative, and controlling of others—asymmetrical in its worldview relationships with others.

TOWARD AN EXPLANATION

It is articulated in the above analysis that there is a contradiction between the fundamental principles of Islamic cultural theory and the fact that they are ignored by the political elite everywhere in the Arab Muslim world. It is most likely that Arab regimes will continue to repress Islamic and other serious opposition groups in order to prevent real change, while allowing less-threatening political forces more participation and freedom in order to maintain a democratic façade. However, insisting on a controlled and selective democracy and the exclusion of a significant force—the Islamic parties—from real participation will discredit the process, disgrace other political forces, and increase social instability (Shahin, 1993: 499).

In search of an explanation for the contradiction between the *Qur'an* and the practice of Arab governments and elite, we would do well to place the phenomenon in its historical perspective.

In modern Arab history, militant Islamic movements have sprung up in several countries—Saudi Arabia, Algeria, Libya, Sudan, and Egypt (Ibrahim, 1996: 23). Most of these movements have used violence to change the status quo. Their members were mostly fundamentalists and ideologically subscribe to Islam and believe that the implementation of the *Shari'a* would be the fundamental solution to all existing social ills. Although their belief is correct, they failed to persuade the Arab people to adopt it in the face of their government. Among the main reasons for this failure is that they do not have detailed operational plans or action programs to implement once in power. They also lack the Islamic diplomatic methods to persuade both the general population and the governments with their claims; instead, they use an ideology and actions that apparently challenge the present social orders. I think that the majority of the Arab people supports the real moderate and tolerant Islamic movements, but the latter are not able to use either the mass media, especially television, to publicize their programs and defend their arguments or the political institutions to compete with the secular elite. A recent survey on democracy in developing countries excludes most of the Islamic world and all of the Arab world because those countries "generally lack previous democratic experience and most appear to have little prospect of transition even to semi-democracy" (Leca, 1994: 59). Another reason that hindered democracy is that for most people it is not a high priority because of their economic struggle to survive.

The contradiction between Islamic cultural theory and practice may also be explained in the light of the fact that contacts between the Islamic world and the West in the nineteenth and twentieth centuries increased the absorption of many Islamic countries into quasi-secular political entities, ranging from hereditary monarchies to modern Western or military-style republics. This contact resulted in pronounced conflicts between modern secularism and the Islamic tradition of *Shari'a*, the canonical law of Islam. Until the nineteenth century, *Shari'a* provided the main, if not the complete, legal underpinnings of social, political, and economic conduct in Muslim societies. The intimate contact between Islam and modern Western industrial countries, coupled with the process of colonization of substantial parts of Muslim countries, introduced a number of Western standards and values to those societies. Thus, at the beginning of the twentieth century and with the introduction of modern means of communication, transportation, and technologies, the fields of civil and commercial transactions proved particularly susceptible to change and new methods of conduct (Mowlana, 1996: 153). Now, most of laws and conduct of ethics—with the exception of a few provisions drawn from *Shari'a*—are indeed direct translations of French and other European codes.

ARAB MEDIA PERFORMANCE AND THE QUALITY OF PUBLIC OPINION

A crucial, yet unexplored, area of the Arab Muslim countries consists of the aspects of media performance and the quality of public opinion. Media in this region are the product of at least two historical components: colonialism and postindependence conditions. These factors, once integrated into a coherent approach, represent the unique characteristics of media in this part of the Muslim world. Rugh's study is probably the most extensive and comprehensive analysis of the Arab media in general. However, Rugh's study was partly simplistic and contains generalities that do not reflect the diversity and complexity of the many facets of the Arab media, especially in terms of its performance and relationship with public opinion (Azzi, 1997: 4).

John Merrill, in a recent reference, argues that the "prevailing trends in the region could send the media off in several directions." He notes "the proliferation of electronically delivered information and entertainment throughout the region provides alternatives to the limited choices previously available, a fact which is breaking former government monopolies of information" (Merrill, 1995: 192).

Three additional aspects of media and public opinion in the Arab Muslim countries need attention. First, no serious research has been done on the political impact of mass media on public opinion even by the governmental institutions. Second, there are almost no regular mechanisms or structures for public opinion to express its views concerning the controversial issues. Third, there is a deep confusion in the Arab public mind, at least about the meaning of democracy and the relationship between information, public participation, civil society, Islam, and the democratic society.

However, four variables—socioeconomic formations, the articulation of civil society, the state, and the external factors—have been acting upon each other to produce a mini-wave of democratization in the Arab world. The interplay varies from one Arab country to another, which accounts for the degree of democratization empirically observed in each at present (Ibrahim, 1995: 37).

Due to the critical role of communication in determining the quality of public opinion, Arab governments—to different degrees—direct, distort, and constrain communication. Mueller states that because open communication can threaten the political status quo, public debate may be limited to topics and issues that are not critical. This type of distorted communication can be effected through censorship, directed communication, and constrained communication (Mueller, 1973: 21). However, governmental direct censorship is decreasing under the pressure of so many factors; the most important of these factors is the spread of Direct Broadcast Satellite Television services (DBS TV).

As mentioned by Aloofy, many of the television officials interviewed remarked that the censorship of programs is on the decrease. One said, "to compete with DBS TV you have to be more open to other cultures and to use new techniques, especially those related to dealing with the audience directly and on air" (Aloofy, 1998: 59).

It seems also important to remember that media and public opinion interact with each other to the extent that the quality of public opinion may determine the performance of mass media. Thus it is difficult to view the influence as unidirectional. It is beyond the scope of this study to numerate and analyze the different components of both media performance and quality of public opinion. Therefore, I emphasize three media components—agenda-setting, media objectivity, and news-framing—to investigate the concept and reality of media performance, in addition to three central public opinion characteristics that would help explain the quality of Arab public opinion.

AGENDA-SETTING

Democratic theory assumes more than knowledge of and participation in government affairs by numerous citizens and groups. Democratic theory also assumes some agreement on what the most important issues of the day are. In fact, any system of government can deal with only a limited set of issues or problems in a given period of time. There must be not only a finite set of issues, but also a sense of priority, or ranking, of these issues that defines an agenda to which governmental institutions can respond by authoritative allocation of resources (McCombs, Einsiedel, and Weaver, 1991: 11).

Research on the agenda-setting process of the mass media stems directly from the notion suggested by Cohen (1963) that mass media "may not be successful much of the time in telling people what to think, but it is stunningly successful in telling its readers what to think about." In other words, even though media may not be very successful in telling us what opinions to hold, they are often quite effective in telling us what to have opinions about. This idea led to an impressive empirical effort to study media agendas, public agendas, and the relationships between them (Brosius and Welmann, 1996: 562).

A number of reviews of the agenda-setting literature since the late 1980s have promoted the idea that a larger effect model has emerged from the wide variety of approaches to agenda-setting research. Rogers, Dearing, and Bregonan (1993) suggest a three-by-three matrix to summarize all of the possible areas of agenda research. The nine resulting cells of the matrix are: Media influence on the media, the public and policy makers; public influence on the public, the media. and policy makers; policy maker's influence on policy, the media, and the public. They point out that most research has concentrated on the media-to-public, media-to-policy, and public-to-policy relationships. In other words, there are four distinct agendas in the agenda-setting process: source agenda, media agenda, audience agenda, and policy agenda. And each of the four agendas has its own characteristic patterns, and each is related to the others by one or more informational, behavioral, or institutional factors (Trumbo, 1995: 5-7).

Most of the media agenda-setting research has been concerned with cognition-public awareness of and concern over issues or problems emphasized by the mass media. Even though the perceived salience of issues and problems by the public is a highly important media effect, it is only one of a number of possible media effects on public opinion (Weaver, 1985: 680). Weaver considers the link between agenda-setting and public opinion and concludes that the few studies that examined the relationship between media agenda-setting with regard to public issues and public opinion suggest that there is likely to be a relationship between media emphasis on an issue, the salience of that issue, and public opinion regarding actors (persons or institutions) associated with the issue. This evidence supports the argument that it is unrealistic to believe that thinking and thinking about can be as cleanly separated as Cohen suggested in 1963. If one subscribes to the idea of an active audience, then one must search for some way to better reconcile thinking and thinking about within a cognitive framework. To apply this framework to the agenda-setting process requires a linkage to the idea of salience. In other words, there must be some way to support the contention of a relationship between changes in the amount of media attention (salience) and changes in an evaluatively based public opinion (Trumbo, 1995: 10-11).

Despite the importance of agenda-setting research in examining the relationship between media performance and public opinion in the Arab world, there have been few systemic studies in this field. The findings of first empirical test of agenda-setting theory in the Arab region in 1986 in Egypt (Hamada, 1997: 53) does not support the main agenda-setting hypothesis. The governmental newspaper *Al Ahram* fails to set its readers' agenda. The data show that the correlation between *Al Ahram*'s agenda and the readers' agenda is very weak (.19) and insignificant. In contrast, the correlation is much stronger between partisan newspaper agenda and that of its readers (the rank order correlation is .85).

The limited effect of *Al Ahram* in setting readers' agenda may be due to the following factors: (1) National press promotes and propagates the government policies and programs. It seldom criticizes the most critical issues and decisions of the government. Readers do not view national press as credible source of news and information. (2) National press adopts almost one-way asymmetric communication from the government to the public. (3) National press self-censorship affects the way journalists gather and publish news and views. (4) National press sometimes provides incomplete stories of events and misleads public opinion. (5) The inability of national press to reach and publish accurate information at the right time negatively affects its credibility. *Al Ahram* is considered among the oldest newspapers in the Arab world; in addition, it is not the readers' agenda-setter. This may lead us to infer that it is the performance of the newspaper that makes its readers distrust it (Hamada, 1997: 332-345).

MEDIA OBJECTIVITY

The notion that competitors maximize their share by maintaining a central position and imitating each other is further applicable to the practice of journalism. Mass media are economic institutions competing in the marketplace for audiences and advertisers. Within a news organization, one important strategy for appealing to a mass audience is objectivity. The convention of objectivity—maintenance of a neutral perspective, detached from political partisanship and ideology—should lead to a perception of journalists as being in the middle of the audience's political preferences. As much as objectivity is defined philosophically, socially, and politically, it is also driven by what Lippmann called the "central motive" for the immediate satisfaction of the largest number of people. Objectivity can be defined also as the media's tendency to seek balance in their treatment of controversial issues (Terkildsen, Schnell, and Ling, 1998: 47). The point here is the perception of lack of bias. If the public perceives the mass media as biased, it will not influence its attitudes and opinions. To complete this argument, the media will be perceived as biased if they represent one side of the conflict. In other words the media will not be seen as credible sources of news and views if they are not independent. Because the Arab mass media are not independent, they are not neutral. Arab public opinion looks at the media system and the political system as one system defending its interests against the public. Media ownership and news values need to change in the Arab world to help media people to work in an objective manner.

NEWS FRAMING

To mention just one example for media framing I would concentrate on the crisis in the Gulf in which the media mobilized public opinion according to frames through which they presented events and individuals. The media employed the frame of popular culture that portrays conflict as a battle between good and evil. According to a study by the Gannett foundation, there were 1,170 examples in the print media and television of linking Saddam Hussein with Hitler. Mainstream media coverage of the crisis in the gulf tended to personalize the crisis as a conflict between George Bush and Saddam Hussein. Although Hussein was presented in purely negative terms, Bush's actions, by contrast, were praised as "decisive," "brilliant," and "masterly." In sexual terms, the narrative of the Gulf war was that Saddam/Iraq were raping Kuwait, refused to pull out, and must be destroyed, with the United States threatening to "cut it off and kill it." The media generally failed to adequately contextualize historical events, tending to simplistic explanations that omit complexity and history. Thus, there was no context to understand the crisis and no big picture or overview of the issues involved (Kellner, 1993: 62, 65, 92). There is relatively little systemic research on framing of news in Arab media, hence there is not enough data on which we can reach specific conclusions.

Another example came from an empirical research on "print media inputs in political decision making," in which 1,746 press items were analyzed, including news stories, investigative reports, editorials, columns, interviews, and articles during the period from 1980 to 1990 (Hamada, 1993: 37). The objective of the research was to examine and identify the role of journalism in making the political decision regarding four important public opinion issues that were very salient in Egyptian newspapers during 1980s. The four public opinion issues are: (1) Parliament election law, (2) Privatization, (3) Islamic money investment companies, (4) the Egyptian-Iraqi crisis in 1989.

This research revealed the following results: first, print media contributed in introducing inputs and dealt with the outputs, but they did not take part in the conversion process. Second, the limited role of national and opposition press in political decision-making is strongly related to the limited role of public opinion in the decision-making process. Third, the role of national press is totally different from that of the opposition press; whereas the first legitimize decisions, the second delegitimize them. The research also concluded that the net impact on decision-making was superficial, tentative, and as a result, there is a gap between political and communication systems. The major suggestion in this respect is that Islamic *Shari'a* should be given the first priority when we consider media laws in Muslims countries, with full confidence that it guarantees freedom of the press as well as the human rights (Hamada, 1993: 37, 316).

Despite the absence of relevant studies covering the Arab countries in general, the performance of the media does not differ from what is happening in Egypt. In his research on "Algerian Journalists and Their World" Kirat concluded that several lessons were learned from this study. First, the poor performance of Algerian journalism is not due exclusively to journalists, but to the organizational and institutional constraints in which they work. When journalists were asked about the weaknesses of the media, a large proportion listed a variety of problems and weaknesses such as unqualified personnel, poor management, unqualified managers, no clear communication policy, uncritical media, no investigative journalism, and lack of credibility. More than one-third also mentioned a lack of protection for journalists, a lack of knowledge of the audience, poor distribution of the print media, and a shortage of modern equipment and facilities (Kirat, 1998: 334, 344).

QUALITIES OF ARAB PUBLIC OPINION

Latent Public Opinion

One can confidently say that in the Arab world there are no continuous, systematic, regular methods by which public officials gauge public opinion. On the other hand, the general political environment does not help create either enlightened public opinion or the channels through which public opinion may express its demands freely and openly.

One may go further to say that in the Arab world there is a clash between the indigenous culture and public opinion surveys. This clash is due to numerous considerations: the most important of them are methodological considerations that focus specifically on conducting survey research, on obstacles both to the collection and analysis of survey data pertaining to Arab society, and also to the maintenance of scientific rigor in the execution of these operations. Among such problems are: (1) obstacles to the construction of appropriate representative and analytical samples; (2) the consideration of validity, reliability, and standardization in measurement, and of measurement equivalence in comparative studies; and (3) issues relating to the development and administration of survey instruments, including matter of language, respondent cooperation, response set, and interview bias (Tessler, 1998: 78).

Political culture and socialization. Arab political culture is by nature authoritarian, and it tends to reinforce the status quo rather than produce change or challenge the political leadership. Furthermore, ineffective political socialization has contributed to acute political ignorance and apathy among Arab masses. The agents of political socialization such as the family, educational system, media, and religious establishment do not focus on direct political socialization, but rather stress ethical and nationalist-oriented values, all within the framework of submission to authority.

Similarly, the media is largely distrusted as it is government-dominated and is believed to provide misleading information as well as propaganda for the government (Goodson and Radwan, 1997: 14). There is no doubt that these ineffective political socialization agents play negative roles vis-à-vis the culture of public opinion pools and surveys.

Contextual and practical limitations. Problems that are contextual rather than methodological also impinge upon the conduct and use of survey research. These include opposition by those who regard survey research as an investigative procedure that cannot be detached from its Western origins, and who thus believe that it inevitably produces inaccurate information; resistance based on political or special-interest considerations from governments and others who fear that surveys will provide information detrimental to their interests; and structural limitations relating to high costs and the absence of suitable data-processing facilities (Tessler, 1998: 78, 79).

Alienated Public Opinion

Another quality of Arab public opinion is that it is alienated. The definitions of alienation suggested by powerlessness and normlessness are the concepts most often utilized by social scientists attempting to delineate political alienation. Political powerlessness suggested that an individual feels that he or she cannot affect actions of the government and has no influence in such matters. When political alienation takes the form of political normlessness the individual perceives that the norms or rules that are intended to govern political relations have broken down (Mutz, 1987: 471).

In a recent research on media use and political efficacy (Hamada, 1995a: 40). I concluded that 66 percent of the respondents feel that political matters are ambiguous and do not make sense, and 75 percent feel that they do not have any say about what government does. As for their perception of decision-makers and their own efficacy, the findings showed that 62 percent feel that public officials do not care about their opinions and 59 percent believe that it is not important to participate in elections because the outcomes are predetermined, and 56 percent believe that they can not affect actions of the government and have no influence in such matters.

Data also revealed that 83 percent had no any previous experience in politics. When we focused on the reasons behind this kind of apathetic public, the research showed that it is the decline in the level of political trust (Hamada, 1995a: 236-244).

Non-Participant Public Opinion

It is supposed that those who hold permanent latent opinions and have negative feelings toward politics (alienation) may not actively participate in political matters. Hence the public opinion preferences may not be transmitted to the process of policy making.

Al Ahram center for strategic studies and research concluded that only 23.6 percent of Egyptian citizens participated in the 1984 parliamentary elections, and there is a steady decline in political participation. This striking result is consistent with what other researchers concluded regarding the major modes of political participation. The following are the results of a eight-level hierarchical model of political participation:

1. Voting: the voting participation (parliament, presidency, professional associations, councils of municipalities, and other societies) ranges from 26 to 6 percent.
2. General interest in politics: 38 percent express their interest in politics.
3. Participation in informal political discussion: 69 percent are involved in political discussions with others.
4. Writing letters or complaint to public officials: 14 percent wrote letters to public officials expressing their views regarding some general issues.
5. Sending articles to newspapers: 14 percent are involved in this activity.
6. Participation in election publicity: 19 percent engaged in election publicity.
7. Active membership in a political organization: 14 percent are actively members in some political organization.
8. Seeking political office: 8 percent sought political office (Hamada, 1995b: 30-45).

What is suggested here is that Arab public opinion is latent, alienated, and nonparticipant. The latent public would lack the motivation to seek information about politics. Lack of motivation in turn helps create an apathetic, inadvertent, and inattentive public. The inadvertent public is largely uninterested in the world of politics. This kind of public would be largely dependent on television for information about political issues and events, learning passively. These people would not acquire any informational base or content to help them form their opinions and attitudes; what they may absorb would just be labels and slogans of any debate, even if the Arab television channels presented any controversial content. The Arab television channels are mostly concerned with entertainment programs. Despite the fact that they are the primary source of information for the uneducated Arab populations they rarely serve the function of public opinion formation. The question in this context is to what extent individuals of the latent public would be alienated and isolated? (It is obvious that the existence of political alienation and isolation is heavily dependent on the latent public). As articulated by empirical studies, the public distrusts the government and feels that it has no say in what it does; hence, it prefers not to involve itself in the world of politics. However, this does not mean that Arab public opinion does not exist. In fact, Arab mass media are encouraged to publish socially useful propaganda that will form and persuade public opinion to adhere to the system; even entertainment programs must serve political purposes. The issue of government ownership of most of the media in the Arab world is very important for understanding the reasons why the media negatively affect public opinion.

ENDNOTES

1.   The author gratefully acknowledges the helpful comments of the editor on an early version of this article.
2.   Numbers in parentheses represent, respectively, chapters and verses from the *Qur'an*.

REFERENCES

Al Barzinji, Suhaib Jamal. 1998. *Working Principles for An Islamic Model in Mass Communication*. Herndon, VA: International Institute of Islamic Thought.

Al-Mehdi, Sadiq. 1978. The Concept of an Islamic State. In Altaf Gauhar Altaf (ed.), *The Challenge of Islam*. London: Islamic Council of Europe.

Ali Nadvi, Abul Hasan. 1978. Islam: The Most Suitable Religion for Mankind. In Gauhar Altaf (ed.), *The Challenge of Islam*. London: Islamic Council of Europe.

Aloofy, Abdellatif. 1998. What Makes Arabian Gulf Satellite TV Programs? A Comparative Analysis of the Volume, Origin, and Type of Program. In *The Information Revolution and the Arab World: Its Impact on State and Society*. Abu Dhabi, UAE: The Emirates Center for Strategic Studies and Research.

American Political Science Association. 1991. Democratization in the Middle East. *American Arab Affairs*, 36.

Ayish, Muhammad. 1998. Communication Research in The Arab World, A New Perspective. *The Public*, 5(3).

Azzi, Abderrahmane. 1997. *Mass Media in the Grand Maghrib*. A Paper Presented at a Conference on Mass Media in the Muslim World, International Islamic University Malaysia.

Britannica Online. 1998. Muhammad and the Religion of Islam, Nature and Significance of Islamic Law, 09/12/98.

Brohi, A.K. 1978. Islam and Human Rights. In Gauhar Altaf (ed.), *The Challenge of Islam*. London: Islamic Council of Europe.

Brosius, Hans-Bernd and Gabriel Welmann. 1996. Who Set the Agenda? Agenda-Setting as a Two-Step Flow. *Communication Research* 23.

Cohen, B. C. 1963. *The Press, the Public and Foreign Policy*. Princeton, NJ: Princeton University Press.

Davutoglu, Ahmet. 1997. *Civilizational Transformation and the Muslim World*. Kualalumpur: Berkauk.

Edelstein, Alex S. 1988. Communication Perspectives in Public Opinion: Traditions and Innovations. In James A. Anderson (ed.), *Communication Year Book, 11*. New York, Beverly Hills, London, New Delhi: Sage.

Goodson, Larry P. and Soha Radwan. 1997. Democratization in Egypt in the 1990s: Stagnant or Merely Stalled? *Arab Studies Quarterly* 19(1), 1-21.

Hamada, Basyouni. 1993. *The Role of Mass Media in Political Decision Making in the Arab World*. Beirut: Center for Arab Unity Studies.

Hamada, Basyouni. 1995a. Communication Behavior and the Political Efficacy of Public Opinion. In Sayed Ghanem (ed.), *Politics and Local System in Egypt*. Cairo: Center for Political Research and Studies.

Hamada, Basyouni. 1995b. *Mass Media Use and Political Participation*. Cairo: Center for Political Research and Studies.

Hamada, Basyouni. 1997. *Mass Media and Politics: Agenda-Setting Function of the Mass Media*. Cairo: Nahdet Al Shark.

Ibrahim, Saad Eddin. 1995. Democratization in the Arab World. In Jillian Schwedler (ed.), *Toward Civil Society in the Middle East*. London: Lynne Rienner Publishers.

Ibrahim, Saad Eddin. 1996. *Egypt, Islam and Democracy*. Cairo: The American University Press.

Kamali, Mohammad Hashim. 1994. *Freedom of Expression in Islam*. Kualalumpur: Berita Publishing SDN, BHD.

Kellner, Douglas. 1993. *The Persian Gulf, TV War*. Boulder, CO: Westview.

Kirat, Mohamed. 1998. Algerian Newsmen and Their World. In David H. Weaver (ed.), *The Global Journalist: Studies of News People Around the World*. Cresskill, NJ: Hampton Press.

Leca, Jean. 1994. Democratization in the Arab World: Uncertainty, Vulnerability and Legitimacy. A Tentative Conceptualization and Some Hypotheses. In Salame Ghassan (ed.), *Democracy without Democrats, The Renewal of Politics in the Muslim World*. London: I.B Tauris.

Maududi, Abul A'la. 1978. What Islam Stands For. In Altaf Gauhar (ed.), *The Challenge of Islam*. London: Islamic Council of Europe.

McCombs, Maxwell, Edna Einsiedel, and David Weaver. 1991. *Contemporary Public Opinion: Issues and the News*. Hillsdale, Erlbaum.

Merrill, John. 1995. *Global Journalism: Survey of International Communication*. New York: Longman.

Mowlana, Hamid. 1993. The New Global Order and Cultural Ecology. *Media, Culture & Society* 15(1), 9-27.

Mowlana, Hamid. 1996. *Global Communication in Transition: The End of Diversity.* Thousand Oaks, London, New Delhi: Sage.

Mueller, Claus. 1973. *The Politics of Communication.* New York: Oxford University Press.

Mutz, Diana. C. 1987. Political Alienation and Knowledge Acquisition. In Margaret L. Mclaughlin (ed.), *Communication Yearbook.* Newbury Park, Beverly Hills, London, New Delhi: Sage.

Pasha, Syed H. 1993. Towards a Cultural Theory of Political Ideology and Mass Media in the Muslim World. *Media, Culture & Society* 15(1), 61-79.

Rogers, E. M., J. W. Dearing, and D. Bregonan. 1993. The Anatomy of Agenda Setting Research. *Journal of Communication,* 43(2), 68-84.

Salem, Azzam. 1982. *Islam and Contemporary Society.* London: Longman.

Shabeer, Abu Buckeer. 1997. *The Limits of Secular Philosophy.* London: Longman.

Shahin, Emad Eldin. 1993. Islam, Democracy, and the West: Ending the Cycle of Denial. In Mona M. Abul-Fadl, *Proceedings of the Twenty-First Annual Conference of the International Institute of Islamic Thought and the Association of Muslim Social Scientists,* Herndon, VA: Institute of Islamic Thought and The Association of Muslim Social Scientists.

Terkildsen, Nayda, Frauke Schnell, and Cristina Ling. 1998. Interest Group, the Media, and Policy Debate Formation: An Analysis of Message Structure, Rhetoric, and Source Cues. *Political Communication* 15(1), 45-61.

Tessler, Mark. 1994. *A History of the Israeli-Palestinian Conflict.* Bloomington and Indianapolis: Indiana University Press.

Tessler, Mark. 1998. The Contribution of Public Opinion Research to an Understanding of the Information Revolution and its Impact in North Africa and Beyond. In *The Information Revolution and the Arab World.* Abu Dhabi, UAE: The Emirates Center for Strategic Studies and Research.

Trumbo, Craig. 1995. Longitudinal Modeling of Public Issues. An Application of Agenda-Setting Process to the Issue of Global Warming. In John Soloski (ed.), *Journalism and Mass Communication Monographs,* 152, 1-50.

Weaver, David. 1985. Media Agenda-Setting and Public Opinion: Is There a Link? In Robert Bostrom and Bruce H. Westley (eds.), *Political Communication.* Beverly Hills, London: Sage.

10

Public Opinion in Socialism

France Vreg

The rise of public opinion in socialism was severely impeded by the social and political structure of "socialist publics," the nature of distribution of political power in society, a paternalistic relationship between the government and the public, and the propagandistic role of mass media. Normatively, public opinion is not a power in itself nor it is the source of all power in society. The political function of the public resides in critical discussion of actions performed by political actors. According to Habermas, the public should translate *voluntas* into *ratio*, which is being reestablished through the opinion process of publicly competing arguments as a consensus about what is the general interest of society (Habermas, 1989: 99).

A reflection on public opinion in socialism leads us to question the nature of relationship between the state and the public. Was the socialist public opinion molded by the party state and its propaganda apparatus, or it was a noninstitutionalized democratic force, as Locke's moral law, the ethical consensus, or Rousseau's "common will?" Was there an open interaction between the public and the government, or was it simply a quasi-interaction between the public and the party propaganda system manufacturing "public opinion?" It is essential to analyze whether socialism was able, and attempted, to establish, however ineffectually, a free and democratic public that would launch a dialogue with political authorities, or whether this would be beyond its premises.

PUBLIC OPINION IN SOVIET "SOCIALISM"

Theories of public opinion developed in the former Soviet Union and other socialist countries in East-Central Europe were based on the assumption that socialism would lead to the elimination of class conflicts. After the October Revolution, the Soviet Union established soviets (a form of direct participation of working people in social management), a delegational system, Workers' Councils and People's Committees. The meetings of the Worker's Councils, and of the People's Committees were envisaged as fora where Soviet people would voice their opinions and interests, whereas the delegational system would promote their interests at higher levels of decision-making.

It was, however, extremely difficult to implement the revolutionary forms of direct democracy on Russian soil, underdeveloped as it was and burdened with the feudal Tsarist tradition and cultural underdevelopment. As a consequence, the statist model of government became ever more firmly established. Power was transferred to higher governmental levels and became anchored in the hands of the top Communist Party and state leaders.

The mechanism of articulating public opinion was rudimentary and limited to Party-controlled organizations and institutions. The Communist Party had a leading role in shaping and articulating public opinion. Komsomol (the organization of Soviet youth) and trade unions also played a role in the development of public opinion. These two organizations together (in addition to the leading Communist Party) were considered as two forms of the public in socialism. It was claimed that only the public rooted in socialism is capable of articulating "the right" public opinion.

The Soviet theoreticians did not speak about "the rule of the public opinion" as the ideal of classic democracy. Nor was there a question of the legislative will of the public or the controlling function of the public opinion. The principle of people's sovereignty had been reduced to the psychological motivation of the people for the efficiency of actions undertaken by the government.

Soviet theoretician A. K. Uledov developed the thesis of a "uniform public opinion" under socialism. He argued that public opinion is always not only the opinion of the majority but—since during the process of articulation, the minority opinions gradually lose the character of public opinion—but also an unanimous opinion. According to Uledov, socialist public opinion was the result of a general agreement among all social classes and groups and, therefore, it was of a higher quality than the opinion of a simple majority (Uledov, 1964: 51-57).

Soviet theoreticians of public opinion were of the view that the freedom of opinion can be ensured only in the socialist society. They rejected American and European theories of public opinion and "capitalist mechanisms" for expressing public opinion. They argued that "the Western bourgeois class" was merely declaring democratic freedoms and did not respect them in practice, particularly freedom of the press: if the press is owned by individual or corporate private owners, it could not express citizens' opinions, but only those held by owners.

In contrast to this, the press in the Soviet Union was claimed to be owned by the people and thus it could, according to the Soviet theorists, provide truthful information. It was argued that with the victory of socialism the press turned into a powerful means of creating public opinion. Accordingly, the media were organized as the "collective propagandist, agitator and organizer," to use Lenin's wording. They were considered an instrument of propaganda and thus aimed to control public opinion rather than express it. The leading Soviet communication scholar Valerij S. Korobeinikov, the director of the Center for the Mass Media and Public Opinion in Moscow, claimed that the mass media in the Soviet Union were the means of building up socialism and communism, and the development of communism would strengthen the role of the mass media in the political, ideological, and moral education of the Soviet people (Korobeinikov, 1978: 10).

After Lenin's death the totalitarian one-party system was stiffening—a process directly accelerated by Stalin. During that period, the articulation of opinions and the opinion-making process in the Party was abolished; the secret service control system and the dogmatic *agit-prop* (agitation and propaganda) method of ideological education were established; and a severe police control and censorship of the press was introduced. Court trials and physical liquidation of a great proportion of party, military, political, scientific, and cultural cadres were the means used to suppress any expression of opinions.

The Stalinist state and Party élites developed into a "state bureaucratic caste." This oligarchic system did away with the possibilities of the working people to participate in decision-making. The state-party model of the "dictatorship of the proletariat" led to the dictator-

ship of the ruling Communist Party structure in the name of the working class. As a closed system, it was bound to concentrate and centralize
the political power, and it gradually excluded other political and social
forces from sharing power. All this created the lifestyle of this élite characterized by personality cult, power politics, political voluntarism, and
ideological indoctrination. A special *state style* of communicating the
Party-bureaucracy symbols of authority was created, and exterior symbols of power and status were cultivated: state limousines, feudal *dachas*,
and so forth.

The alienation of the political, state, and military élites from the
people became the fundamental problem of the system. The political discourse of the élite did not focus on burning social and participation
problems, which concerned the citizens. Until Khruschev, the Soviet
communication system was hermetically sealed and beyond the reach of
external influences. The import of foreign newspapers, magazines, and
scientific books was banned, and external radio broadcasting was systematically jammed.

In all socialist countries, the distribution of political power was
strictly hierarchical: the power elite and administration on the top, powerless masses and a political vacuum at the bottom. A one-way, vertical
state and bureaucratic communication was established. Freedom of
speech was monopolized by mass media that themselves were not
autonomous but directly "accountable" to party and state bureaucracies.
The public was reduced to "the public" of the Communist Party, to
party political activists and representatives of the state, and authorized
interest groups. Public opinion was largely fictitious and had no relevant influence on political system.

ANTI-STALINIST DISSENT AND THE RISE OF
DEMOCRATIZATION

After the Second World War, the Communist system was introduced in
Eastern European countries rather abruptly and entailed wholesale
reconstruction of the entire system of government, economy, and social
organization. East German, Rumanian, and Bulgarian Party theorists,
political scientists, and journalists unquestioningly adopted Soviet theories of public opinion and nurtured the ideological concepts of orthodox
Stalinist socialism. During the first years after social revolution and military victory, the Yugoslav Communist Party (YCP) rigidly copied the
Soviet totalitarian system and spread the Stalin cult. YCP was considered one of the most loyal Soviet satellites. In 1946, Tito himself proposed to Stalin the establishment of an International Information Bureau

as a substitute for the former Communist International. At the founding meeting of Informbureau, the leading Yugoslav Communists, Kardelj and Djilas, went as far as to reprimand the Communist Parties of France and Italy for failing to eliminate the bourgeois system in their countries. However, because of the Soviet Union's attempt to dominate Yugoslavia through the activities of the Soviet trade, military, and intelligence groups as well as through its diplomatic offices throughout Yugoslavia, the relations between Tito and Stalin worsened. Stalin bluntly accused Tito of not following the Soviet line.

At the Informbureau meeting in 1948 in Bucharest, the Soviet representative Zhdanov denounced Tito as a spy of the imperialistic powers. The participants of the meeting adopted a resolution by which the Central Committee of YCP was expelled from the Informbureau. This resolution was practically also a call to all Yugoslav nations to rise against Tito and his government. The break between the Soviet Union and Yugoslavia was a surprise to the West as well as to the people in Yugoslavia, and in particular to the members of the YCP. Yet the reaction of the Yugoslav peoples was exactly opposite to what Moscow expected: they were outraged and gave Tito their plebiscite support.

After the Informbureau incident, Yugoslavia started with gradual democratization: it opened its borders to the West and introduced some forms of direct democracy such as Workers' Councils and other forms of self-management. In that period of the cold war, Tito and Yugoslavia moderately influenced the democratization processes in the countries of the people's democracies in Eastern Europe. Self-management and the politics of nonalignment found many admirers in Western Europe and in other parts of the world. In the words of the French historian François Furet, "the Yugoslav split revived the revolutionary zeal of those who were dissenters from Stalinism. Nostalgic Leninists, the numerous adherents of Trotsky, as well as all those disappointed by the Soviet Union rediscovered the ground they missed. . . . After Russia of the October Revolution, now it was the unlucky Balkan's turn to be heard, rechristened as the avant-garde of European society" (Furet, 1998: 5). The milestone year 1948 was followed by events such as the workers' uprising in East Berlin in 1953, revolution in Hungary in 1956, the Prague Spring and its suppression in 1968, the birth of the Polish Movement in 1980, and Gorbachev's ascent in 1985.

In Yugoslavia, institutes for public opinion research emerged in Belgrade, Zagreb, Ljubljana, and Skopje at the beginning of the 1960s. They were the result of the democratization processes in Yugoslavia that were under way after Tito's conflict with Stalin and the Informbureau in 1948. Yugoslav scholars of public opinion adopted Western concepts of public opinion. Joze Goricar (1969: 716), a pioneer of sociology in then

Yugoslavia, defended a modern definition of public and of pluralist public opinion. Rudi Supek (1968: 45) noted that the process of articulation of public opinion was essentially contradictory and conflicting. In Slovenia, the most developed republic in the former Yugoslavia, public opinion was progressively conceptualized as an interaction between the government and the public, with mass media mediating between them. The political state was required to deploy a two-way communication between the state and its citizens based on the principles of an equilibrium between the two communication streams and participation of political parties and interest groups in the mediating process.

The criticism of this model raises a series of doubts: Is there a communication relationship between two autonomous subjects? What is the social substance of this relationship? Does the public exist as a community of critical and autonomous subjects or is an object of political manipulation? Do the rulers pay attention to the preferences of the ruled? Is the parliament as the traditional institution of "popular will" the supreme expression of this will and public opinion or is it subject to the pressure by the governing political forces? Is the parliament a place where delegated mandataries meet in order to register decisions taken in advance, so that the parliamentary procedure of voting becomes merely a formality?

In a democratic socialism, public opinion was considered a "real power, a constitutive element of policy making," as opposed to a "uniformed public opinion" as a moral ornament to demonstrate the democratization of the system (Vreg, 1966: 22). The public was conceived as the social carrier of public opinion, provided that the basic ingredients of the opinion process were accessible in horizontal interactive communication (e.g., the possibility of identifying facts and alternatives, of public debate, of competition between alternative solutions).

Back in 1962 the Institute for Sociology and Philosophy at Ljubljana University and the Department of Journalism conducted the first public opinion and mass media survey on a sample of 12,000 respondents. The sample was so large because we studied latent structures of the public, public opinion, and media in a way similar to the approach developed by Lazarsfeld in the Institute for Applied Social Research in New York. The project was unique in Yugoslavia and in the Balkans. Political-sociological analyses offered a comparison with public opinion in Europe and the United States. The Center for Public Opinion in Ljubljana built the largest social studies research data bank in Yugoslavia as it then was. Thanks to a more democratic atmosphere in Slovenia—which did not preclude from occasional political interventions in polling—the Slovene public opinion surveys did not share the destiny of similar projects in the rest of Yugoslavia, which were gradually withering away and turning into a servant of politics.

PLURALITY VS. UNIFORMITY IN PUBLIC OPINION

It was only after Stalin's death that in some former East European socialist countries the democratization of political processes and pluralization
of public opinion began. Some individuals and groups became aware of
the existence of a political differentiation in the public, which had its origin in ideological and political traditions, in different concepts of the
road to socialism, in the conflicts shaking society, and in the newly
emerged political and ideological agendas. Increasingly popular became
the idea that socialism should not give birth to an atomized society, but
that it should create conditions for the formation of an articulated society, for the formation of an opinion pluralism of social groups.
"Despotism endeavors to liquidate the articulateness of society and re-
direct it," said Julian Hochfeld in his speech in the Polish parliament
before the elections for People's Committees in 1957. "A characteristic
trait of our socialist construction is the fact that there are being founded,
revived and given increased significance independent unions and associations which organize the life of the population in the spheres of their
own interests, needs and aspirations" (Hochfeld, 1957: 309). The Polish
sociologists defined public opinion as a collection of publicly expressed
opinions on public issues coming from the representatives of different
groups of society. Public opinion cannot be restricted merely to the opinion of the majority, because that would lead to the disregard or underestimation of the views of the minority.

Similar views were present among the Czech and Slovak theorists of public opinion. Both in Poland and Czechoslovakia, national centers for public opinion research were established that tended to shed
light on the pluralism of opinion of social and political groups. Under
Dubcek's chairmanship, the Czechoslovak government instituted in
1968 some forms of democratic socialism. In the system of political pluralism that then developed, several political centers articulated political
opinions. This was the reason that in August 1968 the Soviet army
invaded Czechoslovakia and the politicians who were loyal servants of
the Soviet Union came to power.

The Prague Center for Public Opinion conducted public opinion
polls even after the Soviet invasion. The polls showed that the majority
opinion still supported the overthrown Prime Minister Dubcek. But further research was subdued under political pressure. The Center could
not persist against government pressures and started to present a
proregime and uniform public opinion.

The principle of different and specific ways toward socialism
was increasingly affirming itself in a number of Marxist parties in
Western Europe. The thesis of acceptability of multiparty structure for

West European socialism was gaining ground. At the Congress of the Italian Communist Party in 1969 in Bologna, its president Luigi Longo declared the new society would be a pluralist society. "Socialist society in Italy will allow for the coexistence of several parties and social organizations where views and conflicting forces will confront freely and in a democratic manner."[1]

At the same time, critical Marxists in the socialist countries created theoretical groundwork for the multiparty system of people's democracies in Eastern Europe. The existence of special organizational forms of the Popular Front had become a reality and practice in people's democracies. A process of animating public opinion as a factor influencing the governing process was beginning—in certain socialist countries quite stormily.

The rise of social differentiation of opinions was the foundation of a new political structure which some sociologists termed *political pluralism of a nonantagonistic character*.[2] It was reflected in the form of political polycentrism where several centers relatively freely shaped political opinions and possessed their own propaganda mechanisms that competed in the molding of public opinion. The new organization of society should, to a much greater extent, express and realize the interest of various strata of socialist society which was characterized by nonantagonistic relations. Moreover, in some countries the Communist Party itself became the place where different political trends met, and where, at least up to a certain point, the political differentiation of society was reflected (as for instance, in Poland and former Czechoslovakia).

The political consolidation of society based on the program of the governing party did not exclude different opinions that developed in the internal life of the governing party, whereas different forms of external differentiation into various parties and groups were much less likely to materialize. Parties, political organizations, and groups were institutionalized political opinion centers composing the political pluralism of a "new" type, and this was reflected in the pluralistic structures of the Fronts of Popular Unity, which played different roles in socialist countries. Since the antisocialist opposition had been eliminated from the political system, parties and organizations did not function as a mechanism for gaining power, but as a system of crystallization and representation of interests and opinions of various social groups.

This period marked the beginning of activating public opinion as an agent influencing the mechanisms of government due to favorable conditions for the development of a critical public opinion and for the public expression of political pluralism. Differences existing in every socialist society found their political expression in different forms of political pluralism, which was more and more widely viewed as an indispensable prerequisite for an efficient control over the ruling system. Pluralism appeared either in a *vertical* power structure (parties, political organizations, groups of people holding the same opinion) or in a *horizontal* structure (workers' self-management, local authorities). In some socialist countries, notably in Poland, a bigger role was played by the vertical pluralism of the system, whereas the horizontal pluralism of the political system prevailed in Yugoslavia in the form of self-management. The common denominator of both systems was that they opened the way to political expression of opinions and interests of various classes. (Wiatr, 1966: 216). According to Soviet theoreticians the political pluralism existing in the majority of people's democracies was characterized by the fact that in addition to the Communist Party, there were other active political parties—provided, of course, that they recognized the leading role of the Communist Party, accepted the program of building socialism, and guided and educated the class or social group whose interest they represent.

However, nonantagonistic forms of pluralism did not abolish statism, the bureaucratization of vertical structure and oligarchic tendencies which were the iron law of every organization, including the socialist one. Nor made they possible a direct participation of the people in the process of political decision-making. The socialist theorists disagreed as to the function and durability of political pluralism. Some (for example Wiatr) claimed that pluralism of a nonantagonistic character would remain a permanent form of the crystallization and articulation of opinions, interests, and political will in a socialist democracy. A group of East German scholars initially held the view that the system of a democratic block of parties and mass organizations and people's fronts was very successful and that in the future, it would significantly contribute to the flourishing and strengthening of the German Democratic Republic.

Other people's democracies, however, very soon experienced a formal "withering away" of the nonantagonistic pluralist system and a transition into a one-party system. At the time of the Soviet occupation in Czechoslovakia in 1968, the allied political parties were not consulted by the Communist Party, and in practice, they died out. The articulation of public opinion was extinguished. The ideas of the orthodox Soviet system prevailed in the German Democratic Republic as well as in Bulgaria. In China, during the period of "Cultural Revolution" and the "Gang of Four," the mechanism of a multiparty system sank into oblivion. East German political scientists maintained that socialist democracy in the German Democratic Republic, because of its unique characteristics, could not be reduced to a system of political parties and their participation. This was also the reason why the Constitution of the GDR and the Program of the Unified Socialist Party did not speak of multiparty mechanisms any more.

The Communist Party of the Soviet Union assumed that the process of the development of Communism, based on the common interests of workers, farmers, and (proletarian) intelligentsia would lead to a political and ideological unity of the people in the countries of people's democracies. Along with this, the objective reasons for the existence of a multiparty system would disappear, and the Communist Party would in all those countries grow into the party of all people. However, instead of a genuine public opinion a *quasi-public opinion*, created by political, state, military, and other institutions, prevailed. It was formed through official statements, speeches, and press conferences by statesmen, ministers, parliamentary commissions, political party officials, and state officials. The mass media mainly expressed the official, institutional opinions. Even the secretary-general of the Soviet Communist Party, Leonid Brezhnev, recognized that "the propaganda drumbeat" was full of empty phrases and clichés that made the mass media messages unconvincing. It was not until the late 1970s when in a number of socialist countries the party-state media monopoly was broken, although even during the 1980s a significant part of new and independent media remained illegal or semilegal (Splichal, 1994: 28).

STATE CENTRALISM AND PUBLIC OPINION

In theory, the Yugoslav political system, as conceived by its leading ideologist Edvard Kardelj, ought to allow for political participation in terms of articulation of interests of diverse social groups within a unified socialist organization, The People's Front. But following the Soviet model, he rejected any form of political pluralism. After the Tito-Stalin split and with the introduction of the self-management system, Kardelj considered that the interests and opinions of individual social groups could be structurally incorporated into political system through decisions made by the organs of self-management.

The opposite was argued by Milovan Djilas, who refuted the idea of the People's Front. Democracy, as understood by Djilas, meant the creation of an atmosphere favorable for the articulation of new ideas, for the beginning of an ideological struggle, for the freedom of criticism and open discussion. He was speaking of the possibility of having *two socialist* parties. Thus he created the dilemma of whether political pluralism should be developed in the Yugoslav political system, in which political parties could articulate their opinions and in which authentic public opinion could be formed. At the same time he severely criticized the Yugoslav Communist Party leadership which steadily transformed, along with state bureaucracy, into a new class.[3] Djilas' ideas were criticized by Kardelj who denoted them as attempts to reduce the role of the Communist Party to the role of a discussion club, which could easily lead to the disruption of the League of Communists (the former Communist Party). The critique was followed by Djilas' expulsion from the Party and, incidentally, his imprisonment.

In the former Yugoslavia self-management was the basis of the economic and political system. Workers' Councils were not only consultative, they were also governing bodies and they enjoyed the rights of executive organs. The spread of self-management over all the spheres of public life, including the political process, the system of communication, education, culture, and all segments of the public strengthened those social forces that were able to overcome the tendencies of oligarchy and bureaucracy. According to Serbian political scientist Jovan Djordjevic, "socialist democracy was not reflected only in the degree by which public opinion has become a special institution of society nor by which it has grown as the component part of self-governing society. Public opinion must also remain a factor outside any activity and organizational link. It must be liberated and free from its own institutions as well" (Djordjevic, 1957: 35).

The development of the self-management system in enterprises and in other spheres of social life met with opposition from managerial élites and state bureaucracy. Centralistically oriented Yugoslav forces revived the idea of an "integral Yugoslavhood" embodied in a single "Yugoslav Nation." They tended toward strengthening the power of the centralist structures in the Communist Party and the State. But the ulterior motive was aggressive Serbian aspirations to dominate in Yugoslavia. Antiself-management and centralistically oriented adherents gathered in the circles of the top officials of the Yugoslav State Security Agency. The publics of individual Republics (i.e., federal units based mainly on nationality principle) were supposed to melt into the Great Yugoslav State public, whereby the opinions of individual nations and nationalities living on the territory of Yugoslavia would dissolve in an artificially constructed "average" opinion, which could be presented as an "authentic" Yugoslav public opinion. It was not until the famed Brioni Session of the LCY central committee in 1966 that the trends toward state centralism were defeated.

The conceptualization of social communication in the system of self-management considered public opinion a constituent element of political process. Opinion pluralism included the opinions voiced by grassroots groups, non-Marxist ideological movements, religious associations, ethnic groups, and others. Modest attempts were made to achieve pluralization of opinion and political pluralism which, however, was seen by the hard-core orthodox politicians as the "politicizing of interests" and implementing of the Western political pluralism. State political communication and one-way information flow was preserved in the spheres controlled by the state, for example, the army and foreign affairs, while in the parliamentary bodies and social organizations and associations opened to a dialogue of citizens about current problems.

Public opinion surveys, however, showed that people's participation in politics and the part of the public interested in the issues of general politics were far from the level assumed by the ideologists. Annoying findings stemming from surveys of the Belgrade Institute for Public Opinion Research led the Serbian political regime to denounce them as "politically unacceptable." As a consequence, the Institute continued merely with small-scale, politically irrelevant polls that were geographically confined to the city of Belgrade. In Zagreb, the capital of Croatia, public opinion surveys died away after the so-called national faction within the League of Communists of Croatia had been liquidated in the early 1970s.

Clearly, the political discourse of the Yugoslav political elite was not focused on crucial economic and political problems felt by the citizenry. Citizens' political will was not only a result of their dissatisfaction and disappointment with the material conditions of life, but was primarily related to their powerlessness in decision-making at all societal levels. Political surveys made clear that the system did not meet the expectations of citizens: approximately 80 percent of citizens realized, according to surveys, that they did not have the slightest influence upon government decisions.

Political actors and the mass media failed to consider the citizen an individual, a personality with his or her specific motives and wishes to maintain his or her own identity. Society was only seen as a political and economic system, but not also as a social system, in which the "components of the life-world—culture, society, and personality structures— form complex, sensible collective groups, which communicate mutually, although participating in different substrata" (Habermas, 1988: 98). Vertical distribution (deconcentration) of power and the development of participatory democracy were beyond the scope of political elites. Social institutions did not build their legitimacy on the principle of transparency to the public and an interaction between the state institutions and civil society. This applied particularly to the state security system, especially to its defense, police, and foreign policy subsystems.

NATIONAL DIVERSITIES AND DISCRIMINATION

The ideology of the dictatorship of the proletariat suppressed the nation's question—differences in nations' origin and identity, historical and cultural traditions, levels of development, diverse religions, languages and writings, artistic creativity, and value system. The equality of nations and intercultural communication was an ongoing problem of all multinational socialist states, particularly in the former Soviet Union, Yugoslavia, and Czechoslovakia. Socialist communication systems were not capable of articulating differing interests of nations and nationalities, political and ethnic minorities. Rather, they enhanced the domination of the largest nation, stimulated assimilation, and promoted national stereotypes and national discrimination.

Intercultural communication in the former Yugoslavia reflected the conflicts existing in cultural, media, and other spheres of life. Legal and other forms of regulation only generally covered the use of languages and scripts in public life and in the army. In reality, the great majority of the personnel in the federal administration came from Russian, Czech, and Serbo-Croat linguistic regions respectively, and the language of the dominant nation was *de facto* the official language in the federative institutions, including the army.

The largest nations (Russians, Czechs, Serbs) cherished the ideas on assimilation of the nations and the languages, which would give rise to the so-called state-nation, along with political models of a uniform centralized community with one official language. Mass media were not the articulator of the will of the nations; they were becoming increasingly the agents of government actions. The media primarily distributed information provided by state and Party institutions, or political, economic, military, and other ruling élites.

Although ethnic tensions in the former Yugoslavia ultimately germinated open military conflicts, the Yugoslav system was often taken as an example of proper balance between tendencies toward unity and diversity in a multinational state. The 1974 Yugoslav Constitution definitely affirmed the right of self-government of the nations and national minorities based on their local political institutions (parliaments, governments, courts). The Constitution provided for equality of national languages and alphabets; there was no "state" language—the languages of all nations were in official use. All republics and provinces developed their own educational and mass media systems, and considerable differences existed between them both in terms of quantity (media production and consumption) and quality (e.g., in terms of agenda-setting). However, only newspapers published in Belgrade and Zagreb successfully crossed the republic frontiers and were readily available throughout Yugoslavia. Radio and television broadcasting preserved a traditional uniformity regarding establishment and organizational forms. Although a state monopoly was largely eliminated in the entire communication sphere, legal and statutory regulation remained rather restrictive (Splichal, 1988: 31).

Research into interethnic relations and understanding in Yugoslavia, which started in early 1980s, indicated an insufficient degree of and an imbalanced cross-cultural communication. There was more information about the dominant nations (the Serbs and the Croats) than others (the Slovenians, the Macedonians, and the Albanians) (Klinar, 1985: 6). Public opinion polls in Slovenia showed that the opinions of individuals and groups were articulated also through informal channels. These noninstitutionalized forms of public opinion formation and expression represented an important and sometimes even the predominant opinion. In the process of articulation of public opinion also some dissenting voices were competing, including those of the political opposition that acted beyond the frame of political legitimacy of the system of self-management socialism in the 1980s. During that period, an open democratic opinion atmosphere developed especially in Slovenia, rendering it possible for all kinds of problems to be openly discussed—even those which for decades were held taboo or considered myths. The pluralism of political and cultural groups, nations and ethnic "minorities," ecological and peace movements were gaining strength. The mass media were discussing questions of freedom of the press, censorship, and the violation of human rights (Vreg, 1988: 19–20). Public debates on controversial issues were forcing the local ruling powers to progressively limit and eventually abolish political monopoly.

THE BREAKDOWN OF THE SYSTEM

The crisis of soviet and other communist systems culminated not only because of the "lack" of economic and political democracy, but also because these systems failed to articulate diverse political, economic, and cultural interests of the nations, nationalities, and social and ethnic minorities. The communist rulers controlled the societal information flow and created "public opinion." State propaganda was part of systematic endeavors to influence citizen opinions, to manipulate their knowledge, and to direct their behavior. Political and economic power was concentrated in a few political, state, military, and economic centers. As a result, sentiments of political impotence, breeding anomie, apathy, and political passivity of citizens appeared in the public.

History has shown that large empires were doomed because of the very crude concentration of power in the hands of the political élite of the dominant nations. The same applied to the large multinational federations such as the former Soviet Union, Czechoslovakia, Yugoslavia and other countries where the power was usurped. Multinational federations had a mammoth state administration, powerful repression apparatus, and an immense centralized army. The entire state and economic system was controlled by members of the dominant "supernations" and was filled with statesmen, diplomats, generals, federal officials, and other dominant élite members recruited from the dominant nations.

In the Soviet Union, the "Bolshevik formula" was an "organic" result of a particular civilizational Eurasian milieu. The "Bolshevik code" in essence represents a historically inferior type of "modernization" of societies that did not develop modern forces of production, massive entrepreneurial spirit, and democratic culture. The authoritarian spirit was the social milieu within which the drama of socialism was activated. Political power was taken to be a new Archimedian lever for total reconstruction of the world, society, and human nature. The insatiable logic of unlimited power resulted in the creation of the totalitarian state and the Gulag Archipelago.

But socialism is not to be equated with the Eastern European system of one-party politocracy, because European socialism has been affiliated with democracy ever since its beginnings. The soviet model of socialism was actually a deformation of socialism as a humanistic, pluralist democracy. "The epoch of monism and also political monism in socialism is coming to an end; political pluralism, limited as it may be, is a necessity for any developed complex society that wishes to be rational, democratic and just" (Bibic, 1989: 30).

The shock of almost surrealistic changes in Eastern Europe in 1989 and the early 1990s is comparable with the breakdown of great Empires, with the mid-1800s revolutions. "Socialism is dead," declared many analysts. Others had a contrary vision of the future, as the coming of age of "New socialism" (Gorbachev). Willy Brandt declared that bureaucratic socialism was destroyed and democratic socialism was experiencing a renaissance.

However, the very aim of pluralist society is not self-evident, unproblematic as it appears. We can see this in East Europe. The system of the new society is in some countries seen as "democratic socialism," even though in the new economic and political order numerous dimensions that are civilization achievements of capitalism are being inbuilt. From another angle, the new society is seen exclusively as a return to "old capitalism," in spite of the fact that modern capitalism has evolved through the social struggles of labor and in social-democratic European countries there is a process of the broadening and the strengthening of state power and a process of the erosion of civil society. The power of state and economic corporations has become enormous. The penetration of the state into every sphere of social life means a marginalization of scientific and technical professional influence in the strategy of development. The professional and cultural élites have lost their power and were vegetating on the margins of political and professional decision-making. Educational and cultural institutions and organizations, universities, medical institutions, research institutes, trade unions, and even academies of arts and sciences have become state institutions and directly subordinated to the ministries.

In public life there was no influence of the institutions of civil society, which had very limited and powerless representation in the advisory councils of mass media and other "public-service" institutions. Representatives of political parties have had the decisive role in these organs and transformed them largely into a transmission belt for State and Party bureaucratic élite. In such a bureaucratized, élitist society, citizens remained the object of information flow. The public seemed to be merely "social scenery" in the arena of the struggle for power. They were not given the opportunities of evolutionary changes bringing about citizen participation in decision-making and self-regulation of social groups in a participatory democracy.

A modern pluralist society today should develop on the basis of combination of different principles and life logic. This also holds true for a possible democratic socialist system. To understand the original European idea of socialism, one has to return to authentic ideas about the relationship between the state and bureaucracy already proclaimed by Marx, his arguments for the freedom of the press as a "public eye," and even earlier discussions on the need to establish cooperative and solidary society based on equal rights and equal opportunities of every citizen. (Thus, for example, Solidarity in Poland in the 1980s cannot be interpreted as a battle "against socialism," but against bureaucratic elites and suppression of freedoms.) The fundamental ideas of socialism originally even did not have direct political implications; for example, they were not hostile toward private enterprise as was later communism. For socialist ideas in the twentieth century, the significance of the public and public opinion had a central significance, which is clearly reflected in theorizations of public opinion from Ferdinand Tönnies and John Dewey to Jürgen Habermas in which the public is conceived as the subject presented with the power of judgment and morality, and the free press as the means of public opinion formation and expression.

The fundamental idea of socialism is that of a social state as the guarantor of social justice. This idea emerged from revolts of the slaves, peasant risings, Chartist movements, the French Revolution and mass workers' strikes in Europe and the United States. Before the Second World War French socialists organized the People's Front as a unique bloc of workers and middle classes against the approaching danger of nazism and totalitarianism, and this "model" was replicated in many other countries around Europe where peoples stood up against nazism and fascism. At that time, Edvard Kardelj (one of the leading figures in the Slovene anti-Fascist front and later the ideological founder of Yugoslav socialism) argued that "this people's movement which is today primarily a fighting means of masses, is also an embryo of the alliance of workers, farmers and the so-called 'middle classes' in general that represents the nearest future of any nation" (Kardelj, 1939/1957: 373).

In the system of self-management, public opinion represents a constituent element of political process. The participatory-democratic system of mass communication should enable a dynamic, two-way, pluralistic information flow. The multitude of public and political projects ought to be coordinated on the basis of a cooperative communication activity aiming at consensual decisions. The fundamental condition for such processes is the establishment of a relatively autonomous, self-organized public that would be able to oppose state ideological domination or even repression. In the new type of democracy, the political public is an essential component in legitimization process of the carriers of political and state power.

The idea of self-managerial democracy was included in the political programs of Swedish, French, and Italian socialists; socialist movements in other countries tried to implement the idea in their own specific ways as well. It grew up into the cornerstone of democratic socialism. Future societies will not be uniform. Some will be a combination of authoritarian political regimes and quasi-parliamentary democracy, other will develop a modern pluralism with participatory democracy and effective public opinion. The new information age and the growing complexity make pluralism an inevitable feature of any society. Thus, the dramatic search for a more democratic organization of social and political life will continue, and socialism will have, perhaps the first time in the history of the idea, a chance to compete with capitalism or, actually, with individualism, as the opposite of socialism was not capitalism but individualism (Hobsbawn, 1991: 315).

ENDNOTES

1. *Nasi razgledi* (Ljubljana) 18. 1969. 4(1).
2. The number of parties in people's democracies varied. In Poland there were the Polish United Workers' Party, and two allied parties, the United Farmers' Party and the Democratic Party. In the German Democratic Republic there were five parties with the Socialist Unity Party of Germany at the forefront. In Czechoslovakia there were five parties headed by the Communist Party. In Bulgaria there were two: the Communist Party and the Bulgarian Union of Farmers. Each party had its own newspaper. In China there were nine parties, in Korea three and in Northern Vietnam three.
3. Djilas published his articles from October 1953 till January 1954 in the newspaper *Borba*, which was the newspaper of the League of Communists of Yugoslavia. His political pamphlet "The Anatomy of Certain Morality" was published in the journal Nova Misao. A revised version of his criticism of bureaucratism was published later as a book entitled *New Class—An Analysis of the Communist System* (1957). Western critics assessed the book as "the best anti-Communist document," which superseded the whole of Western anti-Communist propaganda.

REFERENCES

Bibic, Adolf. 1989. Vec obrazov (politicnega) pluralizma. In *Politicni pluralizem in demokratizacija javnega zivljenja*, 16-41. Izola: Slovensko politolosko drustvo.

Djordjevic, Jovan. 1957. *O javnom mnenju*. Beograd: Rad.

Furet, François. 1998, December 2. Preteklost iluzije. *Delo* (Ljubljana).

Goricar, Joze. 1969. Socioloska opredelitev javnega mnenja. *Teorija in praksa* (Ljubljana), 712-721.

Habermas, Jürgen. 1989. *Strukturne spremembe javnosti*. Ljubljana: SKUC. (*Strukturwandel der Öffentlichkeit*. 1962. Neuwied: Hermann Luchterhand Verlag).

Habermas, Jürgen. 1988. *Nachmetaphisisches Denken. Philosophische Aufsätze*. Frankfurt: Suhrkamp.

Hobsbawn, Eric. 1991. Out of the Ashes. In R. Blackburn (ed.), *After the Fall. The Failure of Communism and the Future of Socialism*, 315-325. London: Verso.

Hochfeld, Julian. 1957. Before the Elections for People's Committees. Speech in the Polish Sejm 30. X. 1957 during Debate on the Election Order Bill.

Kardelj, Edvard. 1939/1957. *Razvoj slovenskega narodnostnega vprasanja*. Ljubljana: Drzavna zalozba Slovenije.

Klinar, Peter. 1985. From Ethical Stratification to Multiculturalism—International Meeting. Paper presented at the conference on Communication and Life Styles, Ljubljana.

Korobeinikov, Valerij S. 1978. Mass Intercourse and Mass Information in the Process of Social Development. Paper presented at the World Congress of Sociology, Uppsala.

Splichal, Slavko. 1988. National Diversities, Identity and the Media: The case of Slovenia in Yugoslavia. *Comunicació Social i Identitat Cultural*. Barcelona: IAMCR.

Splichal, Slavko. 1994. *Media Beyond Socialism. Theory and Practice in East-Central Europe*. Boulder, Co: Westview Press.

Supek, Rudi. 1968. *Ispitivanje javnog mnjenja*. Zagreb: Naprijed.

Uledov, A. K. 1964. *Die öffentliche Meinung*. Berlin: VEB. (First published in Moscow, 1963).

Vreg, France. 1966. Drustveno komuniciranje u sistemu samoupravljanja. *Novinarstvo* (Beograd), 2-3, 20-40.

Vreg, France. 1969. Structural and Functional Changes in the Public and the World Community. In *Mass Media and International Understanding*, 34-51. Ljubljana: School of Sociology, Political Science, and Journalism.

Vreg, France. 1980. *Javno mnenje in samoupravna demokracija* [Public Opinion and Self-Management Democracy]. Maribor: Obzorja.

Vreg, France. 1988. Political Communication in Pluralist Society. *Comunicació Social i Identitat Cultural*, 112-137. Barcelona: IAMCR.

Wiatr, Jerzy. 1966. Problems of Pluralism in the Polish Political System. *Socijalizam* (Beograd), 2, 210- 226.

III

POLLING

11

The Election and Influence Frameworks as Arenas for "Reading" Public Opinion

James B. Lemert

Among a large number of conceptual disputes in public opinion scholarship is whether or not the polls have any validity as a measure of public opinion. In his seminal critique of polling's assumptions, Herbert Blumer (1948) seemed to take for granted that polls could indeed predict election outcomes. In that paper and a related 1946 chapter that was reprinted in 1966, Blumer (1966) in effect declared that both polls and elections measured the behavior of a "mass," rather than the deliberation of a "public." Blumer's challenge to the polls, plus the self-promotional efforts of the developing market research/polling industry, have influenced both Blumer's critics and his adherents tacitly to accept the polls-elections linkage (e.g., Blumer critic Phil Converse, 1987, and Blumer adherents Charles Salmon and Ted Glasser, 1995).

Thus the validity of polling as a measure of public opinion has become almost inextricably bound up with whether elections themselves can be taken to express or reflect "public opinion." If elections don't, this reasoning seems to go, polls can't possibly (Blumer, 1948, 1966).

As the title of this chapter implies, in order to present and discuss what I mean by the term "Election Framework" (Lemert, 1981), I'm pretty well committed to taking on the polling/elections side issue as well. On the other hand, I'll also need at least to introduce the concepts of Election Framework and Influence Framework in order to enter the debate about the validity of polls as an indicator of public opinion.

So where to begin? Let me start with some definitions and a vocabulary. Then, using that vocabulary, I'll return to the debate about the validity of polls and, after that, will present a brief summary of some analytical advantages that these concepts bring.

KEY CONCEPTS

Mass Opinion

The concept of a mass—burdened by many excess meanings, such as the "mass society" notions of huge size, alienation from local traditions, individual helplessness, conformity, and pliability—nevertheless remains a useful one (see Beniger, 1987). After discarding these excess meanings, we can say that a mass has three characteristics that are essential to remember when we study public opinion.

1. Following Blumer (1948, 1966), a mass is assembled through a *coincidence* of behavioral or cognitive choices, made at roughly the same time by a number of individuals, each for her or his individual reasons. Thus, members of a mass watch a local television news show tonight, a mass bought shaving cream yesterday, a mass chops wood today, and a mass holds some sort of opinion about whether American President Bill Clinton was being persecuted by his political enemies. Members of the TV news mass may or may not have chopped wood today, or purchased shaving cream yesterday, or have an opinion about Clinton, and so on. Even during a single day, each of us probably is a member of many different masses.
2. Members of a mass lack awareness of who and how many others are doing, or thinking about, the same thing at that time. In essence, members of a mass are cut off from contact with almost all other members of that mass. Direct communication among members of that mass is minimal or nonexistent at the time of the mass behavior. (True, individual members of a mass can log onto the Internet, and then enter into a "chat room" or an interactive Home Page. Similarly, both now and 100 years ago, a mass could have decided to enter an across-

the-fence conversation with a neighbor. But neither now nor 100 years ago does anybody have a way of simultaneously knowing who and how many others are doing the same thing at roughly the same time. Clearly the one-on-one, interactive conversations themselves are not at issue here. Entering into those conversations is.)

3. Members of a mass are disengaged and cut off from the political system but usually very much in contact with the consumer marketing system at the time of the mass behavior. In most societies, the consumer marketing system surrounds us, facilitating mass consumption. Media consumption itself is a mass activity, and in many societies exposure to the media also means exposure to advertising that urges the audience to buy products. If a consumer ad "sells" the consumer on a brand of shaving cream, more than likely there'll be a store selling it just down the street. The mass marketing system makes it as easy as possible for members of the mass to be engaged with it. Retail outlets display large, obtrusive signs; even direct-mail marketing uses self-addressed envelopes and "bill me later" check-off systems to make it as easy to buy as possible. The political system tends to erect barriers to actual (as distinguished from "spectator") participation in it. For example, votes in elections are often treated as if they were consumer decisions, but the grocery store is open almost every day; the voting booth isn't. Beyond elections, consider how difficult it is for an ordinary citizen to contact a government official—no phone number, no address readily available, and hordes of secretaries and other functionaries to get through before the citizen can actually contact that official.

Beyond such barriers as these, news media public affairs content enhances the likelihood that the consumer will mistake *knowing* with *participating* (see Lazarsfeld and Merton's discussion of the media's "narcotizing dysfunction" in this context; 1971: 565-566).

Issue Objects

Mass opinion, then, can be thought of as the views of an aggregate of people about some psychological object they have in common. Their views toward this object may or may not be the same, but presumably they all know enough about the object to have an opinion about it. Some of these objects become *issue* objects in the public opinion process. An issue object is the subject of what is, or could be, a public controversy.

Generally, objects such as Beethoven's music, the family dog, or even the idea of jogging don't become the topic of public discussion and controversy. Issues might concern such objects of controversy as Bosnian Serb leader Radovan Karadzic, Russian President Vladimir Putin, Congressional Republicans' proposal to use part of the U.S. budget surplus to reduce taxes, and so forth.

Participation and Visibility of Opinions

By itself, mass opinion is essentially invisible. The most obvious way for some members of a mass to make their opinion visible is through political participation, which is defined as the effortful act of expressing one's opinion about an issue object (see Lemert, 1981). Participation ranges from voting to demonstrating or picketing, writing letters to the editor, donating time or money, showing up to hear a speaker for a cause, tying yellow ribbons around trees during Jimmy Carter's Iran hostage crisis, harassing women as they enter abortion clinics, interfering with "old growth" logging by perching in the trees, dropping down on a bungee cord to block a war ship from passing under a bridge, and so forth.

Many conventional forms of participation, such as writing letters, petitioning, voting, and showing up to hear speakers, have had long histories of legitimacy and acceptance in Western democracies. With the exception of voting, those histories also mean that such older forms have relatively unambiguous implications for how the people engaging in them feel about the issue object. But some more recent acts of participation, such as putting up yellow ribbons or hanging from bungee cords, have both their issue object and their opinion meanings assigned to them right before our eyes.

Probably, as long as symbolic meanings can be assigned to these otherwise ambiguous acts, there is an almost infinite variety of these newer acts of opinion expression, limited only by participants' imagination and resources.

Is participation the only way that issue opinions can be made visible? No, at least not in principle. Opinions can be made visible through outside intervention:

> if an issues poll is done, *and*
> if the results of the poll are communicated to politicians and
>   other decision-makers, *and*
> if the decision-makers believe the poll results are credible
>   opinion indicators.

Otherwise, participation is the only way.

Majority Opinion

The distinction between majority opinion and public opinion is consistent with Blumer (see especially the 1966 reprint: 48). The polls consistently seem to assign the term "public opinion" to whatever response gets a majority on an issues question. But even in elections, a determined minority can sometimes outweigh a majority when the minority has higher turnout or the minority votes for candidates on the basis of a single issue. In America, it is not at all uncommon for a minority to have turned out to vote. So what does it mean for a majority of a minority to have carried the day?

Even in countries with higher voting turnouts than the United States, the same possible discrepancy between a majority of the mass and "public opinion" is often the case outside of elections, because far greater skills, resources, and motivation often are required for participation in nonelectoral politics.

Effective Public Opinion

Consistent with Blumer (1948), effective public opinion is opinion that is visible to decision-makers as they try to discern public opinion and decide how and whether to react to it (Lemert, 1992). In many cases, effective public opinion reflects the opinions of those who have the access, the confidence, and the skills to make their views visible to those decision-makers. (Although decision-makers' processing of effective public opinion information is unavoidably subjective, it is not idiosyncratic. In other words, their jobs require them to pay attention to opinion input. If that input changes, at some point their perception of public opinion will change.)

In at least two respects, however, my meaning for effective public opinion differs from Blumer's. First, I extend the concept to election results, as noted briefly above. Second, instead of absolutely ruling out the relevance of poll-based information about opinions, I allow the *possibility* that polls can provide part of the opinion information being considered by a given decision-maker in constructing a perception of what public opinion supports or opposes. In other words, whether a decision-maker uses poll data for "reading" the state of public opinion depends on that decision-maker, *not* on public opinion scholars! After all, Blumer himself (1948: 549) asserted that "we ought to begin with those who have to act on public opinion and move backwards along the lines of the various expressions of public opinion that come to their attention." At least in principle, then, polls could be relevant to effective public opinion, but only *if* decision-makers use polls in that way. And as Blumer himself seems to have implied, whether they do is an empirical question, not a prescriptive one.

There is little question that American news media have dramatically elevated the visibility of the polls, often organizing their entire coverage of politics around them (e.g., Frankovich, 1998). And, of course, the major American news media literally have taken on ownership of the polls they publish. But these trends still don't necessarily imply that decision-makers take the polls into account when they try to "read" public opinion.

Empirical research at Oregon and elsewhere with local, state, and national politicians (reviewed by Lemert, 1992: 45) suggests that, regardless of level of office, these politicians don't rely on polls as much as they rely on one or more participation-based types of information about opinions. In addition, writers on both sides of the polls as public opinion issue (e.g., Converse, 1987; Splichal, 1997) suggest that when modern politicians do use polls, it is primarily for tactical/manipulative purposes—very much the way a mass marketer would use surveys—rather than to "listen." Even Converse (1987: S22) concedes that "Few politicians consult poll data to find out what they should be thinking on the issues, or to carry out errands. . . . Such data [instead] give them a sense of what postures to emphasize and avoid."

When consultants do covert polling for politicians, often these polls and/or "focus group" studies are done for the purpose of testing out what are the best ways to frame issues or opponents. The question, which again is an empirical one, is whether and how such essentially manipulative polls are considered by politicians when "reading" effective public opinion.

Election and Influence Frameworks

Issue opinions become visible and are processed in two political arenas, the Election Framework and the Influence Framework.

The Election Framework. The Election Framework occurs only on the day the votes are counted. Normally, only three sets of information are available here: (1) number or percentages of votes that each option on the ballot received, (2) turnout, that is, the percentage of eligible voters who participated, and (3) any exit poll interviews with voters. Unless there are questions about the legitimacy of the vote count, the most valuable use of exit polls is to find out what voters knew and believed about their voting choices.

Why are exit polls so valuable? Modern elections have ambiguity built into them. People can't vote "yes" or "no" on a ballot measure and then write a condition, explanation, or qualification onto the ballot. Without exit poll analyses, candidates who win an election can claim policy mandates that they may not have: It is a fallacy to claim any mandates based on the margin of victory, because several groups of voters each could make the same voting choice, but for quite different—and perhaps even incompatible—policy reasons. Meanwhile, a candidate could win by a single vote, yet every one of his votes could have been obtained for the same policy reason. Exit polls can clarify whether there was a mandate or not, and what kind of mandate it was.

Despite Blumer's objections to elections as public opinion, elections as legitimized expressions of collective opinion have a long history in political theory. More on this topic later.

The Influence Framework. I use the term "influence" here because public opinion is competing with many other possible influences over public policy decisions. These other influences include such things as the decision-maker's own policy preferences, those of colleagues, friends, advisors, and reference groups, and those of powerful interest groups.

In effect, the Election Framework occurs only on election day (the developing new practice of holding elections by mail may extend that period to weeks, however). In any event, the Influence Framework occurs the rest of the time, even including the campaign preceding an election, because the variety of opinion information available during the campaign matches that in the rest of the Influence Framework (IF).

Comparing the Two Frameworks. For the decision-maker in the IF, the perceptual situation for processing information about opinions differs from that of the Election Framework in many ways. In general, these differences between the two frameworks enhance the ability of organized interest groups to dominate effective public opinion in the Influence Framework while strengthening an argument on behalf of the polls in the IF as a corrective to this dominance. (Interest groups have learned to both stimulate and simulate widespread "spontaneous" expressions of opinion in the IF; advocates term it the "grassroots explosion"; critics term it the "astroturf explosion" instead. See Faucheux, 1995.)

Unlike the Election Framework, the IF has available a much greater variety of information about opinion, including both participation-based and more passive, poll-based information. The result is that there is much more room in the IF for decision-makers to selectively attend to some kinds of information about opinions, and not other kinds. This also implies that there will be less consensus among decision-makers about which kinds of opinion information validly reflect public opinion.

Far fewer political resources are devoted to processing information about opinions in the Influence Framework. In the United States, many thousands of employees and millions of dollars are devoted each year to collecting and counting ballots. In contrast, most politicians rarely allocate more than part of one staffer's time to constituents' *opinion* input, though often legislators have learned to allocate multiple staffers' time to contacts from constituents requesting *services*.

There is generally no baseline in the IF to assess what may seem to be a high-participation issue. In contrast, turnout records are kept for most past elections. Generally, the higher the participation is *perceived* to be, the more salient the issue is thought to be to constituents, and thus the more risky the issue to decision-makers.

As a result of both the lack of a participation baseline and the lack of opinion processing resources in the IF, a relatively small increase in participation can create a much bigger impression in the Influence Framework, quickly overcoming available resources and institutional memories. A relatively small number of letters, phone calls, or demonstrators, for example, quickly overwhelms resources ordinarily devoted to them.

Because turnout records are available in the Election Framework, the number of *non*participants is visible as opinion-related information. But in the Influence Framework, nobody is able to tell how many people could have participated, but didn't. For example, if organizers call for a boycott to protest a "sexist" event sponsored by the University of Oregon athletic department, but 100 women show up to participate in the event, does that mean the boycott failed, as the local newspaper declared? How many women could have participated, but didn't? Probably considerably more than 100. And of those nonparticipants, how many stayed away because they agreed the event was sexist? Perhaps a poll could have told us.

Because exit polls are done with actual voters, all the opinion information available in the Election Framework is participation-based. Participation takes the opinion holder's time, knowledge, and other resources. In contrast, telephone and personal-interview survey information in the Influence Framework is passive. Despite their many flaws, polls thus have the potential to provide a "corrective" perspective on how IF *non*participants feel.

What the issue is about, and what the policy options are, is much more subject to change in the IF. What appears on the ballot is fixed, though of course campaigns can be expected to try to find ways of framing the ballot issue to their advantage. The same struggle to control framing occurs in the IF, but in addition such developments as legislative compromises and amendments can radically transform the issues and options. Because their representatives keep close track of such transformations, interest groups adept at quickly mobilizing simulated public opinion have an enormous advantage over those whose previous opinion expressions have suddenly been rendered outdated. Votes in elections have a built-in political legitimacy that most other opinion expressions may lack. Further, for a politician facing the next election, votes are generally the most salient opinion expressions of all.

Despite the differences between the two frameworks, they have several things in common.

First, in both frameworks, opinion information is ambiguous enough to need interpretation. In the case of elections, the ambiguity is created largely by constraints imposed on the ballot by the need for rapid vote counting. Standardized vote tallies don't allow many nuances. In the IF, ambiguity is created largely by (1) an overload of possible information about opinions and (2) the lack of resources for processing opinion input.

Second, public opinion in both frameworks is therefore *constructed*, the result of an interpretation imposed by the decision-maker on some or all of the opinion information that reaches him or her. In an interesting analysis of how the meaning of electoral outcomes is socially constructed, Mendelsohn (1998) reported that in six Canadian elections, "policy mandates" tended to be given in the media to Conservative Party victories, but only when the party's campaign emphasized ideology. "Personal" mandates tended to be given when a newly elected party leader had won his first election.

The third similarity between the two frameworks is that both of them emphasize participation-based opinion information. In the IF, this emphasis is based on the enormous variety of such participation and the aforementioned preference by decision-makers for participation-based information. In the Election Framework, even the exit polls usually intercept only voters as they leave their voting place.

We return now to the seminal arguments about polls raised by Blumer in his 1946 and 1948 articles. They still resonate today (e.g., Althaus, 1998; Salmon and Glasser, 1995; Splichal, 1997; Verba, 1996).

THE ARGUMENT ABOUT POLLS/ELECTIONS

I began this chapter by implying that Blumer may have mistakenly constrained future debate among public opinion scholars by linking pre-election polls—and, by extension, all polls—with elections. Having been linked, if one is irrelevant to public opinion, then the other must be, too. A second assumption in his argument is that public opinion occurs only in what I'm calling the IF. Ever since Blumer's 1948 article, the debate has largely proceeded without reexamining either of these two assumptions.

Even when we look at elections from the perspective of pollsters, one of the clues that there ought to be a conceptual disconnect between pre-election polling and elections is that pre-election polls tend to hide the fact that they are not sampling a population of voters. Even when they draw their original sample from lists of registered voters, they have (at best) a sample of those eligible to vote. The expected voters have to be sorted out, after they and likely nonvoters all have been interviewed. Strictly speaking, the population of actual voters cannot be identified and sampled until after they've voted. Pollsters use various proprietarial systems to try to identify which of their respondents will vote, but inevitably there will be errors.

Although this poll-election disconnect may seem to be a narrow, technical point, it is not. I propose to separate consideration of whether polls reflect public opinion from arguments about whether elections do. It may be that the answer is the same to both, neither, or one, but the two issues require somewhat different arguments for and against.

Elections as Public Opinion

The arguments against elections as public opinion expressions fall into several categories, each of which will be examined below.

One person, one vote. For Blumer, voting is mass behavior. Elections reflect "an aggregation of equally weighted individual opinions" (1948: 548), rather than public opinion. Public opinion instead reflects differences in power to influence effective opinion and in access to organized groups; elections don't allow either to play a part:

> the formation and expression of public opinion giving rise to effective public opinion is not an action of a population of disparate individuals having equal weight but is a function of a structured society, differentiated into a network of different kinds of groups and individuals having differential weight and influence. (Blumer, 1948: 547)

Of course, Blumer wrote this passage long before the development of the modern campaign industry, but even at the time he wrote this there was reason to question whether the outcome of elections (effective public opinion?) reflected the actions only of equally weighted individuals.

To begin with, not everyone votes, not even in Blumer's era. Demographics such as wealth and education play a significant role in influencing both who bothers to vote and how they will vote. In that sense, at least, social structure is reflected in the vote. If electoral turnout continues to decline in America, the efficacy feelings and social characteristics of voters more and more will come to resemble those of the knowledgeable and savvy IF participants. Second, even in Blumer's time, the two major American parties were actively engaged in determining who was on the ballot, who had enough funds to run strong campaigns, which initiative measures made the ballot, how those ballot measures were entitled in the Voter's Guide, and so on.

More recently in America, interest groups, political action committees, fund-raising consultants, pollsters, direct-mail experts, political advertising specialists, candidate recruiters, and others all have very large influences on what and who gets on the ballot, on voter turnout, and on the sometimes unpalatable choices voters have in front of them. As V.O. Key (1966: 2-3) put this point so memorably, "the people's verdict can be no more than a selective reflection from among the alternatives and outlooks presented to them. . . . If the people can choose only from among rascals, they are certain to choose a rascal."

In 1902, one of America's first initiative processes was adopted by the state of Oregon as part of the Progressive reform movement. Today, about half the states now have an "Oregon plan" initiative process (Broder, 1998). The initiative was intended to give voters a chance to repeal obnoxious legislation as well as to enact laws the state's legislature had refused to. The initiative is put on the ballot by petition. If enough signatures are declared valid, Oregon voters will then decide its fate at the next general election. But what has happened to the initiative process in Oregon and elsewhere may be a perfect example of how not everybody counts equally in modern elections. Oregon political analyst Russell Sadler put it this way:

> This year interest groups trying to influence legislation actually spent more money on initiatives than they did lobbying the Oregon legislature. . . . [Paying petition circulators] strips the initiative of any pretense that petitions reflect the spontaneous uprising of frustrated Oregon voters and express the will of the people. (Sadler, 1998)

When the U.S. Supreme Court declared that campaign money should be treated as unfettered free speech, the way was cleared in future court cases to legalize paying petitioners by the number of signatures they obtain. If money is speech, it talks with a ventriloquist's voice in the voting booth.

A BRIEF ASIDE

By now, the astute reader should be challenging my argument against the "one person, one vote" position taken by Blumer. The first challenge would go something like this: Wait a minute! Most of the power inequalities you've mentioned occur in what you have already defined as the Influence Framework, not in the voting booth itself.

To answer this challenge requires me to distinguish between information about opinion and factors affecting the outcome of an election. My distinction between the IF and the Election Framework rests on the differences between the two frameworks in opinion information processing. Blumer's exclusion of elections rests on the illusion of equality, allowing power and inequalities a role only in what I'd call the IF. It appears to me that the only way Blumer can argue that power is equalized in elections is to assume that nothing happening before election day makes a difference in terms of how those "equal" votes are cast. In contrast, he does not impose such a narrow time frame on what I'm calling the IF.

There's a second possible challenge that would say something like this: Even if not everybody votes, and even if the ones who vote might be more affluent than those who don't, when they enter the voting booth, the ones who vote are all equal.

Are they? Some states, Oregon and Washington among them, have something like what is called here a "double majority rule" when all tax proposals are put to a vote. In order to be approved, a tax proposal in Oregon must not only receive a majority of those voting, it must also have had a turnout of a majority of registered voters. Thus people wishing to prevent a tax increase can win two ways: by not turning out or by voting no. Proponents of the tax have only one way to win. "Yes" voters remain invisible if they don't vote, and their not voting helps the "no" side, whereas if "no" voters stay at home, their not voting still registers them on the "no" side.

In America, the votes of National Rifle Association members or anti-abortion voters are thought to be more disciplined and unforgiving of decision-makers who "stray" on those single issues, whereas gun control and women's choice supporters have the reputation of being more "forgiving" if a candidate's other positions are attractive. As a voter, then, who has more clout?

In addition, voting by mail and widespread absentee voting also allow family members, friends with stronger views, and interest groups the opportunity to discuss and influence how others vote. Recently in Oregon, a husband was charged with forging his wife's signature and filling out her ballot. Political organizations can even contact mail/absentee voters while they have their ballots nearby. And if the organization convinces voters to change how they voted, it can give detailed instructions about how voters can invalidate their already returned ballot—and get a new one.

I return now to the arguments against elections as public opinion.

Two Private Acts. In an interesting elaboration of Blumer's second argument about elections and polls, Salmon and Kline (1984), Salmon and Glasser (1995), and Splichal (1997) assert that both polls and elections elicit "private" opinions whereas public opinion processes require expressions in public. Because both polls and elections elicit similar "private" behavior, it's no surprise that pre-election polls generally predict election outcomes, they argue.

Let's look at the survey interview situation first. When a pollster asks questions on the telephone or in a face-to-face interview, there is considerable evidence that the race, status, and mannerisms of the interviewer can make huge differences in the answers given. So, even if respondents are told their answers will never be linked to them personally and regardless of whether the poll's information about opinions ever reaches decision-makers, the interview still approaches a "social," nonprivate situation.

Regarding the "privacy" of voting: perhaps in principle, but not always. Why not?

Universal vote-by-mail for all elections already has been institutionalized in Oregon; in five other states mail-in "absentee" ballots are readily allowed for any reason.

Often, people living together all receive their ballots at the same time. To say the least, these ballots are not necessarily filled out by each person in privacy. As electoral turnout continues to decline in the United States, the movement toward voting by mail and virtually unrestricted "absentee" voting will also continue to spread to more states in a perhaps vain attempt to encourage voting and maintain the legitimacy of elections.

More generally, elections where you have to show up in person have some social aspects that don't resemble the social aspects of the survey interview. In many countries, you show identification to clerks, sign in, and are handed ballots, but you aren't encouraged to express your opinions aloud. In the survey interview, the interviewer may not even know your name, but you *are* expected to express your opinions aloud when asked.

"Normative" Pleas. Although Blumer (1948: 547-548) articulates what he terms a "very important" (547) argument for elections as public opinion, his rebuttal of this argument actually seems to concentrate on

polls, rather than elections, calling the argument ". . . a normative plea and not a defense of *polling* . . ." (548, emphasis added). Nevertheless, he does say about elections that:

> Many important questions could be raised about how and to what extent public opinion is expressed at the election polls, and, more important, whether it would be possible, or even advisable for public opinion, in the form of an aggregation of equally weighted individual opinions, to function meaningfully in a society with a diversified organization. However, such questions need not be raised here . . . (ibid.: 548)

"Advisable?" To a certain extent doesn't that sound like a "normative plea" on the part of Blumer about what "ought" to be?

Elections an Outcome; Public Opinion a Process. Although he didn't emphasize this distinction as much in his 1948 article as he did in his 1946/1966 chapter, Blumer tended to regard public opinion as a process—"always moving toward a decision even though it never is unanimous" (1966: 48). Meanwhile, elections are more static; they're held at a specific time, and then they're over. (See Salmon and Glasser, 1995: 442, for an especially strong statement of this view.) My distinction between Influence and Election Frameworks also recognizes this difference; where we differ is what to make of that difference. However, when in 1948 Blumer emphasized decision-maker perceptions as an "end point" for the study of public opinion processes, he in effect undercut his own absolute distinction between process and outcome.

In fact, past elections may even be treated as part of the information about opinions being considered currently in the more complex IF. The November 1998 Congressional election results manifestly were interpreted as a rebuke to House Republicans who had been pushing for impeachment of President Clinton and this interpretation heavily influenced the ensuing impeachment debate.

An NBC News report by Joe Johns (1998) also illustrates how possible *future* election results can influence legislators to push for action in the IF:

> Johns: . . . [I]n an election year, many on Capitol Hill believe that if Congress does not pass some sort of [health care] reform, voters may show their wrath this November.

Arguably, this same report may illustrate the power of past elections as well. Republican members of the U.S. House of Representatives remembered that they had just barely retained their majority in the 1996 election because they were seen as uncaring about several issues salient to voters. In other words, interpretations of the meaning of the 1996 election were influencing IF perceptions in 1998. That those IF perceptions also related to possible future elections also suggests that even future elections may be thought of by decision-makers as definitive expressions of public opinion. In a *New York Times* article that ran in the June 30, 1998 Eugene (Oregon) *Register-Guard*, Israeli president Ezer Weizman is quoted as follows:

> The [Israeli-Palestinian] peace process is limping. . . . If I were in his [Prime Minister Netanyahu's] place, I would move for early elections. The sooner we go to early elections, the sooner we'll know what the public thinks.

The idea of future elections being treated as expressions of public opinion has been related by Zaller (1994) to V. O. Key's concept of "latent opinion," the feared possibility of electoral revenge being taken at a future election for an IF decision that itself is still being considered. It is well known that past election results often are interpreted as public opinion "mandates," and used to provide a policy justification in the IF.

In summary, democratic theory gives elections considerable legitimacy as an opportunity for letting the "will of the people" be expressed. There is considerable evidence, both anecdotal and quantitative, that what past elections "mean" and what future elections might produce can figure prominently when politicians consider their options in the IF. On balance, the existence of elections also heightens the salience, at least for elected politicians who feel at risk, of every other kind of information about constituent opinions, including the participation-based types that Blumer himself cites as examples of public opinion input. In short, the case against elections isn't made.

I return now to the other issue in the argument: Do the polls measure or reflect public opinion?

Polls as Public Opinion

Here the evidence and the argument is a much closer call, especially when polls' general ability to predict elections has been removed from the argument, as I've already tried to do.

Blumer's contention (1948) that the polling industry has continued to define its subject matter tautologically—public opinion is what we poll, therefore polls measure public opinion—remains as true today as when he first made it.

It's also as true as ever that the polls treat all eligible citizens alike, making no distinctions having to do with differences in political skills and clout. The model that polls implicitly apply to public opinion is a "simple reductionist" one (Lemert, 1981) that reduces public opinion to majority opinion and thereby distorts the nature of the public opinion process in the IF. This simple reductionist model has greatly interfered with our understanding of how mass media can (and do) alter public opinion.

It's also true that polls capture mass opinions and that there is no logical reason to believe that the assumed ability of polls to predict election outcomes says anything about the validity of polls concerning the many issues where no election is available to provide a validation test. However, we know that polls are used by at least some decision-makers. Based on her examination of poll-related memos, Heith concluded that polling in the Nixon, Ford, Carter, and Reagan White Houses served both "informational" and "strategic" purposes, but it had not yet been determined whether polls were used during policy making for "responsive leadership, [or] followership, or an effort to manipulate the public . . ." (1998: 187).

Clinton's high job approval in the polls seemed to influence many of the political choices made by Congressional Republicans in the summer and early fall of 1998. For example, they released videotapes of Clinton's grand jury testimony in an apparent effort to test whether the tapes would drive down support for Clinton's remaining in office. Clinton's job rating actually went up.

Thus, it's still possible that, if those poll results are made visible to decision-makers, and if decision-makers are inclined to use polls as an indicator of public opinion, polls become part of effective public opinion. This is a very conditional, qualified and contingent endorsement, to be sure, though hardly the only one in the field. For example, Verba makes the same distinction I do between participation-based and poll-based opinion information, and then concludes that if decision-makers wish "the closest approximation" of everyone's views, they should choose polls. But "if the voices of activists are louder because of their greater intensity of concern, then they deserve the greater clout they have" (1996: 6). Similarly, Althaus (1998: 2) argues that the Blumer-Converse debate hides a "fundamental normative tension between . . . two important conceptions of public opinion . . . representation of interests and representation of voices: the closer an indicator of collective public opinion comes to representing all voices in a public [i.e., polls], the less likely it will be to reflect the interests of that public." He then goes on (1998: 3) to argue that the more important questions about polls concern: "What sort of opinion might surveys be particularly good at revealing, and which political functions might surveys be particularly suited to fulfill?" Answering these two questions also would produce conclusions about when opinion surveys would *not* be "particularly good."

For better *and* for worse, polling has become thoroughly institutionalized in politics (Converse, 1987; Frankovich, 1998; Miller, 1995; Moog, 1997; Moog and Hauser chapters in this volume; Splichal, 1997). What about polls that deliberately present different types of presumably accurate information about the opponent in order to diagnose how best to frame the debate? The best way to answer this is to interview the decision-makers who commission these polls. If such diagnostic polling leads decision-makers to present themselves differently, we need to know whether they consider that to be an adjustment to the dictates of public opinion—or just a way to "market" themselves. Given the penetration of polling into our media and political institutions, questions such as these will be much more productive ones for us to investigate now than will be whether or not polls "are" public opinion. As Blumer himself put it, we should ask decision-makers about the opinion information they consider when they are constructing their interpretations of public opinion.

RESEARCH USING THE CONCEPTS PRESENTED HERE

The vocabulary and viewpoints discussed in this paper offer many productive opportunities for those interested in either quantitative or qualitative study of the public opinion process. These opportunities occur at two levels:

1. Interviews and observation of decision-makers concerning:
   - their processing of information about issue opinions, including the modalities (e.g., letters, meetings, polls) they might prefer;
   - the impact (if any) of perceived public opinion on their (a) tactical decisions and/or (b) substantive decisions;
   - developing techniques of identifying, issue by issue, who are the decision-makers, who are the ones who can provide linkage, if there is any, between public opinion and their decisions; and
   - whether decision-makers' perceptions of public opinion are idiosyncratic or constrained by political reality.
2. Factors influencing whether and how mass issue opinions become visible to decision-makers.

Briefly, here are some examples of research that has already touched on many of the broad areas listed above.

First Level

Although an interpretation is imposed on opinion information, decision-makers' interpretations tend not to be idiosyncratic. They will reflect the opinion information received. A number of sociopolitical pressures on decision-makers tend to limit how idiosyncratic such interpretations can be (see Lemert, 1981: 12-16). In contrast, voters have no such constraints imposed on their interpretations. Thus, political decision-makers seemed much less prone than voters to wishful thinking (Lemert, 1986). These constraints make it possible to argue that the mass media change public opinion by changing the amount and/or "tilt" of the opinion information being received by the decision-maker. As information about opinions changes, decision-makers' ideas about the state of public opinion on that issue will change as well.

Political scientists Warren E. Miller and Donald E. Stokes (1963) asked members of the U.S. House of Representatives to estimate the preferences of their respective districts in certain policy areas, then looked at those legislators' roll-call votes to see if they reflected perceived opinion in those districts. This pioneering research design, though not without flaws, has been used by many subsequent researchers.

My students and I have done several studies of local and state politicians, asking them about their preferred sources of opinion information. Consistently, participation-based information is chosen most often. Others have asked members of Congress or their staffers similar questions, and again participation-based information is mentioned most often (for reviews of this research, see Lemert, 1981, 1986, 1992).

As a self-appointed surrogate for "The People," the news media very frequently publish information about issue opinions, such as polls or declarations of electoral "mandates" (Mendelsohn, 1998). Similarly, letters to the editor and items about such things as petitions, testimony at public hearings, or demonstrations each contain information about public opinion. The media also communicate information about issue opinions indirectly, such as by portraying the U.S. health industry's "Harry and Louise" ads against Clinton's health care reform plan as being very effective with the mass audience, thus convincing a key Congressional decision-maker to compromise with the industry in exchange for its withdrawal of the ads (Jamieson and Cappella, 1998).

Second Level

Here, what moves people from the mass to visibility—or keeps them invisible to decision-makers—is an especially important question for public opinion scholars and media critics to ask.

In his classic *Democracy without Citizens*, Entman (1989) discusses numerous ways that American news media reduce participation, including the lack of "accountability news," that is, lack of news that would enable citizens to hold decision-makers responsible for their decisions.

In a series of experiments, Ansolabere and Iyengar (1995) reported that political attack advertising reduced intent to vote, especially among people without ties to a political party. Lemert, Wanta, and Lee (1997), using actual turnout records for a special Senate election, reported that attack ads reduced turnout among Republicans, not necessarily people without party ties. This line of research isn't likely to end soon.

Through content analysis, Hungerford and Lemert (1973) showed that Oregon newspapers displaced the locale of environmental issues outside their own circulation zones, thus reducing the saliency of any environmental threat and reducing ordinary people's motivation to express opinions about those controversies.

In a series of studies using content analysis, an experiment, elite interviews, and survey methodologies, we have shown that the U.S. news media systematically exclude content from political coverage that would allow people to find the ways and means to participate in the IF. This content, which I define as mobilizing information (MI) includes things such as addresses and phone numbers of decision-makers (Lemert, 1981). In addition, two studies of opinion expressions sent as letters to a newspaper editor and as "Free Speech Messages" to San Francisco Bay Area broadcast media found that gatekeepers at newspaper and broadcast stations systematically eliminated or reduced MI before these submissions were published (Lemert and Cook, 1982; Lemert and Larkin, 1979).

ANALYTICAL ADVANTAGES

The two-level approach recommended here provides several advantages to public opinion analysts.

1. This approach isn't dependent on any single "ideal" model of social interaction. Herbert Blumer and Salmon and Glasser

emphasize the importance of group processes in the formation and expression of public opinion. But some—for example, Coleman, 1986—argue that society is evolving away from extended group interactions (Coleman, 1986: 1319): "Society has become more individualistic, with individuals pursuing paths disconnected from family and community." Regardless of which society one envisions, the narrowed definition of a mass—and the difference between mass opinion and effective public opinion—works.

2. The approach leads to a huge variety of research opportunities at both the decision-maker level and the level of how and whether mass opinion becomes visible as information about issue opinion.

At the decision-maker level, for example, such questions as these need to be addressed: How do politicians use polls? What types of information about opinion do private sector decision-makers prefer, compared to elected politicians? Does perceived salience of an issue affect how much care is taken to gather and study information about opinions on that issue? Do appointed decision-makers in government process information about opinions differently than elected ones do? Among elected politicians, does their processing of information about opinions change as the calendar nears their next election?

At the mass level, participation as a dependent variable has not received sufficient attention from mass media scholars. How do the media interfere with participation? And how may they enable it, especially in the IF? Which sense of political efficacy—internal (roughly, political self-confidence) or external (roughly, confidence in the political system)—is it easier for media messages to alter? And which sense of efficacy, if it can be changed, has greater power to change participation? (This question is of central importance to newspapers in the public journalism movement, whose content seems aimed at improving external efficacy, whereas internal efficacy seems to be a more powerful predictor of continued attention to the news.)

By focusing on how effective public opinion can be changed by mass media, the approach opens up strong opportunities for developing the correspondence rules that we will need to link effects on individuals with social-level effects on public opinion. The approach continues to recognize that there are differences between the IF and the election framework, as did Blumer and more recent scholars such as Salmon and Glasser. The approach doesn't foreclose the possibility that certain kinds of polls may be taken into account as effective public opinion. It also allows the possibility that decision-makers may spend heavily on political polling for manipulative purposes, rather than to "listen" to *vox populi*. How and whether decision-makers use polls should be a high-priority research item.

By focusing attention on decision-makers, the approach may help lead to more sophisticated—and realistic—approaches to the study of linkage between public opinion and decision-making. For one thing, it may be necessary to distinguish between what might be termed "tactical linkage" and "policy linkage," a distinction implied by Converse (1987) when he discussed how political polls are used by politicians.

I hope this too-brief sketch will lead readers to explore a rich agenda of qualitative and quantitative research possibilities.

REFERENCES

Althaus, Scott L. 1998. What Can Surveys Tell Us about Public Opinion? A Normative Perspective on the Blumer/Converse Debate. Paper presented at annual meeting, American Association for Public Opinion Research, 14-17 May, St. Louis, Missouri.

Ansolabehere, Stephen and Shanto Iyengar. 1995. *Going Negative: How Political Advertisements Shrink & Polarize the Electorate.* New York: The Free Press.

Beniger, James R. 1987. Toward an Old-New Paradigm: The Flirtation with Mass Society. *Public Opinion Quarterly* 51(Supplement), S47-S66.

Blumer, Herbert. 1948. Public Opinion and Public Opinion Polling. *American Sociological Review* 13(5), 542-555.

Blumer, Herbert. 1966. The Mass, the Public, and Public Opinion. In B. Berelson and M. Janowitz (eds.), *Reader in Public Opinion and Communication*, 2nd ed., 43-50. New York: The Free Press.

Broder, David. 1998, August 2. Oregonians Debate Merit of Initiatives. *The Register-Guard*, Eugene, Oregon, pp. 1A, 15A.

Coleman, James S. 1986. Social Theory, Social Research, and a Theory of Action. *American Journal of Sociology* 91(6), 1309-1335.

Converse, Philip E. 1987. Changing Conceptions of Public Opinion in the Political Process. *Public Opinion Quarterly* 51(Supplement), S12-S24.

Entman, Robert M. 1989. *Democracy Without Citizens: Media and the Decay of American Politics.* New York: Oxford University Press.

Faucheux, Ron. 1995. The Grassroots Explosion. *Campaigns & Elections* 16(1), 20-25, 53-56, 66-67.

Frankovich, Kathleen A. 1998. Public Opinion and Polling. In D. Graber, D. McQuail, and P. Norris (eds.), *The Politics of News: the News of Politics*, 150-170. Washington, DC: CQ Press.

Heith, Diane J. 1998. Staffing the White House Public Opinion Apparatus: 1969-1988. *Public Opinion Quarterly* 62(2), 165-189.

Hungerford, Steven E. and James B. Lemert. 1973. Covering the Environment: A New "Afghanistanism"? *Journalism Quarterly* 50(3), 474-481, 506.

Jamieson, Kathleen Hall and Joseph N. Cappella. 1998. The Role of the Press in the Health Care Reform Debate of 1993-1994. In D. Graber, D. McQuail, and P. Norris (eds.), *The Politics of News: The News of Politics*, 110-131. Washington, DC: CQ Press.

Johns, Joe. 1998, June 28. Public Calling for Reform of Health Care Industry and Health Maintenance Organizations. NBC News Transcripts. Lexis/Nexis.

Key, V. O., Jr. 1966. *The Responsible Electorate: Rationality in Presidential Voting, 1936-1960*. New York: Vintage.

Lazarsfeld, Paul F. and Robert K. Merton, 1971. Mass Communication, Popular Taste, and Organized Social Action. In W. Schramm and D. F. Roberts (eds.), *The Process and Effects of Mass Communication*, rev. ed., 554-578. Urbana: University of Illinois Press.

Lemert, James B. 1981. *Does Mass Communication Change Public Opinion After All? A New Approach to Effects Analysis*. Chicago: Nelson-Hall.

Lemert, James B. 1986. Picking the Winners: Politician vs. Voter Predictions of Two Controversial Ballot Measures. *Public Opinion Quarterly* 50(2), 208-221.

Lemert, James B. 1992. Effective Public Opinion. In D. Kennamer (ed.), *Public Opinion, the Press, and Public Policy*, 41-61. Westport, CT: Praeger.

Lemert, James B. and Roxana J. Cook. 1982. Mobilizing Information in Broadcast Editorials and "Free Speech" Messages. *Journal of Broadcasting* 26(1), 493-496.

Lemert, James B. and Jerome P. Larkin. 1979. Some Reasons Why Mobilizing Information Fails to Be in Letters to the Editor. *Journalism Quarterly* 56(3), 504-512.

Lemert, James B., Wayne Wanta, and Tien T. Lee. 1997, May. Going Positive: A Case Study of the Smith-Wyden Senate Campaign in Oregon. Paper presented at annual meeting, International Communication Association, Montreal, Canada.

Mendelsohn, Mathew. 1998. The Construction of Electoral Mandates: Media Coverage of Election Results in Canada. *Political Communication* 15(2), 239-253.

Miller, Peter V. 1995. The Industry of Public Opinion. In T. L. Glasser and C. T. Salmon (eds.), *Public Opinion and the Communication of Consent*, 105-131. New York: Guilford.

Miller, Warren E. and Donald E. Stokes. 1963. Constituency Influence in Congress. *American Political Science Review* 57(1), 45-56.

Moog, Sandra. 1997. Television, Mass Polling and the Mass Media. *Javnost—The Public* 4(2), 39-55.

Sadler, Russell. 1998, June 28. Oregon Can Teach Congress a Lesson. *The Register-Guard*, Eugene, Oregon, p. 3B.

Salmon, Charles T. and Theodore L. Glasser. 1995. The Politics of Polling and the Limits of Consent. In T. Glasser and C. Salmon (eds.), *Public Opinion and the Communication of Consent*, 437-458. New York: Guilford.

Salmon, Charles T. and F. Gerald Kline. 1984. The Spiral of Silence Ten Years Later. In K. Sanders, L. Kaid, and D. Nimmo, *Political Communication Yearbook 1984*, 3-30. Carbondale: Southern Illinois University Press.

Splichal, Slavko. 1997. Political Institutionalisation of Public Opinion through Polling. *Javnost—The Public* 4(2), 17-38.

The New York Times. 1998, June 30. Israeli President Raps Netanyahu.

The Register-Guard, Eugene, Oregon, p. 4A.

Verba, Sidney. 1996. The Citizen Respondent: Sample Surveys and American Democracy. *American Political Science Review* 90(1), 1-7.

Zaller, John. 1994. Positive Constructs of Public Opinion. *Critical Studies in Mass Communication* 11(3), 276-287.

12

Distorting Democracy: Public Opinion, Polls, and the Press

Steven Barnett

> The material for opinion research . . . is not already constituted as
> public opinion simply by becoming the object of politically relevant
> considerations, decisions, and measures. The feedback of group
> opinions, defined in terms of the categories employed in research on
> governmental and administrative processes or on political consen-
> sus formation . . . cannot close the gap between public opinion as a
> fiction of constitutional law and the social-psychological decomposi-
> tion of its concept. (Habermas, 1989: 244)

Concepts of public opinion, how it is manifested, and how it impacts on
different structures of democracy has been a fascinating and complex
area of analysis since the Enlightenment, when it first became accepted
philosophy that the process of opening up the machinery and legislation
of government to critical scrutiny distinguished autocracies from
democracies. For Jeremy Bentham it was "the tribunal of public opinion" that prevented misrule, and for John Locke the law of opinion or
reputation was overwhelmingly powerful in judging the rectitude of
men's actions (Speier, 1995: 26).

Whereas the legacy of Enlightenment thinking was the primacy of public opinion in the abstract, this posed (and continues to pose) a number of key theoretical and empirical questions about how "public opinion" evolves, how it is manifested, and how it can be accommodated within the machinery of democratic government. This question, in turn, is bound up with the different forms that democracy can take and which models are more or less able to take account of the popular will. Today, opinion polls have become an almost universally accepted currency for interpreting the popular will, despite their many methodological drawbacks. This chapter reviews the theoretical link between polls, public opinion, and democracy and some of the problems associated with opinion measurement. Its main thrust, however, is a case study of the mediatized nature of most opinion polling and the dangers this poses of confusing proprietorial agenda-setting with the press's claims to represent the *vox populi*.

PUBLIC OPINION AND DEMOCRACY

Writing at the end of the nineteenth century after studying the United States, James Bryce defined four different models of democracy in terms of the efficacy of public opinion (Bryce, 1984). The first model, that of "direct popular government" derived from the Athenian *polis*, was relevant only to small communities and only of historical interest. It was inapplicable to large nation-states. The second model was representative or parliamentary democracy in which public opinion only manifested itself through those elected to speak on behalf of a constituency of people. This was how Bryce saw the United Kingdom, where representatives could operate independently of public opinion. In the United States, however, the third model prevailed, where public opinion was "the great source of power, the master of servants who tremble before it." Although Bryce was unclear about the precise mechanisms through which elected representatives were sensitized to the popular will, there was no doubt about the source of real legislative power:

> Where the power of the people is absolute, legislators and administrators are quick to catch its wishes in whatever way they may be indicated, and not care to wait for the methods which the law prescribes. (1984: 267)

The fourth model was aspirational rather than real, an ideal-type reinvention of direct popular rule that would eliminate the need for elected representatives. This fourth stage "would be reached if the will of the majority of the citizens were to become ascertainable at all times, and without the need of its passing through a body of representatives." Thus, as Fishkin has said, Bryce anticipated both the invention and the influence of opinion polling. What is important about Bryce's model, however, is that it elevates public opinion to this sovereign role in its *abstract* form; because the ascertainability of majority will was no more than an ideal form of democracy, he was not required to address the problems of how it came to be ascertained. Although the weaknesses of a representative system were well established because of the filtering process of popular opinion, little thought was given to whether a different kind of filtering process would be applicable to a more precise calculation of where majority opinion lay. One of the inherent weaknesses of this model of public opinion and democracy was outlined by Fishkin:

> The movement towards more direct democracy . . . in fact results in the decision-making power, in the large nation-state, being brought to a people who are *not a public*. The locus of ostensible decision resides in millions of disconnected and inattentive citizens, who may react to vague impressions of headlines or shrinking soundbites but who have no rational motivation to pay attention so as to achieve a collective engagement with public problems. (1995: 23; emphasis in original)

This problem of disengagement should be distinguished from the paternalistic and absolutist Platonic tradition that the masses are not capable of reaching decisions about the common good and therefore not entitled to be involved in the process. It should also be distinguished from the philosophy of those who, like Edmund Burke, believed that a representative model of democracy allowed—even entitled—elected representatives to defy the local opinions of their constituents if they felt they were acting in the national interest. Burke's classic speech to his constituents on being elected in November 1774 made his position on the role of public opinion abundantly clear: "Your representative owes you, not his industry only, but his judgement; and he betrays, instead of serving you, if he sacrifices it to your opinion" (quoted in Hampster-Monk, 1987: 109). Although electors' opinions might be "weighty and respectable" it is Parliament that hears the arguments, that allows MPs to deliberate, and that attempts to look after "the general good, resulting from the general reason of the whole."

A similar approach was taken by James Madison who, as one of America's founding fathers, was concerned that the people's voice should be heard but also that it should be "refined" by the deliberations of representatives. As with Burke, Madison believed that factional or partial considerations needed to be resisted and that "the public voice, pronounced by the representations of the people, will be more consonant to the public good than if pronounced by the people themselves" (quoted in Fishkin, 1985: 58).

This position therefore accords public opinion due respect, accepting both that it is somehow ascertainable, and that it may well reflect a thoughtful, rational, and engaged debate among electors. It remains, however, the right (and duty) of representatives to give such opinion serious consideration rather than feeling mandated by or subservient to it. Modern examples of this model of democracy in action are the running debates about capital punishment in the United Kingdom or gun control in the United States. There is considerable survey evidence in Britain that public opinion has long favored the reintroduction of capital punishment for certain categories of first degree murder (of policemen or in pursuit of terrorist activities, for example). In America, again if we accept polling evidence, public opinion favors some form of gun control. In both cases (for different reasons) the legislative representative assemblies have apparently defied the popular will. We will address later the issue of to what extent we can trust the "measured" aggregation of British and American opinion, but the principle is well established that elected assemblies need not be slaves to the perceived or "measured" popular will.

A further argument in defense of representative democracy advanced by theorists like Schumpeter and de Tocqueville—writing from different eras and within different social and historical contexts—is the protection it can offer against the "tyranny of the majority." Both recognized that majorities are quite capable of undermining basic rights and freedoms, and that certain principles should be above even the rights of considered majority opinion. In the words of de Tocqueville: "I am not the more disposed to pass beneath the yoke [of despotism] because it is held out to me by the arms of millions of men" (quoted in Speier, 1995: 46). Joseph Schumpeter hypothesized about a country in which Christians were persecuted and Jews slaughtered on the basis of decisions made through established democratic practice. At this point, he concluded, it was proper to "speak of the rabble instead of the people and to fight its criminality or stupidity by all the means at ones command" (Schumpeter, 1976: 242). There is, therefore, an issue of basic individual rights that should not be infringed; by implication, a representative system in which such rights are enshrined are more consonant with the proper conduct of political life than a populist majoritarian system in which such rights are potentially at risk.

This theme is echoed by Walter Lippmann, who combines fear of dangerous irrationality with a belief in civic disinterest as the natural order of things: "when public opinion attempts to govern directly it is either a failure or a tyranny. It is not able to master the problem intellectually, nor to deal with it except by wholesale impact" (Lippmann, 1925: 51). The only positive force that public opinion exercises, for Lippmann, is as a bulwark against crises in public affairs. If no crisis arises, there is no role nor necessity for public opinion to hold sway because "the work of the world goes on continually without conscious direction from public opinion." Again, this theory arises from a natural disinclination by ordinary citizens to apply themselves to matters of state:

> The public will arrive in the middle of the third act and will leave before the last curtain, having stayed just long enough perhaps to decide who is the hero and who the villain of the piece. Yet usually that judgement will necessarily be made apart from the intrinsic merits, on the basis of a sample of behaviour, an aspect of a situation, by very rough external evidence. (Lippmann, 1925: 48)

THE RISE AND RISE OF POLLING IN BRITAIN

The legitimacy and rise in popularity of opinion polls fits—on the face of it—squarely into the populist and majoritarian tradition of democracy rather than the parliamentary or representative tradition. This was certainly the position of polling's founding father George Gallup after he had demonstrated the power of scientific sampling methods by predicting the outcome of the 1936 presidential election on the basis of a few thousand respondents (as opposed to the *Literary Digest*, which made a wrong call on the evidence of several million responses to its self-completion question). He visualized a democratic nirvana of representative polls and neutral mass media bringing the nation together "literally in one great room . . . the people, having heard the debate on both sides of every issue, can express their will" (quoted in Fishkin, 1995: 79).

In America and throughout Europe, we have seen the legacy of that vision. In late 1990s Britain, the recent political domination of a resurgent and rechristened "New" Labour Party has accompanied a much wider and more explicit use of polls and focus groups. This has its roots in the growing emphasis on professional marketing and advertising skills, which political parties throughout Europe are importing from the United States and employing to "sell" themselves to their electorates. Although the origins may be in campaigning, the newly elected Labour government appears to be ready to extend such techniques from political maneuvering into the very mechanisms of government. The Labour Party's embodiment of marketing and presentational techniques, Peter Mandelson, made his name as the party's director of communications before being appointed to one of the most senior government positions. He said in 1998:

> It may be that the era of pure representative democracy is coming slowly to an end. . . . Today people want to be more involved. Representative government is being complemented by more direct forms of involvement from the internet to referendums. [There will be] more citizens' movements, more action from pressure groups. This requires a different style of politics and we are trying to respond to these changes. (quoted in Tyrrell and Goodhart, 1998)

The authors of the article from which this quote is taken refer to the evolution of Britain's political system in which ideology is being superceded by public opinion—what they call "opinion poll democracy." Their assessment of current political trends is that "classical, elite-mediated, representative democracy has increasing difficulty representing anything," that party activists who might a generation ago have been relied upon to convey something of the general will are now atypical and unreliable channels of communication for politicians, and that anyway a society that used to be relatively homogeneous has been transmuted into something altogether more "opaque, fragmented and individualised." We need to beware the somewhat idealized historical view presented by the authors both of the unified nature of public opinion and the efficacy of political party machines as its conduit. In addition, Mandelson's assumptions (common among senior Labour politicians in Britain) that we are witnessing a great democratic resurgence in the body politic— with new technology acting as initiator and catalyst—are at best questionable.

Nevertheless, these sentiments do exemplify an increasingly pervasive sense that politics are being popularized, and that citizen-based research—in the form of opinion polls and focus groups—is a positive step towards creating an "inclusive" as well as consultative political environment. Tyrrell and Goodhart offer in partial support of this thesis their own opinion poll evidence on the electorate's view of the role of opinion polls in the democratic process. Nearly a third of those questioned believed that government took more notice of polling data than Parliament and MPs, and a majority of these people (58%) felt this was a good thing. On the other hand, two attitude questions displayed a measure of electoral schizophrenia: over two thirds agreed with a statement that government policy was often too difficult for ordinary people to understand, and over three quarters agreed that public opinion is fickle and to follow it too closely is not a good way to run the country; but three quarters also agreed that polls are more in touch with the general public than MPs. Although it would therefore be wrong to suggest that "opinion poll democracy" has the unequivocal support of the public, there is certainly a sense that it has some merit.

These findings contrast with the results of Herbst's qualitative research in America when she found "much cynicism about the role of polls, media and corporations in warping and limiting America's public space" and that "[p]olls are believed to suppress critical thinking, and to dictate the questions a society asks itself as well as the range of possible answers" (Herbst, 1993). This fairly sophisticated general public critique of the problems associated with polling (of which more below) could equally be applied to Tyrrell and Goodhart's poll about attitudes to polls, at which point we are in danger of entering an Alice in Wonderland world of ever-decreasing circular arguments. It may be that a more sophisticated series of questions—or indeed a more qualitative approach—would have produced more comparable responses in the United Kingdom to those elicited by Herbst in America, but taken at face value these poll data suggest a more benign disposition to the democratizing potential of polls in Britain.

We might fairly conclude, then, that within the governing classes and the body politic in Britain there is a growing belief in the role and legitimacy of opinion polls. Indeed, these two trends are almost certainly interrelated. The huge campaigning investment in polls, in particular by the Labour Party (see Butler and Kavanagh, 1997: 128-132) has seeped into areas of policy-making and populist rhetoric, which in turn is likely to create an expectation that more apparently authoritative and "objective" mechanisms of discovering and satisfying the public view will be incorporated into the legislative process. No empirical evidence has so far been collated, but it is a fair working hypothesis that in Britain in the last five years more public opinion polls have been commissioned and disseminated, and more reference has been made to the results in the press and Parliament, than at any time this century. A process that was anyway growing in uncritical acceptance as well as sheer volume has found its apotheosis in a new Labour government desperate to reclaim the middle ground of politics and profoundly influenced by a consumerist political culture that has enabled the leadership to embrace "the people" while simultaneously bypassing a traditionally more radical grassroots membership. To be a good democrat in Britain at the end of the millennium is to listen to and then act on results of focus groups, polls, and referendums. The new democracy is the politics of consumer-led pragmatism, rather than ideology, but its gaping weakness is the sovereign place such pragmatism assigns to a fundamentally flawed method of democratic accountability: consumer research.

Just over ten years ago, Philip Converse also concluded that in America there was a "mounting tide of acceptance of public opinion data" at all levels of public office and identified some of the dangers in transferring these data from those who generated them to those who interpreted them (Converse, 1987). In particular, he warned about an "excess faith in the precision of results" and an "inappropriate reification of the results, lending them more homogeneity or stability than is usually wise." Although a mild qualification of the usefulness of opinion polls in terms of how they entered public debate, his argument accepted polls as an "external validation" and as a means of achieving "greater sensitivity to public opinion." The measurement process through which public opinion came to be established was therefore not in dispute; the problem was in the dissemination of these data and in the more philosophical question of whether their increasing prominence improved "the quality of governance."

Converse's semicritical stance suffers on two counts, both of which require more exploration. The first is that, although acknowledging some drawbacks, he glosses over both the number and severity of methodological problems involved with employing polls as an accurate barometer of public opinion. The second, more significantly, is that (like most other critics) he makes a clear distinction between polls as an efficient measurement system and the process of dissemination or representation of those polls. The link that is rarely made explicitly and that requires more rigorous enquiry is the symbiotic and mutually dependent relationship of the conduct of opinion polls and their exposition through the mass media, particularly through the press. As Splichal (1997) has said, "The idea of public opinion is inseparable from techniques, instruments and institutions related to the expression and representation of opinions." What needs to be spelled out more clearly is the interdependence of the techniques, the institutions of representation, and the subsequent interpretation (or reification) of the popular will among the nation's policy thinkers and lawmakers.

SOME PROBLEMS WITH POLLING

A number of methodological problems around the distortive effect of polls have been explored by critics in the past, from the very technical to the more highly philosophical. It is important to examine these briefly in order to understand fully the context for a critique of the presentational and interpretational role of the mass media. Broadly speaking, they can be placed under two headings: first, problems associated with the *quality* of public opinion in polls; and second, problems associated with the circumstances of commissioning and publication of polls.

Questions about quality have long persisted among critics of the political significance of polls, and indeed among those who have tried to theorize the relationship between public opinion and the problems of democratic, collective decision-making (see Price and Neijens, 1997, for an interesting summary). These are not questions about the relative merits of different kinds of polls, but about the nature of the opinions being measured. It is axiomatic that a well-constructed poll—that is, one that takes an approximately random sample of the population—will involve members of the electorate who may have very little interest, understanding, or concern about the issues being investigated. It is populist in the absolutist sense that everyone's opinion is regarded as equally valid, but it takes no account of the fickle nature of opinion when unprepared respondents are presented with questions about issues to which they have given very little or no consideration. Responses become suspect not because these individuals have no right to express an opinion, but because such solicited opinions are highly susceptible to the nature of the questions and the reporting environment in which they are being asked. In the words of William Miller, polls (including academic surveys) "may reflect the view of the unaffected, the inexpert, the uninterested, or the irresponsible, and may merely echo the output of the media" (1983: 87). This problem is exacerbated, says Miller, by the fact that giving responses to hypothetical questions (for example, about the balance between tax cuts and maintaining hospitals or schools) have no real consequences. Hence, "A populist regime in which top politicians communicate to the masses by television and gauge responses by sample surveys . . . might be a highly defective democracy."

When opinions are not passionately held or are uninformed or have not been subjected to thoughtful disputation, they are more likely to be influenced by the vagaries of phraseology or question order. There is experimental evidence that opinion statements that are elicited from people on issues to which they have given little thought "give every indication of being rough and superficial" and "vacillate randomly across repeated interviews of the same people" (Zaller, 1992: 28). The result is that the smallest changes in question order or phrasing can produce large differences in the resulting "public opinion." Further evidence for the artificiality of polls comes from studies that have introduced entirely fictional subject matter. Famously, in 1975, one third of respondents in America were prepared to give their opinion on the (entirely fictitious) Public Affairs Act. Twenty years later, when people were asked whether this (still fictitious) Act should be repealed, opinions were dramatically affected by whether the proposal was presented as sponsored by the Democrat President Clinton or the Republican congress (Fishkin, 1995: 79). The danger of such fickleness is that, having tested little more than respondents' desire not to look foolish, the "majority view" thus established from the random responses can actually serve to inhibit the more considered opinions of minorities. Noelle-Neuman (1984) found evidence of what she called a "spiral of silence," where those who believe themselves to be in a minority were less inclined to speak out against a perceived majority will, thus further reducing support for their own position. It is therefore feasible for pressure groups to use this fickleness to engineer an apparent consensus in support of their own views which then becomes self-fulfilling.

As other critics have observed, public opinion is therefore *created* by the process of asking questions of a large number of disengaged people. The results give an illusion of coherence on issues where opinion is at best complex and at worst supremely indifferent. The fact that those being asked their opinion might be scientifically representative of the population as a whole does not mitigate the problem nor make the data more valid. It simply means that the poorly informed or disinterested respondents are present in roughly the same proportion as in the population as a whole. It is a spurious definition of "scientific."

Over the last few years some scholars, explicitly recognizing the inherent problems of poll-based research, have tried to overcome their weaknesses by experimenting with ways of eliciting more engaged, informed, or reasoned opinions. Some of these, like a so-called "mushiness index," are contained within orthodox questionnaire techniques and simply assess how stable or consistent individual opinions are on particular issues. Others are more ambitious and attempt to draw people into discussion and to understanding the consequences of the hypothetical positions they are initially inclined to take. Price and Neijens (1998) describe some recent examples of informed or deliberative opinion polls. These include surveys by the Americans Talk Issues Foundation (ATIF) that attempt to achieve considered responses at an early stage of policy formation. One technique is to offer respondents a number of policy options and expose them to persuasive arguments for and against each proposal before asking them to come to a conclusion. Another example is the Choice Questionnaire, developed in the Netherlands, which tried to ensure that respondents had adequate information about a number of different policy options and evaluated not just the consequences of these options but the trade-offs involved.

Two other approaches attempt to compensate for the lack of opportunity to discuss or reflect on the issues under investigation. The "Planning Cell" was a technique pioneered in Germany in the 1970s that involved small representative groups of citizens brought together in different locations to discuss issues of regional or national importance. More recently, Fishkin has attempted to recreate the Habermasian "ideal speech situation" through deliberative polls that bring together much larger representative samples and give them the opportunity to interrogate experts and then engage in intense debate on a particular issue. The first, for example, involved a carefully selected sample of 300 people in the United Kingdom who spent a weekend discussing the policy options involved in dealing with rising crime. Of particular interest was not only the pioneering nature of this experiment (and the critique of orthodox polling that informed it) but the fact that it was sponsored by two media organizations: Granada television, one of Britain's leading commercial television companies, and the broadsheet newspaper the *Independent*. It is instructive that although the program that emerged from this study created substantial interest and publicity, it made little impact on the way in which standard polls were subsequently commissioned or interpreted by media organizations.

This brings us to the second category of critique: the circumstances in which polls are undertaken and their results disseminated. We have seen that even under the most controlled and benign circumstances, the inherent weaknesses of polling methodology make them little more than a contrivance. Under circumstances in which organizations or individuals have a vested interest in the results, they can be a potent public relations weapon. Miller quotes one example from Britain in the late 1950s of a deliberate attempt by an antinationalization pressure group to design a questionnaire that would give them the answers they wanted. The fact that this survey was conducted through one of the leading commercial research companies suggests, says Miller, that "the most reputable of polling organisations provide no guarantee against biased questions and distorting surveys designed to influence rather than report public opinion" (1983: 94). A similar example is given by Catherine Marsh from 1978 when proposals to nationalize agricultural land were under public discussion. The Country Landowners Association, representing large land owners, used a reputable agency to ask the question "How strongly do you agree or disagree that it is important for a free society that agricultural land should be privately owned?" The overwhelming majority who agreed was then trumpeted in a press release as a demonstration of public opposition to the government's proposals. What was missing from subsequent reports was a fairly crucial piece of information from the same poll: less than 10 percent were aware of the government's proposals (Marsh, 1982: 132)!

A second example from Marsh illustrates how the same research company can unwittingly produce apparently contradictory results depending on the client. In this case, the issue under debate was abortion and the political context was an attempt in 1980 by anti-abortion MPs to reduce the permitted fetal age of abortion from twenty-eight weeks to twenty weeks. Gallup conducted polls for two different clients: first, for the magazine *Woman's Own*, which was being advised by a pro-abortion activist who opposed the new initiative; and a little later for a medical anti-abortion pressure group that supported the new bill. One of the questions asked by Gallup in the first survey on behalf of the pro-abortion lobby was (of women):

If you had suffered rape and as a result became pregnant, do you think you would:
    Continue with the pregnancy and keep the child?
    Continue with the pregnancy and offer the child for adoption?
    Seek an abortion?
(Men were asked the question in terms of their partner, if applicable).

One of the questions asked in the second survey on behalf of the anti-abortion lobby was:

Do you think that abortions:
    Should be available on demand?
    Should only be allowed in certain circumstances?
    Should never be allowed?

The suggestion is not one of deliberately unprofessional conduct, but rather of time and resource limits combined with the influence that will inevitably come with holding the purse strings. It may have been possible—given unlimited resources, no deadline, and a completely neutral agenda—to devise a more sophisticated research instrument that would be less obviously manipulative. But in the end, as Marsh concludes, "the search for unbiased question-wording is a particularly fruitless and philosophically naive quest" (1982: 145).

For this reason, we have to ask some searching questions about the motivation behind polls that are prominently reported. In an earlier essay, Marsh illustrates the way in which polls were used in the run-up to a referendum in 1975 on whether Britain should stay in the Common Market—an issue that, as we shall see, has some fascinating echoes twenty-five years on. The pro-Common Market "Britain in Europe" group invested considerable sums of money in commissioning polls to generate positive publicity about support for their position, which they believed would reinforce their support. Marsh reports a quote from Bob Worcester of the research company MORI that the pro-Europe group's growing lead in the polls "should have considerable impact on the strategy of the campaign. When you are ahead (as we are) you reassure people and encourage them to cast their vote" (Marsh, 1979: 278). This cycle of positive reinforcement is, of course, the corollary of Noelle-Neumann's spiral of silence. As Marsh goes on to observe, the political agenda can thus be dominated by the particular organization or pressure group that has taken the polling initiative: "The sponsors take all the important decisions. They can choose what to have a poll about, how to word it, when to have it, whom to ask the question of; and newspaper owners can control how and when and whether it is reported" (Marsh, 1979: 283). In all these cases, there is one important potential obstacle for the sponsor seeking publicity: there is no guarantee that newspaper owners (or TV companies or any other media owner) will report the results with the prominence or uncritical interpretation that the sponsor might like. That position changes radically when sponsor and media owner are one and the same.

POLLS AND THE PRESS

Although there has been no systematic study, there is anecdotal evidence that the number of polls being commissioned by media owners and the amount of space being allocated to their reporting—particularly in the British national press—has increased markedly over the last twenty years. This is certainly true at election time: Norris reports twenty opinion polls published during the 1959 British general election, rising during the 1970s and 1980s, and peaking at fifty-seven during the 1992 campaign (1997: 82). Similar trends have been reported in the United States where concern has been expressed for some time (as increasingly in European countries) that the resulting "horse-race" nature of election coverage displaces more informational and democracy-enhancing policy analysis. Almost certainly, the same process of proliferation applies to polls between elections. Following Suhonen (1997), we can divide them into three broad categories: the regular, voting-intention polls that trace the fluctuating support for political parties or individual leaders; more broadly based—often comparative or longitudinal surveys—that offer "state of the nation" information, such as the annual British Social Attitudes surveys or the General Household Survey; and ad hoc polls on particular social, economic, or political issues.

This fairly crude typology has a parallel (and equally crude) typology of sponsorship. The first, though sometimes funded through regular contracts between newspapers and research companies, are often conducted by the agencies themselves as a means of creating press publicity and maintaining (in some cases) a very long run of longitudinal data. Particularly at times of fevered political activity or heightened political tension—as with President Clinton's impeachment trial in

America or in the run-up to the 1997 election in Britain when support for the Conservative government had apparently collapsed—such polls are gratefully seized upon by the media and will ensure that research company names are frequently in the public eye. The second, "state of the nation" surveys, are usually better resourced, better thought through and sponsored through government agencies, grant-giving trusts, or academic programs. They are often used as a statistical basis to inform policy thinking on a wide range of issues from crime prevention policy to transport planning.

The third category, one-off polls on a wide variety of issues, can have a range of different sponsors from pressure groups wanting to influence government policy (as on abortion) to advertising agencies seeking some free publicity for themselves or a client. Increasingly, however, it appears that such polls are being commissioned by and then prominently reported in newspapers (or, less frequently, television and radio programs).

There are a number of reasons for this profusion of media-inspired and media-funded polls. First, as column inches and airtime expand, space needs to be filled. Polls and their analysis can provide plenty of copy to sit alongside the exponential increase in lifestyle journalism, opinion pieces by named columnists, and other "softer" forms of editorial content. Second, as the media environment becomes more competitive and more aggressive, polling data can provide news stories in their own right that give welcome free publicity to a newspaper or program. Compared to the costs of sponsorship or buying airtime, even the most expensive polls would be cheap. Third, on stories which have been running for some time or on which rival publications or programs seem to have won a competitive advantage, polling information can provide a quick and easy angle that will often be picked up by competitors. In this sense, it is an alternative to the orthodox journalistic practice of uncovering or developing the "facts" of a story to give it fresh impetus. Fourth, and perhaps more significantly, the use of polls allows newspapers to fulfill one of their traditional fourth estate roles as "tribunes of the people." The British tabloid press in particular likes to see itself as a vigorous campaigning force that can stand up for the rights of "ordinary people" against the might of governments, corporations, or other elite bodies that exercise power over individual citizens. Describing the media's role in commissioning ad hoc polls, Suhonen argues that "[i]n this way the media represent the people's will and act as organs of the civil society who deal with the power of the state and the economy."

All of these functions that polls fulfill for a burgeoning mass media tend to disguise one fundamental point: that in most instances, individual publications or programs will be carrying out polls according to their own political or editorial agenda. In the vast majority of cases, because such polls are necessarily rushed and inexpensive exercises and because they are often conducted within a particular political context, they will suffer from all the problems of manufacturing public opinion outlined above. Much more importantly, this process of contrived opinion formation will take place along lines that are consonant with the particular interests or agenda being promoted by the commissioning publications.

CASE STUDIES

Two examples from Britain in the last three years illustrate the point. In September 1997 the *Independent on Sunday*, a national broadsheet newspaper that was struggling to survive in a highly competitive newspaper environment, launched a campaign to decriminalize the drug cannabis. To what extent this was a marketing strategy based on knowledge about its readership and to what extent the personal crusade of its then editor Rosie Boycott was not clear, but it succeeded in generating both hostile and favorable publicity. It recruited several medical specialists in support of cannabis legalization for medicinal purposes, held a well-attended conference in December 1997, and organized a march and rally in London in March 1998. At one point the Lord Chief Justice, Lord Bingham, added his authoritative voice to the campaign by calling for a debate on the issue. All these initiatives succeeded in raising the profile of the *Independent on Sunday* as a newspaper and in keeping the legalization of cannabis on the political agenda. This was an achievement, given that the new Labour government and Conservative opposition were publicly unyielding even in considering the appointment of a Commission to look at the legislative position. There was, however, some suggestion that elements within the Labour Party were sympathetic to the arguments but had been prevented by party leaders from speaking out because of the importance of holding a firm "law and order" line in public. For the campaign to make any headway, it was clear that only the weight of public opinion was likely to put any political pressure on the government.

On 12 October, the *Independent on Sunday* led its front page with the banner headline "Huge majority want cannabis legalised." The subheadline read "Government isolated as 80 per cent back our campaign for radical change in law." These figures came from a poll carried out on behalf of the *Independent on Sunday* by the research company MORI, and although the precise wording of questions and responses are not given, the sense is plain enough from the text:

> Almost half those polled, 45 per cent, said they were in favour of the current restrictions being relaxed for those who needed cannabis for medicinal purposes, while more than one in three, 35%, wanted it to be legally available for recreational use. The Government's policy of maintaining the status quo, that all cannabis possession should remain illegal, received the approval of one in six, 17 per cent.

This was interpreted by the newspaper both as the *Independent on Sunday* speaking out on behalf of the nation, and as the nation supporting the newspaper: "The British public is firmly behind the *Independent on Sunday* campaign to decriminalise cannabis—and opposed to the Government's obdurate stand" ran a companion piece on the same day. Moreover, the article suggested that popular support, which the newspaper had identified, was indeed having some political impact: "There are signs that the Government may be preparing to rethink its drugs strategy." Here was a newspaper, then, positioning itself as tribune of the people, speaking out on behalf of a clearly established popular will against an obdurate government.

Five days later, the campaign was taken up by the *Daily Mail*, a mid-market tabloid that has recently become Britain's second most popular newspaper, selling well over 2 million copies. The *Mail* and its stablemate *Mail on Sunday* has a very well-established political identity: pro Conservative in its politics, although somewhat ambivalent around the last general election, but unshakeably conservative in its approach to moral issues. It has a clearly stated commitment to "family values" and will invariably take a hawkish line on issues like divorce, immigration, homosexuality, or crime. The *Mail*'s editorial position was and remains implacably opposed to relaxing the law on drugs.

On Friday 17 October, the second lead story on its front page was headlined "Most Britons oppose making drugs legal." Its opening paragraph met the *Independent*'s claims head-on: "The vast majority of Britons are opposed to the legalisation of cannabis despite a high-profile campaign to change the law." It then reported the results of an opinion poll commissioned from ICM—a research company as reputable as MORI—in which respondents had been asked for each of six different drugs whether they should be made legal or remain illegal. For cannabis, 62 percent said that it should remain illegal whereas for the other five drugs—ecstasy, amphetamines, LSD, cocaine, and heroin—the figure was over 90 percent.

Although the *Independent* had used standard methods and a respected agency, the *Mail* attempted by implication to discredit the data by comparing the two methodologies: "[*The Independent*'s] results were based on a sample of 600 people who were asked complex questions over the phone with many possible multiple choice answers." By contrast, the *Mail's* survey "asked 1108 adults simple and clear questions during face-to-face interviews. Participants had the opportunity to keep their replies confidential by filling out a questionnaire which could not be traced to them." In polling terms, telephone interviewing is accepted practice and sample size is much less important than how representative the sample is. Given the research companies being employed, it is fair to assume that standard and methodologically acceptable sampling techniques were used by both. Confidentiality would also have been guaranteed by both companies.

In other words, the only significant difference between the two polls was in the phrasing of questions and the interpretation of results. For the *Mail*, it was important to demonstrate the "real" position of public opinion in order to compensate for what it called the "bogus 'facts' foisted on the public" and to deflect any ministerial moves towards greater leniency under the banner of popular support. Its editorial agenda became clear in its leader column that day:

> The *Mail* survey establishes that most people are firmly on the side of Home Secretary Jack Straw in opposing any relaxation in the law. They want more of a police effort in cracking down on pushers. They want harsher penalties. And they are unmoved by the argument that crime levels would fall if drugs became legally available.

Neither the *Independent on Sunday* nor the *Daily Mail* was really motivated by a desire to uncover the "true" state of public opinion, nor to put themselves at the service of the public by acting as unbiased conduits of the popular will to government. They each had a highly developed editorial agenda, to which their respective uses of opinion poll data was subservient.

The second example of newspapers' exploitation of polls involves another contentious moral issue: the public acceptability of homosexuality and in particular the peculiarly British debate about whether homosexual politicians should be "outed"— that is, revealed as being gay without their permission.

In October 1998 a British cabinet minister, Ron Davies, was the alleged victim of a robbery on Clapham Common in South London. The circumstances of the robbery remained vague, but the fact that Davies admitted to meeting and willingly going off with a stranger in an area renowned for its casual homosexual encounters—and then immediately tendered his resignation—triggered much speculation about his personal life. A day later, an openly gay former MP turned political columnist, Matthew Parris, was being interviewed on an influential BBC program about the issue of homosexuality in politics. He mentioned that there were at least two other gay MPs in the cabinet, one who had already declared his homosexuality and another—Trade Secretary Peter Mandelson—who had not. This unprompted revelation about a high-profile cabinet minister caused something of a stir, even though it had been canvassed in a popular newspaper at least ten years earlier. It was certainly common knowledge among journalists.

Within a week, the issue was given fresh impetus by a fourth cabinet minister "voluntarily" declaring his homosexuality after being threatened with exposure by the tabloid *News of the World*. In combination with the Ron Brown and Peter Mandelson stories, the whole question of "gays in the cabinet" became a hot topic.

At this point the *Sun*, Britain's top-selling tabloid newspaper owned by Rupert Murdoch, felt it appropriate to run a front page editorial on behalf of "the public" that clearly threatened a wholesale campaign of outing. Addressed to Prime Minister Tony Blair and headlined "TELL US THE TRUTH TONY," it was given the ominous subheadline "Are we being run by a gay Mafia?" and stated unequivocally that "the public has a right to know how many homosexuals occupy positions of high power." Underlining its self-proclaimed role as a mouthpiece for concerned public opinion, it continued "there are widespread fears that MPs, even ministers, are beholden to others for reasons other than politics." The *Sun* even provided—apparently with a straight face—a telephone hotline for "ministers and MPs who are secretly homosexual" and wanted to come out. Although offensive to many, this overtly illiberal approach by the *Sun* was consistent with its attitude throughout the 1980s and 1990s, where it would speak unapologetically about "poofters" and made no pretense about its distaste for homosexuality (Chippindale and Horrie, 1990). In this respect, it reflected the views of its editors and proprietor. More importantly, the paper was convinced that its attitude was firmly rooted in a widespread sense of public disapproval, particularly among its core working-class readership.

The following day the *Guardian*, a liberal broadsheet, published the results of a commissioned opinion poll that appeared to contradict the *Sun*'s long-standing view of public intolerance. It announced that "Exclusive poll shows majority not concerned by homosexuality." In response to the question "Do you think homosexuality is morally acceptable or not?" 56 percent of respondents answered yes. When asked "Do you think being openly gay is compatible or incompatible with holding a cabinet post?" 52 percent said compatible. The paper concluded unequivocally that "The days when it was assumed that the British public was overwhelmingly intolerant of homosexuals are over."

Within two days, the *Sun* had performed what was widely seen as a spectacular U-turn. It issued a "new policy statement" to the effect that the paper was opposed to the outing of gay politicians, and confirmed its position on its own leader page: "From now on the *Sun* will not reveal the sexuality of any gays, men or women, unless we believe it can be defended on the grounds of overwhelming public interest." Taken with the *Guardian's* opinion poll, this was widely seen as a triumph for a more progressive public mood over a newspaper's historically bigoted and uncompromising editorial approach to homosexuality.

In fact, all was not quite how it seemed. As many commentators pointed out in the days following this editorial *volte face*, there were other proprietorial agendas at work. First, Rupert Murdoch's daughter Elisabeth was known to be close friends with Peter Mandelson. According to a *Guardian* report, she was "thought to have complained, with other senior News International executives" about the *Sun's* position. More importantly, it was Mandelson as the minister responsible for Trade and Industry who would be ultimately responsible for sanctioning News International's proposed and hugely controversial takeover of Manchester United football club. As many observers of the Murdoch empire have observed in the past, his newspapers' editorial positions tend to owe less to a consistently applied ideology than to a pragmatic view of what will further his corporate interests (e.g. Shawcross, 1992). It would not have been very politic (nor characteristic of Murdoch himself) to offend a key member of the government. So was the *Sun* bowing to a tide of new liberalism that was sweeping away decades of British prejudice against homosexuality? Or were a few senior editorial staff, under proprietorial pressure, taking out a corporate insurance policy? What exactly was the state of public opinion?

According to one report, many *Sun* reporters maintained that their "mafia" angle was legitimate because there was still widespread disquiet about homosexuality. The *Guardian* quoted one as saying "If you go outside the M25 a lot of people have serious concerns about gays." This may not have been supported by the *Guardian's* editorial agenda, nor its opinion poll findings, but it is supported by more considered attitudinal research in Britain. According to the 1996 *British Social Attitudes*, an academic program of longitudinal research in the United Kingdom, 55 percent of the population believe that sexual relations between two adults of the same sex is "always wrong" (Barnett and Thomson, 1996). The discrepancy between this figure and the *Guardian's* may be explained by differences in question wording in the two surveys—that being gay is acceptable as long as it doesn't involve sex!—but it again highlights the dangers of newspapers' use of opinion polls in trying to interpret "public opinion." Had the *Sun* decided to justify its first editorial position through reference to overwhelming public support, it could easily have duplicated a BSA-style question.

In the end, what the British public really *think* about homosexuality is probably unfathomable and certainly unquantifiable. What the British newspapers *wrote* about the public's view on homosexuality in October 1998 in the aftermath of government "outings" had less to do with trying to gauge true public opinion and much more to do with the newspapers themselves—in this case, the ownership of the *Sun* and the liberal agenda of the *Guardian*.

Whereas these are two examples of the media's use of polls in the arena of moral and relatively apolitical issues, there is also evidence of similar techniques being used increasingly in one of Britain's most serious political debates since the war: whether or not to join the Single European Currency and sign up to the Euro. Because the Labour government has pledged to hold a referendum before coming to any decision, and given the perceived success of the Britain in Europe group twenty-five years ago in creating a bandwagon effect, we can expect a plethora of polls using a variety of differently worded questions in the run-up to this long-awaited referendum (everything from "Do you want to scrap the British pound?" to "Do you want to be the only European country left out of the European currency?"). Most newspapers in the United Kingdom have taken sides, and it is already apparent that those opposed to monetary union give a prominent place to polls that appear to show public opinion moving against it (and, by definition, very little publicity to polls which show the opposite).

For present purposes, the most interesting question is what prompted both political parties to concede a referendum at all, given Britain's tradition of Parliamentary sovereignty. The answer almost certainly lies in the large number of polls being published in the run-up to the last election showing heavy majorities in favor of a referendum on the single currency. These were, inevitably, being commissioned and published by the "Eurosceptic" newspapers, in particular the *Sun*, and helped to create a climate where it became impossible politically for any of the main parties to argue that this decision should be left to the elected representatives. When the apparent "consensus" emerged that a referendum would indeed precede any government decision on the single currency, it was widely interpreted as a victory for true populist democracy—political parties surrendering to the overpowering might of popular opinion.

In fact, it is much more likely that these polls were tapping a general sense that referendums were, like motherhood and apple pie, a "good thing." Curtice and Jowell quote previous surveys as finding high levels of support for referendums, adding that questions "tend to ask respondents merely whether they are in favour of or against referendums, so it may not be surprising that most people say they want a vote for themselves" (1997: 104). In their own survey, they posed the question on three separate issues as a choice between a vote by MPs and "everyone having a say" in a referendum. On all three issues—joining the single currency, restoring the death penalty, and changing to a proportional representation system of voting—there were large majorities in favor of a referendum. In other words, the *Sun*'s polls were tapping a seemingly widespread approval for more voter involvement in decision-making generally, rather than a groundswell of feeling on the single currency issue. In this case, however, the commissioned polls and the self-generated publicity built around them were part of a systematic campaign to influence the political decision-making process. Once again, the motivation had little to do with representing the people's will to Parliament. Polls merely offered the opportunity to elicit predictable responses to a "motherhood" question that could then be exploited to further the newspaper's firmly held editorial and proprietorial convictions.

CONCLUSIONS

Herbst has attempted to conceptualize four different definitions of public opinion, the last of which was public opinion defined as "reification or fictional entity." By this definition, supported in the writings of writers as diverse as Lippmann and Bourdieu, public opinion does not exist but is manufactured as "a rhetorical tool used by the powerful to achieve their goals." Although the argument presented here appears to support that definition, it is too simplistic. To demonstrate that the media can and do represent public opinion in a way that is consonant with their own corporate or editorial line does not necessarily preclude either the validity of other concepts of public opinion or some representation of it that might be less mediated by self-interested elites. It would be legitimate, for example, to state that within most Western European countries at the end of the millennium there is overwhelming agreement that pedophilia is wrong and that those involved in its practice should be prevented from doing so. There are a number of criminal justice policy outcomes that flow from this consensus—in contrast to, say, a less clear-cut public opinion on this issue in ancient Greece. In addition, more dynamic concepts of public opinion such as those propounded by Habermas on will formation or Fishkin on deliberation are crucial to discussions of modern democracy and the role of the media.

Even on less obviously contentious issues, where opinion may be complex or evolving or fragmented, we cannot dismiss the notion of a general will simply because the instruments of its measurement are unsophisticated or prone to distortion or deliberately manipulated by elite opinion formers. There are many examples, usually from well-funded and long-term programs of academic or government research, of genuinely unbiased attempts to assess the state of public opinion. These probably have most legitimacy in tracking attitudinal shifts, because longitudinal surveys using repeat questions can iron out methodological deficiencies. In other words, simply because the instruments of measurement are usually manipulated does not of itself vitiate their usefulness or relevance in understanding something of the general will.

The problem of reification, then, is particularly (although not solely) applicable to the media institutions involved in the commissioning, processing, and publishing of opinion data using measurement methods that are flimsy and manipulable. Through judicious exploitation of such weaknesses, these institutions can lend a spuriously populist credibility to their own agendas. The kinds of experiment funded by Granada TV, which have more claim to legitimacy, will not be taken up by newspapers that want their data quickly, cheaply, and in accordance with their own campaigning priorities or political affiliations. These spurious renditions of public opinion are then fed into the "opinion-formation" process through other communication outlets, and in many cases into the policy-making and legislative process through debates in Parliament. A research project urgently required is some examination of how many parliamentarians and government ministers mention "a recent opinion poll" to demonstrate public backing for a measure they are currently promoting—and precisely where they read the results of this poll. Even lawmakers are probably unaware that their attempts to ground legislative initiatives in the general will are more likely to come down to vested interests masquerading as popular opinion through the distorting mirror of mediatized opinion polls.

REFERENCES

Barnett, Steven and Katarina Thomson. 1996. Portraying Sex: The Limits of Tolerance. In R. Jowell et al. (eds.), *British Social Attitudes: The 13th Report*. Aldershot: Dartmouth Press.

Bryce, James. 1984. *The American Commonwealth*. New York: Macmillan.

Butler, David and Dennis Kavanagh. 1997. *The British General Election of 1997*. Basingstoke: Macmillan.

Chippindale, Peter and Chris Horrie. 1990. *Stick It Up Your Punter! The Rise and Fall of the Sun*. London: Heinemann.

Converse, Philip. 1987. Changing Conceptions of Public Opinion in the Political Process. *Public Opinion Quarterly* 51, 512-524.

Curtice, John and Roger Jowell. 1997. Trust in the Political System. In R. Jowell et al. (eds.), *British Social Attitudes: The 14th Report*. Aldershot: Ashgate Publishing.

Fishkin, James. 1995. *The Voice of the People: Public Opinion and Democracy.* New Haven: Yale University Press.

Habermas, Jürgen. 1989. *The Structural Transformation of the Public Sphere.* Cambridge: Polity.

Hampster-Monk, I. 1987. *The Political Philosophy of Edmund Burke.* Harlow: Longman.

Herbst, Susan. 1993. The Meaning of Public Opinion: Citizens' Constructions of Political Reality. *Media, Culture and Society* 15, 437-454.

Lippmann, Walter. 1925. *The Phantom Public.* London: Macmillan.

Marsh, Catherine. 1979. Opinion Polls—Social Science or Political Manoeuvre? In J. Irvine et al. (eds.), *Demystifying Social Statistics.* London: Pluto Press.

Marsh, Catherine. 1982. *The Survey Method: The Contribution of Surveys to Sociological Explanation.* London: Allen and Unwin.

Miller, William. 1983. *The Survey Method in the Social and Political Sciences: Achievements, Failures, Prospects.* London: Frances Pinter.

Noelle-Neumann, Elisabeth. 1984. *The Spiral of Silence: Public Opinion, Our Social Skin.* Chicago: University of Chicago Press.

Norris, Pippa. 1997. Political Communications. In P. Dunleavy et al. (eds.), *Developments in British Politics.* Basingstoke: Macmillan.

Price, Vincent and Peter Neijens. 1997. Opinion Quality in Public Opinion Research. *International Journal of Public Opinion Research* 9(4), 336-356.

Price, Vincent and Peter Neijens. 1998. Deliberative Polls: Toward Improved Measures of "Informed" Public Opinion? *International Journal of Public Opinion Research* 10(2), 145-175.

Schumpeter, Joseph. 1976. *Capitalism, Socialism and Democracy.* Suffolk: George Allen and Unwin.

Shawcross, William. 1992. *Rupert Murdoch: Ringmaster of the Information Circus.* London: Chatto and Windus.

Speier, Hans. 1995. The Rise of Public Opinion. In R. Jackall (ed.), *Propaganda.* Basingstoke: Macmillan.

Splichal, Slavko. 1997. Political Institutionalisation of Public Opinion through Polling. *Javnost/The Public* 4(2), 17-38.

Suhonen, Pertti. 1997. The Media, Polls and Political Process: The Case of Finland. *European Journal of Communication* 12(2), 219-238.

Tyrrell, Robert and David Goodhart. 1998, October. Opinion Poll Democracy. *Prospect*, 50-54.

Zaller, John. 1992. *The Nature and Origins of Mass Opinion.* Cambridge: Cambridge University Press.

13

Opinion Polls and Journalism: The Case of Finland

Pertti Suhonen

Now that the mass media are every day publishing the results of opinion polls commissioned by themselves or sponsored by others, they are in many ways fulfilling some of the functions that are mainly considered the domain of political parties, pressure groups, elections, and other political institutions. Because poll journalism constructs and expresses public opinion, it, for its part, expresses the will of the people, shapes the citizens' identities, and controls the use of power.

Opinion polls and the public presentation of their results convey to the decision-makers in both politics and economy a picture of the mood in society and the opinions of citizens on whatever the controversial issues may be under political debate. Political decisions are thus made in the knowledge of what the public opinion is. The decision-makers must also bear in mind that the media and their audiences are aware of the state of the public opinion as well (Lemert, 1981: 214).

So polling and journalism together fulfill the same representational function as elections and referendums. In the production and presentation of public opinion they also compensate for the functions of civil society based on people's active participation and organization (see, for example, Lemert 1981: 32).

The role of polls in view of the democratic representation of civil society has been analyzed in starkly different ways. In one extreme there are ideas of opinion polls as genuine direct democracy (Gallup and Rae, 1940). The opposing view highlights the fact that the development and increase in opinion polls has in part undermined the democratic institutions (Beniger, 1992; Salmon and Glasser, 1995).

The polls shape people's identities, that is, fulfill the identity function, when the results of opinion polls are published with great visibility and provide people with an opportunity to compare their own opinions, attitudes, and values with those of the majority, the minority, or some other reference group. Such comparison may strengthen or weaken citizens' identities and opinions. Those who vacillate in their opinions agree more easily with the majority than with the minority (McAllister & Studlar 1991; Noelle-Neumann 1984).

Being aware of the poll results enables the citizens to evaluate the performance of decision-makers by comparing their actions to the public opinion. In some cases journalists intentionally arrange opportunities for comparison to their audiences. It is quite usual that the media commission polls on the central issues under political debate and on the issues being voted in the parliament. When publishing the results, the journalists pose the question whether the representatives of the people agree with the public opinion or act against it (Suhonen, 1997). The results that are not published and remain with the researchers and financiers do not have such a control function. In these cases it is rather a question of the fact that polling is a means for the economic and political power machineries to control the public opinion from behind the scenes (Beniger, 1992; Peer, 1992).

The fulfillment of these functions—representing public opinion, shaping the identity of the public, and controlling decision-making—depends on one hand on the number of public opinion polls carried out, their subjects, and results. On the other hand, it is also crucial how the surveys and their results are presented in the mass media. The bigger the headlines and the more channels through which an opinion poll on some social issue is presented, the more difficult it becomes for decision-makers to ignore it and the more people's political attitudes the poll either strengthens or undermines. The large number of polls, their promotion to the main news pages of the newspapers or to top news on radio or television, and also the public debate on the basis of the results strengthens the position of poll results as the public opinion.

The weight of poll news is not, however, only decided on the basis of the publicity it receives. The interpretation and commentaries that the journalists make of the results also has its own effect on the reception of the news. The linguistic strategies that are used in news headlines or when the results are published are a fundamental part of the journalistic signifying of poll news.

As far as the production of public opinion based on polling is concerned, journalism has five crucial roles:

1. Commissioning the polls and the choice of subjects;
2. Selection of news items from other poll material available;
3. Evaluating the results with means of news visibility;
4. Offering a certain interpretation to the audience with headlines and other linguistic strategies of the text;
5. Critical evaluation of the research methods, results, and their social significance.

Poll journalism may also be examined from the point of view of the media itself, where the most important question is to which purposes the media actually needs polls.

HOW MASS MEDIA USE POLLS

In the 1930s the rapid increase of opinion polls in the United States was to a great extent due to the fact that journalists became interested in them. Later polls and journalism have increasingly become intertwined in ways both apparent and subtle (Gawiser and Witt, 1994: 1-2). This is the situation not only in the United States but all over the Western world, including Finland.

When the Finnish Gallup Company was founded in 1945 its operation was critically dependent on its cooperation with the media. *Helsingin Sanomat*—the biggest daily newspaper—and fourteen other newspapers agreed with Gallup to regularly commission opinion polls and to publish their results. Under the circumstances of economic depression after the war there would not have been such a demand for market research that it would have given cause to found a separate research institution (Suhonen, 1995).

At least four purposes can be named for which the media use opinion polls: First, the media try to influence political decision-making by commissioning opinion polls and by publishing their results. *Helsingin Sanomat* acted in just this way in the 1970s when it attempted to influence Finnish foreign policy. At the beginning of the decade the newspaper appealed strongly to the results of its poll for a free trade agreement between Finland and the European Economic Community, now known as the European Union (Suhonen and Haapasalo, 1975). At the end of 1978 there was an exceptionally lively public debate on Finnish foreign policy and the public opinion about it. A poll carried out by *Helsingin Sanomat* showed that there was increased discontent among people with the country's foreign policy and especially with what was thought to be its excessive allegiance to the Soviet Union. The former editor-in-chief of *Helsingin Sanomat* (Nortamo, 1997) said that through the opinion poll the newspaper attempted to democratize the foreign policy debate in order to voice the citizens' critical opinion, which otherwise would have remained unknown.

Second, poll results make interesting subject matter for news. For example, the results of polls commissioned by television news are often newsworthy in many different ways. Polls are often carried out on very topical subjects connected to the political agenda or current election campaigns. The results are new because they have never been made public before. The results are doubly new if they show a change in the public opinion or in support for parties or politicians. Often other media quote the news on polls and thus make them available to their own audiences. When the media publish the results of opinion polls that they have commissioned they are not only reporting the news but creating it too (Atkin and Gaudino, 1984; Cantril, 1991: 65-68).

In the 1980s the term "horse-race journalism" was coined in the United States to denote the ceaseless follow-ups made by the television and newspapers of the support for presidential candidates. The daily competition and its changes became more important than the candidates' characteristics and political opinions (Atkin and Gaudino, 1984; Maarek, 1995: 82).

In Finland both of the two biggest national TV companies and the country's biggest newspaper publish the political parties' support polls at regular intervals, and when elections get nearer they do this almost every week. Poll results were published almost daily in the week before the first round of votes in the 1994 presidential elections. Several media also follow the citizens' satisfaction with the policies of the president and the government.

Publishing poll results produces journalism that in one way differs from traditional news journalism. Whereas news usually tells people what has already happened, the support figures for parties or candidates also predict the future—in other words, the outcome of the elections.

Third, well-planned and conducted opinion polls may be used by precision journalism as a part of a larger story. Polls are conducted in order to get a reliable and deep understanding of the society and its changes (Ismach, 1984; Meyer, 1990).

Fourth, it is worth remembering that journalists sometimes use opinion polls in order to find out what the audience expects of the media. What things are important or interesting and how should they be reported? This practice could be compared with the politicians' interest in the public opinion (Gawiser and Witt, 1994: 4-5).

Susan Herbst (1993: 115) summarizes all these points in the following: "Journalists have always been interested in evaluating public opinion, since in democracy, public opinion matters—it is a news. Rigorous assessment of popular opinion helps editors figure out what the public wants to hear or read about, and therefore shapes news content. Also people like to read and hear about themselves, and opinion polls enable social comparison on a mass scale."

From these two perspectives—the political functions of opinion polls and the use of polls by media—I examine Finnish poll journalism of the late 1990s in the light of empirical data.

RESEARCH DATA

In order to analyze opinion poll journalism, Finnish mainstream media was monitored over a period of three weeks, 28 February-20 March 1997. The research object was five wide-circulation newspapers, four daily national news broadcasts (Finnish Broadcasting Company), and the four television news broadcasts reaching the largest audiences. For the period under investigation everything written in the newspapers was examined except for the classified ads and the cartoons. Everything related to opinion polls was included in the research data. The selection was based on the headlines of the articles.

Radio and television data were selected according to the same principles. Headlines were taken to be the subjects named at the beginning of the news broadcast and also the opening sentences of each individual item.

Strictly interpreted, opinion polls are used to discover what is on people's minds: opinions, attitudes, values, beliefs, intentions, cognitive concepts, and so forth. In this research the interpretation is somewhat more liberal. Items about people's activities, behavior, and conditions surveyed through a large sample were also included if the data had been collected by a questionnaire or an interview. The research data therefore includes, for example, research on television viewing, smoking, and surveys on health and employment.

OPINION POLLS ON THE MEDIA AGENDA

The newspapers examined included 145 items on opinion polls in the three-week period. Television news broadcasts carried twenty items on opinion polls and radio news broadcasts carried twenty-three. The media investigated for the three weeks included seventy different polls, that is, somewhat more than three per day.

Naturally, publicity was not evenly distributed among the subject matter of the news items. Only a small fraction of the opinion polls appeared in so many media that it could be said that they made it on the media agenda. The most prominent poll was that concerning Finns' attitudes to the Swedish-speaking minority in the country. This occurred fourteen times in the media investigated. Some ten other surveys appeared at least five times. Approximately one half of all the polls were addressed only once, in one newspaper or one radio or television news broadcast.

In addition to frequency, another dimension that defines the position of some issue on the agenda of publicity is its generic status. For example, a survey of the confidence placed in the President of Finland is more obviously on the agenda the more widely its results are published on the main news pages of the papers or page one news of the electronic media or the more papers that address it in its editorial.

In the period investigated the newspapers only deemed 9 percent of the poll news to be so significant as to merit a headline on the front page. Almost four fifths of the press data are news. They also include news elements addressing other matters whose paragraph headline refers to a poll or its results. One typical example of this is the news about Britain preparing for a general election, part of which reports the most recent support figures for the political parties (Table 13.1). The promi-

Table 13.1. Types of Newspaper Articles Dealing with Polls (in Percentages.

News, over 2-column headline on front page	2
News, 1-2-column headline on front page	7
Other news	63
Part of news with paragraph headline	6
Editorial	12
Other article, story, etc.	7
Letters to the editor	3
Total percentage	100
Total number	145

nence of opinion poll news on the inside pages of the newspapers varied considerably. Of these, 30 percent had headlines over four columns. There was the same amount of one-column news. One fifth of the items were editorials or other articles commenting on the results of the polls.

The number of editorials was fairly high (12%). This figure indicates that more than one out of ten news items on polls gives the newspaper cause to discuss it in its most prestigious forum. Taking into consideration the other articles written by journalists one may state that the newspapers take the poll results seriously.

Both radio and television news broadcasts begin by naming some important news items. The list resembles the front page of a newspaper, condensing the newscasters' idea of which of the news of the day are the most important and of greatest interest to the audience. Of the news on the electronic media over one third of the news about opinion polls made it to this important position.

On radio and television news broadcasts results of opinion polls achieved the status of important news relatively more frequently than in the newspapers. This is due to the fact that of the opinion polls addressed in the electronic media news a considerably larger proportion had been commissioned by the media themselves than by the newspapers. All the media attach major news value to their own opinion polls (Atkin and Gaudino, 1984; Cantril, 1991: 65-68).

WHO COMMISSIONED POLLS AND WHO CONDUCTED THEM?

Public opinion constructed with the aid of opinion polls is heavily dependent on which actors in society finance the surveys and determine which subjects are surveyed. When the mass media select their news material, they ultimately determine what the public opinion looks like in the public sphere and in the eyes of the citizens and decision-makers. Of course it must be kept in mind that a considerable proportion of the results of opinion polls goes no further than the use of those commissioning them and that they are not even offered for public consumption.

Throughout the history of opinion polls the media have been active in commissioning them and have thus contributed to the construction of public opinion and its reflection on the public and decision makers.

In March 1997 over one quarter of the opinion poll news in Finland was concerned with surveys commissioned by the media. However, in some of these cases the role of the media is fairly passive and confined to purchasing the results offered by commercial research institutions for publication (Table 13.2).

Table 13.2. The Division of Opinion Poll News According to the Actor Commissioning Them (by Percentage).

Commissioned by	Newspapers	Radio and television	All
Sample media	1	20	7
Other media	26	11	21
Political party	2	2	2
NGO	14	22	16
Business	5	4	5
Commercial research institute	1	7	3
Public authority	17	4	13
University	10	7	9
Statistics Finland	8	13	10
Unknown source	17	9	14
Total percentage	101	99	100
Total number	101	44	145

Nongovernmental organizations (NGOs) are also prominent in commissioning surveys, at least measured by the quantity of news. By having citizens' opinions measured on issues that they regard as important the organizations are able to get their voices heard. Moreover, they can generate public discussion on subjects which, without the opinion polls, would not be raised in the public debate. For the NGOs, commissioning opinion polls is one way to keep them on the public agenda.

One third of the news in the research data concerned opinion polls carried out on taxpayers' money. In Table 13.2 they are divided into three groups. Public authority commissioning surveys means central government, local government, and municipal organizations. Follow-ups by public authority on citizens' attitudes to defense policy have the longest tradition in Finland. The Planning Committee for National Defence Information, which operates under the Ministry for Defence, has since 1964 annually investigated the citizens' confidence in the country's foreign policy, opinions on the country's international agreements and readiness for military defence. Universities and Statistics Finland engage in survey activities defined by their own respective missions. Thus they both commission and conduct opinion polls.

The proportion of opinion polls in the news financed by businesses and economic organizations is very small and does not give a true picture of their activity in commissioning surveys. It may be that a smaller proportion of their survey findings is released for public consumption than in the case of the NGOs, for example.

Almost half of the news items in which it was possible to deduce who had conducted the survey were those conducted by commercial research institutions. Next in prominence came surveys by the universities and Statistics Finland. In news about foreign surveys it is frequently left unspecified by whom the survey was carried out.

SUBJECTS OF THE OPINION POLLS

The role of poll journalism in the production of public opinion is essentially linked to the opportunity to select news items from the survey results available and to decide on the subjects for surveys commissioned by themselves.

In the context of this chapter it is justified to classify the subjects of the polls according to what kind of a relationship they have to the operation of the decision-making system(s) in the society. Support polls and issue polls are directly connected to decision-making.

Support polls have a strong association with representational politics. They measure the competitive situation between political parties and presidential candidates and the confidence placed in the government, the ministers, the parliament, the president, and in other political actors. They have a certain analogy with elections. Support polls also serve the political campaigners in the run-up to the elections. On the other hand, support polls also operate between elections by monitoring the stability of support for those in elected positions and the reactions of voters to the decisions they make.

Issue polls have a closer resemblance to direct democracy such as referendums. They measure citizens' opinions on issues which are either politically decided or which have the goal of becoming politically decided or which for other reasons are under public debate. In Finland recent examples of such issues are the country's membership in the European Monetary Union (EMU) and NATO, the legalization of euthanasia, Sunday shopping, the levels of taxation and social security, the best uses for tax revenue, and so forth.

People's values and attitudes form their own subject category within poll research. On a more general level than single issues they measure the citizens' social and political orientation and the overall ideological atmosphere.

The reality of everyday life is an exception to the research themes mentioned above. It does not deal with people's cognitive categories but their real-life situations and practices. This kind of research sets out to investigate people's lifestyles and actions such as employment, working conditions, socioeconomic status, social relationships, health, consumer habits, media following, hobbies and so on (Table. 13.3).

In spring 1997 the share of support surveys in Finnish mainstream publicity was a good fifth of all poll headlines. Almost half of the support surveys in the data were concerned with the popularity of the political parties and prime ministers in Britain and Sweden. At that time the British were preparing themselves for the general election and the support surveys predicted a landslide victory for Labour after a lengthy period in opposition. The number of domestic support polls was relatively low partly because of the fact that in 1997 no elections were organized in Finland. Elections always arouse interest in the support for political parties and other political actors.

Twenty-two percent of all headlines concerned polls eliciting people's opinions on questions of policy issues. The share of headlines about value and attitude surveys was 24 percent.

Polls on people's life situations and everyday activities—including media following—accounted for one third of the subjects for headlines in the data as a whole. Although these are not opinion polls in the literal sense of the term, their uses in politics and journalism are to a great extent the same as in polls measuring people's cognitive aspects. These, too, provide decision-makers with information on people's lives and enable social comparisons to the audience of the media.

Table 13.3. Subjects of Opinion Polls in Headlines (by Percentage).[a]

	Newspapers	Radio and television	All
Support enjoyed by political actors	24	19	22
Policy issues	18	32	22
Values and attitudes	15	11	14
Reality of everyday life	19	30	22
Media consumption	13	3	10
Something else	11	5	10
Total percentage	100	100	100
Total number	120	37	157

[a]The table includes only those news items whose headline mention some researched topic.

MEANING STRUCTURES OF THE HEADLINES

In accordance with the strong generic conventions, headlines have a crucial position in news. The size of the headline is a message on the importance of the news and of its newsworthiness. The headline presents the most significant aspect of the news or what the publisher wants to be perceived as such. Headline status is in poll news usually given to the result which, according to the journalistic interpretation, is the most notable.

The prominent appearance of the results of opinion polls in big headlines on the front page is one means of their journalistic signifying. The other one comprises the linguistic and rhetorical devices through which journalism presents the results. Results produced as percentages, group comparisons, or time series can be examined from many perspectives and the same numbers can be used in many different ways. Linguistic means can be employed, for example, to create an image of a unified public opinion or to emphasize a division of the nation into two. It is rhetorically possible to play up some findings and play down others and to enhance or detract from the credibility of the poll.

Both journalistic and political motives can be found behind the expressions used in poll news headlines. When the aim is to convey the central results of the survey, or to play up the newsworthiness of a poll conducted by the selfsame media, one is talking about journalistic motives. When the headline is designed to influence decision-makers, political processes, or the general opinion, one can talk about political motives. Moreover, poll news may have political consequences even without political motives. Headlines written on purely journalistic basis can be found appealing by the audience if they contain sensationalism or bias that the writer has included without expressly political goals.

The way in which the results are presented suggests to the audience an interpretation of their meaning. It also reveals something of the attitude of the media and journalists to opinion polls in general and to the matter at hand in particular.

What now follows is an analysis of the ways the Finnish mainstream journalism uses headlines in poll news. The aim is to describe the different structures of meaning in the most typical headline types from the point of view of what political consequences one can assume them to have.[1]

Here follow brief descriptions of twelve types of opinion poll news headlines illustrated by examples picked out from newspapers in 1996 and 1997. These twelve types are named as follows:

1. Generalization
2. Majority/minority
3. Percentages
4. Polarization
5. Comparison
6. The will of the people
7. Intensification
8. Factualization
9. Change of subject
10. Change/permanence
11. Competition
12. Research

The headline types form several dimensions that are to some extent independent of one another. Thus the same expression may find its way into several headline types.

The first five ways of presenting poll results describe the division of opinion or its concentration among the people. The result of an opinion poll is most likely a percentage that conveys the generality of the opinion measured.

1. Generalization is a linguistic strategy whereby a result describing how widely an opinion is held can be made to look as if this opinion were unanimous—public opinion in the most demanding sense. Generalization most frequently presents the object of the research as a collective (grammatical) subject such as Finland, the Finns, women, men, the nation, citizens, and so forth.

> "Finns still suspicious of EMU"
> "Men make no sacrifices to the environment"
> "One man not enough for a Chinawoman"
> "Nation against to new nuclear power plant"
> "Mothers avoid the Internet"

The opinion of the greater or smaller majority—sometimes of a clear minority—is generalized in such headlines to become a collective characteristic. Such a mode of presentation in a poll on opinions about the environment offers the interpretation by which self-centered indifference to environmental problems is an essential part of a man's characteristic being. A man reading the headline is compelled to either accept the environmental attitude expressed or doubt whether he is indeed a man.

Almost without exception such generalizing headlines give a wrong picture of the survey results at hand. Very seldom do the results report an entirely unanimous public opinion.

Generalizing headlines may also either confirm or undermine the opinion of the reader, listener, or viewer, depending on whether s/he is of the same or of different opinion with the nation, Finns, women, or men, and so forth, presented in the headline. The question is also one of identity: femininity, masculinity, nationality, and so forth. The generalizing mode of representing poll results is also likely to strengthen the bandwagon effect (McAllister and Studlar, 1991).

2. Speaking about majority or minority is a more precise means than generalization of making headlines on opinion polls. It, too, stresses the status of opinions by implicitly presenting the majority opinion as the public opinion. This expression, too, offers the audience a place in the majority or in the minority through the opportunity to make comparisons.

"Majority of motorists accept winter speed limits"
"Over half in favor of free sale of wines"
"Majority dreams of freedom from working life"

Because the democratic ideal stresses the role of the majority and demands that its will be done, such headlines carry a political statement. This kind of headline, like the generalization, may be used consciously or unconsciously to reinforce the picture of the acceptability of a dominant opinion and to undermine the minority view.

3. Speaking about percentages is the most neutral means of describing the division of opinions. "Fifty-six percent of citizens support EU membership" sounds different from such headlines as "The majority supports . . ." or " Finns support . . . ." This category includes headlines in which the results of opinion polls are stated in percentages or in which the ratio is expressed in words.

"Over one third of consumers in favor of Sunday trading"
"Every fifth young person thinks racism patriotic"
"Yeltsin's popularity again at 7 percent"
"86 percent in favor of lower taxes"

Discourse analysis has frequently turned its attention to the meaning potential in percentages or other exact numerical information. The use of numbers is one of the most common factualization strategies through which an attempt is made to imbue a text with credibility (Potter, Wetherell, and Chitty, 1991). Numbers are a natural part of poll news and so in this context they do not greatly serve to impart convincing meaning. The exception is news in which decimal points in percentages are used to create an impression of precision and reliability of results (Gawiser and Witt, 1994: 109).

Presenting very high or very low percentages in headlines may also serve as an intensifier of expression. The opinion of 86 percent sounds stronger than if the headline were merely to mention a majority.

4. Polarization as a type of headline is the opposite of generalizations that create seeming unanimity. In markedly polarizing headlines the emphasis in the interpretation is on the division of the people into contradictory camps. Milder polarization is at hand when the headlines report a fifty-fifty situation numerically.

"Support and opposition equal on nuclear power"
"For and against EMU—evenly balanced"
"Finns in two minds on EMU membership"
"Support for main parties splits Albania in two"

It is characteristic of polarization that the image of controversy is based on an even division of percentages, which does not yet convey the intensity of the differences of opinions. In opinion polls on both EMU membership and issues of nuclear power, wavering supporters and opposers together constitute a majority in whose ranks there is very little controversy.

Describing public opinion as highly polarized is, especially in political journalism, connected to the general conception of the news value of controversy (Gamiser and Witt, 1994: 106).

5. The comparison in the headlines stresses differences between the groups being surveyed in opinions, attitudes, values, and behavior. Describing one of the groups is usually enough to underline its difference and deviance from the others.

"Women and men on different roads in security policy"
"Education increases positive attitude to the EMU"
"Young girls smoke and drink hard"
"Finnish woman seeks out sex like a man"

The attempt at times in this kind of headlines to stress the differences between the groups by rhetorical means may mislead the audience. Compared groups are made to appear completely different, although the result may show relatively small percentual differences. For example, women are referred to generically as a united group with men as their opposite, although opinions may divide in almost the same way in both groups. Stressing the difference may be based on the language of the original report's "statistically significant differences," which in surveys with a large sample may be of the order of only a few percent (Gawiser and Witt, 1994: 121-123).

6. Speaking in the headline about the will of the people appeals to the core idea of democracy by stressing the weight of public opinion in decision-making in the society.

"The people want the present government to continue"
"People's opinion against the EMU line"
"Finns demand lower taxation"

Opinion polls are presented as the will of the people on occasions when they concern social controversies, current social policy, or issues to be decided by public authority. Headlines appealing to the people contain an implicit demand that the decision-makers abide by the rules of democracy and obey the will of the majority.

7. The intensity of expression in headlines or other news text is a linguistic dimension all on its own. At one end of the dimension are expressions revealing intense emotions, thus stressing the force of the opinions. At the other end, headlines express the results by diluting the opinions and obscuring the people as the subjects of the opinions. The former utterance can be called intensification. The distinctly neutral expressions of opinions, attitudes, and values are replaced by expressions of feeling: fear, longing, concern, faith, and so forth.

"Majority dreams of freedom from working life"
"Nuclear power still frightening"
"Pollution causes concern"
"Brits repel EMU"

In certain cases the questions in the surveys are already emotionally loaded or otherwise intensify the respondents' signifying. Significance is sometimes intensified at the point when results are interpreted—in research reports, press releases, or news headlines.

The purpose of intensification is usually to breathe life into the language of the news and use of headlines in order to make the news item or article more appealing. In the same process the headline imparts an erroneous idea of the results of the survey. Extreme intensification may also be a rhetorical device to make people's conceptions appear excessively emotional instead of being a rational opinion.

8. Factualization is a linguistic strategy that instead of reporting opinions speaks of what they concern; for example, by declaring the majority belief or situation supported to be the truth. Examples are helpful to clarify the nature of this discourse.

> "Price control more important than ever"
> "Soviet Union a greater threat to independence than EMU"
> "Kekkonen the greatest Finn"
> "Santa Claus is a democrat"
> "Finland should be defended with arms"

The remaining part of the headline may refer to the survey carried out or otherwise indicate that this concerns an opinion poll. Even so, the reader easily gets the impression that the opinion in the headlines is the truth or that this is the newspaper's idea of the truth.

9. Change of linguistic subject is another way to dilute the opinion. It is a strategy whereby citizens as the subject who have the opinions are replaced by the object of the opinions the newspaper is talking about.

> "Center Party overtakes the Social Democrats"
> "Ahtisaari still leads the polls"
> "Fathers still not up to expectations"
> "Protection of the environment should not cost"

Compared to factualization, change of subject is a more transparent way of diluting opinions. It can at least indirectly be determined from all the examples above that in the background there are expressions of people's opinions arranged in some way or other—support, expectations, criticism, popularity, and so forth. However, the focus of interpretation has shifted from the people surveyed to the actions or actors about which they were asked; for example, from the electorate to the political parties.

10. Change/permanence is a perspective of the headline that generally originates in the setup of the survey. The survey sets out to describe a change in opinions or a single cross-section survey may be placed after a series of other, earlier surveys.

"Prime Minister loses popularity"
"Support for EMU grows"
"Consumers happier than last spring"
"Growing sympathy for fur farming"

According to journalistic news criteria change is generally more noteworthy and therefore more interesting than permanence. No change is news only when it runs contrary to expectations of change. Especially when the media publish the results of polls they have themselves commissioned there is an attempt to make much of even a minor change by emphasizing this in the headlines (Cantril, 1991).

Stressing a change in public opinion in the headlines offers the readers, viewers, and listeners of the news an opportunity for social comparison. The change presented as the major result of the survey may set in motion possible changes in people's opinions in the same way as the generalizing discourse. When support polls anticipate changes in the parliament these may turn out to be self-fulfilling predictions.

11. Emphasizing competition is a metaphorical means of describing the results of opinion polls with words borrowed from sports reporting. This closely resembles the so called "horse-race journalism" described above.

"Ahtisaari still leads the polls"
"Round break in the presidential game"
"Support for the Conservatives closing in on the Centre Party"
"Chirac even with Lionel Jospin"

The metaphors adhere to the subjects and competitive settings of the surveys. When monitoring several competitors, the expressions are frequently different from a struggle between two rivals.

Also in Finnish opinion poll journalism the competition discourse is most frequently used in connection with polls on the political parties and politicians. It portrays well one side of representational politics. However, it also offers the citizens only the passive role of the armchair sportsperson.

12. In addition to the above mentioned expressions, which all refer to the content, there is good reason to add one more dimension that is also used in the signifying the poll news. Fairly often the headline includes a reference to the poll carried out. This gives important ideas to the audience of how the public opinion has been constructed.

Here, too, the choice of words shows how seriously the media itself takes the results and what kind of a reaction it expects of the audience. When the words "public opinion research" are chosen it shows higher esteem than speaking of "opinion polls." The equivalent of the latter in the Finnish language is the use of the word "gallup" without the capital G in the spelling. Between these two extremes such generally used expressions as opinion "survey" or "measurement" can be found.

The preceding qualitative analysis of headlines reveals the alternative linguistic strategies and rhetorical means by which journalists signify the results of polls. The analysis also paid attention to the politically interesting consequences that can follow from the use of such rhetorical means, however unintentional these may be. As such, typologies do not, however, yet cast much light on the totality of poll journalism. In addition to the microanalytical description of the headlines quantitative content analysis is also necessary to show the position of each headline type in the news media (Fairclough, 1995: 105). With regard to the interpretations of the audience the significant discourses are those which are repeated often enough.

Generalization and emphasis on change were the most common headline types in the poll journalism of the Finnish mainstream media in March 1997. Both of them occurred in one third of the headlines (Table 13.4).

The opinion poll news included on average two of the headline types defined. There were more expressions in radio and television news headlines. The difference is partly due to the fact that in electronic media the delimitation of the headlines is not so clearcut as in the press.

Many widely used headline types contain some kind of exaggeration or beside-the-point interpretation that give the audience an inaccurate picture of the poll results. It is exactly in these cases where the journalists' intentions of writing sensational and sexy headlines may lead to unexpected and unintended political consequences; the public opinion presented in the headlines seems more unanimous, contradictory, or intense than what the original results would actually have suggested.

Journalists often accept the claim of exaggeration, as some Finnish studies have found (Hakkarainen, 1998; Kostiainen, 1998). However, they are not very willing to give up their style of writing. The attractiveness of poll news might suffer if the headlines were written in keeping with the everyday reality of the results.

Table 13.4. Linguistic Strategies of Poll News Headlines (in Percentages).

	Newspapers	Radio and television	All
Generalization	32	26	31
Majority/minority	6	18	8
Percentages	18	35	22
Polarization	7	15	9
Comparison	15	9	14
Will of the people	15	38	20
Intensification	11	12	11
Factualization	9	3	9
Change of subject	24	15	22
Change/permanence	25	56	32
Competition	16	18	17
Research	20	35	24
Total percentage	198	280	219
Total number	123	34	157

A CRITICAL STANDPOINT WANTED

What is expected of quality journalism as a matter of course is a critical stance to its sources, to the credibility of the information offered, and to the newsworthiness of the information for the media itself and for its audience. Naturally, journalism should also be expected to be self-critical of its own work; for example, of its style of writing headlines.

This demand for a critical stance is especially important when the media publish the results of opinion polls. It is important for two reasons. When presenting the poll results the media take on the position of representing the public opinion—the will of the people—and thereby it fulfills an important political function. Representing the public in a reliable way predisposes journalism to have a critical attitude.

Another thing that demands that poll journalism be critical is the complexity of polling as a form of information production. The different stages of the research process—the sample, formulating the questions, analyzing and interpreting the data, and so forth—are prone to mistakes that affect the results. A journalist of good professional calibre should be able to recognize the margin of error and know how to estimate it and also be able to give the audience an opportunity for a critical reception of poll news.

The demand for a critical stance has been known very early. This is shown by the multitude of books over the decades on the problems of the methods of opinion polls and of presenting them in public (for example, Cantril, 1991; Gawiser and Witt, 1994; Rogers, 1949). The organizations of both researchers and media have given guidelines on the critical assessment of polls and their results.

The first widely accepted guidelines on publishing the results were given in 1968 by the American Association for Public Opinion Research (AAPOR) (Sabato, 1981: 315, 338). The guidelines included an eight-point list of minimum requirements that the research institute had to report to the body commissioning the research. At the same time the list was a recommendation for what the media should publish when presenting the results.

The list was a catalogue of the significant points that, if checked, increase the reliability of the results. The long list showed the researchers and journalists—and sometimes also the audience—the problems causing uncertainty inherent in the research. On the other hand, this kind of transparency increased the trust in pollsters and their research.

The American Newspaper Publishers Association (ANPA) doubled the AAPOR's eight-point checklist in their guidebook on the publication of opinion poll results. The Finnish Newspaper Publishers Association published their own guidebook according to the model of the ANPA guidebook along with the checklist borrowed from them (Liimatainen and Sinkko, 1983; Suhonen 1991: 119-121). The checklist has been further expanded and clarified by Gawiser and Witt (1994: 161-162).

The everyday life of Finnish news journalism does not seem to include the recommended elaboration of research methods in connection with poll news. Although half of the news—according to the Finnish data—do mention the size of the sample or the number of interviewees, the sampling method is named or explained in only a couple out of a hundred. What suffices instead is a mention of the research data representing the whole voting-age population or some other population as the object of research. The number of people who have refused or who have been unable to be contacted or other such deficiencies are also hardly ever mentioned.

From the point of view of interpreting the survey results and estimating their reliability, it is very important to know how the questions have been posed to the people. Therefore the poll result publication guidelines require that the actual expressions of the questions are published with the news. Finnish journalists have not been very good at adopting this practice. In only one out of ten poll news could it be read what was asked and how. It was even more rare to present the margin of error of the results, which is a mathematical estimation based on statistics of how the sample has effected the results and how well they represent the whole population (Gawiser and Witt, 1994: 85-90).

The abovementioned checklists are also meant to steer journalists when they commission opinion polls, choose surveys sponsored by others as subject matter for news, and criticize the quality of research and the reliability of results. On the basis of the textual analysis it can be said, however, that poll news rather seldom include critical assessments.

Of the poll news on radio and television, only 5 percent included commentary on the research methods. In newspaper journalism such criticism was nearly double the amount. The difference is most probably caused by the fact that the text volume in electronic news is much smaller than in newspapers. Newspaper text thus allows more space for scrutinizing the methodological problems of the research.

In slightly over 10 percent of the news analyzed there were estimations of the purposes, meanings, and effects of the polls published. In some cases polls were criticized for the fact that they aim to influence decision-making or people's opinions. Sometimes polls were regarded as trivial entertainment. The social role of individual results and the whole opinion poll apparatus were relatively more frequently analyzed in editorials and commentaries.

DISCUSSION

This chapter has presented an empirical analysis of the opinion poll journalism in mainstream Finnish media. The starting point was the widely held view that polling has strengthened its position in the construction and representation of the public opinion. Opinion polls fulfill an ever more visible part of the functions of the civil society and political system by communicating the will of the people to decision-makers and by giving the citizens a chance for social comparisons.

The strong position of opinion polls is partly due to their sheer numbers. What is more essential, however, is their highly visible position on the agenda of media publicity. Polls earn their political power from the very fact that the knowledge of their results is widely shared among both the public and the decision-makers. It is much more difficult to ignore a majority opinion known to all than a research result that remains unknown to but a few behind the scenes.

The media commission opinion surveys and choose news topics from other poll supply mainly by using journalistic criteria. In general the aim is to produce attractive and salable news without a conscious effort to influence politics. In spite of this, poll journalism does have political consequences. The public agenda is being controlled by choice of news topics and by means of visibility. Headlines and the rest of the text suggest to the audience a certain interpretation of the poll results.

The analysis of poll news headlines showed several linguistic strategies that made the news seem attractive but simultaneously gave an exaggerated or otherwise biased picture of the results. The generalization of an opinion to make it reflect on the whole population or emphasizing the changes in opinions offer the citizen a point of reference that either strengthens or undermines his or her own opinion. Headlines may also, directly or indirectly, appeal to decision-makers and their democratic hearts. Headlines can also be used to highlight the intensity of the opinion or to fade out the citizens as the actual "owners" of the opinions.

According to the quantitative analysis, more than half the poll news headlines in Finnish mainstream media contain, compared to the actual results, exaggerated or other biased expressions that can be assumed to have political consequences. This is rather usual especially when the media itself has sponsored the research and wants to benefit from its first claim to the results.

Another trademark characteristic of poll journalism—at least in Finland—is lack of criticism. The guidelines made by the organizations of both pollsters and the media, which recommend the inclusion of basic methodological facts of the research into the news, have hardly produced any results. It is also very seldom that poll news include reflective arguments by the journalists of the polls' subject matter, goals, or research methods. The lack of criticism and self-reflection in connection to the publication of poll news is a bigger problem than it is in connection to most other news topics. It is hard to imagine that the way other news topics are handled by the media would have as significant political consequences as opinion polling.

To some extent it is understandable that journalism is not very interested in including profound methodological check-ups in poll news. It could lead to the rejection of the whole news, or the quick wit with which the news is reported would suffer. However, news is not the only journalistic genre. Instead, other types of texts or TV and radio programs could be used more often and for more forceful debates on the reliability of opinion polls, methodological problems, and the social significance of polling.

The public debate on both the reliability and social role of opinion polling becomes active in Finland from time to time. Such debates are most often started when the survey results show a clear contradiction between the public opinion and government policies or when different surveys produce contradictory results.

For example, such a debate was going on in fall 1997 when the bigger media published several opinion polls on Finland's EMU membership. Most results showed that the majority of the people were against the positive EMU stance promoted by the government. The prime minister, Mr. Paavo Lipponen, criticized the research institutes for methodologically unsound surveys and the media of populism that forgets the principles of representational democracy when appealing to poll results as the voice of the people. The media answered Mr. Lipponen by blaming him for having contempt for the citizens.

Poll journalism and the problems therein—such as the ones dealt with above—are not a singularly Finnish phenomenon. The ideals of present-day Finnish journalism have largely been adopted from the United States, Britain, and Sweden from where the poll industry also came to Finland. Although the numbers of published polls vary from one country to another, their subject matters resemble one another. It is highly probable that the same basic interpretations that are offered to the audience of the poll results can also be found in the mainstream media of other Western democracies. It is nearly impossible to form an exact picture of the situation because, so far, there is little research on the subject.

ENDNOTE

1   The specification of the headlines was done in two stages. In the first stage various discursive practices were sought in an extensive data corpus covering news material from 1996 and a tentative classification of discourse types was made. In the second stage the classification was tested on the data from March 1997, adjustments were made, and the headlines in the new data were classified.

REFERENCES

Atkin, Charles K. and James Gaudino. 1984, March. The Impact of Polling on the Mass Media. *The Annals of the American Academy of Political and Social Science* 472.

Beniger, James R. 1992. The Impact of Polling on Public Opinion: Reconciling Foucault, Habermas, and Bourdieu. *International Journal of Public Opinion Research* 4(3).

Cantril, Albert H. 1991. *The Opinion Connection: Polling, Politics, and the Press*. Washington, DC: Congressional Quarterly Press.

Fairclough, Norman. 1995. *Media Discourse*. London: Longman.

Gallup, George and Saul Rae. 1940. *The Pulse of Democracy*. New York: Simon & Schuster.

Gawiser, Sheldon R. and G. Evans Witt. 1994. *A Journalist's Guide to Public Opinion Polls*. Westport: Praeger.

Hakkarainen, Pirkko. 1998. *Yleisen mielipiteen paradoksi. Yleisön, toimittajien ja tutkijoiden käsityksiä mielipidemittauksista*. Tampereen yliopisto, Tiedotusopin laitos, Julkaisuja, Sarja A 91.

Herbst, Susan. 1993. *Numbered Voices. How Opinion Polling Has Shaped American Politics*. Chicago: The University of Chicago Press.

Ismach, Arnold H. 1984, March. Polling as a News-Gathering Tool. *The Annals of the American Academy of Political and Social Science* 472.

Kostiainen, Riikka. 1998. *Mielipidemittausten käyttö journalismissa. Toimittajien näkemyksiä gallup-journalismista ja mielipidemittausten sekundaarikäytön analyysi*. Tiedotusopin pro gradu -tutkielma. Tampereen yliopisto.

Lemert, James B. 1981. *Does Mass Communication Change Public Opinion After All? A New Approach To Effects Analysis*. Chicago: Nelson-Hall.

Liimatainen, Eila and Risto Sinkko. 1983. *Mielipidetutkimukset ja sanomalehti*. Helsinki: Sanomalehtien Liitto.

Maarek, Philippe J. 1995. *Political Marketing and Communication*. London: John Libbey.

McAllister, Ian and Donley T. Studlar. 1991. Bandwagon, Underdog, or Projection? Opinion Polls and Electoral Choice in Britain, 1979-1987. *Journal of Politics* 53(3).

Meyer, Philip. 1990. Polling as Political Science and Polling as Journalism. *Public Opinion Quarterly* 54(3).

Noelle-Neumann, Elisabeth. 1984. *The Spiral of Silence. Public Opinion— Our Social Skin*. Chicago: The University of Chicago Press.

Nortamo, Simopekka. 1997. Toukokuu Gallup-demokratiaa kansanvallan vajeeseen. Helsingin Sanomien kuukausiliite.

Peer, Limor. 1992. The Practice of Opinion Polling as a Disciplinary Mechanism: A Foucauldian Perspective. *International Journal of Public Opinion Research* 4(3).

Potter, Jonathan, Margaret Wetherell, and Andrew Chitty. 1991. Quantification Rhetoric—Cancer on Television. *Discourse and Society* 2(3), 333-265.

Rogers, Lindsay. 1949. *The Pollsters. Public Opinion, Politics, and Leadership.* New York: Alfred A. Knopf.

Sabato, Larry. 1981. *The Rise of Political Consultants: New Ways of Winning Elections.* New York: Basic Books.

Salmon, Charles T. and Theodore L. Glasser. 1995. The Politics of Polling and the Limits of Consent. In T.L. Glasser and C.T. Salmon (eds.), *Public Opinion and the Communication of Consent.* New York: Guilford.

Suhonen, Pertti. 1991. *Kaksisuuntainen peili. Mielipidetutkimukset julkisuudessa ja politiikassa.* Helsinki: Hanki ja jää.

Suhonen, Pertti. 1995. Kansan tahto välittömässä demokratiassa. In I. Ruostetsaari (ed.), *Vaalit, valta ja vaikuttaminen.* Tampere: Tampere University Press.

Suhonen, Pertti. 1997. The Media, Polls and Political Process. The Case of Finland. *European Journal of Communication* 12(2), 219-238.

Suhonen, Pertti and Jukka Haapasalo. 1975. Tajunnan tutkimus joukkotiedotuksen palveluksessa: Manipulaatiota vai demokratiaa? In Y. Littunen and R. Sinkko (eds.), *Yhteiskunnallinen tieto ja tiedotustutkimus.* Tapiola: Weilin + Göös.

IV

MASS MEDIA

14

Changes in Mass Media and the Public Sphere

Winfried Schulz

Among the most salient developments in present societies are fundamental and rapid changes of mass media. Public discussions as well as the academic literature are speculating on the societal consequences of these changes. There is a concern that the media changes contribute to a deterioration of political processes in general and to a fragmentation of the public sphere and an increase of political cynicism in particular. Blumler (1990) has listed several other consequences as characteristics of "the modern publicity process," a formula that he uses to summarize the fundamental changes that political systems are undergoing in our time. In this chapter, I look at the empirical evidence of such changes and their consequences. Preceding this is a discussion of the key terms related to my research—public sphere and fragmentation.

EMPHATIC MODELS OF THE PUBLIC SPHERE

Abreast with an increased attention paid to the transformation of politics and mass media, classical sociological terms like "public," "public sphere," and "public opinion" have been revived. A notable example of this academic fashion is an attempt of the German sociologist Gerhards (1997) at clarifying the terminology by contrasting two concepts of publics that he calls the *discursive* and the *liberal* model, respectively. The former has been fostered by Habermas in his widely recognized study on the transformation of the public sphere and in his more recent reflections and modifications of his concept (Habermas, 1962, 1992a, 1992b). The latter can be found more or less explicitly outlined in many political science text books as a central element of Western liberal democracies. Gerhards enhances the academic aureola of the liberal model by referring, among others, to the writings of Luhmann (1970) and Rawls (1993). Because both concepts concentrate on some basic features of the public sphere in a rather abstract and idealized way, they have the function of "ideal types" in the sense Max Weber has introduced this term. Nevertheless, both Habermas and Gerhards claim that the concepts have empirical validity and are thus appropriate for a description of observable phenomena (Gerhards, 1997; Habermas, 1992b: 451).

The two models have some key features in common. Both originate from the age of Enlightenment and are closely linked to the demand for civil rights and freedom of expression. Due to this heritage the concept of the public sphere has an "emphatic" character (Luhmann, 1996: 186). *Public* is not just a descriptive feature or a special category of social formations among other categories like the group, the crowd, or the mass (Blumer, 1939). *Public* is also—and in many contexts primarily—a postulate, a political demand, a state to strive at.[1]

Both models look at the public sphere as an intermediary system that links the periphery with the center of the political system or, as Habermas puts it, the private and collective actors of the periphery with the political institutions in the center. Both conceptions have some obvious resemblance with political systems models of the Easton type (Almond and Powell, 1966; Easton, 1965). Systems models of this type contrast input processes, output processes, and conversion processes. Mass media are considered in these models as just one of several channels or agents through which the interests and the will of the people are transformed or converted into political decisions.

The models are different with respect to the position and the role of political actors, particularly of interest groups. According to the liberal model, organized collective actors such as interest groups and political parties dominate the public sphere and provide inputs to the political decision center. These groups are part of the conversion processes. Their function is to aggregate the different preferences of individual citizens, represent their opinions in the political arena, and mirror the variety of interests in a pluralistic society. In contrast to this, the Habermas model implies that individual citizens and collective actors of the civil society infuse the relevant political input into the public sphere. Habermas makes a sharp distinction between actors of the civil society on the one side and *powerized* (*vermachtete*) actors on the other.[2] Social movements and voluntary associations are exemplary actors of the civil society. Interest groups such as labor unions, religious bodies, and professional associations, are categorized as *powerized* actors. Habermas is rather skeptical of the media and draws a somewhat ambivalent picture of their role in society. On the one hand, at least in "moments of mobilization" and under conditions of a perceived crisis they could give platforms to the actors of the civil society or even promote their interests. On the other hand, he suspects that the mass media are infiltrated by interest groups and instrumentalized for manipulating the public.

Another difference of the two models refers to the style of communications in public. In the context of the liberal model all communications and the actions of all actors are considered to be legitimate as long as they respect other actors with different opinions. In contrast, Habermas with his discursive model is quite demanding as to the style of public communications. He expects that reasons are given for issues and positions and that actors who put forward certain arguments refer to the respective arguments of their opponents. As a result, a public discourse of a higher level of rationality is expected to emerge. This is the precondition for reaching a consensus on political decisions, or at least a majority opinion that is based on arguments. The legitimacy of political decisions is dependent on a rational discourse in public. In the context of the liberal model, on the other side, public opinion is simply the outcome of aggregating individual opinions. Majority opinions deserve no special quality whether they are based on a rational discourse or not (Gerhards, 1997).

A MACHIAVELLIAN MODEL OF THE PUBLIC SPHERE

Like these two models most other concepts of publics and the public sphere, particularly in sociology and political science, refer to mass media only as technologies, instruments, or (neutral) agents with the function of publicizing, distributing, or aggregating information and opinions. The metaphoric terminology is quite telling. Mass media are referred to as mirrors, windows, platforms, forums, and the like. Distinctive of this view is a notion of mass media and the public sphere that has its advocates mainly in the field of mass communication research (see, e.g., Blumler, 1990; Mancini and Swanson, 1996;

Schönbach and Becker, 1995). For lack of a better term I call it a model of a *media-constructed public sphere*. The label signals that mass media are at the center of this concept. They are seen as playing an *active* role in the formation of publics and the public sphere. In order to highlight the differences to the former two models in more detail, I adopt the descriptive scheme that Gerhards (1997) uses in his article and expand it by one more column, which refers to the third model. Also, a few labels are added to Gerhards' scheme as well as the new subcategory "role of mass media" (see Table 14.1).

Other than the advocates of the value-laden, "emphatic" models both of the discursive and liberal type, those who prefer the concept of a media-constructed public are primarily interested in "unsentimental" analysis, as Blumler (1998) qualifies the approach. He therefore calls it a "Machiavellian theory" and adds two further aspects in order to justify this designation.

> First (like *The Prince*), it can be received at either of two levels: simply as a description of how "mediatized" politics works nowadays; or as an account of unavoidable constraints to which even idealists must submit in order to stand a chance of advancing their ends. Second, it gains empirical validity to the extent that powerful actors subscribe to it and apply its precepts in practice. (Blumler, 1998: 85)

The perspective of the media-constructed notion is different from the other two models in several respects. The most important difference is that mass media are regarded as *constitutive* of a public sphere. This does not neglect that there are some social arenas in which persons interact face-to-face in order to exchange information and opinions, such as, for example, coffee houses, club meetings, and party conventions. However, as empirical data demonstrate, the relevance of such interactive publics for the formation of a public sphere falls far behind the relevance of the media publics that are constituted by mass communication.

For instance, during election campaigns almost every voter is reached by mass communicated messages, and most of the voters many times, whereas only a relatively small minority participates in interactive publics like meetings or conventions. During the 1994 campaign for the German parliamentary elections only 7 percent of the voters attended a party event. The respective figures for the United States are quite similar, for Great Britain even lower (Dalton, 1996: 49-50). When people are asked to rank different sources according to their importance for political information and opinion formation, television and the press are mentioned most often. Personal interactions play only a minor role (Schulz and Blumler, 1994: 212; Semetko and Schönbach, 1994: 73, 78).

Table 14.1. Models of the Public Sphere.

	Liberal Public	Discursive Public	Media-Constructed Public
I. Input			
Actors	Collective actors	Individual actors or collective actors of the civil society	Mass media as gate-keepers deciding on the public access of protagonists and collective actors
Representation of actors	Equal access of all actors, reflecting the preferences of the people	Domination of the actors of the civil society	Selected and mediatized actors according to news value criteria and media formats
II. Communication in public			
Style	All communications and actions are acceptable as long as they respect other actors with different opinions	Communication - with reference to other actors - giving reasons - on a high level of rationality	Emphasis on aspects which fit news factors and media formats,
Role of mass media	Part of the intermediary system	Platform for individual or collective actors, manipulator of the public	Constitutive of a public sphere
III. Results			
In the public sphere	Public opinion as a communicated majority opinion determined by aggregation of individual communications	Consensus or majority opinion backed by arguments	Fragmentation
In the political system	Issues on which a consensus cannot be reached are disregarding	Legitimacy of decision Community-building by discourse	Decline of political trust and of social capital, political cynicism

This holds also for everyday situations. For taking part in the public discourse on current events, people rely much more on the mass media than on personal interactions.[3]

In addition to these data the hypothesis of media dependency and related research support the argument of a preponderance of media publics over interactive publics. Even nonmediated, interactive publics are very much dependent on information and viewpoints which people pick up from mass media. As Kepplinger and Martin (1986) show, mass media are frequently mentioned in personal conversations as sources of information or for substantiating one's own opinion. Moreover, public events that form interactive publics, such as political meetings, party conventions, or demonstrations, usually become part of the general public sphere only through mass media. By spotlighting only a few of a large number of events, the media not only selectively "upgrade" interactive publics to a higher level of publicity; they also have considerable control over the timing and the format by which interactive publics are transformed into media publics. As powerful gatekeepers they mediatize the images of actors as well as the framing of issues and arguments in the process of publicizing. They actively construct the public according to a specific media logic and to news media criteria such as personalization, negativism, drama, and emotion (Galtung and Ruge, 1965; Schulz, 1990).

The following remarks and data concentrate on two aspects: (1) changes in mass media and the public sphere in recent decades, and (2) the consequences of these changes. I concentrate on the model of a media-constructed public sphere in order to confront some implications of this model with empirical data.

MASS MEDIA AND THE PUBLIC SPHERE IN TRANSITION

Changes of publics are the focal point of Habermas' famous book on the transformation of the public sphere (Habermas, 1962). He analyzed the transformation processes that took place between the seventeenth and the nineteenth centuries (with a few critical looks on our century until the late 1950s). In his more recent publications he expands his perspective somewhat and adds, among other aspects, a few remarks on the impact of television (Habermas 1992a, 1992b).

Social and political changes resulting from television have been a central topic of mass communication research for decades. Whereas early studies focused on the impact of television as a completely new technology, more recent research quite often deals with possible consequences of an expanding program supply and of concomitant changes in the style of journalism. The studies of Robinson (1975, 1976, 1977), for instance, seem to demonstrate that voters who rely on television for political campaign information are prone to develop a feeling of political inefficacy, distrust, and cynicism. He coined the term "videomalaise" in order to express that television gives rise to political malaise among the public. The findings of Gerbner and his collaborators seem to justify the interpretation that television viewing "mainstreams" the outlook and social reality beliefs of the public and "cultivates" fear, alienation, and interpersonal mistrust (Gerbner, 1990; Gerbner and Gross, 1976).

In Europe similar concerns became an issue in public debate and an object of study in the late 1970s and early 1980s in the course of deregulating and commercializing the broadcasting sector. Attempts to replicate the results of Robinson and others in a European setting arrived at negative or mixed results (see, for instance, Holtz-Bacha, 1990). This may be due to the differences between the American and the European media systems at that time. Whereas American television was —and still is—highly entertainment-oriented and saturated with crime and violence, in practically all European countries television was information-oriented and committed to the principles of public service and social accountability. This changed during the 1980s when the broadcasting sector was deregulated in almost all European countries. Usually, the new commercial television channels adopted American TV formats and soon conquered the viewer market with a heavy load of entertainment, crime, and violence. As a consequence, the viewing habits and the television intake of the population have changed dramatically.

The following changes are well documented for Germany as well as for other European countries:

Television viewing time increased, particularly among the younger generations.

Many people make use of a wide range of different TV channels and programs.

Many people watch TV more superficially and as a secondary activity.

The overall supply of TV programs became very much entertainment-oriented.

Entertainment viewing increased much more than information viewing.

Information programs on television became more tabloidized with more emphasis on sensationalism, negativism, personalization, and soft news.

It is quite likely that changes of this kind have an impact on the political system and on the public sphere. Depending on what role is assigned to mass media for "communication in public," different consequences are hypothesized. The three models discussed above approach this question differently. They look at mass media either as a part of the intermediary system, as a platform or manipulator, or as a precondition of the public sphere, respectively. Some consequences resulting from these different perspectives are listed as examples at the bottom of Table 14.1.

The following analysis refers to two hypothesized consequences of a media-constructed public sphere, the fragmentation of publics, and a decline in political trust.

THE FRAGMENTATION HYPOTHESIS

Several authors assume that a fragmentation of the public will be the result of a proliferation of channels in an expanding media environment (e.g. Holtz-Bacha, 1997; Mancini and Swanson, 1996; McQuail, 1994: 71; Neuman, 1982). "Fragmentation refers to the process whereby the same amount of audience attention is dispersed over more and more media sources" (McQuail, 1997: 133). Not only the enormous expansion of program choices, but also an increasing diversification and specialization of TV programs are hypothesized to contribute to audience fragmentation. Quite similar tendencies are expected from an increase of radio programs, magazines, local papers, and internet and online media, at least in media-affluent societies.

Such expectations are based on the presumption that people concentrate on certain media or channels and neglect others. In case that there is only little or no overlap of the audiences, different segments of the society are attuned to different streams of information, worldviews, and value systems. The public sphere may dissolve into a large number of subcultures and the common ground of experience for all members of society disappears. Very often fragmentation tendencies are inferred from aggregate data of media market shares. The market structure, however, is an ambivalent indicator of the behavior of individual viewers. Totally different selection patterns may result in similar market structures. For instance, if there is a supply of thirty different channels and each individual allocates his or her total viewing time to just one channel, this may result in exactly the same aggregated structure as would arise if each individual spreads out his or her viewing budget over all thirty channels. In the first case, we have an extremely fragmented audience, but in the second case there is a high potential for overlap among audiences.[4]

Individual-level data provide a more valid account of how much concentration or diversification is manifested in people's media choices and of the degree to which different audiences actually do overlap. The concept of *channel repertoire* provides a helpful approach in this respect. Channel repertoire refers to the number of available TV channels that individual viewers choose to watch (Ferguson and Perse, 1993). Figure 14.1 applies this concept and represents, in a rather abstract and idealized way, the presumptions of the fragmentation hypothesis with reference to potential structures of a media-constructed public sphere.

The *integrated* structure is the ideal pattern of a media public in a public service broadcasting system. Until the 1980s, this was the dominant normative paradigm for media policy in many Western European postwar societies. Since then it has been substituted by the *expanded* structure as the ideal pattern. The other two constellations, the *segmented* and the *fragmented* patterns, are different audience structures with little overlap.

To illustrate this approach by the situation in Germany: A typical German household has some thirty different TV channels available via cable and more than fifty channels via direct broadcasting satellite.[5] The market is split into many small and mid-size segments. The bigger channels have a share of around 15 percent of the daily viewing time,

Size of the Channel Repertoire

		low	high
	little	segmented	fragmented
Overlapping of the Channel Repertoire			
	big	integrated	expanded

Figure 14.1. Implicit presumptions of the fragmentation hypothesis

several smaller channels hold between four and twelve percent, and the rest is dispersed among more than two dozen marginal channels. A closer look at the German TV audience on the individual level discloses, roughly speaking, three different selection patterns. About one fourth of the population has a small repertoire of only two channels or less (watched regularly or frequently). These are the old-fashioned viewers who watch mostly the two main public service programs of ARD and ZDF. In spite of the expansion of offerings the channel repertoire of these viewers remains quite low and their viewing habits still correspond with the "integrated" pattern that was typical for the time when most people had a choice of only two or three public service channels.

The other extreme is the "avant-garde viewer" who makes extensive use of the range of offers with a repertoire of six or more channels. A considerable segment of about one third of the population belongs to this type. In most cases, the repertoire includes commercial channels as well as public service programs. In addition, there is the large middle group of viewers with a repertoire of three to five channels who concentrate on the major programs of both systems. With reference to the typology of Figure 14.1, it seems to be appropriate to characterize this viewing pattern as expanded rather than as fragmented.

Neither in the group with a medium-size repertoire, nor among the "avant-garde viewers" with a high channel repertoire can we find clear signs of audience fragmentation, at least not in terms of channel selectivity. The development rather seems to go in the opposite direction. Increasingly, more viewers expand their repertoire to more channels and to the same channels so that it is quite likely that they are exposed to the same program (though probably not all at the same time).

MEDIA CHANGE AND POLITICAL TRUST

Even if the media usage behavior in an expanding media environment does not seem to follow the fragmented pattern, this does not necessarily preclude the public sphere from being affected by the media changes. Problematic effects may particularly result from changes in TV program content and in journalistic style that characterize the media transformation processes in Europe. These changes have often been labeled "Americanization." The label is referring to an obvious convergence of European and American TV program formats, partly due to a filling up of the new commercial television channels with cheap Hollywood productions. In view of these developments the question arose whether the concomitants of American television that Robinson, Gerbner and others observed have been imported together with the commercial programs.

For the first time since the deregulation of the German broadcasting system a representative survey of the German population provides data to test this question.[6] The results that I present here focus on just one aspect, namely on people's trust in political institutions, which is the essence of the "videomalaise" hypothesis. Political trust is measured by questions that have been used quite often in other studies, particularly in the United States (see McKean et al., 1995; Pinkleton et al., 1996; Vetter, 1997).[7] The data base of the following analysis includes a large number of media use measures that allow for several potential correlates of political trust.

As Table 14.2 shows, each of the television viewing indicators is negatively related to political trust. Although the percentage differences between the total population and the population segments characterized by a specific media use behavior are not dramatic, the pattern of results seems to be quite consistent. Other than for the TV indicators, people with high attention to newspaper information as well as those who mention personal conversations as a source of "much" or "very much" political information are less inclined to subscribe to the negative statements about politics. The results for people with high attention to information on the radio are mixed.

The results shown in Table 14.2 might be spurious, because certain patterns of media use are systematically linked with demographic factors, such as age and education, and with different levels of political competence. To control for possible spuriousness and to find out about the specific relationship of each media use indicator to political trust, I have included in a multiple regression analysis all media use indicators together with eight demographic factors and two indicators of political competence as independent variables.[8] This quite rigorous test, which is documented elsewhere in more detail (Schulz, 1998), singled out three factors as particularly relevant for people's trust in politics. Whereas channel repertoire and high attention to TV information display a negative (and statistically significant) relationship, only high attention to newspaper is positively related to political trust.

If we rely on the data available so far it seems as if the "avant-garde" in an expanding media environment—that is, people with a high channel repertoire who make extensive use of a broad range of TV information genres—show a decline in political trust. In other words, the higher and the more diverse the dose of information people get from television, the more negative is their image of politics. However, this tendency is counteracted if people attend to information in the newspaper.

These results are only partly in line with an implication of the model of a media-constructed public sphere. A decline in political trust as a presumed result from a media-constructed public sphere seems

Table 14.2. Media Use and Political Trust.

Question: On this show card we have listed a number of frequently heard opinions about politics. How much do you personally agree or disagree with these opinions?

	"Politicians never tell what they actually have in mind"		"Politics is a dirty business"		"The parties only want the votes; they don't care about the opinions of the voters"	
	agree[a] %	disagree %	agree %	disagree %	agree %	disagree %
Total respondents	57	9	45	19	54	11
Respondents with -						
access to cable or satellite transmission	59	9	46	18	55	11
preference for commercial TV channels	61	8	49	16	58	11
heavy TV viewing	63	7	49	16	58	10
high channel repertoire	60	8	49	16	58	10
high attention to TV information[b]	61	9	48	18	57	11
high attention to TV entertainment	63	7	51	15	60	8
high attention to information on the radio	59	9	46	19	53	11
high attention to newspaper information	51	12	41	21	46	12
personal conversations are a source of much/very much political information[c]	53	11	44	22	53	14

Table 14.2. Media Use and Political Trust (con't.).

[a]Respondents had the possibility to differentiate their answers according to five categories: completely agree, mostly agree, partly agree-partly disagree, mostly disagree, completely disagree. The figures in the table combine the two agree/disagree categories. The percentages for the intermediate category (as well as the nonresponses) are omitted ($n = 6,000$; the number of cases in each of the media use groups exceeds at least 1.100).

[b]Attention to different content types was measured in the same way for each medium. Respondents were presented a show card that listed some twenty different content genres. They were asked to indicate—by a five-category scale ranging from regularly to never—for each of the genres how often they read, heard or watched it, respectively. Attention to TV information, for instance, was categorized as high if a respondent mentioned an above average number of TV information genres as regularly or frequently watched programs. A similar procedure was applied to categorize how extensively respondents use other media and entertainment genres.

[c]The question asking about the importance of personal conversations was: "There are a number of possibilities to hear about political events. How much do you personally hear about politics from magazines, television, newspapers, radio, and from conversations with friends, people you know, and colleagues?"

(yet) to be confined to those segments of the public that are highly attuned to politics as presented by television and that are not counterbalancing their information intake with high attention to the newspaper.

Does watching TV information cultivate political cynicism or do people with a negative attitude towards politics expose themselves extensively to TV information? The latter seems to be less plausible than the former, although there is no way of deciding this question definitely on the basis of a single survey. To be precise, the results presented here are just correlations. Correlation is a precondition of causality, but at the same time it is open to an interpretation in both directions.

Moreover, even if the results are statistically significant and plausible, their magnitude does not seem very impressive. If we compare the population average on the top of Table 14.2 with the segments in the lines below, the differences in the "agree" categories hardly exceed three percentage points. Also, the multiple regression analysis explains less than 1 percent of the total variance in the dependent variable by media use factors. However, it can be argued that even such small margins form a considerable group of people if the percentages are projected to the total population. It may also play a role that the changes in the German media system were quite new in the mid-1990s when the survey was fielded. Commercial radio and TV, although introduced in the 1980s, conquered substantial market shares only in the early 1990s. One might speculate that the impact of these changes on people's political orientations accumulates only slowly over time.

If a causal interpretation is valid—namely, that watching information programs on German TV contributes to a decline in political trust—how could such a finding be explained? A possible explanation is that an expanded attention to TV information which the change of the media system brought forth exposes viewers more often to the spectacular, the sensational, and negative aspects of politics. These are the most salient aspects of information programs, and these aspects are particularly promoted by the new commercial channels (Bruns and Marcinkowski, 1996; Pfetsch, 1996). Because people with a high channel repertoire watch commercial channels *in addition* to public channels, it is more likely that they are affected by the tabloidized TV information, as compared to the old fashioned viewers who still stick to only a few public service channels. Zapping and hopping through the channels and picking up bits and pieces from different programs, which is a characteristic of the "avant-garde viewers," may be disadvantageous to contextualizing and digesting the information properly.[9]

When comparing these results with research in the mid-1980s when there was still a monopoly of public service television, such an interpretation gains support. The indicators of political trust were unrelated to television viewing at that time (Holtz-Bacha, 1990).

SUMMARY AND CONCLUSION

The fragmentation hypothesis, which holds that people concentrate on certain media or channels and neglect others as the availability of channels proliferates, does not seem to match the empirical data. An analysis of media-use behavior in Germany rather suggests that the public expands its attention and accommodates to an expanding media system, though obviously with different speed in different segments of the population. Particularly the "avant-garde viewers" of television, who have acquired a high channel repertoire, are making use of a broad spectrum of new program offers and do not, as has been assumed quite often in the literature, confine their choices to a small number of specialized channels. Hence, one of the presumptions of the model of a media-constructed public sphere can be called in question.

On the other hand, there is some empirical evidence that the changes of the media system have a bearing on people's political trust, especially among the "avant-garde" of TV viewers who make extensive use of the range of choices. Such consequences would indeed be compatible with assumptions about a media-constructed public sphere. If the interpretation is valid that a high channel repertoire and high attention to TV information programs contribute to political cynicism, the outlooks for future changes in the media system are not particularly benign. There may be more channels and programs available that proliferate the diversity of information supply. But this does not necessarily mean that we can expect positive results for the political culture. On the contrary, problematic consequences seem to be more likely if we are facing a further decline in the quality of mass media information as a by-product of an increasingly stronger competition in a deregulated media system.

ENDNOTES

1. Authors quite often concentrate on qualifying the desired state and on the functions it serves or should serve and mix up different perspectives, e.g., empirical and normative, descriptive and prescriptive, causal and functional arguments.
2. "Vermachtet," a term coined by Habermas, is derived from the German word for power (*Macht*). The word form connotates "powerful" and probably also "corrupt." I suggest translating it by "powerized" although this word form may not arouse the same associations as the German "vermachtet,"
3. For example, when people in Germany were asked "Where do you get most of your information on what is currently happening in the

world?" 87 percent answered "on television" and 68 percent "in the newspapers," as opposed to only 25 percent who said "from conversations with other people." These are results from a representative survey of the German population aged 14 years and over and fielded in autumn 1995 (n = 6.000); for more details of this study see Kiefer (1996).

4. To be more precise, actual overlap is dependent on the additional condition that channel selection is synchronous.
5. In 1995 almost 80 percent of the population was hooked to either cable or satellite.
6. See note 3
7. Other terms that are in use for this concept are "political cynicism" and "political efficacy." The three questions used and presented in Table 14.2 were selected on grounds of a factor analysis from a more comprehensive set of statements tapping political efficacy (for methodological details, see Schulz, 1998).
8. The demographic factors are gender, age, formal education, occupational status (working versus nonworking), occupational group (workers versus others), household income, community size, place of residence (East versus West Germany). The indicators of political competence were a self-assessment of respondents' interest in politics and a scale made up of three indicators of "internal political efficacy." The latter concept measures people's feeling of being capable to understand politics. As dependent variable in this multiple regression analysis an index was used that was built from all three indicators of political trust shown in Table 14.2.
9. The data we have available provide only an indirect test of this interpretation. The survey included a question that asked people to characterize TV viewing. Among the statements the respondents were given on a show card there was one which read: "Can be combined with many other activities." It is likely that people who agree with this statement as a characterization of television viewing tend to use television rather superficially and often as a secondary activity. The analysis actually shows that agreement with this statement is highly correlated with extensive usage of TV information programs, particularly among population segments with little interest in politics.

REFERENCES

Almond, Gabriel A. and G. Bingham Powell, Jr. 1966. *Comparative Politics: A Developmental Approach*. Boston: Little, Brown and Company.

Blumer, Herbert. 1939. Collective Behavior. In Alfred McClung Lee (ed.), *New Outline of the Principles of Sociology*, 167-224. New York: Barnes & Noble.

Blumler, Jay G. 1990. Elections, the Media and the Modern Publicity Process. In Marjorie Ferguson (ed.), *Public Communication. The New Imperatives. Future Directions for Media Research*, 101-113. London and Beverly Hills: Sage.

Blumler, Jay G. 1998. Public Spheres in Contention: Reflections from Britain, 1997. In Christina Holtz-Bacha, Helmut Scherer, and Norbert Waldmann (eds.), *Wie die Medien die Welt erschaffen und wie die Menschen darin leben*, 83-101. Opladen and Wiesbaden:Westdeutscher Verlag.

Bruns, Thomas and Frank Marcinkowski. 1996. Konvergenz Revisited. Neue Befunde zu einer älteren Diskussion. *Rundfunk und Fernsehen* 44, 461-478.

Dalton, Russell J. 1996. *Citizen Politics. Public Opinion and Political Parties in Advanced Industrial Democracies*. Chatham, NJ: Chatham House .

Easton, David. 1965. *A Systems Analysis of Political Life*. New York: Wiley.

Ferguson, Douglas A. and Elizabeth M. Perse. 1993. Media Audience Influences on Channel Repertoire. *Journal of Broadcasting and Electronic Media* 37, 31-47.

Galtung, Johan and Mari Holmboe Ruge. 1965. The Structure of Foreign News. The Presentation of the Congo, Cuba and Cyprus Crises in Four Norwegian Newspapers. *Journal of Peace Research* 2, 65-91.

Gerbner, George. 1990. Advancing on the Path of Righteousness. In Nancy Signorielli and Michael Morgan (eds.), *Cultivation Analysis. New Directions in Media Effects Research*, 249-262. Newbury Park: Sage.

Gerbner, George and Larry Gross. 1976. Living with Television: The Violence Profile. *Journal of Communication* 26(2), 173-199.

Gerhards, Jürgen. 1997. Diskursive versus liberale Öffentlichkeit. Eine empirische Auseinandersetzung mit Jürgen Habermas. *Kölner Zeitschrift für Soziologie und Sozialpsychologie* 49: 1-34.

Habermas, Jürgen. 1962. *Strukturwandel der Öffentlichkeit. Untersuchungen zu einer Kategorie der bürgerlichen Öffentlichkeit*. Neuwied and Berlin: Luchterhand.

Habermas, Jürgen. 1992a. Further Reflections on the Public Sphere. In Craig Calhoun (ed.), *Habermas and the Public Sphere*, 421-461. Cambridge, MA: MIT.

Habermas, Jürgen. 1992b. *Faktizität und Geltung. Beiträge zur Diskurstheorie des Rechts und des demokratischen Rechtsstaats*. Frankfurt a.M.: Suhrkamp.

Holtz-Bacha, Christina. 1990. *Ablenkung oder Abkehr von der Politik? Mediennutzung im Geflecht politischer Orientierungen*. Opladen: Westdeutscher Verlag.

Holtz-Bacha, Christina.1997. Das fragmentierte Medien-Publikum. Folgen für das politische System. *Aus Politik und Zeitgeschichte. Beilage zur Wochenzeitung Das Parlament*, B42/97, 13-29.

Kepplinger, Hans Mathias and Verena Martin. 1986. Die Funktionen der Massenmedien in der Alltagskommunikation. *Publizistik* 31, 118-128.

Kiefer, Marie-Luise. 1996. *Massenkommunikation. Eine Langzeitstudie zur Mediennutzung und Medienbewertung 1964-1995*. Baden-Baden: Nomos.

Luhmann, Niklas. 1970. Öffentliche Meinung. *Politische Vierteljahresschrift* 11, 2-28.

Luhmann, Niklas. 1996. *Die Realität der Massenmedien*. 2nd enlarged ed. Opladen: Westdeutscher Verlag.

Mancini, Paolo and David L. Swanson. 1996. Politics, Media, and Modern Democracy: Introduction. In David L. Swanson and Paolo Mancini (eds.), *Politics, Media, and Modern Democracy. An International Study of Innovations in Electoral Campaigning and Their Consequences*, 1-26. Westport, CT: Praeger.

McKean, Michael L., Glenn Leshner, Robert Meeds, and Ashley Packard. 1995, August. Using TV News for Political Information: Effects on Political Knowledge and Cynicism. Paper submitted to the annual convention of the Association for Education in Journalism and Mass Communication, Radio-TV Journalism Division.

McQuail, Denis. 1994. *Mass Communication Theory*. 3rd ed. London: Sage.

McQuail, Denis. 1997. *Audience Analysis*. Thousand Oaks, CA: Sage.

Neuman, W. Russell. 1982. Television and American Culture: The Mass Medium and the Pluralist Audience. *Public Opinion Quarterly* 46, 471-487.

Pfetsch, Barbara. 1996: Konvergente Fernsehformate in der Politikberichterstattung? Eine vergleichende Analyse öffentlich-rechtlicher und privater Programme 1985/86 und 1993. *Rundfunk und Fernsehen* 44, 479-498.

Pinkleton, Bruce E., Erica Weintraub Austin, and Kristine Kay Johnson. 1996, May. Relationships of Political Disaffection, Voter Sophistication, and Information Seeking to External Efficacy and Political Behavior. Paper presented to the Political Communication Division of the International Communication Association, Chicago.

Rawls, John. 1993. *Political Liberalism*. News York: Columbia University Press.

Robinson, Michael J. 1975. American Political Legitimacy in an Era of Electronic Journalism. Reflections on the Evening News. In Douglas Cater and Richard Adler (eds.), *Television as a Social Force: New Approaches to TV Criticism*, 97-139. New York and London: Praeger.

Robinson, Michael J. 1976. Public Affairs Television and the Growth of Political Malaise: The Case of "The Selling of the Pentagon." *American Political Science Review* 70, 409-432.

Robinson, Michael J. 1977. Television and American Politics. *Public Interest* 48, 3-39.

Schönbach, Klaus and Lee B. Becker. 1995. Origins and Consequences of Mediated Public Opinion. In Theodore L. Glasser and Charles T. Salmon (eds.), *Public Opinion and the Communication of Consent*, 323-347. New York and London: Guilford.

Schulz, Winfried, 1990. *Die Konstruktion von Realität in den Nachrichtenmedien. Analyse der aktuellen Berichterstattung.* 2nd ed., Freiburg and München: Alber.

Schulz, Winfried. 1998. Media Change and the Political Effects of Television: Americanization of the Political Culture? *Communications. The European Journal of Communication Research* 23, 527-542.

Schulz, Winfried and Jay G. Blumler. 1994. Die Bedeutung der Kampagnen für das Europa-Engagement der Bürger. Eine Mehr-Ebenen-Analyse. In Oskar Niedermayer and Hermann Schmitt (eds.), *Wahlen und Europäische Einigung*, 199-223. Opladen: Westdeutscher Verlag.

Semetko, Holli A. and Klaus Schönbach. 1994. *Germany's "Unity" Election: Voters and the Media.* Cresskill, NJ: Hampton Press.

Vetter, Angelika. 1997. Political Efficacy: Alte und neue Meßmodelle im Vergleich. *Kölner Zeitschrift für Soziologie und Sozialpsychologie* 49, 53-73.

15

American Political Communication
in the Information Age: The Mixed
Promises of the New Media and
Public Journalism*

Sandra Moog

Beginning in the 1960s, technological innovations such as the television and new methods of mass opinion polling have ushered in a new era for political communication in the United States. At the same time that these new modes of political communication have been gaining ascendancy, American political parties have been gradually losing power as mediators between the electorate and their representatives, leaving the mass media as the primary arena for political communication in the United States. In many ways, the political communication regime formed by new communication technologies would seem to offer possibilities for greater democratization of the political process. With a television in

*The first three sections of this chapter are a condensed version of an article entitled "Television, Mass Polling and the Mass Media: The Impact of Media Technologies on American Politics, 1960-1996," published in *Javnost—The Public*, 4(2): 39-55, 1997.

almost every American home, individual citizens can now hear political statements and rebuttals first hand, and they can follow the actions of their representatives in real time. Through the use of more and more sophisticated polling techniques, leaders can measure the interests and reactions of the electorate more often and more accurately than was ever before possible. Paradoxically, however, although these new forms of political communication might seem to offer the possibility of a less mediated and therefore more directly democratic politics, the dynamics of the interactions between politicians, pollsters, the media, and the American audience/electorate have developed in ways that may actually serve to undermine the capacity of voters to make intelligent decisions about whom to elect for office, and of politicians to make policy in the best long-term interest of the electorate.

The new political communication regime, dominated by the logics of television coverage and opinion measurement and management has, in fact, come to present new challenges to the possibility of in-depth, sustained analysis of candidates and policy options on the part of the media, and therefore, on the part of the citizenry as well. Political communication in the mass media has come to be dominated by increasingly superficial and cynical coverage of politics, in which the actions of politicians are more often than not interpreted as constant ploys for popularity and good press coverage. Journalistic coverage of politics has become increasingly "hyper-reflexive" focusing more and more on the game of politics itself, as it is played out in the media, at the expense of either extensive reporting of the activities or statements of politicians, or careful analysis of social problems or policy initiatives.

Contemporary observers of the American political scene have expressed pessimism about the role that these new communications technologies have come to play in national life. After years of such superficial and cynical presentation of politics in the mainstream media, they note, many voters are becoming cynical about press coverage of politics, about their elected representatives, and about the very capacity of government to handle social problems. A new generation of technologies, however, is just beginning to enter the American mainstream, technologies which seem to offer mixed promises for communication in the electronic public sphere. The proliferation of cable and direct satellite television programming, Internet web pages, chat rooms and electronic mail, for example, while offering new opportunities for interactivity and citizen-directed access to news sources, are helping to erode the common public sphere located in network television and local and national newspapers and magazines. At the same time, new formats for political news coverage and analysis are proliferating (such as talk radio and television talk shows, and the new "public journalism"), some of which seem to exacerbate problematic trends, whereas others conscientiously orient themselves towards trying to overcome them.

In the two sections that follow, I will first discuss how the mass media have come to be the primary arena for political communication in the United States. I will then discuss the kind of dynamics that have come to characterize this electronic public sphere due to the increasing dominance of television and mass opinion polling since the 1960s and 1970s.[1] The remainder of the chapter will be dedicated to an exploration of the role that new media technologies and new formats for media use may be expected to play in either exacerbating or ameliorating trends towards more superficial, negative, and hyper-reflexive communication in the public sphere.

THE RISE OF THE MASS MEDIA AS THE "SPACE OF POLITICS"

The rise of an independent press in the late 1800s, followed, in the 1920s and 1930s, by the development of journalistic commitment to more analytical and critical coverage of politics, meant that by the middle of this century the mass media had come to play an important role as an arena for the public discussion of political issues (Schudson, 1973: 144-151). But the role of the mass media as an arena for public debate and as a medium for communication between politicians and the electorate was always limited by the dominance of the political parties in American political life. Before 1968, the selection of candidates and the development of political platforms took place, in a majority of states, in closed-door meetings of party elites.[2] There was little opportunity for the average citizen to express his or her preferences, except on voting day.

In the decades after Watergate and the riots at the 1968 Democratic National Convention in Chicago, a series of political reforms were enacted, which began to slowly erode the power of the political parties. In state after state, both major parties opened up the candidate selection process to the general membership, and campaign finance reform weakened candidates' reliance on parties for financial support. Candidates, substantially cut loose from party support, had to begin looking directly to the electorate for money as well as votes. They have begun to rely heavily on the mass media as a means to communicate with voters and to garner support.

As the political parties have been weakening in their role as arenas for political communication and bargaining, the mass media has become the dominant site for political struggle. As Manuel Castells explains in *The Power of Identity*, the media has become the "privileged space of politics": "The key point is that electronic media (including not only television and radio, but all forms of communication, such as news-papers and the Internet) have become the privileged space of politics. Not that all politics can be reduced to images, sounds or symbolic manipulation. But, without it, there is no chance of winning or exercis-ing power" (1997: 311). However, as the parties have receded as the cen-tral organizers of political communication, and this function has been ceded to the mass media, the postwar information revolution has been rapidly transforming the nature of the mass media. The increasing dom-inance of television and of mass opinion polling have created a peculiar logic of communication in this new electronic public sphere.

TELEVISION, MASS OPINION POLLING, AND THE DYNAMICS OF THE NEW ELECTRONIC PUBLIC SPHERE

John F. Kennedy has been hailed as the first "modern media president" (Entman, 1989: 129). It was during his 1960 campaign for the presidency and during his tenure in office that the use of television and of mass opinion polling first became decisive strategic tools in national level pol-itics. With his media blitz during the West Virginia primaries and his telegenic victory over Nixon in the first televised presidential debate, Kennedy demonstrated the power of the new medium, a lesson he car-ried into his presidency, during which he held the first televised press conferences in White House. Kennedy was also the first presidential can-didate to directly employ a polling agency, using the results of seventy-seven private polls to make strategic decisions during his campaign, a practice which he carried into his presidency as well (Jacobs and Shapiro, 1995: 164; Moore, 1992: 78-88).

Since Kennedy's time, these two new technologies have come to play a more and more dominant role in American politics. Television has become the most important source of news for most Americans: in 1990, 58 percent reported it to be their only news source; in 1992, 60 percent reported it to be, in their opinion, the most credible source of news as well, compared to fewer than 20 percent who reported newspapers to be the most reliable source (Ansolabehere et al., 1993: 44-45). As television has become the dominant source of news for most Americans, politicians have come to dedicate more and more of their resources towards trying to get their messages across via television. Representatives and their media strategists carefully plan public events and statements, tailoring them to the requisites of the medium. Television has come to dominate campaign strategizing as well: by 1990, television advertising was, according to the *Los Angeles Times*, the "single biggest expenditure for the average Senate campaign" (Ansolabahere et al., 1993: 89). In 1996 the

Clinton campaign and the Democratic National Committee spent $85 million on ads for Clinton alone (Morris, 1997).

Computer-assisted mass opinion polling, the second pillar of the new electronic political communication regime, has become more and more central to political communication in the United States since Kennedy's time as well. Whereas Kennedy only used polls occasionally while in office, his successors Johnson and Nixon made frequent use of them, routinizing the use of a "public opinion apparatus" (Jacobs and Shapiro, 1995: 164).[3] With the advent of new technologies, such as computer analysis of data, poll data could be used strategically to target messages to different subgroups of the population; in the 1970s and 1980, pollsters such as Patrick Caddell, Peter Hart, Robert Teeter, and Stan Greenberg used these new technologies to became key political strategists, playing important roles as close advisors to presidential candidates during elections and to presidents in office (Moore, 1992: 128-129). The new computer technologies also allowed for such quick tabulation of poll results that polls could begin to be incorporated into regular news stories as well; during the 1970s major national newspapers and television networks began to establish in-house polling operations. By the 1980s, polling data had come to dominate much news coverage of politics: in a three week period in October 1988, poll data was found to appear in 53 percent of *Washington Post* stories and 37 percent of *New York Times* stories about the 1988 elections (Scott Razan, cited in Patterson, 1993: 81).

As television and mass polling have become so central to the way that politics is covered in the mass media and the way that politicians try to communicate with the electorate, new dynamics have come to dominate in this electronic public sphere. In part, these new technologies have served to amplify some of the problematic tendencies already inherent in the logic of the news business. As Todd Gitlin pointed out in his 1980 book on coverage of the New Left, there are four key "traditional assumptions in news coverage": "news concerns the event, not the underlying condition; the person, not the group; conflict, not consensus; the fact that 'advances the story,' not the one that explains it" (Gitlin 1980: 28). If these tendencies often result in the simplification of complicated issues in print and radio journalism, they are further exacerbated in television coverage of politics. Prisoner to its need for fresh pictures to accompany dialogue, television news coverage of politics tends to be much more superficial then other forms of mass media, presenting stories in short sound bites, and three- or four-sentence "voice-overs." It is therefore even more reliant on devices that can quickly frame a story in one of these standard traditional formats, tending to personalize politics, framing it in terms of basic conflicts between political figures that can be followed day after day, as minor developments break. One unfortunate result is that political coverage tends to reduce the acts of campaigning for office, or of making policy, to rather superficial popularity ploys and partisan warfare. Stories that frame the news in terms of "horse-race" and "spin control" tend to overshadow the issues behind the politics. Politicians themselves are forced to try to simplify their messages and to frame them in simplistic terms in order to break through to the audience/electorate.

As a result, an unfortunate dialectic is set in place: public relations considerations come to dominate more and more of politicians' attempts to communicate with the electorate, and the media responds by framing more and more political activity in terms of PR ploys and "spin control" efforts. Communication in the new electronic sphere becomes "hyper-reflexive": less attention is dedicated to legislation and government policies or the social problems they are intended to address, while communication strategies themselves become the central concern of public discussion. Political discussion in the mass media increasingly comes to revolve around interpretations of, and reactions to, yesterday's interpretations and reactions, and more and more of politicians' attention becomes oriented towards trying to figure out how to direct that discussion (Moog, 1997: 48-49).

The frequent public opinion polling employed by major news organizations and politicians' staffs reinforces this hyper-reflexivity. Opinion polls can create a series of pseudo-events, allowing for stories that often do no more than track public reactions to recent public opinion statistics. During primaries, for example, voters are often asked to rank candidates before they have had a chance to assess those candidates' records or promises. A common response is to rank candidates in terms of their "electability." Such assessments will inevitably be based on interpretations of recent opinion polls. The result is that such figures tend to be ephemeral and volatile, and it is often not clear what they really mean. Daily tracking polls during elections, for example, have begun to be seriously questioned by a number of scholars and prominent journalists, due to the extreme volatility of such figures during the 1996 elections (Morin, 1995; Mundy, 1996).

One unfortunate result of the hyper-reflexivity of the contemporary public sphere is that it reinforces trends towards more negative and cynical politics. Journalism's tendency to try to frame stories in terms of conflict consistently presents political struggles in a negative light. But other aspects of the new system reinforce this negativity. Research and campaign experience have shown that not only does television lend itself more forcefully to personalized, image-oriented messages, but that the audience is more likely to remember negative than positive messages (Ansolabehere et al. 1993: 84, 88). As a result, many candidates have turned to negative campaign tactics. Once in office, they often continue to employ methods learned during their campaigns in their attempts to win battles over appointments and the drafting of legislation. According to Manuel Castells, in fact, we have reached the point where "scandal politics is the weapon of choice for struggle and competition in informational politics" (Castells, 1997: 337). The Clinton administration has certainly faced a continuous barrage of scandal investigations throughout both terms of its tenure, each nicknamed in the press, in the attempt to invoke the public excitement of the Watergate era, from "Travelgate" and "Troopergate" to Whitewater, and culminating, of course, in the impeachment proceedings of 1999.

The very dynamics of the new communications regime seem to encourage negative and cynical coverage of politics. Journalists and politicians have, in a sense, become sparring partners, as politicians try to "spin" how they are covered in the news and journalists, trying to read through such efforts, are constantly trying to interpret how they and the American public are being manipulated by their representatives. As a result, journalists have resorted to more intensive framing of stories, dedicating less and less space to the unmediated presentation of the news as it is being made by politicians. From forty-two seconds in 1968, the average television sound bite had shrunk, by 1992, to less than ten seconds. In network news presentation of the 1992 general election, for example, anchors and reporters spoke six minutes for every minute that candidates were shown speaking. And not only are journalists speaking more, but what they are saying about politics and politicians is increasingly cynical: whereas 75 percent of the news coverage received by Nixon and Kennedy in the 1960 presidential elections was positive, 60 percent of the discussion that Clinton, Bush, and Perot received in the 1992 election was negative in content (above statistics cited in Patterson 1993: 74-75, 68, 20).

Thus, although the new electronic public sphere might seem to offer the possibility of a more informed and more participatory public, the reality is that the dialectic set in place as television and mass opinion polling have come to dominate in the presentation of political discourse has come to undermine much of this promise. In fact, as political scientist James S. Fishkin points out, the result is a far cry from George Gallup's original vision that public opinion polling, in conjunction with the unification of political discourse through the mass media, might, in effect, reinstate the ideals of the New England town meeting, but on a national scale. On the contrary, a more apt metaphor for the resulting political discourse, as V.O. Key, Jr. and Milton Cummings presciently remarked in 1966, is that of the public sphere as "echo chamber" (Fishkin, 1996: 133-135).

The increasing superficiality and negativity of communication in the public sphere may turn out to have serious implications for political culture in the United States. Public alienation from both the media and the political process is at an all-time high in the United States. Since 1966 confidence ratings for government have fallen drastically; confidence in the White House has dropped from 46 percent in 1966 to 18 percent in 1994, confidence in Congress, from 35 percent to 18 percent. Confidence in the press has dropped as well; for the press in general, from 30 percent to 13 percent, and for television news, from 43 percent to 24 percent. And these figures do not seem to represent merely a general sense of pessimism, or postmodern malaise, in the country: in 1992 an ABC/Money Magazine poll found that only 22 percent of Americans were dissatisfied with their own lives, whereas 72 percent expressed dissatisfaction with "things in the country these days" (reported in *The Public Perspective*, 1992).

A number of critical voices within the journalistic community have recently raised themselves above the din to make calls for more responsible journalistic practices and greater involvement of the public in the political process. Prominent political writers and pollsters, like the *Washington Post*'s David Broder and Richard Morin, have made calls for less reliance on poll stories and less horse-race (Morin, 1995; Mundy, 1996). In his recent book, *Breaking the News*, James Fallows, a *U.S. News and World Report* editor, admonishes his peers and calls for greater public accountability of journalists. Even Cokie Roberts has made public pleas for more responsible practices in the mainstream press:

> In her 1994 Theodore White lecture at Harvard's Joan Shorenstein Center, ABC's Cokie Roberts recalled the belief of some that "the press won Watergate." She added, "My question is, what have we won lately, and have we made it harder for the system to work? And is that clash, between politicians and the press, undermining our institutions so fundamentally that their very survival is called into question?" (from Capella and Jamieson, 1996: 84)

Thus it seems that the promise of the new electronic public sphere, the opportunities it might offer for greater access of the citizenry to informed public discourse and for better communication between politicians and the electorate, are being undermined by many of the dynamics that have been established over the last thirty-five years. But what kinds of developments might we expect in the next few decades, as new media technologies alter the composition of that electronic public sphere, and new formats for news presentation and analysis offer new opportunities for public participation? Will the dynamics described above, the increasing superficiality, hyper-reflexivity, and negativity of the contemporary public sphere be reinforced or undermined? The next section examines the advent of new media technologies and new forms of political communication that have been becoming increasingly dominant throughout the course of the 1990s.

THE "NEW MEDIA" AND THE FUTURE OF THE ELECTRONIC PUBLIC SPHERE

The information revolution has brought in its wake a second generation of media technologies that many have come to call the "new media" (Graber, 1996; Patterson, 1993; Weaver, 1994). The proliferation of satellite and cable television, the introduction of the Internet as a new source for information and personal communication, and the development of more audience-driven forms of news analysis, such as talk radio, have begun to offer alternatives to the mainstream press with which the public has become so disenchanted. As the public has become increasingly frustrated with the presentation of politics in the mainstream media, many have flocked to new media and new media formats that seem to offer greater opportunities for more in-depth coverage, for information more tailored to individual interests, or for more interactivity and audience participation. Some of these innovations do, indeed, offer ways for citizens to avoid the frustratingly superficial and cynical news analysis that has come to dominate in the mainstream media. However, although some of these new forums offer exciting new possibilities for access to political information and deliberation, others actually serve to exacerbate the troubling dynamics described above. The characteristics of the new media seem to offer mixed blessings for political communication in the United States.

Instant Access. A number of new media formats that have become increasingly popular throughout the 1980s and 1990s allow the audience instant access to political news in ways that were never before possible. New cable television formats, such as CNN and C-Span, for example, offer continual political coverage, twenty-four hours a day, seven days a week. New Internet formats, as well, allow citizens to obtain up-to-the-minute information on political events whenever they choose to access it.

These new news formats allow citizens to bypass some of the frustratingly superficial fare found in typical mainstream news coverage. However, the ascendance of these new instant access formats actually serves to exacerbate some of the problematic dynamics of that have come to characterize the public sphere. Cable television, for example, has proven to have diverse implications for the hyper-reflexivity of the contemporary public sphere. CNN's continuous daily coverage of politics, in formats similar to those used on network stations (news hours, pundit shows, etc.), has served to speed up the news cycle of newspapers and television stations, exacerbating some of the problems inherent in an already fast-paced news business. As James Fallows points out in *Breaking the News*, the nonstop news cycle fostered by institutions such as CNN has sped up the deliberative process of office holders, and has handicapped policy-making processes:

> The most obvious effect of the non-stop news cycle is to force government officials to spend their time in non-stop response. Ideally public officials would be able to think decades ahead, in considering national savings rates and environmental challenges; or years ahead in planning school reforms and industrial growth; or months ahead about trade negotiations or foreign policy statements; or at least beyond the next weekend's political talk shows, with their verdicts on "good" or "bad" weeks. In reality it can be hard for officials to think more than fifteen minutes ahead, as they look through the mountain of phone slips on their desk and try to answer congressional objections, kill off rumors or leaks, and put their spin on stories in the minutes before the next deadline arrives. (Fallows, 1996: 185)

Unmediated Access. Not only do some of these new technologies offer instant access to political events, they also offer new possibilities for less mediated access to news and information. C-Span is, perhaps, the best example of this new form of political communication. C-Span, which began seventeen years ago as a cable channel, provides direct, usually unmediated, coverage of political activities, from filming the floor of both houses of Congress during regular daily sessions, to covering other political events of national importance, such as the annual governor's meeting, or national conferences on issues such as education or welfare reform. By providing direct, unmediated access to the actual processes of government and gatherings of public significance, C-Span offers an opportunity for dedicated citizens to assess political leaders, their policies, and many governmental institutions, outside of the constraints of dominant journalistic conventions.[4]

The Internet offers new opportunities for more direct communication between political actors and the public as well.[5] For example, as more and more organizations in society—government bureaus, businesses, social movements, interest groups, think tanks, and political campaign organizations—are rapidly setting up Internet information sites, and as search engines like *Yahoo!* and *Gopher* are becoming more user friendly, citizens find they can research political issues themselves;

they can find texts of political speeches, arguments about policy issues presented by a variety of interest organizations, and various sources of information to compare and contrast in their own fact-checking ventures. Increasingly, they can also find information about particular political campaigns: candidate platforms; texts of speeches; and information prepared by candidates' campaign organizations, including information about how to donate time or money to a candidate's campaign. According to Edward Epstein of the *San Francisco Chronicle*, 1996 was a "breakthrough year for the marriage of the Internet and politics" as "hundreds—perhaps thousands of candidates on the local, state and national levels [had] their own sites on the World Wide Web" (Epstein, 1996). According to a postelection poll released on November 21, 1996, a full 9 percent of American voters said that information they found on the Internet influenced their vote in the 1996 elections (Chandrasekaran, 1996).

As more people take advantage of these new sources of less mediated political communication, citizens and political actors regain a certain amount of control over their access to one another, circumventing the limitations of short sound bites and cynical coverage. Of course, what may be lost in the process is the positive role that a more critical public sphere can play in civic life. As citizens are finding it easier to access specifically that information which interests them, be it weather reports, sports news, or political news on topics of special interest, it seems that many of them may be bypassing the kinds of traditional news formats that might potentially offer in-depth news analysis on a variety of topics of public interest. In a March 1995 national survey conducted by the Times Mirror Center, for example, only 45 percent of Americans said they had read a newspaper the previous day, compared to 58 percent only a year earlier, and 71 percent in a similar study from 1965 (cited in Rosen, 1996: 19). And a recent survey by the Pew Research Center indicated that the percentage of Americans getting news from the Internet at least once a week more than tripled from 1996 to 1998— going from 11 to 36 million news users, whereas the percentage of Americans who watched nightly network and local television news had fallen from 30 percent in 1993 to 15 percent in 1998 (Pew Research Center, 1998: 1).[6] As people turn to a variety of less mediated sources for their news, we may begin to lose the sense of a single national public sphere, with central problems to be discussed and analyzed by citizens and experts alike. This brings us to the issue of the rise of new forms of interactive media and the cultivation of a variety of more specialized publics.

Interactivity and Demassification. A number of the new media formats have been celebrated by scholars and news analysts for their ability to provide new, more interactive formats for citizen participation in news-gathering and analysis.[7] The Internet, for example, not only serves as a locus for instant and unmediated access to various sources of news and information; the interactivity of the Internet has also allowed it to become a new kind of forum for political action. Responding to Internet polls on political sites, spreading information to friends and colleagues through E-mail, and signing and circulating electronic petitions are just a few of the ways in which Internet activity can become political activity, rather than just the consumption of political information. Through participation in politically oriented chat groups, citizens can take a more active and participatory role in political discourse. This opportunity to actively participate in political discussion, beyond the confines of their own daily social circles, may well inspire citizens to more actively and more thoroughly inform themselves about political issues.[8] And the capacity to regularly and inexpensively communicate with other citizens far beyond one's own locality has allowed for the formation of a number of social movements and interest groups that otherwise might have found the barriers to organization too high.

Such new forms of interactivity allow people to come together to form specialized publics around particular kinds of interests. For example, the American militia movement and other related "patriots" movements (such as the county rights movement and many anti-environmentalist organizations) have used the Internet as a primary locus for membership recruitment and organizational activity and communication (Castells, 1997: Ch. 2).[9] In fact, the flourishing of these organizations over the last decade has probably been significantly aided by their adoption of the Internet as a central organizational tool, as many members of these groups are rural residents and do not have the resources to travel to frequent meetings in order to maintain group solidarity.

However, the growing power of these "patriot" groups, in particular, culminating in such events as the 1995 Oklahoma City bombing of a federal building and the deaths surrounding the showdown between militia zealots and the FBI in Montana, point to the darker side of these new forums for interactive communication and organization. The legitimacy of sources of information on the Internet is not always verifiable. And the dialogue that is fostered by these forums often creates a rather insular worldview. The flip side of the benefits of interactivity and the cultivation of specialized publics is the danger posed by the failure to incorporate contrasting visions and voices into public dialogue. Thus, the single echo chamber of the mass media may come to be complemented by a multitude of isolated peripheral echo chambers as well.

Talk radio, another new media format that has blossomed in the United States in recent years,[10] has this same Janus-faced quality. Like the Internet, talk radio shows allow citizens to find a political niche that they may find more suited to their own views and to play a more interactive role in public discourse. And as in the case of the Internet, this new development has led to celebratory assessments on the part of some observers of the public scene. Susan Herbst, for example, in a recent article entitled "Public Expression Outside the Mainstream," actually goes so far as to call these shows modern day, democratic "electronic salons," asserting that the shows provide a space for public discussion, but without the elite barriers to entry that characterized the salons of eighteenth century Paris (Herbst, 1996: 125, 129).

However, although many voters may find these new mass media formats more engaging than traditional radio and television news programs, in tone and format the shows often fall prey to many of the same symptoms that plague the mass media political communication regime. It is as if the pundit shows have been recreated on the airwaves, except that average citizens get to sit in for the pundits. Many of these shows—the ever-popular Rush Limbaugh show is an excellent example—encourage superficial and vitriolic assessments of the game of politics. Although some of these shows do attempt to foster an atmosphere in which various sides of an issue will be explored (see, for example, talk show host Diane Rehm's impassioned plea for more of this kind of format; Rehm, 1989), many of them thrive on angry and cynical attacks on politicians and the political system. Even boosters of talk radio, such as Michael Harrison, editor of the trade-publication *Talkers*, concede that the medium is not striving to create a particularly informative or politically balanced forum for political discussion: "Talk radio is, by its own definition, not fair. . . . Fair means giving equal attention to all sides. Talk radio is a parade of biases, a hodgepodge of truth and opinion" (Hudis and Heuton, 1996).[11] Not surprisingly, talk radio listeners tend to be more cynical about government than the average voter.[12] Thus, although these new, more interactive venues for more specialized publics hold much promise, and for many citizens provide a fresh alternative to the cynical and tightly packaged coverage they find in traditional news commentary, the development of these specialized public forums are plagued by their own kinds of shortcomings.

CONCLUSIONS: THE MIXED PROMISES OF THE NEW MEDIA AND THE NEW PUBLIC JOURNALISM

What clearly emerges from these speculations about the impact of the "new media" is that they do not promise to offer a simple solution to the problematic dynamics that plague our political discourse. A shift towards more instant and unmediated access and towards more interactivity and niche-oriented narrowcasting by means of a variety of the new media sources has created opportunities for citizens to access specifically that information that is most relevant to their lives, and for them to become more active participants in their pursuit of knowledge. But it also means that the national public sphere is becoming more fragmented. With the rapid proliferation of news providers, it is becoming harder for citizens to assess the objectivity of the news they receive. Whereas news sources like C-Span have begun to offer less mediated presentations of political leaders and processes, they have also sped up the news cycle, further accelerating the breakneck pace which politicians and traditional media sources must keep. And a shift towards more interactive venues for news analysis, such as interactive internet formats and talk radio, can foster more interest and responsibility on the part of citizens, but many of these forums simply recreate the superficial, cynical approach to politics that has come to dominate much mainstream press coverage.

In a recent article, Ellen Hume, a reporter and executive director of the Democracy Program at the Public Broadcasting System, discusses some of the dangers of the fragmentation and proliferation of news sources today. She insists that in the new climate, in which the public's confidence in the news has dropped precipitously and audiences are no longer captive, but can seek out their own sources for information and political debate among the proliferating new interactive and niche-oriented media formats, the public, more than ever before, needs mainstream news providers to act as responsible gatekeepers. In order to win back the confidence and attention of the American public, she claims, mainstream newspapers, newsmagazines, and television news programs must solidify their reputations as objective and reliable news sources by rejecting trends towards cynicism, superficiality, and tabloid-style ploys for large audiences. They also must try to move beyond the hyper-reflexive tendency to present all of politics as an insider's game: "The old journalism delivers the old politics: the insider's game, full of sound and fury, but remote from citizen's concerns" (Hume, 1996: 143). Rather, she insists, traditional news sources must try to orient the news more towards the real problems that people experience in their everyday lives.

Overcoming the current superficiality, frenetic pace, and hyper-reflexivity of mainstream news sources will require more than just new technologies and new formats for the presentation of political news; it will require new commitments to in-depth, analytical coverage. If we are to begin to overcome some of the corrosive trends that have beset our political discourse, we must find ways to refocus the gathering and analysis of the news, regardless of whether that news is presented via the Internet, talk radio, or via more traditional news sources such as newspapers and television news programs. Political coverage must become less superficial; more dedicated to in-depth analysis of social problems, political issues, and policy options; and more committed to both addressing those issues that most concern the average citizen, and to showing the average citizen the relevance of political events for his or her life.

One movement, or series of movements within journalism that has been attempting to address these problems through innovative methods for setting the news agenda and for gathering and reporting the news, is a movement that has come to be known as the new "public" or "civic" journalism. A loosely associated group of local newspaper editors, journalists, and academics, supported by a number of different charitable foundations, including the Knight Foundation, Kettering Foundation, and the Pew Charitable Trusts, are experimenting with ways to avoid cynical horse-race and poll-driven coverage of politics, in favor of new approaches that attempt to involve citizens more deeply in the political process and in setting the news agenda. According to Merritt Davis, the editor of the *Wichita Eagle* and one of the pioneers in the movement, this search for new forms of journalistic coverage is being driven by the recognition that journalism and public life are codependent, and that, especially in an age of information glut such as our own, a journalism that truly addresses citizens' concerns is essential if we are to maintain an active and critical public sphere (Davis, 1995: 4, 7).

During the 1992 campaign, various attempts were made to devise mechanisms by which voter concerns would be used to set the news agenda for more in-depth coverage of issues. Newspapers like the *Washington Post* employed focus groups to infuse news coverage with in-depth attention to the concerns of average voters (Morin, 1995). In another fascinating experiment, the *Charlotte Observer* sent reporters out on door-to-door canvassing missions to ask voters what issues the paper should discuss in their coverage of the presidential elections, and then tried to let this "grass-roots agenda-setting" determine editorial policy. As a result of the experiment, coverage in the *Observer* almost doubled, column for column, compared to coverage of the previous presidential election in 1988. According to an outside study by the Poynter Institute, coverage of campaign strategy fell from 21 percent of total campaign coverage in 1988 to 11 percent of the total in 1992, and horse-race polls declined from 6.1 percent to 1.4 percent (Rosen, 1996: 45). The Charlotte experiment has generally been considered a success. One study showed that in those districts served by the *Charlotte Observer*, voter registration went up by 10 percent to 12 percent (Weaver, 1994). These kind of constructive, community-oriented projects have continued, both at the *Charlotte Observer*, and at other local papers such as the *Wichita Eagle*, the *Dallas Morning News*, the *Virginia-Pilot*, and at the *Akron Beacon Journal*, which received a Pulitzer Prize in 1994 for its constructive coverage of racial issues (see Hume, 1996: 148-151; Merritt, 1995: 101-102; Weaver 1994).

The movement has been intensely criticized by many in the mainstream media and in academics. And much of the concern is legitimate. In an effort to revive civic life in their localities, a number of newspapers have crossed the line into activism, in ways that could be problematic. For example, a project spear-headed by the Columbus, Ohio *Ledger-Inquirer*,[13] called "Columbus beyond 2000" began with a town meeting, held at the newspaper's expense, intended to put pressure on local government. The effort culminated in the creation of a citizen's movement, called "United Beyond 2000," supported by a regular bulletin board in the newspaper, and led by a number of journalists and newspaper employees. Although the *Ledger-Inquirer* staff, after the initial paper-sponsored town meeting, continued to participate in the movement only in their capacities as private citizens, many have raised concerns about the dangers of such alliances between newspapers and local activists, especially because, in this age of mergers and acquisitions, so many local newspapers now have monopoly markets.[14] At the *Asbury Park Press* in New Jersey, for example, community activists are reported to have been holding regular monthly meetings at newspaper offices, bringing one commentator to ask: "If the local newspaper doesn't keep a critical eye on community leaders, who will?" (Sherman, 1998: 55).

Another question that needs to be asked about civic journalism is to what extent reader-generated agendas really succeed at creating the kind of critical, analytical coverage that could improve the level of public discourse in the press. When reader polls are used as a helpful guideline to assist editors in choosing topics for in-depth analysis, as in the election coverage experiments conducted at the *Wichita Eagle* or the *Charlotte Observer*, they can serve as a helpful tool to assess reader interest and to orient coverage away from the strategic narrowing of the agenda attempted by many campaign PR experts. But attempts to let polls drive the content of coverage can be problematic, perpetuating some of the problems indicated in the public sphere as echo chamber model. Majority-driven agendas can be oppressive, raising the old

Tocquevillian concerns about the fate of minority concerns in populist democracies that pander too much to the majority (for a similar argument from a slightly different perspective, see Heikkila and Kunelius, 1996). And the intensive focus on local citizens' local problems can lead to a limited vision of the national and international scope of most social problems afflicting our very complicated, globalizing society today (Parisi, 1997). Losing sight of the importance of news analysis by experts, and of the perspective that critically informed journalists need to continue to bring to bear on public issues, is a danger to which much public journalism can too easily fall prey.[15]

However, despite a number of misguided experiments in this direction, as the movement seeks to define for itself how to engage local citizens and create new forms of political coverage that avoid the traps of superficiality and hyper-reflexivity that plague mainstream coverage, the best efforts in the movement have much to recommend them. The most ambitious efforts have been those that manage to provide readers with informed analysis of issues on the public agenda, and those that create in the press a space for sustained public deliberation. In the words of New York University's Jay Rosen, the main academic proponent and theorist of the movement, journalism needs to find ways, not just to make "a perfunctory stab at consulting 'real folks' without demanding too much from them" but to facilitate public deliberation, using contact with citizen concerns to help direct the kind of sustained, multistage projects that can help readers to educate themselves and to feel personally engaged by political issues (Rosen, 1996: 49-58).

University of Texas professor James Fishkin's National Issues Convention, held in January 1996 in Austin, Texas was a particularly ambitious project in the spirit of the new civic journalism. A representative sample of Americans from all over the country were chosen, given nonpartisan materials to read on the major social and political issues at stake in the 1996 elections, and then flown into Austin by Fishkin and PBS. Once in Austin, they participated in a number of small focus groups, in which, with the help of a moderator, they discussed those issues with fourteen other voters of diverse race, gender, and socioeconomic background. Later, the participants had an opportunity to pose questions to the presidential candidates or their representatives in a series of televised meetings. The goal, according to Fishkin, was to circumvent the problems that plague standard opinion polling, especially the fact that opinion polls are known to elicit volatile "phantom opinions," which are formulated quickly by respondents who are given no time to deliberate about their opinions, seek further information, or discuss them with others. The intention is, through providing information and allowing for deliberation, to create a prescriptive assessment of public opinion, an assessment of "what the public would think, if it had a better chance to think about the questions at issue" (Fishkin, 1996: 134). The broadcasting of the event to the general public is then intended to inspire further public discussion of the issues at stake and to publicize the results of the deliberative poll. Although the event in Austin was not as well attended by the candidates as had been hoped, and did not garner the ratings that would signal it as a clear popular success, it was one of the most successful examples of an effort to bring public deliberation into the mainstream media. (For more information, see Fishkin, 1996; also Burke, 1996.)

Whether these new forms of civic journalism will be integrated into the mainstream press remains to be seen. The voices calling out the most strongly for reform belong to some of the most powerful and well-known representatives of the most well-respected media institutions, people like ABC's Cokie Roberts, the *Washington Post*'s David Broder, and *US News and World Report*'s James Fallows. But change comes hard, especially in an industry facing such intense market pressures, making both the time and financial resources that would be needed to carry out such innovative projects scarce.[16] The success of these projects will, in the end, depend not just on the values of individual journalists, but on the capacity for these new formats of political coverage to attract audiences and to fit into the budgetary restraints of the businesses that run news organizations. It remains to be seen to what extent the efforts of the journalism profession itself may eventually succeed in reversing some of those dynamics of the mass media political communication regime that are most damaging to our political discourse, and therefore to our ability to carry out the kind of constructive national political projects that are now called for as we enter the twenty-first century.

ACKNOWLEDGEMENTS

I would like to thank Manuel Castells for providing the inspiration and much of the theoretical framework for this piece. This work began as a research project for his recent, three-volume work on the information revolution and the network society, *The Information Age: Economy, Society and Culture*, and it was through my work with Castells that I first began to think about the media's new role as the dominant "space of politics" (see Volume II, *The Power of Identity*), and to speculate about the role that new media technologies and new communication formats have played in reshaping political discourse within that space.

ENDNOTES

1. For more detailed analysis of the issues discussed in the first two sections of this paper, please see my article in *Javnost—The Public* 4(2), 1997. See also Castells, 1997: Chapter Six.

2. In 1968, only sixteen or seventeen states allowed for the direct participation of average party members in the selections of candidates through direct primaries.

3. Although Kennedy did continue to commission private opinion polls while he was in office, his reliance on opinion polls decreased significantly once he assumed office: during his years as president, Kennedy employed only sixteen opinion polls. Johnson and Nixon made more frequent use of opinion polling (each averaging about twenty polls per year) (Jacobs and Shapiro, 1995).

4. Of course, the cameras' very presence turns these same political events into opportunities for staging and spectacle on the part of politicians. Nevertheless, citizens and politicians are provided through this medium with new opportunities for direct communication, without the normal mediation of journalists' intensive selection of quotes and careful framing of events.

5. Other modes of providing less journalistically mediated forms of political communication have been experimented with in recent years as well. During the 1996 elections, an experiment in completely unmediated television presentation of the candidates was carried out for the first time in America by three of the four major networks, as well as PBS and CNN. For the first time (perhaps since the 1952 presidential elections), the major presidential candidates were each given free airtime during the last campaign. On Fox, NBC and CBS, PBS, and CNN each candidate gave one- to two-and-a-half-minute answers to questions on a number of different topics, which were broadcast a number of times throughout the month before the election. The free air time did not have as big of an impact on voters as had been hoped; nevertheless, a study by the Public Policy Center of the Annenberg School of Communication reported that the candidates' statements (1) devoted less time to attacking opponents than the candidates' advertisements, (2) were more factually accurate than statements in the candidates' advertisements or in the nationally televised debates, and (3) addressed a wider range of topics than either the advertisements or the debates (Mifflin, 1996).

6. Pew researchers insist that the rise in the number of Internet news consumers is unrelated to the decline in consumers of traditional news sources: "The survey finds no evidence that going online for news leads to less reading or viewing of more traditional news sources. People who go online for news say that their news habits are unchanged. Analysis of the polling confirms this in finding that their news consumption patterns do not differ significantly from

non-users, all other things being equal" (Pew Research Center, 1998). It seems however, that some group must be changing its habits, as audiences for newspapers and network news programs are in decline. Either the Internet users are, indeed, relying on traditional sources less, or the non-Internet users are relying on them less (in which case the users and nonusers would, indeed, have quite dissimilar consumption patterns).

7. For a discussion of some recent celebrants of Internet interactivity, see Greenwood, 1997: 6-7.

8. Many scholars caution, however, that technologies such as the Internet are less likely to inspire the politically inactive to participate in civic life than to provide a new venue for those who are already politically active. As a result, technologies such as the Internet and C-Span may only serve to widen the gap between the 10-15 percent of the voting age population that is politically active (beyond just voting), and those who are not. For an excellent discussion of these issues and review of the current literature on the promises of the Internet as a democratizing force, see Greenwood, 1997.

9. The Internet has proven a valuable resource to many other groups who would have otherwise faced barriers to organization, such as the environmental justice movement.

10. A *Times-Mirror* survey in 1993 found that four in every ten of those surveyed reported listening to talk radio with some frequency, and one in six reported listening regularly (Balz, 1993). These figures seem to have remained fairly steady throughout the 1990s: according to Mary Matalin, during the 1996 elections, 44 percent reported getting some or all of their political information from talk radio (Hudis and Heuton, 1996).

11. The public recognizes that this is the case as well, rating (in February of 1996) talk radio as second to last in terms of "fairness" when presented a list of fourteen news outlets (Hudis and Heuton, 1996).

12. *Times-Mirror*'s 1993 survey, cited in Hudis and Heuton, 1996.

13. On the *Ledger-Inquirer* project, see Rosen, 1991: 271.

14. On mergers and acquisitions in the newspaper business, see Davis, 1995: 41.

15. The *Spokesman-Review* of Spokane, Washington seems to have taken a dangerous step in this direction when it abolished editorials on its op-ed page in favor of running only op-ed pieces written by readers (Sherman, 1998: 50).

16. The fate of public journalism is at present rather precarious. Although a number of local experiments have served to encourage civic participation and have helped to increase reader satisfaction at local newspapers, there is no indication that they are helping to increase circulation rates (Sherman, 1998: 55).

REFERENCES

Ansolabehere, Stephen, Roy Behr, and Shanto Iyengar. 1993. *The Media Game: American Politics in the Television Age.* New York: MacMillan.

Balz, Dan. 1993, July 19. Misleading Medium of U.S. Politics: Talk Radio Listeners Often "Caricature Discontent," Survey Finds. *The Washington Post*, A7.

Burke, Terri. 1996. People Spoke; Who Listened? *The Quill* 84(2), 33-35.

Capella, Joseph N. and Kathleen Hall Jamieson. 1996. Political Cynicism and Media Cynicism. *Annals of the American Academy of Political and Social Science* 546, 71-83.

Castells, Manuel. 1996. *The Rise of the Network Society. The Information Age: Economy Society and Culture. Volume I.* Cambridge, MA: Blackwell.

Castells, Manuel. 1997. *The Power of Identity. The Information Age: Economy Society and Culture. Volume II.* Cambridge, MA: Blackwell.

Chandrasekaran, Rajiv. 1996, November 22. Politics Finding a Home on the Internet. *The Washington Post*, A4.

Davis, Merritt. 1995. *Public Journalism and Public Life: Why Telling the News is Not Enough.* Mahwah, NJ: Erlbaum.

Entman, Robert. 1989. *Democracy Without Citizens: Media and the Decay of American Politics.* New York: Oxford University Press.

Epstein, Edward. 1996, October 14. Internet Alters the World of Campaigning: Candidates Use World Wide Web to Reach Voters. *The San Francisco Chronicle*, A7.

Fallows, James. 1996. *Breaking the News: How the Media Undermine American Democracy.* New York: Vintage.

Fishkin, James S. 1996. The Televised Deliberative Poll: An Experiment in Democracy. *ANNALS of the American Academy of Political and Social Sciences* 546, 132-140.

Gitlin, Todd. 1980. *The Whole World is Watching: Mass Media in the Making and Unmaking of the New Left.* Berkeley: University of California Press.

Graber, Doris A. 1996. The New Media and Politics—What Does the Future Hold? *PS-Political Science & Politics* 29(1), 33-36.

Greenwood, Linda L. 1997. American Politics in the Age of Information: Promise or Peril? Paper given at the International Conference on Media and Politics, Katholieke Universitet, Brussels, February 27-March 1, 1997.

Heikkila Heiki and Risto Kunelius. 1996. Public Journalism and Its Problems—A Theoretical Perspective. *Javnost-The Public* 3(3), 81-95.

Herbst, Susan. 1996. Public Expression Outside the Mainstream. *ANNALS of the American Academy of Political and Social Sciences* 546, 120-131.

Hudis, Mark and Cheryl Heuton. 1996. Talk Ratings are Stronger Than Ever. *Mediaweek* 6(15), 4-6.

Hume, Ellen. 1996. The New Paradigm for News. *ANNALS of the American Academy of Political Science and Sociology* 546, 141-153.

Jacobs, Lawrence R. and Robert Y. Shapiro. 1995. The Rise of Presidential Polling: The Nixon Whitehouse in Historical Perspective. *Public Opinion Quarterly* 59, 163-195.

Merritt, Davis. 1995. *Public Journalism and Public Life: Why Telling the News is Not Enough.* Hillsdale, NJ: Erlbaum.

Mifflin, Lowrie. 1996, November 3. Free Experiment Wins Support, If Not Viewers. *The New York Times,* Sec. 1, 38.

Moog, Sandra. 1997. Television, Mass Polling and the Mass Media: The Impact of Media Technologies on American Politics, 1960-1996. *Javnost—The Public* 4(2), 39-55.

Moore, David W. 1992. *The Superpollsters: How They Measure and Manipulate Public Opinion in America.* New York: Four Walls Eight Windows.

Morin, Richard. 1995. The 1992 Election and the Polls: Neither Politics nor Polling as Usual. In Paul J. Lavrakas, Michael W. Traugott, and Peter V. Miller (eds.), *Presidential Polls and the News Media.* Boulder, CO: Westview Press.

Morris, Dick. 1997, January 15. Inside the White House. *The Guardian,* sec. 2, p. 6.

Mundy, Alicia. 1996. Taking a Poll on Polls. *Media Week* 6(8), 17-20.

Parisi, Peter. 1997. Toward a "Philosophy of Framing": News Narratives for Public Journalism. *Journalism & Mass Communication Quarterly* 74(4), 673-686.

Patterson, Thomas E. 1993. *Out of Order: How the Decline of the Political Parties and the Growing Power of the New Media Undermine the American Way of Electing Presidents.* New York: Alfred E. Knopf.

The Pew Research Center. 1998. Event-Driven News Audiences—Internet News Takes Off. Pew Research Center Biennial News Consumption Survey, 24-May 11, 1998. Source, http://www.people-press.org/med98rpt.html.

The Public Perspective. 1992, July/August.

Rehm, Diane. 1989, February 26. Our Master's Voices? Talk-Show Hosts Should Stay out of Politics. *The Washington Post,* C7.

Rosen, Jay. 1996. *Getting the Connections Right: Public Journalism and the Troubles in the Press.* New York: Twentieth Century Fund.

Rosen, Jay. 1991. Making Journalism More Public. *Communication* 12(4), 267-284.

Schudson, Michael. 1973. *Discovering the News: A Social History of American Newspapers.* New York: Basic Books.

Sherman, Scott. 1998, April. The Public Defender—A Journalism Professor's Crusade to Bring the Community into the Newsroom. *Lingua Franca* 8(3), 49-56.

Weaver, David. 1994. Media Agenda Setting and Elections—Voter Involvement or Alienation. *Political Communication* 11(4), 347-356.

16

Media as Political Actors: The Role of Consonance in "Policy Agenda-Setting" in Germany*

Christiane Eilders

Due to the growing demand for more transparency in complex modern democracies it has become increasingly important for political actors to generate attention and acceptance for their concerns. A favorable public opinion has become a central factor for legitimation. Yet, the term "public opinion" is still contradictory and poorly defined. Instead of following the common assumption that public opinion is the aggregate of individual attitudes this paper proceeds from the theoretically more substantial concept of public opinion as output of public communication (Neidhardt, 1994). Because the role of nonmediated public communication has continuously declined, the mass media constitute the most important subsystem of the public sphere in modern societies (Gerhards and Neidhardt, 1991). Public communication—that is, the open

*This chapter relates to some theoretical assumptions of the empirical project "Mass Media's Voice in the Political Process: Issues and Opinions in Editorials" by Friedhelm Neidhardt, Barbara Pfetsch and the author. It is currently conducted at the Wissenschaftszentrum Berlin für Sozialforschung (Social Science Research Center).

exchange of issues and opinions noticeable by a large audience—is organized and structured by the media according to professional criteria and norms. Public opinion as output of public communication thus becomes visible through the contributions of various actors who advance their views on certain issues in print and electronic media. These contributions may cover a variety of issues or concentrate on a few; they may represent consonant or dissonant opinions.

The crucial role of media in public communication mainly builds on its function of information dissemination between the political system and the audience. However essential and undisputed the dissemination of information through the mass media, the reduction of media activity to the information function assigns media a predominantly passive role in the political process. Restricting the role of the media to an exclusive information agency is not only a deficient description of the media but also means distorting and underestimating the legitimate active role of the media in the process of opinion formation. Recent contributions on media performance in modern democracies drew attention to the more evaluative functions of the media (Gurevitch and Blumler, 1990; Page, 1996a). In political communication processes the mass media are participating actors with genuine political interests and goals. In Germany—as in many other modern democracies—mass media are explicitly expected to watch critically over the political process and thereby provide accountability. This assignment puts media in a slightly more active position. Like any other actor in society, media have the right to make their views and concerns public and express their opinions on issues, events and actors.[1] Confounding the two aspects of media messages—the neutral dissemination and the media's autonomous contribution of opinion—leads to the perception of media as an uncomfortably diffuse factor in political communication. As long as opinion is marked as such, the media have the right to take their own view and openly try to influence public opinion formation and even policy. The claim of neutral information dissemination and the media's right to contribute to the political discourse as autonomous actors thus have to be treated separately.

The notion of media as participating actors in the political process directs the attention to the media's opinion rather than to their performance regarding the information function. In editorials media communicate their genuine views on the relevance of issues and express their particular opinions on actors and policy options. Through editorials the media are explicitly authorized to publicly express their opinions and by noticeably commenting on public affairs they make use of their right to present themselves as autonomous actors. Because editorials stand for the collective opinion of a media outlet[2] they allow for an efficient assessment of the media's autonomous contribution to the political discourse. Focusing on editorials in German national newspapers, this chapter first discusses the strategies the media employ in communicating their specific views. Second, the role of correspondences across different media outlets is addressed. Media opinion can be described on two basic dimensions; the relevance assignment for certain issues or subissues, and the evaluation of actors and policy options. The degree of correspondences across different media outlets on these dimensions implies different chances for the perception of the "media's voice" as unified factor in political discourse. Regarding possible political effects the chapter discusses under what circumstances the media might be successful in finding resonance for their relevance assignments, interpretations, and opinions in the political system.

MASS MEDIA AS PARTICIPATING ACTORS IN POLITICAL COMMUNICATION

Whereas we have considerable knowledge about media regarding their performance as information agencies, only little is known about the media's autonomous acting in the political process, about their genuine "voice" on the relevance of issues and events, on their interpretations and evaluations of public affairs. Because editorials are the legitimate place for explicit opinion, an examination of evaluation strategies most likely starts out with an assessment of the open judgments of actors or policy options. Yet, editorials—just like the articles from the news section—carry much more opinion than what is covered by the obvious evaluative statements. There are various implicit evaluation strategies suggesting a certain interpretation or giving an issue a certain slant. Establishing an issue hierarchy by assigning more or less relevance to an issue is one of the central implicit evaluation strategies. Relevance assignment is usually achieved by selecting a specific issue out of the stream of events continuously taking place. The criteria employed in this selection process are generated from professional norms but also underlay the specific political goals and interests of the media outlet. Editorials mean an additional chance to emphasize particular issues and reinforce the relevance assignment of the news section. By selecting an issue for the editorial section the media indicate that the selected issue is important enough to be commented on and given extra space.

In political science the assignment of relevance to an issue is debated as a strategy of political parties to establish an ideological profile and position themselves in relation to competing parties. Scholars supporting this "salience model" hold that parties do not compete through different positions regarding particular issues but rather occupy certain issues, presenting them as the most relevant problems. In this view competition between political parties can consist of attempts to assert the saliency of different issues that favor one or the other side. It is assumed that "there is no point at which particular issues have to be discussed by both sides" (Budge and Farlie, 1985: 269). This view stands in sharp contrast to the traditional view of party competition, which assumes that parties offer different policies on the same issues. Applied to the media system and the media's strategies to position themselves in the political spectrum,[4] the salience model implies that different media outlets differ in issue selection rather than ideological positions on particular issues. Different editorial positions of media outlets should be reflected by a different issue repertoire rather than by arguments and evaluations. Editorials offer the chance to establish an issue agenda that is largely independent of daily politics and other external events and thus enable media outlets to employ issue selection as a means of political positioning similar to parties. It should be interesting to find out whether or not different media outlets do in fact position themselves through issue selection rather than through the expression of opinion on an issue.

The notion of relevance assignment and issue selection as implicit political statement is impressively illustrated by findings on framing strategies in news reporting. Framing from this perspective can be seen as a further subtle way of communicating opinion without explicit evaluation. The concept of framing can be traced back to Goffman (1974), who sees frames as a means to organize experience by supplying the context within which a particular occurrence or event is interpreted. Frames thus enable individuals "to locate, perceive, identify, and label occurrences within their life space and the world at large" (Snow et al., 1986: 464). Framing in communication research refers to the more or less intentional selection of context information in reporting an event or commenting on an event. Editors can thereby influence the interpretation and evaluation of an event. There are two main framing strategies in media coverage. The episodic frame describes issues in terms of specific instances, whereas the thematic frame depicts issues more abstractly by placing them in some appropriate context. Results of a number of experiments showed that episodic framing leads to individualistic as opposed to societal attributions of responsibility (Iyengar 1996). The significance of framing strategies in political contexts can be explained by the complexity of political issues, the ambiguity of political discourse, and the low levels of public knowledge and interest in politics. Because people are "exquisitely sensitive to contextual cues when they make decisions, formulate judgements, or express opinions" a particular frame may profoundly influence opinion formation (Iyengar, 1991: 11).

The accentuation of issues and specific aspects of an issue can also affect the judgment of a political actor. According to the concept of priming, the performance of a political actor is measured against the issues or subissues previously highlighted by the media (Iyengar and Kinder, 1987; Krosnick and Kinder, 1990). The reception of a media report on unemployment would then have a different effect on the audience's perception of the performance of a political actor than the reception of a report on economy. Priming—like framing effects—can be explained on the basis of information processing theories. When faced with a judgment or choice, people rely upon information that is easily accessible in memory and comes to mind spontaneously instead of taking all information into account and analyzing it. Using such shortcuts and heuristics allows a "low-effort" decision-making (Krosnick and Kinder, 1990).

The findings on framing and priming demonstrate the possible impact of a certain issue selection or even slightly different accentuations of subissues. The emphasis of particular contents indicates an assignment of relevance that might affect either the perception of issue salience in general or specific evaluations of the reported issues, events, or actors. In order to assess the particular editorial stance of a media outlet special attention has to be directed to issues and subissues rather than to explicit evaluations only. It may be assumed that media outlets differ in terms of both issues and opinions according to their position on the left-right scale and to their affinity to political parties. As media opinion can be described as a significant part of the collective phenomenon of public opinion, not the single editorial or the views of one particular media outlet but the entity of issues and opinions in the media system come into focus. From a macroperspective the degree of correspondence between different media outlets represents a central factor in political discourse regarding the consistency of public opinion as well as the probability to succeed in finding resonance in the political system.

CONSONANCE IN PUBLIC OPINION

In contrast to Noelle-Neumann's concept of public opinion[4] our notion of public opinion as output of public communication does not necessarily imply high degrees of correspondence between the contributions of different actors who speak in public. Public opinion may be highly diverse in terms of both issues and opinions. Yet correspondences might develop in a discoursive process as the public speakers relate to each other and possibly modify their views. Thus, public opinion is not static but rather underlies constant change as new issues appear on the agenda, opinions are formed, and correspondences between the ones who publicly speak increase or decrease over time. Applied to media opinion as reflected in editorials of different newspapers correspondences might develop as the papers observe each other, relate to each others' arguments, and thus establish a political discourse. Regarding the possible effects of public opinion on the audience and the political system, the constantly changing degrees of correspondences play an important part in the political process. Public opinion becomes a consistent and politically effective factor as a high level of correspondence develops regarding issues as well as opinions.

Correspondences between the contents of different media outlets are generally referred to as consonance and regard the uniformity of political positions of two or more media outlets. Consonance finds its expression in the selection of identical issues and the expression of the same opinions on these issues. Most discussions on consonance relate to the idea of pluralism and diversity in the media system and see consonance as a potential threat to the audience's free and unbiased opinion formation. It is assumed that the media will provide diverse information and opinions needed for an independent opinion formation as long as a pluralistic media structure is guaranteed. Whereas a pluralistic media structure and high degrees of content diversity have persistently been unquestioned as a presupposition of free opinion formation and a well-functioning democracy, recent developments such as individualization and disintegration have led to a more critical discussion of diversity in the media system. Evidently, a common identity or a feeling of solidarity only develops on the basis of shared issue repertoires and common universes of discourse. Media contribute to integration as they provide common experiences, mutual reference points, and shared agendas. So far, mass media have nourished the coherence of communities by focusing on common issues, but with the expansion of programs in the electronic media and the internet the audience threatens to become increasingly fragmented. Shaw and Hamm (1997) see this fragmentation as a drop in common focus leading to a disruption of social union.

It need not be emphasized that a total uniformity between the issues and opinions in the media is as dysfunctional as the total lack of mutuality.[5] The media system has to be open for new problem definitions and relevance assignments. A new issue will be addressed by a single media outlet first—thereby reducing the degree of common focus—and then possibly be adapted by others if it finds resonance and support. Correspondingly, a certain opinion on an issue might be expressed by a single paper first and then spread to the other media outlets. The question is not whether or not diversity is a substantial condition of democracy, but how much diversity is desirable without sacrificing integration. Pluralism and diversity have their limits when the cohesion of society dissolves and the different segments are likely to move away from each other. Thus, pluralism and diversity on the one hand and social integration on the other hand seem to be conflicting ideals that have to be carefully weighted against each other in order to ensure the functioning of democratic society.

One step towards solving the dilemma is the analytical differentiation between the two underlying dimensions of the concept of correspondence. In media research high degrees of correspondence are predominantly referred to as consonance. Consonance includes both correspondences of issues and opinions. Because these two dimensions imply different assumptions about the condition of public opinion, a terminological differentiation is suggested. Consonance refers to the evaluative dimension. It is defined as corresponding opinions. The degree of correspondence on the issue dimension is referred to as focusing. Thus, focusing denotes a correspondence of issues, whereas consonance denotes a correspondence of opinion. Regarding the formation of public opinion it is assumed that a low degree of focusing implies a fragmentation of public opinion with highly dissipated issue agendas, whereas a lack of consonance points to considerable conflict between different segments of society. The partisanship might follow the established structures of the party spectrum or develop along the groups and movements not represented in the party system. Correspondingly, the line of conflict can be located between media with left and right party affiliations, or between the media, the political groups and movements on the one hand and the established political parties on the other hand. This would be the case if the positions in the media system develop regardless of party affiliations—for example, in terms of new conflicts between materialism and postmaterialism. Without a common focus, however, conflict is unlikely to become manifest. Its latent character will show in the struggle of salience assignment to a particular issue.

According to the terminological differentiation, focusing strongly relates to the integration aspect whereas consonance is more central for the idea of pluralism and diversity. If media mutually cover a highly focused repertoire of issues and express corresponding opinions on these issues, the media's "voice" is highly integrated and unified in its evaluation. It seems unlikely that this constellation will develop in democratic societies. If they do, however, it is interesting to find out for which issues this constellation nevertheless exists, meaning which problems and conflicts are unanimously seen as relevant and evaluated consonantly. In contrast, a constellation of high common issue repertoires but low consonance indicates a structure of public opinion that is integrated in terms of issues but heterogeneous regarding the respective opinions about these issues. The structure of the public sphere as reflected by the media then not only represents the pluralistic character of society, but also shows the constellations of conflict in the political system and the divergent interests of social groups and movements. High fragmentation of the public sphere or disintegrated and structurally heterogeneous public opinion indicates an anomic condition of society. Public communication in which the different contributions relate to each other on the basis of common issues and opinions does not develop under such conditions. If media address only few common issues, however, but comment on these unanimously, a selective public consonance becomes visible with unanimous opinions concentrating on few key issues. It will be interesting to investigate which issues this applies to.

In spite of the controversial debates on pluralism and diversity in the media system a research tradition investigating the actual degree of correspondence in the media has not developed. The empirical efforts to assess the common issues repertoires and opinions across different media outlets remained few. Except for single-issue comparisons across different media outlets focusing on the opinion rather than on the issue dimension, there is basically no information on the general degree of correspondence in the media system. One has to depend on assumptions about media markets, audiences, and professional journalistic processing strategies to obtain a picture of the current condition of focusing and consonance in media. Considering the pluralistic structure of society and the marketing strategies of competing media outlets—including binding segments of the audience through their editorial stance—the degrees of focusing and consonance are likely to be low. High degrees of focusing and consonance, on the other hand, can be expected if some structural characteristics of media systems are taken into account: the corresponding standardized attention criteria, the uniformity of professional and class interests, the media's observation of each other and their reciprocal co-orientation as well as the opinion leadership of the prestige media (Kepplinger, 1985; Noelle-Neumann and Mathes, 1987).

THE IMPACT OF MEDIA OPINION ON THE POLITICAL SYSTEM

The degree of correspondence in media coverage and editorials gains special significance with regard to media's impact on politics. Focusing on the relation between media and politics indicates a macrolevel approach that is not interested in the impact of single editorials on individual recipients but regards the impact of collective media opinion on the collective reaction of the political system. Research on media effects in general, and on the role of correspondence in media messages in particular, has predominantly dealt with microlevel phenomena. Some findings on audience effects, however, can contribute to a deeper understanding of the significance of focusing and consonance in communication processes and can easily be applied to macrolevel research approaches. In the study of opinion formation and attitude change the degree of correspondences—with a strong focus on opinions rather than issues—is mostly referred to as consonance. It describes the degree of correspondence between two or more cognitions, mostly the relation between an individual's position on an issue and the perceived position of an external representation of opinion, such as a single person, a collective actor, or a media message. Various theories (e.g., Heider's balance theory or Osgood's and Tannenbaum's model of congruency) assume a desire for cognitive balance and self-assurance as an explanation of certain selection strategies in information processing, in particular the phenomenon of selective exposure to media messages. Consonance as conceptionalized in this chapter—that is, the correspondence between different external representation of opinion (e.g., in the media system)—is addressed as a specific condition that forces individuals to perceive information dissonant to their own cognitions. Highly consonant media messages are likely to penetrate the selective filter usually warding off the messages dissonant to one's own cognitions. Empirical findings indicate that in addition to the consonance between external messages, the individual usefulness of information (Atkin, 1973) and a high credibility of the source (Donsbach, 1991), both very typical characteristics of political media messages, also facilitate a bypass of the selective filter. Because political actors unlike ordinary citizens are expected to be responsive to critique, carefully consider the arguments, and explain and justify their particular views on the controversial issue, the chances of credible and useful information to be processed should be fairly good. If politicians nevertheless disregard the above information-processing mechanisms and tend to ignore deviant messages, it may be assumed that high degrees of consonance in media messages will increase the chances for dissonant messages to pass the selective filter and find resonance in the political system.

Although the controversial discussion on the power of the mass media in general has drawn considerable public attention to macrolevel effects, the empirical efforts to investigate the collective resonance of the political system to the universe of issues and opinions expressed in the media system seem rather weak. A large body of research deals with the structural effects of the interdependence of media and politics. It focuses on the professionalization of political public relations, on the quantity and quality of interpersonal contacts between political actors and media professionals, and on the general modifications of the political process through the anticipation of the media logic. Only few studies have investigated substantial content effects between media and politics and assessed the reciprocal influences of the two agendas on each other. Agenda-setting research, originally concerned with media impact on the issue salience in the audience, has broadened its focus and increasingly addresses questions regarding the media impact on the political agenda (Rogers and Dearing, 1988). Rogers and Dearing distinguish this approach from the larger body of audience-oriented research: "Agenda-building" or more precisely "policy agenda-setting" refers to the assumed impact of media content on issue salience among political actors and sometimes even on policy decisions themselves. The majority of studies on agenda-building processes indicated a considerable impact of media coverage on policy makers.[6]

Although some of these effects might be direct consequences of media messages, a great deal of media impact is mediated through the the anticipation of effects in the audience. Political actors expect the electorate to be strongly influenced by media messages and therefore adapt policy according to the expected majority opinion. A close observation of the media is a rational means for the assessment of public sentiments. When politicians want to find out about the distribution of opinions on a particular issue among the electorate they cannot always rely on opinion surveys. Because poll data are not readily available for every issue and at all times, the news media serve as surrogates for it (Entman, 1989; Kennamer, 1992; Pritchard, 1992; Sigal, 1973). Mass-media content can thus be instrumentalized as a sort of feedback agency to check how the problem definitions and solutions put forward by politicians are accepted (Fuchs and Pfetsch, 1996). In Germany, the most important information sources for political actors are the national prestige newspapers (Herzog et al., 1990; Puhe and Würzberg, 1989).[7] As they can be characterized as opinion leaders in the German media system, it may be assumed that their effect exceeds the effects on their immediate audience (Kepplinger, 1985).

Agenda-building research has so far mainly restricted its investigations on the effects of particular issues and opinions on politics and disregarded macrolevel concepts such as the entity and constellation of issues and opinions across the different media outlets. If media are seen as watchdogs of the political process, and if they are expected to address legitimate concerns and social problems not yet being processed to the political system, they need sufficient power to find resonance. Therefore it becomes relevant whether papers select and comment unanimously or whether they refer to different issues and express divergent opinions. It is assumed that high degrees of correspondence in the media system translate into power. Only through corresponding contributions in political communication can the media be perceived as a collective actor and effectively influence the political system. Page relates the question of media power to the notion of media as autonomous actors in the political process: "The concept of 'political actor,' applied to the media or anyone else, implies observable action that is purposive and sufficiently unified, so it makes sense to speak of a single actor. A critical question, therefore, concerns whether—or to what extent—media outlets do in fact use their publications and broadcasts in a purposive and unified fashion to pursue policy objectives" (Page, 1996b: 20). It may be assumed that the structure of correspondences in the media system affects the chances of finding resonance in the political system insofar as the degree of focusing relates to agenda effects in the political system and the degree of consonance influences the direction of the political effects. Distinguishing between issues and opinions leads to four constellations of correspondences in the media system, each implying different chances to find resonance in the political system (Figure 16.1).

Under the condition of high degrees of both focusing and consonance we expect a strong political pressure to develop due to the

| Consonance | **Focusing** | |
	High (Different Media Outlets Address Same Issues)	**Low** (Few Media Outlets Address Same Issues)
High (Different Media Outlets Express Same Opinion)	Processing is highly probable—effects likely to correspond with the position of the media	Processing only under certain conditions depending on issue and media outlet—with selective effects on direction.
Low (Few Media Outlets Express Same Opinion)	Processing is probable —only partially parallel to the position of the media	No processing

Figure 16.1. Constellations of focusing and consonance in the media and their assumed impact on the political system

homogeneity in the media system. The particular issue is likely to be processed by the political system and the resulting decisions will follow the unified media position. If an issue is addressed by several media outlets but evaluated differently, the chance of being processed by the political system is still considerably high, but the resonance will be diverse and probably restricted to certain political parties or fractions that agree with the editorial stance of the particular media outlet. If an issue is addressed by few media outlets only, but these share the same opinion on the particular issue, the chances of political processing depend on further conditions. It is central which media outlets addressed the issue, which kind of issue was addressed, and between which media outlets with which editorial stances consonance was obtained. If under the condition of low degrees of focusing only low degrees of consonance develop, the political system is not likely to respond at all. This constellation implies much noise, but efficient pressure will not develop.

Finally, regarding the political macroeffects of media opinion, the persistence of focusing and consonance in the media system over time needs to be highlighted. Only by considering the persistence over time it can be settled whether "issue-attention cycles" (Downs, 1972) do in fact take place within short time periods (Funkhouser, 1973) and whether the "half-life" of issues on the media agenda is shorter than the respective time period on the political agenda; a question that has serious implications for the political effects of the media (Kingdon, 1984). Noelle-Neumann also considers stability over time as an important condition for media effects. In her view media effects on attitude change of the audience cannot be accounted for by the singular reception of one specific news item. Effects rather develop through slow cumulation of repeated messages (Noelle-Neumann 1973). This idea not only concerns the chances of media messages to affect the audience but also represents an important factor in the perception of the media's "voice" by the political system. If issues and opinions in editorials constantly change, their effect should be relatively small. If, however, stable issue focusing and opinion consonance develop over time, an increasing pressure on the political system can be expected. This pressure will be stronger the more persistent focusing and consonance are.

SUMMARY AND CONCLUSION

It was argued that media in modern democratic societies organize and structure the open exchange of issues and opinions and thus constitute public communication. Public opinion can be described as the output of this communication process. Among other actors the media themselves take an active part in the political discourse. They not only disseminate other actors' views, but also advance their own relevance assignments, interpretations, and evaluations, trying to influence policy decisions either directly or indirectly through the process of public opinion formation in the audience. The notion of media as political actors calls for a systematic analysis of the opinion section of the media in order to assess the media's autonomous contribution to the political discourse. In editorials media are explicitly authorized to openly express their opinions and present themselves as participating actors in the political process. This chapter therefore suggests a close examination of editorial impact on the policy decisions of the political system. This not only regards the explicit evaluation strategies in editorials. Special attention has to be directed on the issue repertoire across the different media outlets— which according to the "salience-model" might be a significant means for the media to communicate their political position to the audience market. Applying a macrolevel agenda-building perspective to the collective phenomenon of public opinion, the degree of issue and opinion correspondences in the messages of different media outlets should come into the focus. It is assumed that professional selection criteria and coorientation mechanisms in the media system provide a great deal of correspondences in editorial coverage. Yet the expansion of programs in the electronic media and new internet-related communication technologies might lead to an ever increasing diversity of issues without considerable overlap between the media outlets. Low degrees of issue focusing and opinion consonance indicate social fragmentation and disintegration as well as a considerable amount of conflicts between the different segments of society.

The differentiation between issue focusing and opinion consonance leads to four different constellations regarding the condition of public opinion, each indicating different chances to find resonance in the political system. The macrolevel concepts of focusing and consonance thus not only indicate the condition of society in terms of fragmentation and disintegration, they also relate to the possible impact of media opinion on politics. Although the relation between media and politics is a much disputed field, research has predominantly focused on microlevel audience effects instead of investigating the collective resonance of media opinion in the political system. It is assumed that the central supposition of media impact is the visibility of the media as a unified actor speaking with one voice. The higher the degree of issue focusing and opinion consonance between the different media outlets and the more persistent this constellation, the more pressure builds up and the more likely a reaction in the political system should be provoked. Only high levels of correspondence in the media system provide the media with sufficient power to comply with the role of a critical watchdog and successfully address their concerns. With these elaborations on the relation between the constellations in media opinion and media's impact on the political system we moved beyond the current state of the art. Evidently, more theoretical and empirical effort is needed to validate our assumptions. Further research will need to investigate the constellations of issues and opinions in the media system in a long-term perspective rather than the particular single issues and opinions. Special attention has to be directed to the national prestige newspapers, as they are important reference points for the political elite and serve as opinion leaders in the media system.

ENDNOTES

1. The explicit assignment of a critical observation and evaluation of politics has not led to a clarification of the desirable amount of media opinion. Media are often considered as manipulative and manipulated agencies influencing public attitudes and policy decisions without democratic legitimation (Donsbach, 1982; Noelle-Neumann, 1977).

2. In Germany, editorials do not represent individual views of single journalists, but indicate the editorial stance of a media outlet. Editorials reflect the political views of the papers and serve as a forum of presentation for the media's own view of public affairs. Because the opinion section does not have to comply with the information function of neutral reporting, it can be expected that the different political positions of media outlets become most visible and distinguishable in editorials.

3. Media regard their editorials as a means to position and stabilize themselves on the audience market, as the editorial stance corresponds with certain political segmentations of the public. This applies in particular to national prestige newspapers whose editorial stance can be located on a left-right scale. There are more liberal and more conservative media outlets and their distance to political parties differs considerably.

4. Noelle-Neumann basically conceptionalizes public opinion as opinion that can be expressed in public without fear of isolation. Public opinion in her work on the "spiral of silence" represents a perceived majority opinion based on the observation of media opinion (Noelle-Neumann, 1982).

5. The antagonism between pluralism or diversity and integration is vividly reflected by the contrasting appraisals of any given degree of correspondence in the media system. Depending on the particular reference point, high degrees of correspondence are character-

ized using either positive synonyms such as consent, cultural mutuality, and harmony or negative synonyms such as conformity, adaption, assimilation, uniformity, standardization, stereotyping, collectivism, monopolization, and monologization. Low degrees of correspondences are either positively labeled as diversity and pluralism or devalued as fragmentation, heterogenization, segmentation, dissipation, atomization, specialization, individualization, and polarization.

6. Cohen (1973), Gilberg et al. (1980), Cook et al. (1983), Leff et al. (1986), Protess et al. (1987), and Pritchard and Berkowitz (1993).

7. Almost half of the federal and country representatives view the national prestige newspapers as important or very important for their parliamentary work. Their significance is also reflected in their frequent use by political actors. This group not only reads national prestige papers disproportionately often but also spends disproportionately much time reading them.

REFERENCES

Atkin, Charles K. 1973. Instrumental Utilities and Information Seeking. In P. Clark (ed.), *New Models for Communication Research*. Beverly Hills, 205-242.

Budge, Ian and Dennis Farlie. 1985. Party Competition—Selective Emphasis or Direct Confrontation? An Alternative View with Data. In H. Daalder and P. Mair (eds.), *Western European Party System. Continuity & Change*, 267-305. London: Sage.

Cohen, Bernhard L. 1973. *The Public's Impact on Foreign Policy*. Boston: Little Brown and Company.

Cook, Fay Lomax et al. 1983. Media and Agenda Setting: Effects and the Public, Interest Group Leaders, Policy Makers, and Policy. *Public Opinion Quarterly* 47, 16-35.

Donsbach, Wolfgang. 1982. *Legitimationspropbleme des Journalismus. Gesellschaftliche Rolle der Massenmedien und berufliche Einstellung von Journalisten*. Freiburg: Alber.

Donsbach, Wolfgang. 1991. *Medienwirkung trotz Selektion. Einflußfaktoren auf die Zuwendung zu Zeitungsinhalten*. Köln: Böhlau.

Downs, Anthony. 1972 . Up and Down with Ecology—The "Issue-Attention Cycle." *The Public Interest* 28, 38-50.

Entman, Robert M. 1989. *Democracy without Citizens: Media and the Decay of American Politics*. New York: Oxford University Press.

Fuchs, Dieter and Barbara Pfetsch. 1996. Die Beobachtung der öffentlichen Meinung durch das Regierungssystem. In W. van den Daele and F. Neidhardt (eds.), *Kommunikation und Entscheidung. Politische Funktionen öffentlicher Meinungsbildung und diskursiver Verfahren*, 103-138. Berlin: Edition Sigma.

Funkhouser, Ray. 1973. The Issues of the Sixties: An Exploratory Study in the Dynamics of Public Opinion. *Public Opinion Quarterly* 37, 62-75.

Gerhards, Jürgen and Friedhelm Neidhardt. 1991. Strukturen und Funktionen moderner Öffentlichkeit: Fragestellungen und Ansätze. In S. Müller-Doohm and K. Neumann-Braun (eds.), *Öffentlichkeit, Kultur, Massenkommunikation. Beiträge zur Medien und Kommunikationssoziologie*, 31-89. Oldenburg: bis.

Gilberg, Shelton et al. 1980. The State of the Union Address and the Press Agenda. *Journalism Quarterly* 57, 584-588.

Goffman, Erving. 1974. *Frame Analysis: An Essay on the Organization of Experience*. Cambridge: Harvard University Press.

Herzog, Dietrich et al. 1990. *Abgeordnete und Bürger. Ergebnisse einer Befragung der Mitglieder des 11. Deutschen Bundestages und der Bevölkerung*. Opladen: Westdeutscher Verlag.

Iyengar, Shanto. 1996. Framing Responsibility for Political Issues. *Annals, American Association for Political Sciences* 546F, 59-70.

Iyengar, Shanto. 1991. *Is Anyone Responsible? How Television Frames Political Issues*. Chicago: University of Chicago Press.

Iyengar, Shanto and Donald R. Kinder. 1987. *News that Matters*. Chicago: Chicago University Press.

Kennamer, J. David. 1992. *Public Opinion, the Press, and Public Policy. An Introduction*. Westport, CT: Praeger.

Kepplinger, Hans Mathias. 1985. *Die aktuelle Berichterstattung des Hörfunks. Eine Inhaltsanalyse der Abendnachrichten und politischen Magazine*. Freiburg: Alber.

Kingdon, John W. 1984. *Agendas, Alternatives, and Public Politics*. New York: Little Brown.

Krosnick, Jon A. and Donald R. Kinder. 1990. Altering the Foundations of Support for the President through Priming. *American Political Science Review* 84, 497-512.

Leff, Donna, David L. Protess, and Stephen C. Brooks. 1986. Crusading Journalism: Changing Public Attitudes and Policy Making Agendas. *Public Opinion Quarterly* 51, 166-185.

Neidhardt, Friedhelm. 1994. Öffentlichkeit, öffentliche Meinung, soziale Bewegungen. In F. Neidhardt (ed.), *Öffentlichkeit, öffentliche Meinung, soziale Bewegungen*, 7-41. Opladen: Westdeutscher Verlag.

Noelle-Neumann, Elisabeth. 1973. Kumulation, Konsonanz und Öffentlichkeitseffekt. Ein neuer Ansatz zur Analyse der Wirkung der Massenmedien. *Publizistik* 18, 26-55.

Noelle-Neumann, Elisabeth. 1977. Öffentlichkeit als Bedrohung. Über den Einfluß der Massenmedien auf das Meinungsklima. In Elisabeth Noelle-Neuman (ed.), *Öffentlichkeit als Bedrohung. Beiträge zur empirischen Kommunikationsforschung*, 204-233. Freiburg: Alber.

Noelle-Neumann, Elisabeth. 1982. *Die Schweigespirale. Öffentliche Meinung—unsere soziale Haut*. Frankfurt: Ullstein.

Noelle-Neumann, Elisabeth and Rainer Mathes. 1987. The "Event as Event" and the "Event as News": The Significance of

"Consonance" for Media Effects Research. *European Journal of Communication* 2, 391-414.

Page, Benjamin I. 1996a. Public Deliberation, The Media, and Democracy. Paper presented to the International Communication Association. Chicago, May 1996.

Page, Benjamin I. 1996b. The Mass Media as Political Actors. *Political Science & Politics* 29, 20-24.

Pritchard, David. 1992. The News Media and Public Policy Agendas. In J. D. Kennamer (ed.), *Public Opinion, the Press, and Public Policy. An Introduction*, 103-112. Westpoint, CT: Praeger.

Pritchard, David and Dan Berkowitz. 1993. The Limits of Agenda-Setting: The Press and Political Responses to Crime in the United States, 1950-1980. *International Journal of Public Opinion Research* 5, 86-91.

Protess, David L. et al. 1987. The Impact of Investigative Reporting on Public Opinion and Policymaking. Targeting Toxic Waste. *Public Opinion Quarterly* 51, 166-185.

Puhe, Henry and H. Gerd Würzberg. 1989. *Lust und Frust. Das Informationsverhalten des deutschen Abgeordneten.* Eine Untersuchung. Köln: informedia.

Rogers, Everett M. and James W. Dearing. 1988. Agenda-Setting Research: Where Has It Been, Where Is It Going? In A. Anderson (ed.), *Communication Yearbook* 11, 555-594. Newbury Park: Sage.

Shaw, Donald L. and Bradley J. Hamm. 1997. Agendas for a Public Union or for Private Communities? How Individuals Are Using Media to Reshape American Society. In M. McCombs, D. Shaw, D. Weaver (eds.), *Communication and Democracy. Exploring the Intellectual Frontiers in Agenda-Setting Theory*, 209-230. Mahwah, London: Erlbaum.

Sigal, Leon V. 1973. *Reporters and Officials: The Organization and Politics of Newsmaking.* Lexington, MA: D.C. Heath.

Snow, David A. et al. 1986. Frame Alignment Processes, Micromobilization, and Movement Participation. *American Sociological Review* 51, 464-481.

Author Index

Subject Index

AES-0289